To my husband, Paul.
I wouldn't be the same without you,
and neither would this book.

CONTENTS

CREEPY CUTE

DRAWING CLASS

LEARN TO DRAW 70 SWEETLY SPOOKY CHARACTERS AND COZY CREATURES

MARCIE DRIESSEN

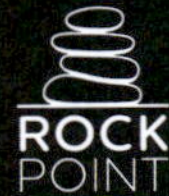

INTRODUCTION

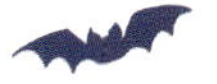

hello!

I'm Marcie, a chronically ill artist from the Netherlands. Before I ever started taking traditional art classes, I often turned to my large collection of illustrated books during the days when I didn't feel so great. They kept me company and brought me great comfort. Those books led me to my first venture into art through realistic art classes. For many years, I drew photorealistic portraits, but there was always a part of me that loved ghost stories and the more whimsical, fantastical art of my illustrated books.

Growing up in a small village in the woods, I spent much of my time reading and drawing, or, on my good days, exploring the forest and marsh near my house, where I would pet toads and talk to crows. These small joys soon bled into my art, and I began to draw ghosts and skeletons for fun outside of my classes. Eventually, I realized it made me so happy and felt rewarding to invent my own little world full of all the things I loved that I made the switch away from portraiture and never looked back. From learning how to draw from a book much like this one, I am extremely excited to get to make my own for you.

What Is Creepy Cute Art?

In this book, I combine cute, cozy, and wholesome elements with dark and creepy ones. My characters usually resemble baby animals with large heads, big sparkly eyes, and chubby bodies. To make it a little bit creepy, I give these characters eyes that are entirely black or white, fangs, a gaunt face, or grayish skin. Then, I tie it all together in a comforting scene, which can include candles, string lights, flowers, hot drinks, and soft blankets. Sometimes I leave the project black and white, only adding shading and highlights. If I add color, I go for a twilight look using dark and muted colors.

You can make these drawings your own by including objects that are comforting to you and favorite animals. Make them even creepier by drawing characters of cute ghosts and zombies or placing the cuddliest animals in haunting settings like graveyards, overgrown forests, or

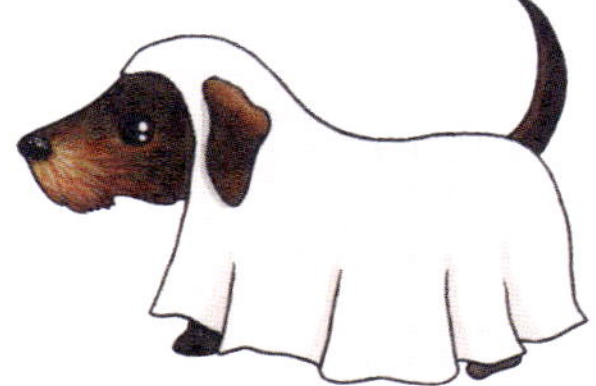

abandoned buildings. The opportunities are endless.

Afterwards, I hope to give you the inspiration to create your own world of everything creepy and cute.

Finding Inspiration

Inspiration can be found everywhere, but for me, I find it in the things that bring me joy. Art becomes more enjoyable and meaningful when you make it personal. You have already taken the first step in picking up this book, but there is so much more to explore. Find inspiration in the aesthetics of your favorite books or movies; in the photos you take of the things that catch your eye; or on social media, where you can find prompts or lists of ideas that give you a starting point. Creating creepy cute art can be as simple as drawing a haunted version of your house. Once you figure out what inspires you the most, you'll never run out of ideas.

How to Use This Book

This book includes seventy-one step-by-step projects teaching you how to create the animals of the Mulberry Forest, the creatures of the Gourd Hamlet, the places on Hollow Lanes, and all the Spooky Celebrations. You can follow

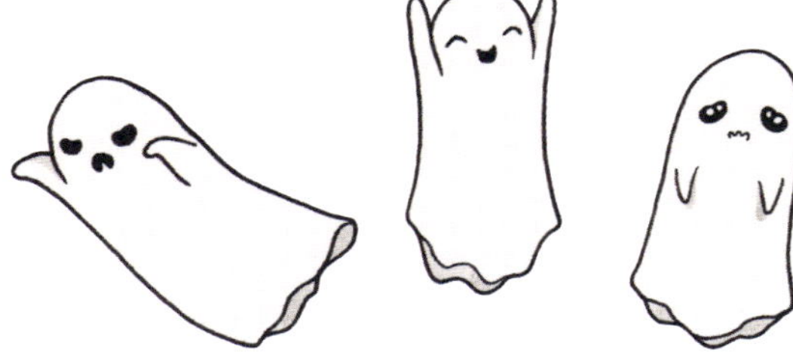

along exactly, but don't feel like you have to. I encourage you to grab a sketchbook and experiment by taking what's in this book and combining little pieces of various designs to make scenes of your own. A great way to start is by giving your characters different facial features to make them wicked, happy, or sad.

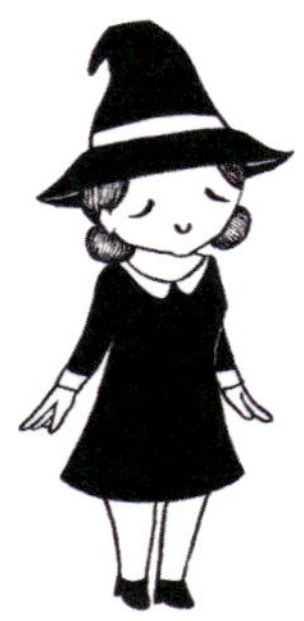
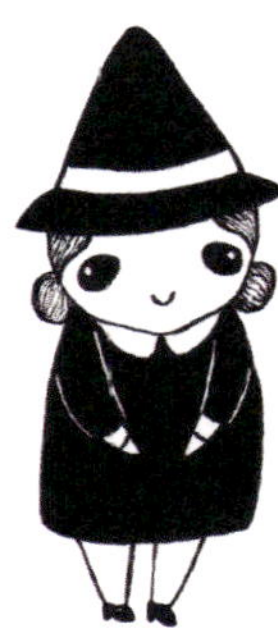
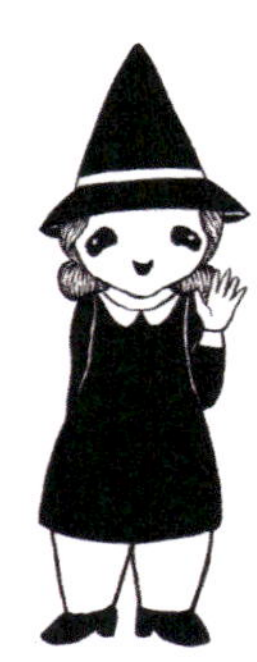

You can also change their body shapes to make them look more realistic or chubbier (and therefore cuter), or even have them doing something. Find the kinds of looks you like and add your personal touch in whichever way your inspiration pulls you.

Materials

Most often, I create my artwork with traditional art supplies, but there are so many options out there for you to use. If you would like some tips on what supplies to begin with, here are some of my recommendations.

PAPER: Basic printer paper works nicely for sketching. However, for final artwork, use watercolor or mixed media paper. If you're like me and make your drawings small with tiny details, try hot press paper, which has a smoother texture. If you want paper with tooth to it, try cold press.

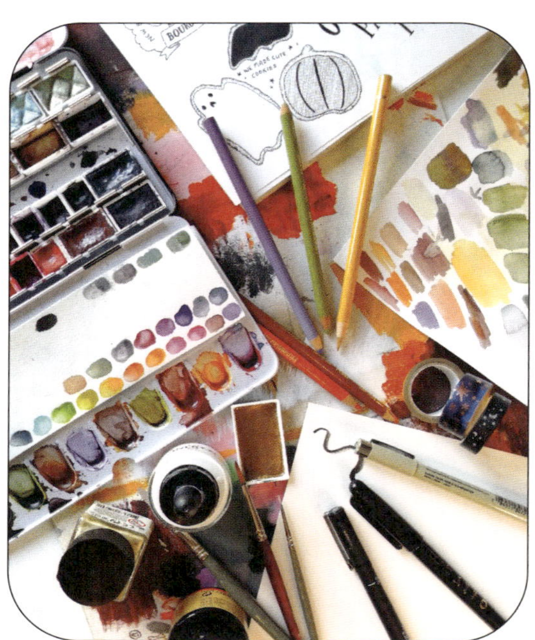

PENCIL AND PEN: I sketch with pencil because it's easy to modify and erase. In the tutorials in this book, you will use pencil twice: first for the sketch, and then again when transferring it onto a clean sheet of paper. This way you can get as messy as you want when sketching. After transferring, trace all the lines in pen and color over a nice, clean sketch.

MARKERS: For adding color and shading, use markers that are permanent. Try alcohol-based markers such as Ohuhu. They offer great quality, a large range of colors, and have both brush and fine tips for an affordable price. Or you can use water-based markers for a versatile, watercolor effect. I love Tombow because they have soft and hard tips in gorgeous colors.

COLORED PENCILS: If you choose to color with colored pencils, pick an oil-based brand such as Polychromos. They have 120 colors and are easy to blend and sharpen. You can also use a wax-based pencil, but keep in mind that they are quite opaque and will cover your ink lines. If you don't mind that, I recommend Prismacolor for their vibrant colors and the ability to create texture. But be aware that their soft tips are harder to sharpen.

BRUSHES: For coloring using inks or watercolors, choose some round brushes in a few thicknesses. These will be useful for creating texture. My favorite brush sizes are 8 for coloring large areas, 3 for creating rougher textures like leaves and tree bark, and 3 or 0 for creating finer textures like grass and fur.

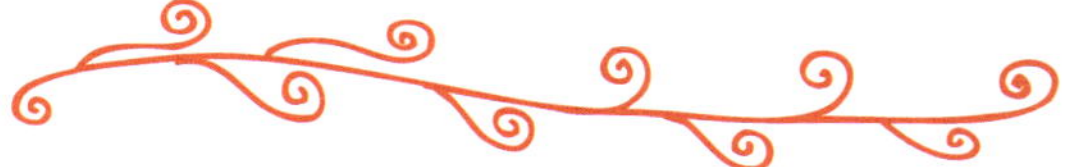

A TRANSFER METHOD

In each tutorial, trace your sketch with pencil on watercolor paper before inking. There are many ways to get your sketches onto heavier paper, including transfer paper, a lightbox, or just a window on a bright day. Personally, I use a sun lamp, which is cheaper and portable. If none of these options are available to you, you can sketch directly on the watercolor paper; just be sure to do some preplanning in order to keep erasing to a minimum.

coloring your Drawings

When it comes to picking colors for my artwork, I like to combine colors that remind me of autumn or Halloween. This palette usually includes yellow, orange, red, brown, green, dark blue, and violet. You can use these as a starting point but, of course, feel free to use whatever colors summon those feelings for you. Another option is to use black and white and only one other color. For this, I usually use orange.

You'll find that there are many kinds of black pigments, and the one you choose can have a surprisingly dramatic effect on the overall feel of the drawing. I recommend doing some research to see what kind of pigment you like best. My favorite is India ink, which is made of wood ash. The color has a touch of brown that adds a subtle warmth and resembles the ink used in old sepia photographs.

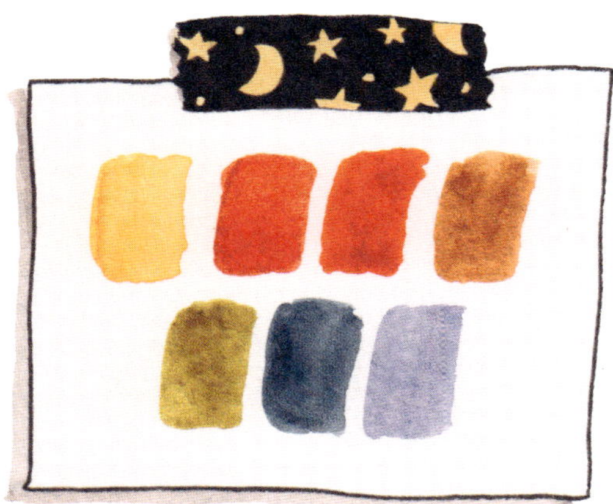

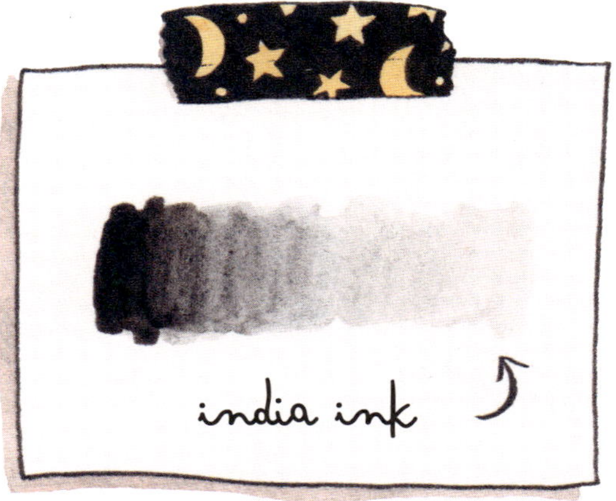

That Twilight Look

Do you know what cozy and eerie settings all have in common? Darkness. An easy way to add darkness is by shading. When you add shading, make sure to decide where the light is coming from and position the shading on the opposite side of the objects in the drawing. A shading technique I use often is called stippling, which uses dots clustered together or spread apart to create a textured shadow.

As mentioned earlier, the projects that have color use dark and muted colors. They not only bring that spooky atmosphere to the drawing, but they also create opportunities to add beautiful lighting effects, like moon- or candlelight.

If you don't have dark or muted colors, there are two ways you can create them yourself. One option is to mix it with a bit of the color that is on the opposite side of the color wheel, also known as its complementary color.

I've supplied a color wheel for your reference. See the mini diagram for how I mixed two opposite colors, orange and blue, and toned it down to make a muted orange.

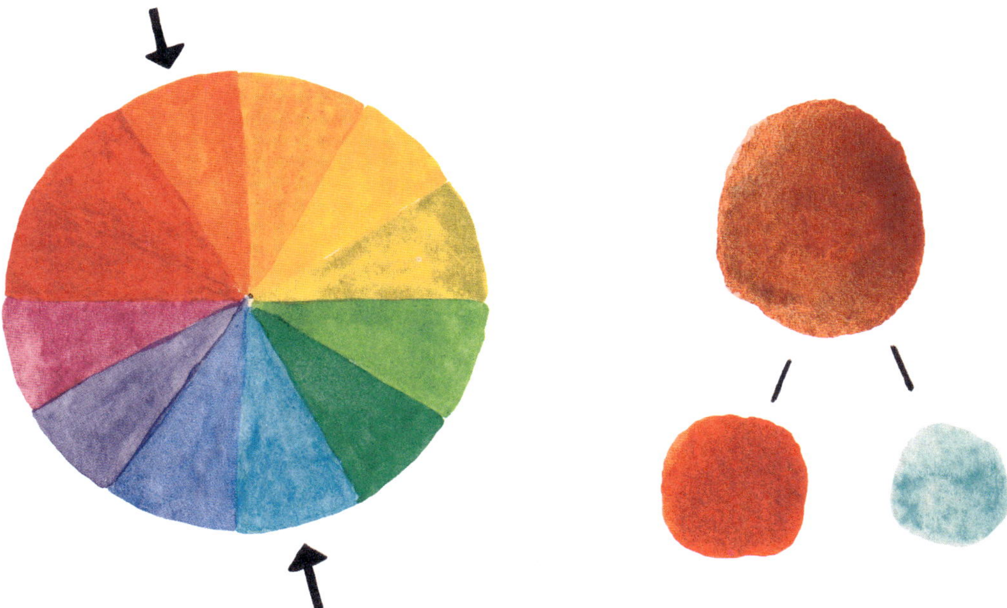

The second option is to first paint the picture black and white and then add color on top. This is a much faster way if you don't want to mix a range of colors until you find the perfect shade. The images below show how I used this method when coloring a pumpkin.

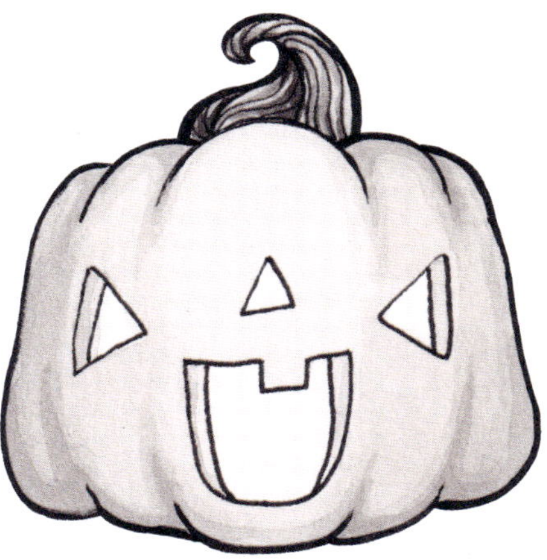

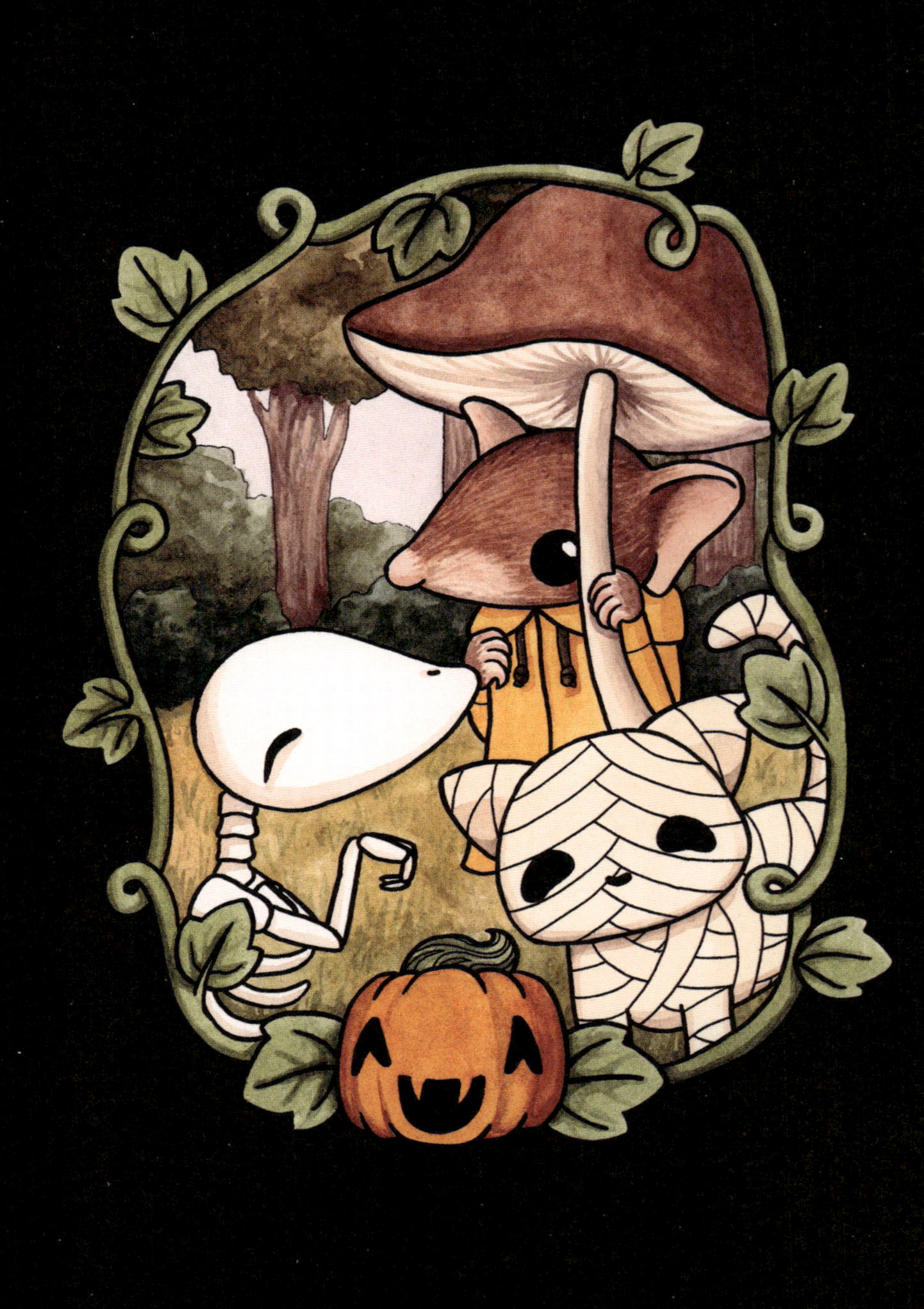

mulberry forest

WITCHY TOAD

1. Start with a droopy witch hat. Draw an oval with a curved line across for the hat's brim. Then add the triangle top with the point curved to the right. Add a star charm.

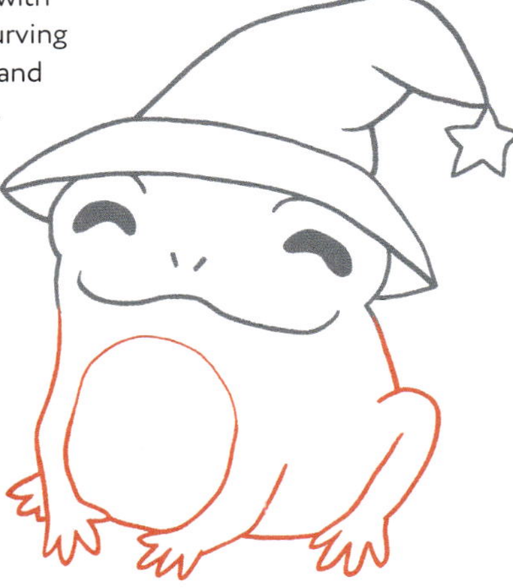

2. Outline the face on the sides with curved lines. Add the eyes with two thick arches, the nose with two slanted dashes, and a wide, smiling mouth in a W shape.

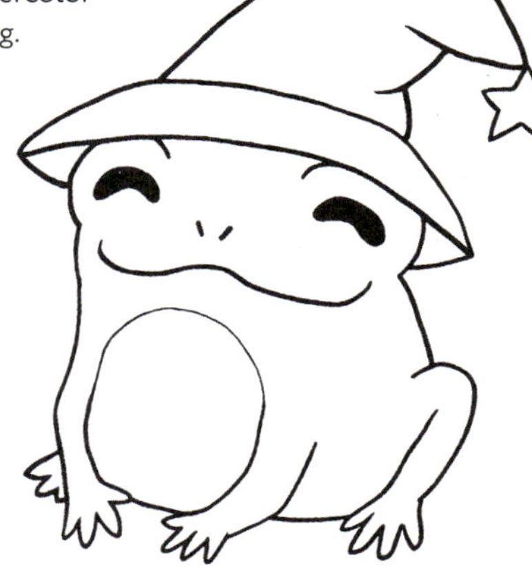

3. Add a round body with the two front arms curving in toward the center and the legs on the sides. Give each paw four spiky claws.

4. Cleanly trace your sketch with pencil on watercolor paper before inking.

5. I used watercolors of brown for the hat, yellow for the star charm, and green and cream for the body. Add shading under the hat, mouth, and body.

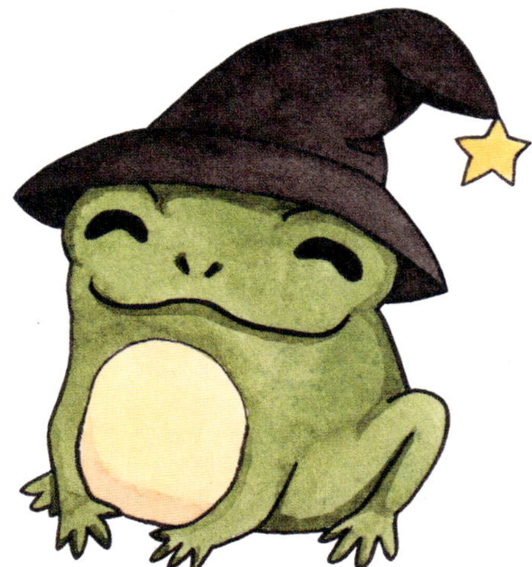

SKELETON DOG

1. Draw a tilted teardrop shape for the skull. Add two dashes for an eye and a nose.

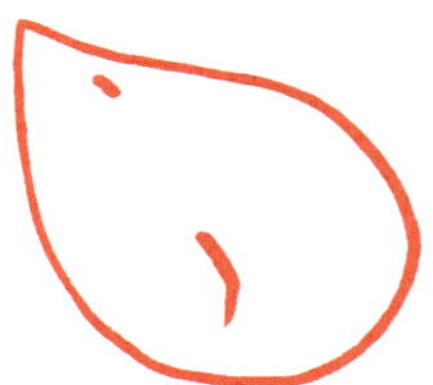

2. Add a spine with many connected rectangles. Curve the end into a tail.

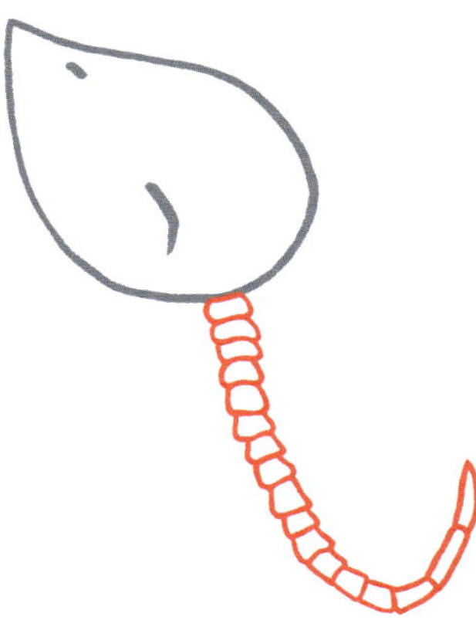

3. Draw a partial rib cage along the left side of the spine with four curved ovals.

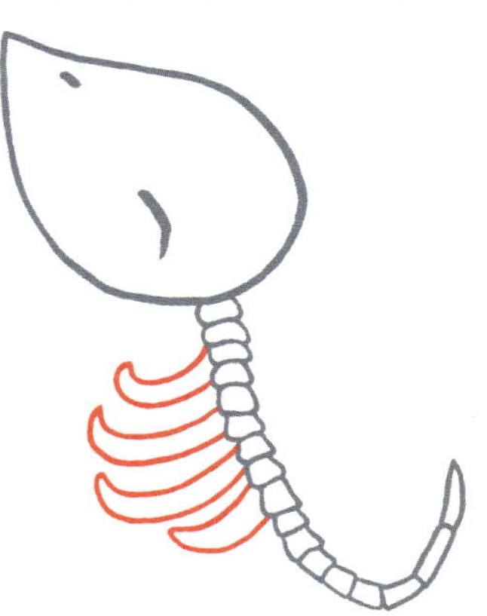

4. Draw the front leg starting with an oval, two rectangles, and a pointed oval for the foot. Add a back leg below. Make it bend at the knee so that it makes an upside-down V.

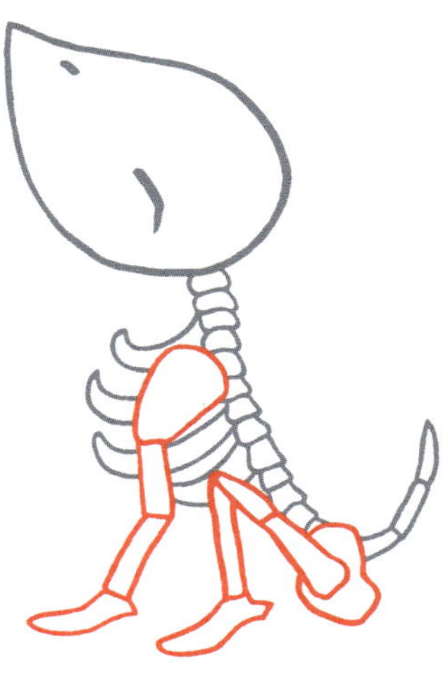

5. Cleanly trace your sketch with pencil on watercolor paper before inking.

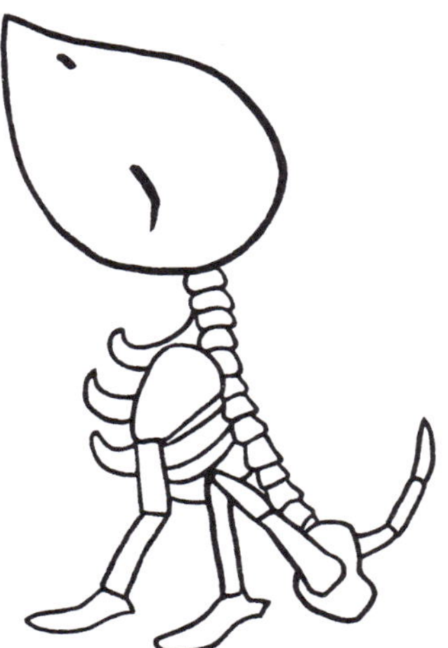

6. Color your drawing. Create some shadows along the bones such as the spine, ribs, and tail. I used diluted ink.

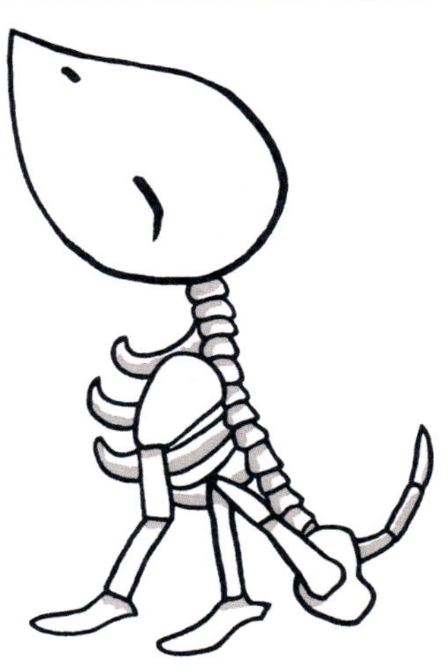

GHOST RAT

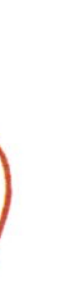

1. Draw a teardrop shape for the head with a rounded tip for the nose. Leave a small gap where the neck will connect. Add a solid eye.

2. Add triangle ears on the top and the side of the head.

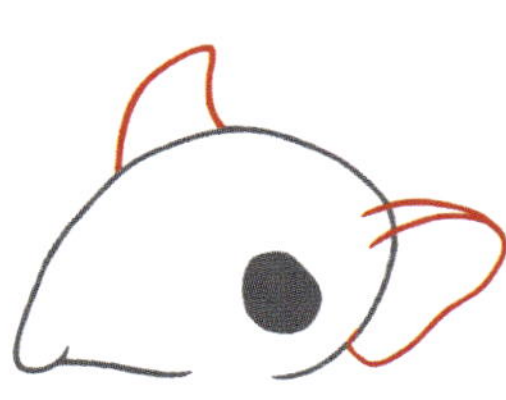

3. Add a wispy ghost body with curvy lines that taper toward the bottom.

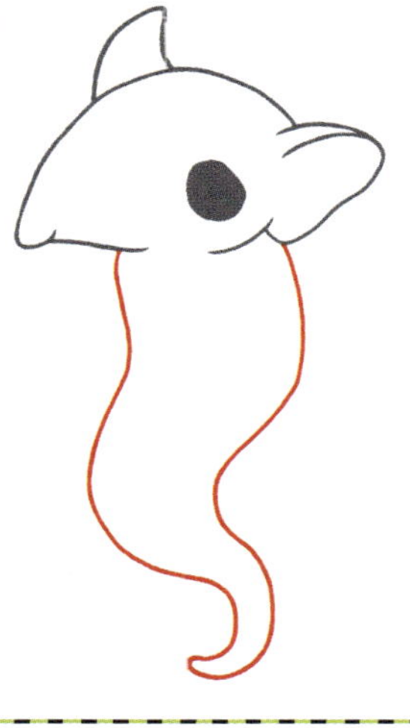

4. At the top of the body, draw two paws, each with four claws, pointing to the left.

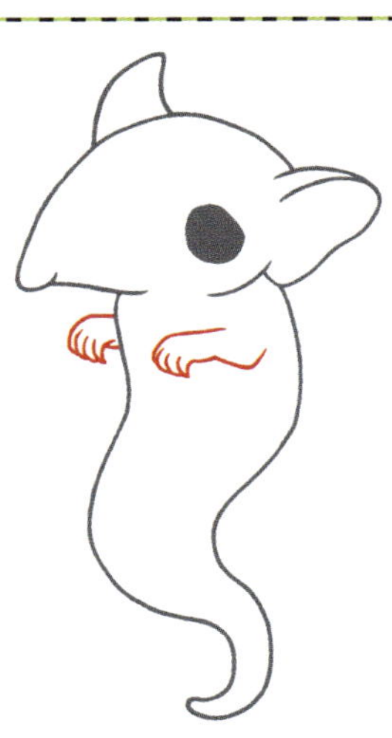

5. Cleanly trace your sketch with pencil on watercolor paper before inking.

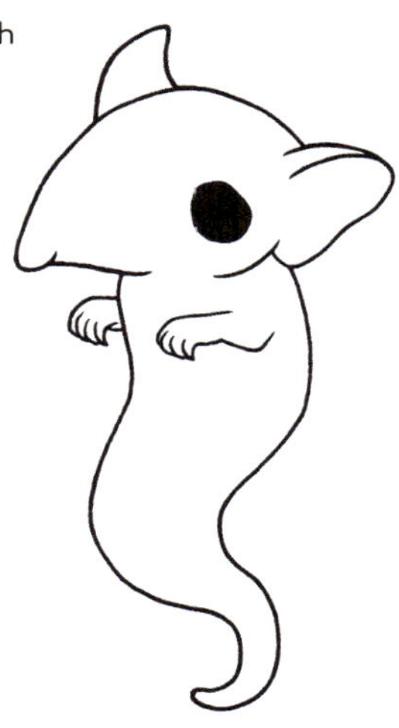

6. Color your drawing and add some shading in the ears, at the mouth, and under the arm. I used diluted ink.

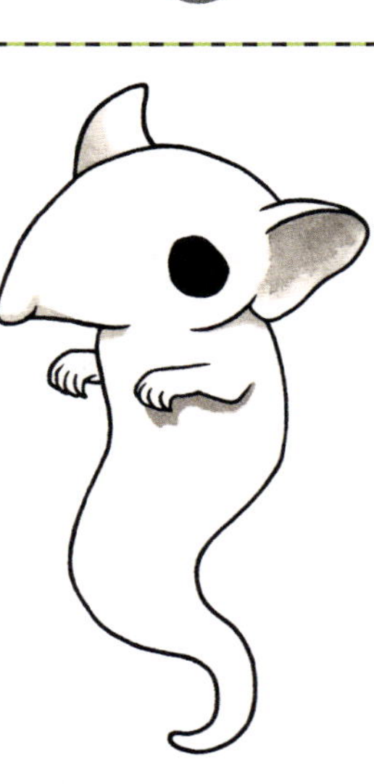

RAINY DAY SPIDER

1. Draw a leaf with three corners curled upward. Add wavy lines along it for veins.

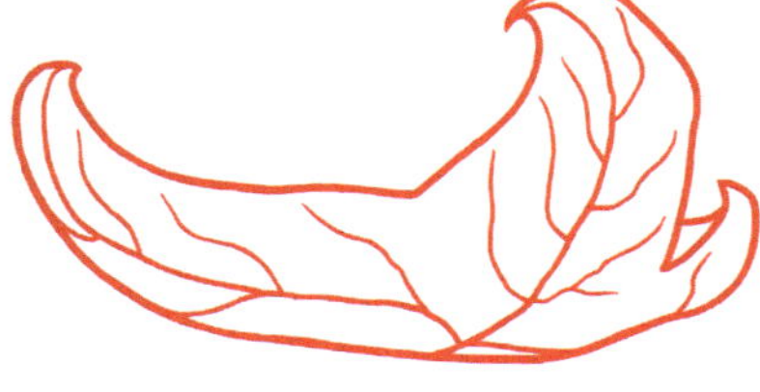

2. Add an oval head underneath with a curve to the left for the body.

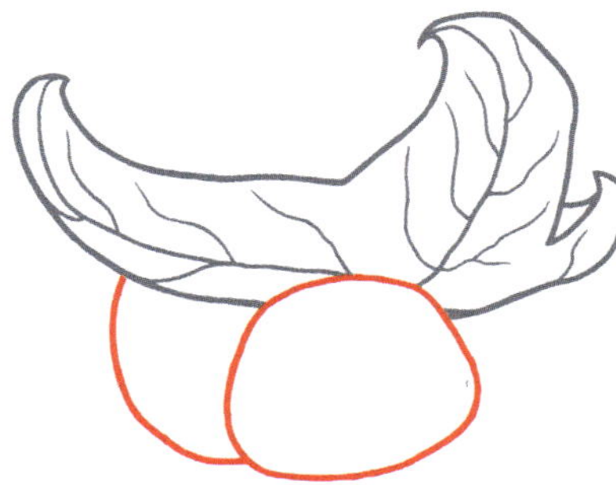

3. Draw the face with solid eyes with two highlights and a small smile with two triangle fangs.

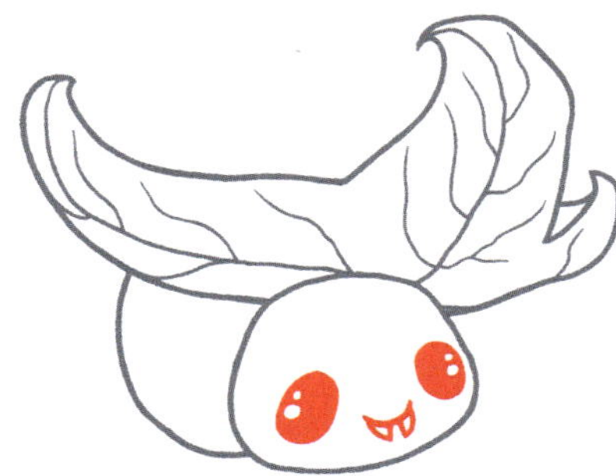

4. Make two oval arms on the left and right holding up the leaf.

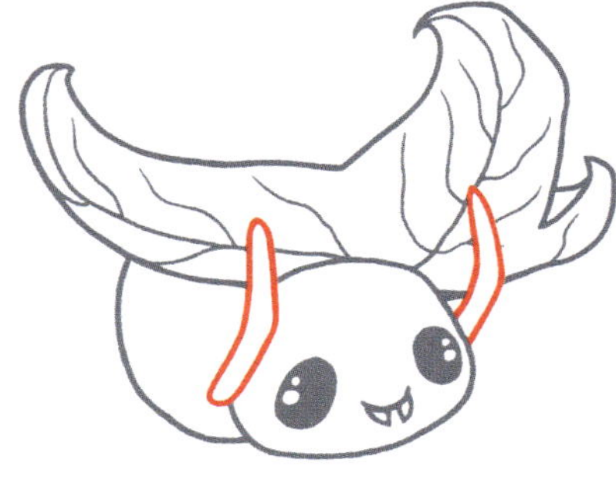

5. Add three bent legs on the left and two feet on the right.

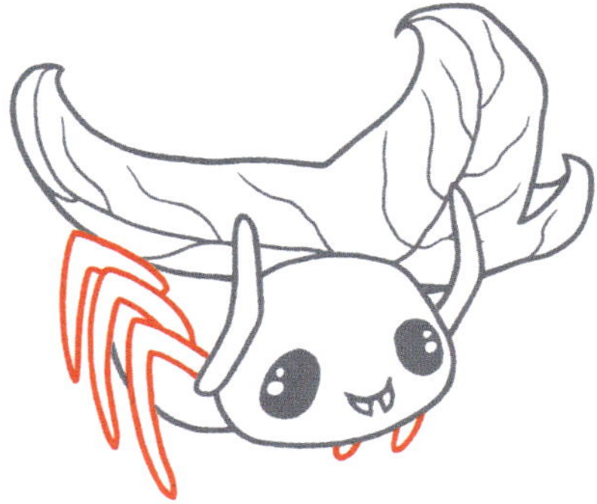

6. Cleanly trace your sketch with pencil on watercolor paper before inking.

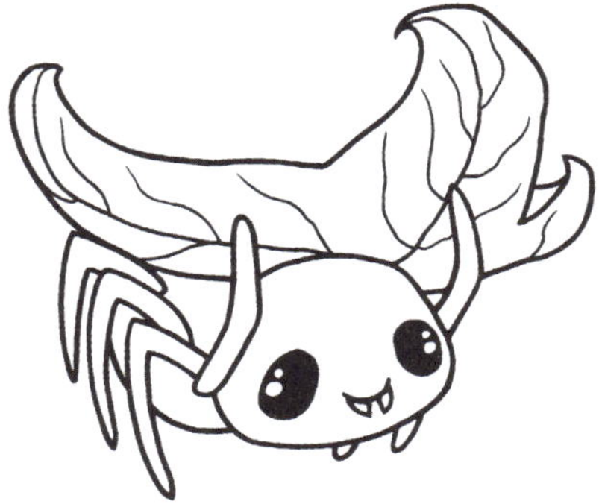

7. I used watercolors to make the background a muted violet, the leaf a dark yellow, and the spider gray. Add shading using brown on the underside of the leaf and gray on the spider. With white ink or paint, add rain splashing in the background with lines and curved splash marks.

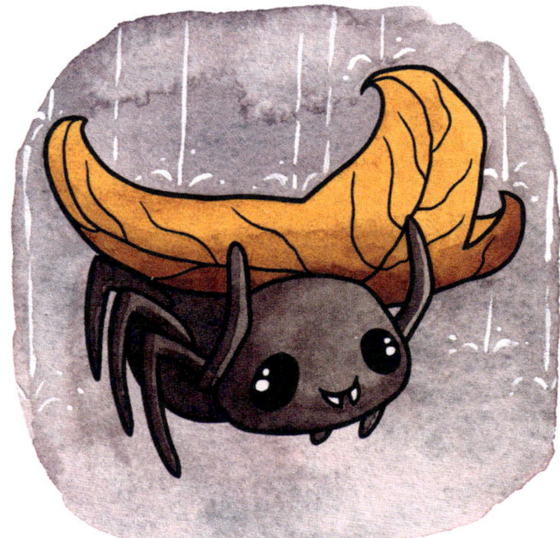

FLYING FAMILIAR

1. Draw two overlapping ovals.

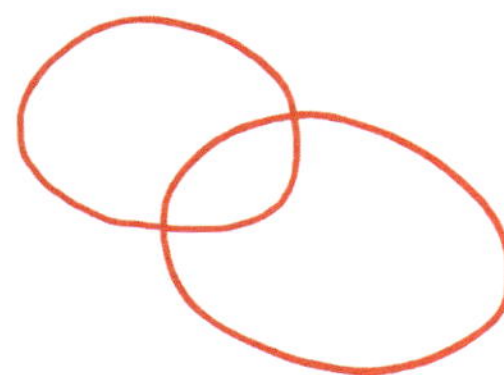

2. In the smaller oval, draw two solid oval eyes with highlights, an upside-down heart for the nose, and two curves with triangle fangs for the mouth.

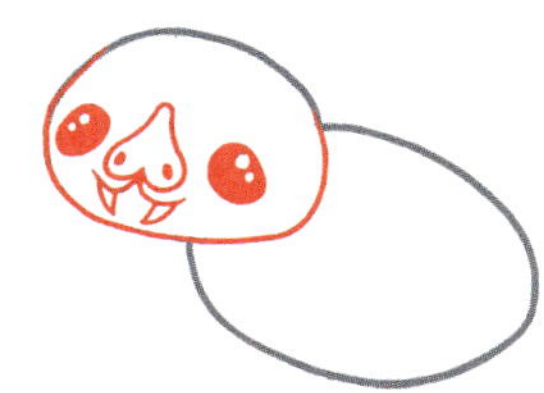

3. Add large triangle ears with a curved line down the middle. Draw a small witch hat with an oval and a triangle.

4. Draw two flared wings, one in front of the other. Make a wide triangle then divide it into three triangles. Connect the bottom with a scalloped line. Draw only a partial back wing.

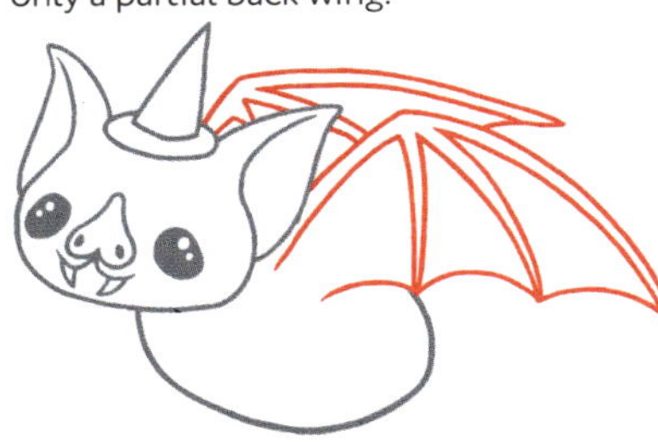

5. Add two feet with three curved claws. Connect to the body with lines.

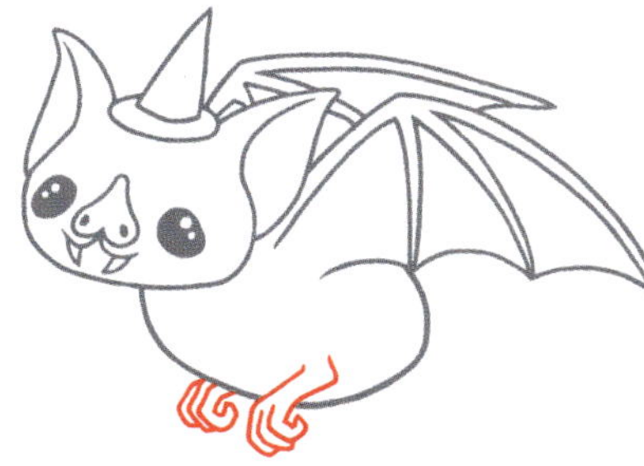

6. Cleanly trace your sketch with pencil on watercolor paper before inking.

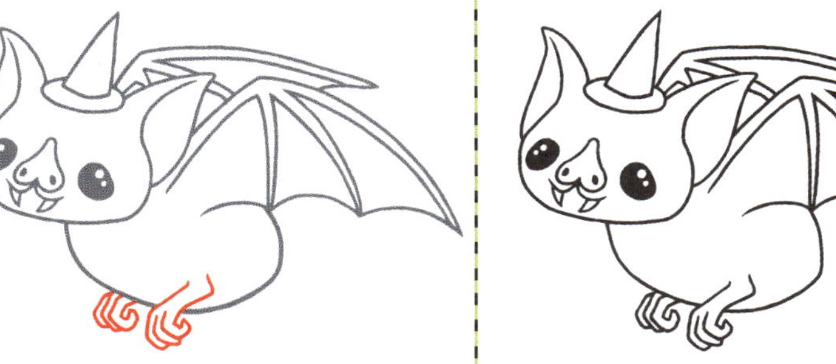

7. I used watercolors to make my bat brown and muted pink. For the hat, I used black. With a very thin brush or pen, create furry texture with short lines across the face and body. Add shading as if the light is coming from the top left of the page.

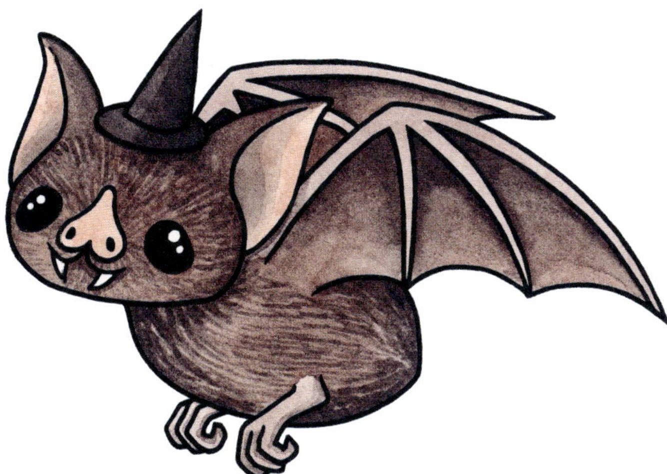

PUMPKIN PEEKABOO

1. Draw two overlapping ovals.

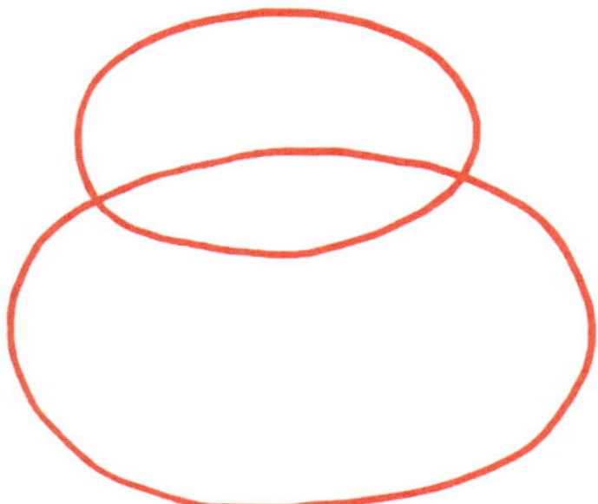

2. Draw triangle ears with a line in the middle on the sides of the top oval. Add two solid oval eyes with highlights, a heart-shaped nose, and two curved lines for the mouth.

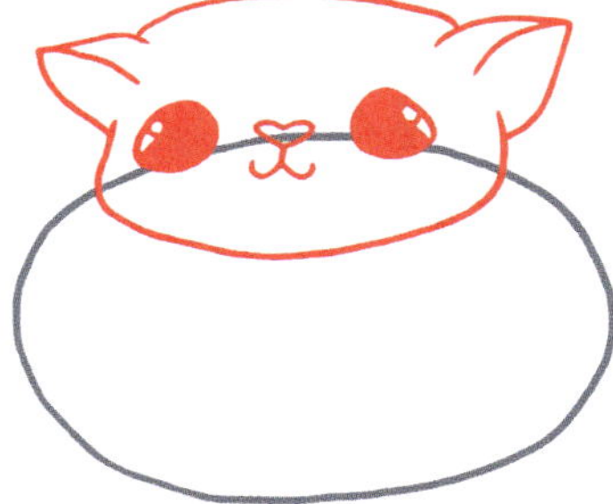

3. Add paws on the sides of the face with four toes each.

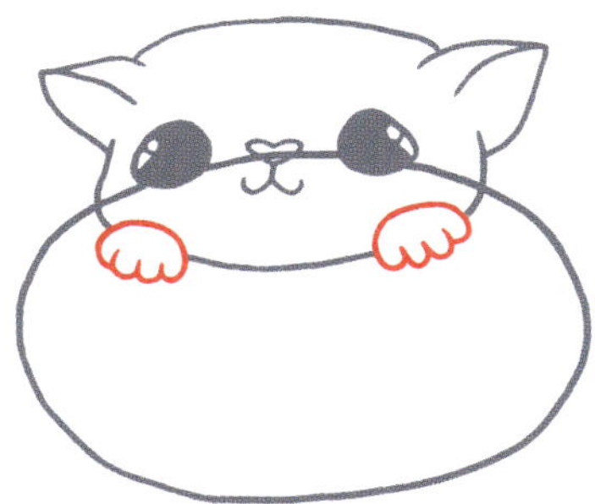

4. Add ridges to the bottom oval.

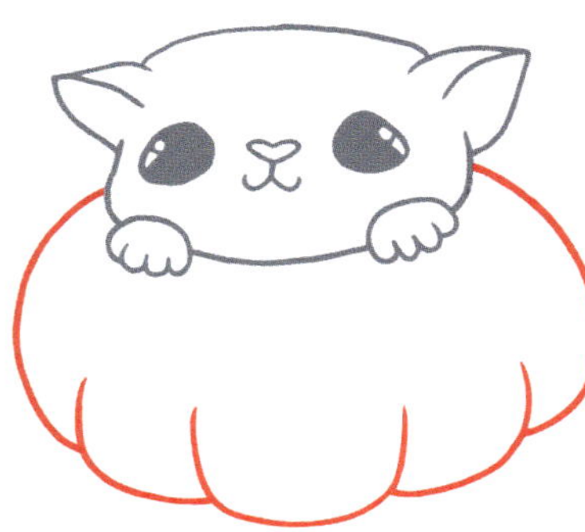

5. Draw a pumpkin hat with a curved stem. Add detail to the stem.

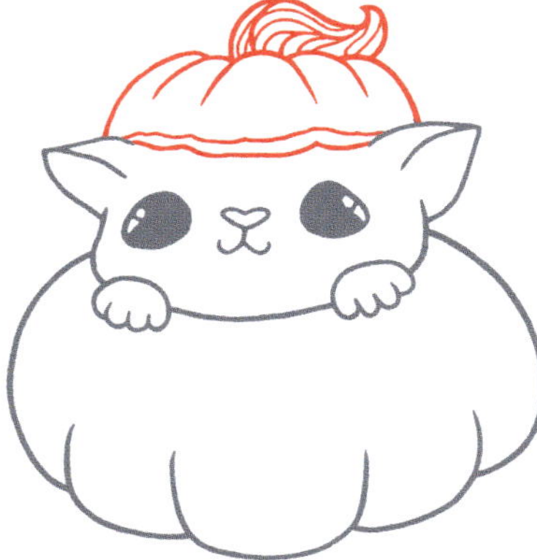

6. Cleanly trace your sketch with pencil on watercolor paper before inking.

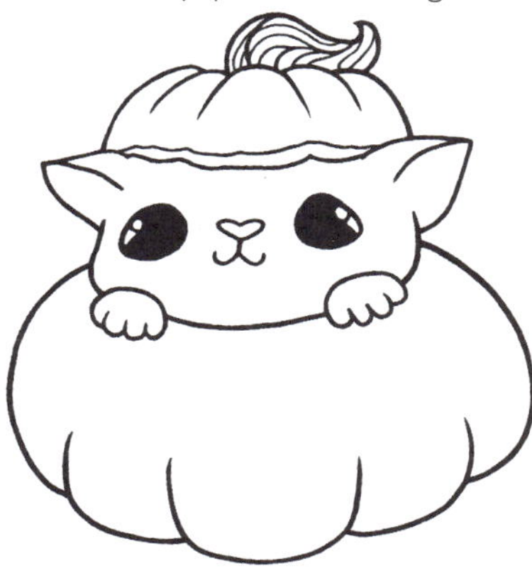

7. I used watercolors to make the pumpkin a bright orange with a green stem. For the cat, I used light gray with pink inner ears and nose. Add furry texture to the face with light lines. Add shading to the ridges of the pumpkin and the underside of the head and paws.

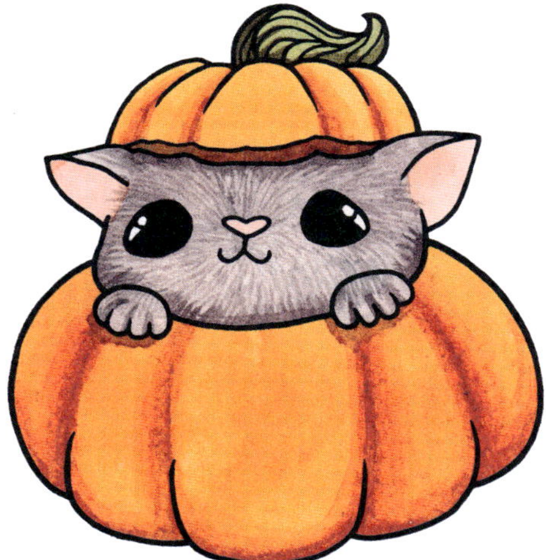

SUGAR RUSH SKUNK

1. Draw a rounded triangle for the head and a rectangle that flares out at the bottom for the body.

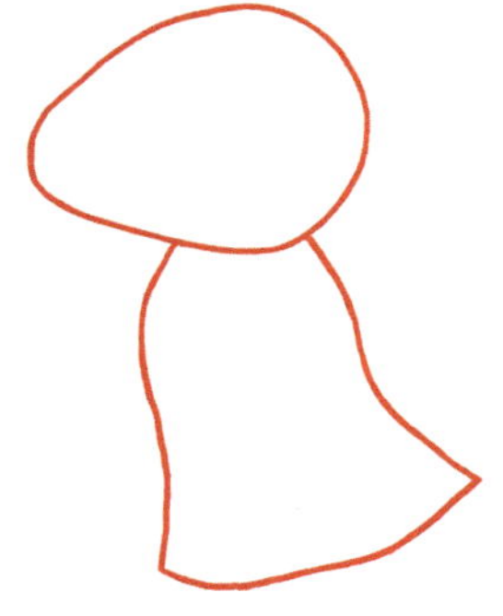

2. Add an arm with an oval divided into three sections: upper arm, forearm, and hand. Then add two legs with two ovals.

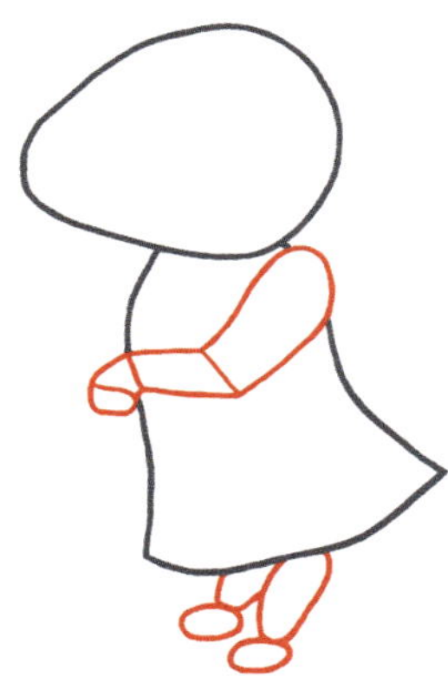

3. Add curved lines for the eyes, an oval nose, and two rounded ears.

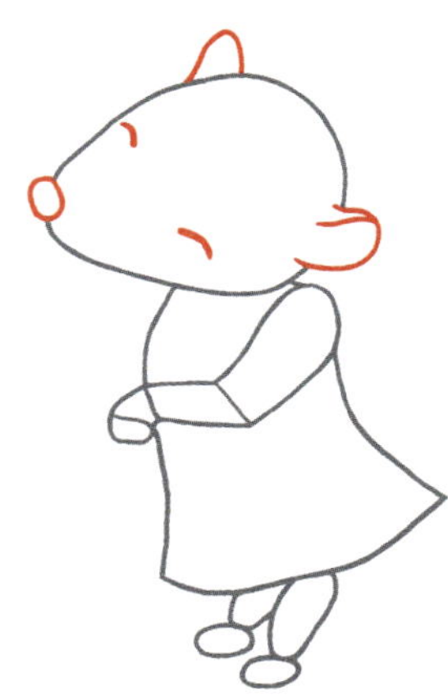

4. Make the dress with a rounded neckline and a pleated skirt with two bows.

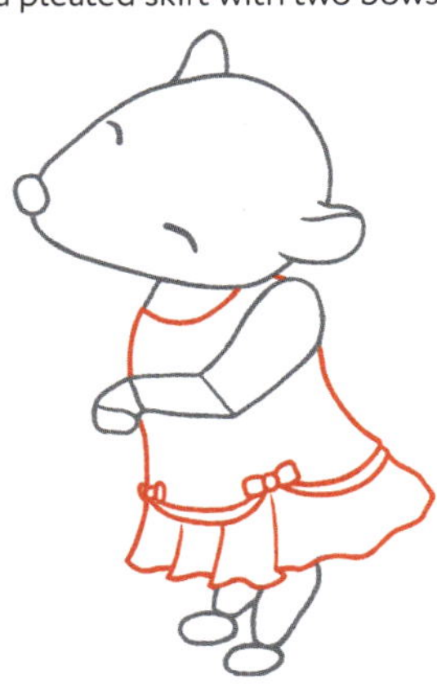

5. Add two arched paws with two toes. Then draw a large tail behind the body.

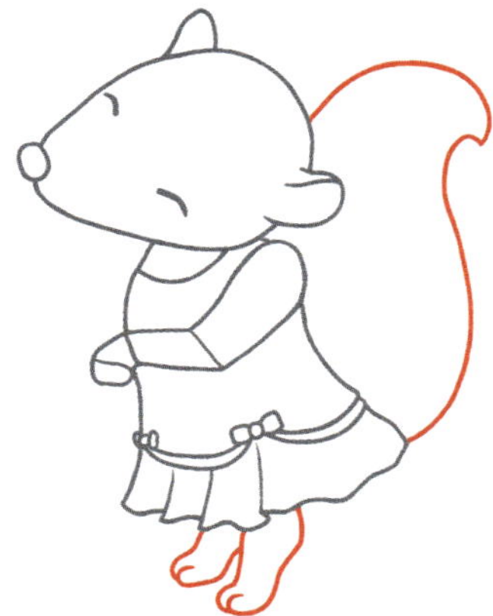

6. Draw a puffy sleeve at the shoulder and add the arm. Make the hand curve down.

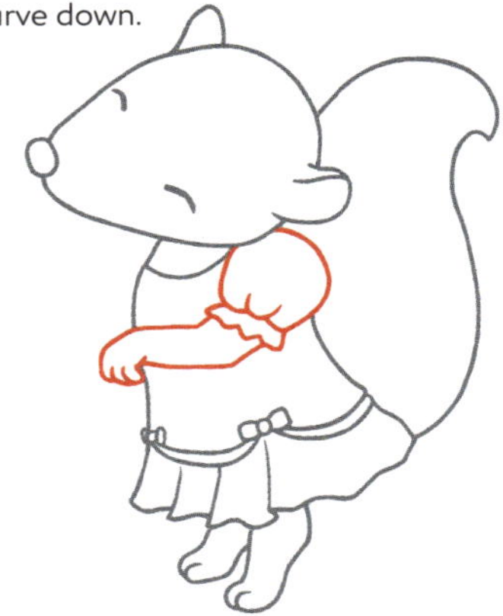

7. Add a bucket in the shape of a cat's head with the handle in the hand.

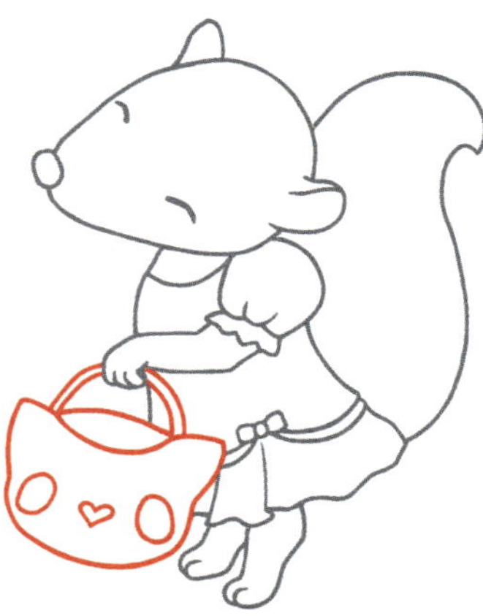

8. Cleanly trace your sketch with pencil on watercolor paper before inking.

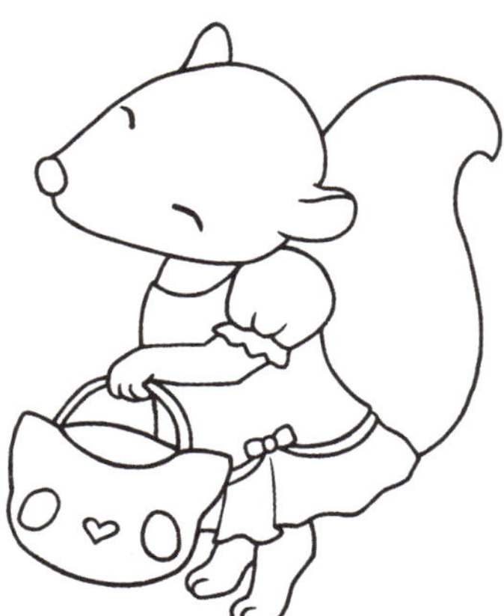

9. I used watercolors to make a traditional black and white skunk holding a black cat basket. I used dark yellow for the dress, cream for the skirt, and red for the details.

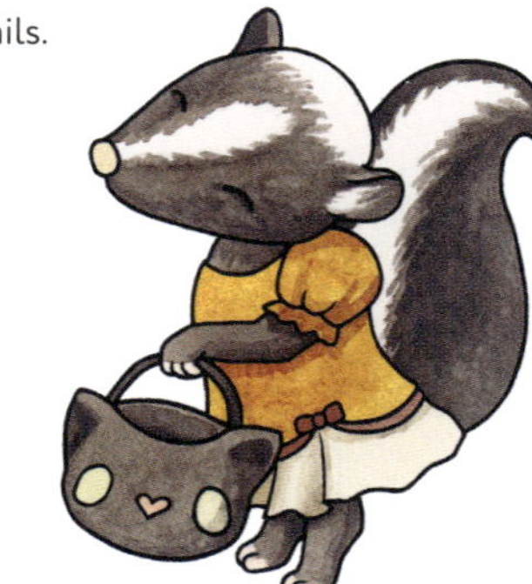

MUMMY CAT

1. Sketch a peanut shape for the body.

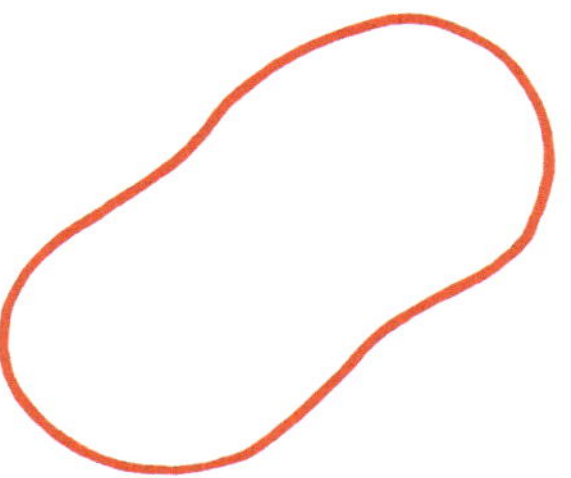

2. Add a rounded square head and triangle ears to the left of the body. Make a sleepy expression with thick arches for the eyes and a solid oval mouth.

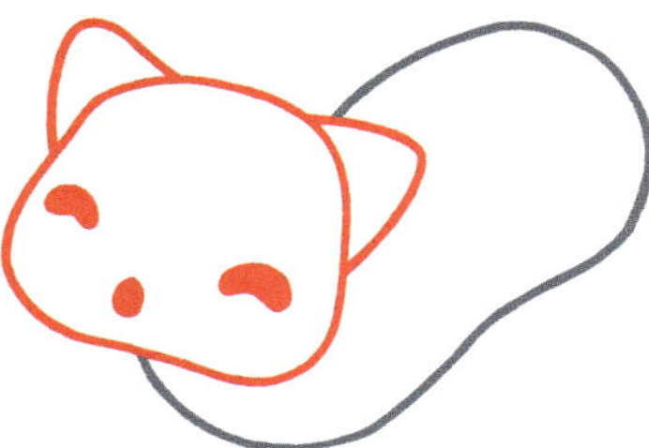

3. Draw two ovals for the front paws below the head.

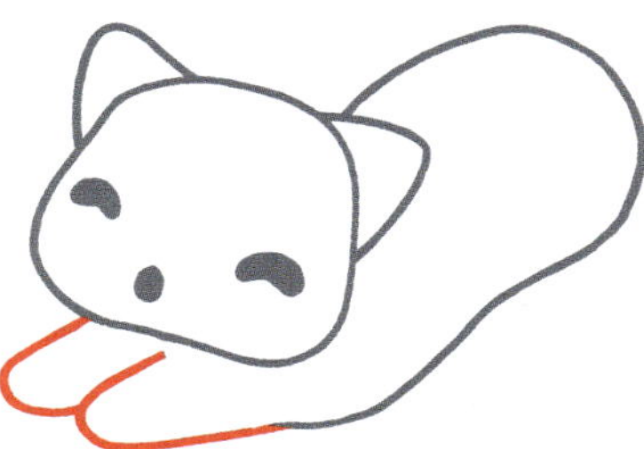

4. Draw a stretched-out back leg with curved lines.

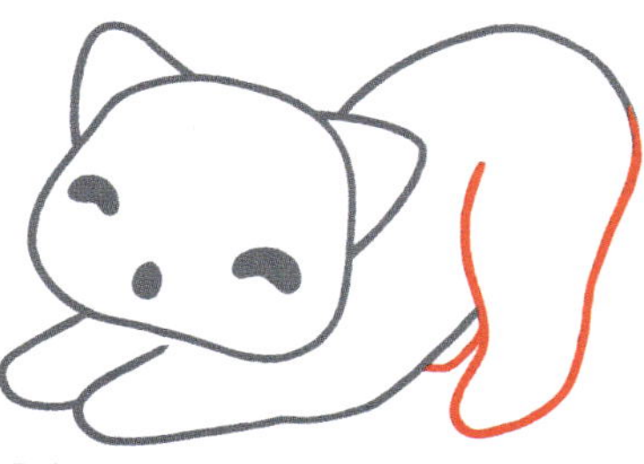

5. Make a curved tail at the end of the body that bends toward the head.

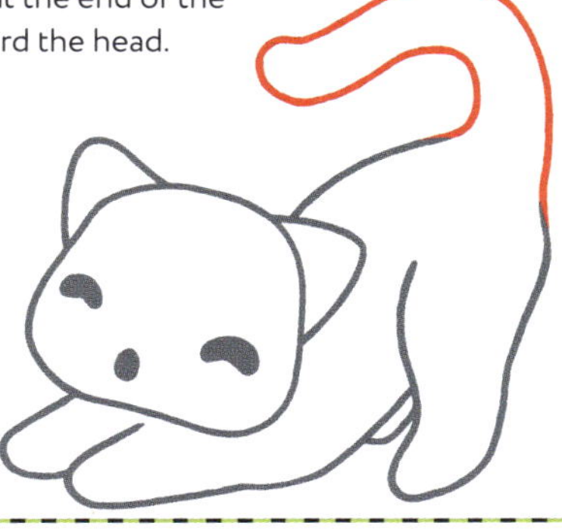

6. Add a crisscrossing pattern with curved lines for the bandages. Do one body part at a time.

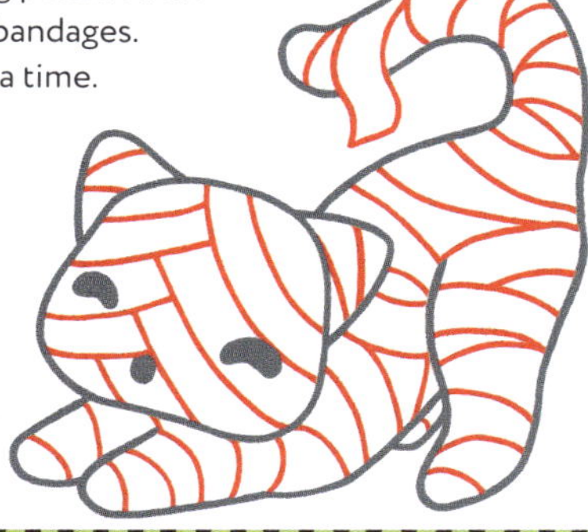

7. Cleanly trace your sketch with pencil on watercolor paper before inking.

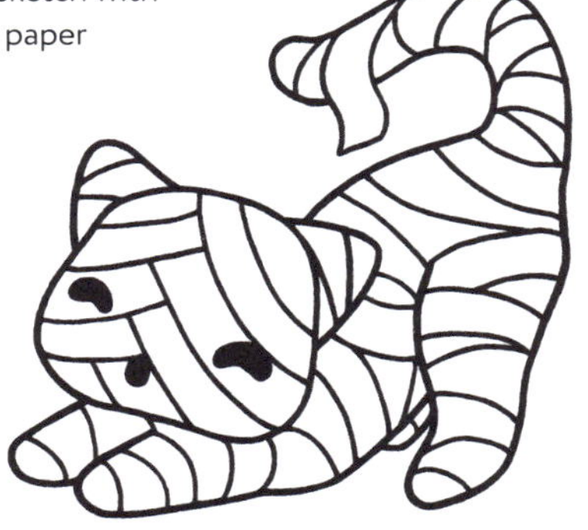

8. I made the bandages a pale beige color. Add shading on the right side of the body.

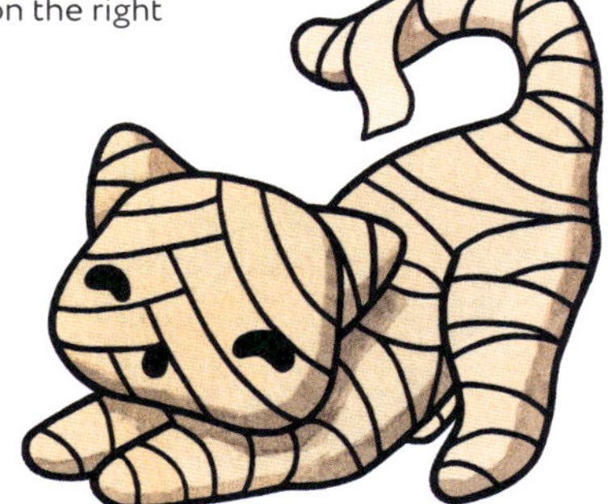

SKELE-FOX

1. Sketch two overlapping ovals, one horizontal for the head and one vertical for the body.

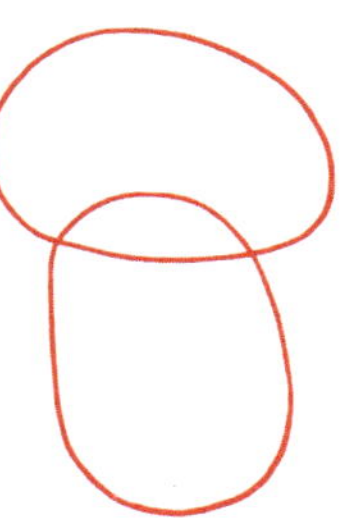

2. Add triangle ears with a line down the middle and fuzzy cheeks on the sides of the head.

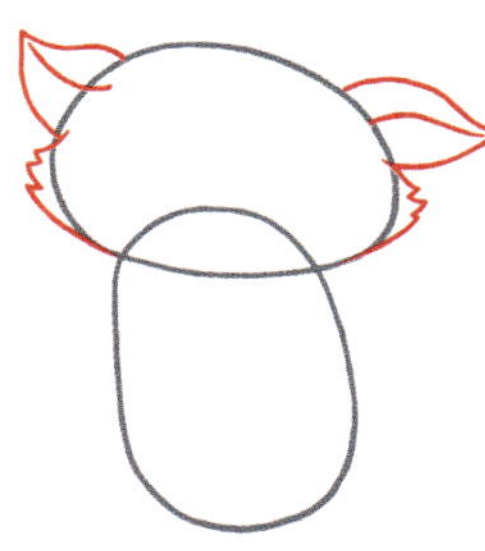

3. Draw solid oval eyes with a pupil, a triangle nose, and curved lines for the mouth.

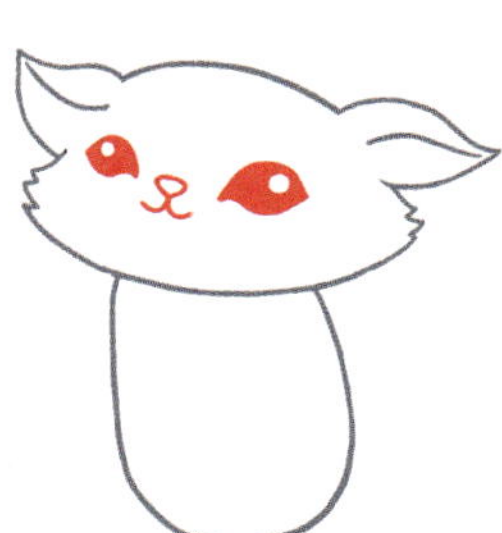

4. Draw a skull on top of the head in the shape of a mushroom. Add two oval eyes, an upside-down heart for the nose, and lines for the teeth.

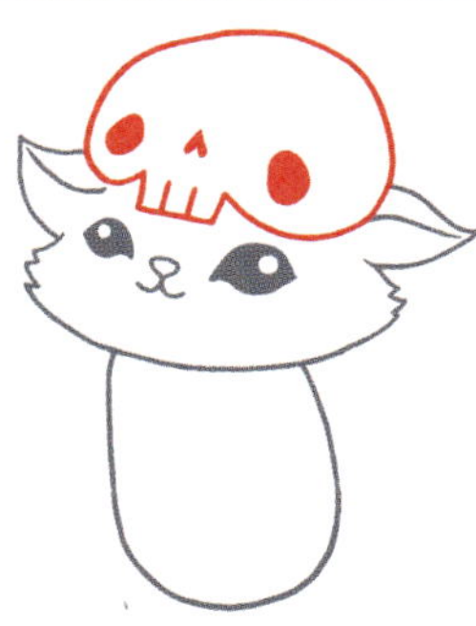

5. Add a big fluffy tail wrapped in front of the body. Draw lines for the front legs.

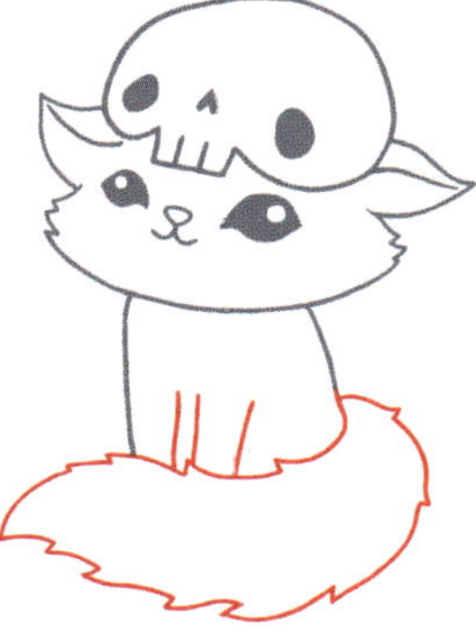

6. Draw bones on the torso with ovals for the collarbones and arms, and teardrops for the chest and ribs.

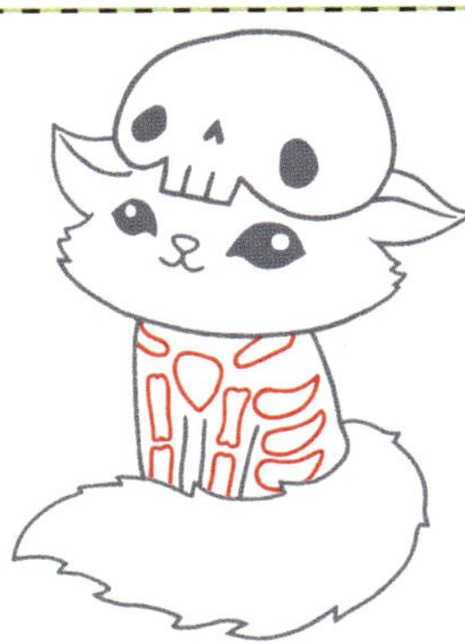

7. Cleanly trace your sketch with pencil on watercolor paper before inking.

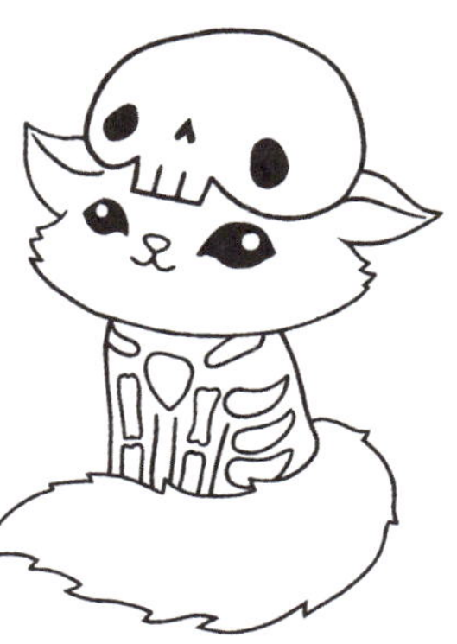

8. I made the fox a dark orange with white patches. Make the edges uneven for fuzzy texture. I used brown for the tops of the ears, and black and white for the skeleton shirt. Add shading on the skull, fox, and costume.

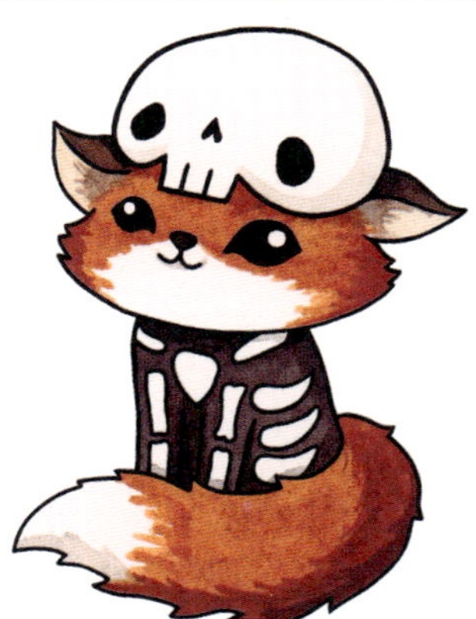

HOCUS POCUS POSSUM

1. Draw a broomstick with an oval stick and a bristled end. Add oval bindings where the stick and bristles meet.

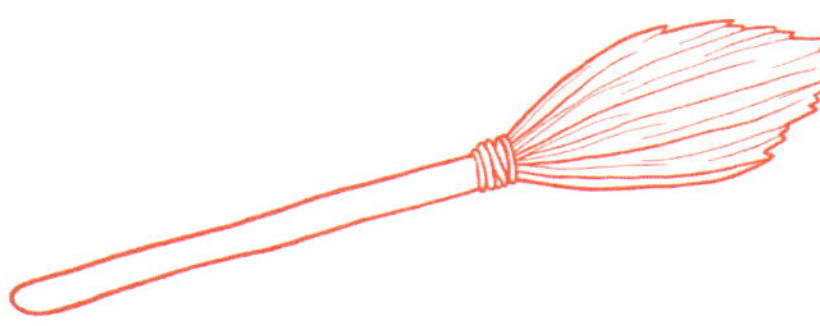

2. Draw a teardrop shape for the head with a rounded tip for the nose. Add rounded ears on the sides and teardrop-shaped eyes with highlights.

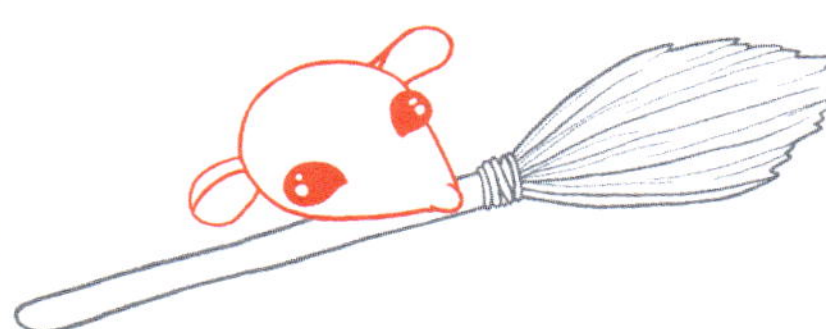

3. Draw a witch's hat on top of the head with a pointed oval and a triangle.

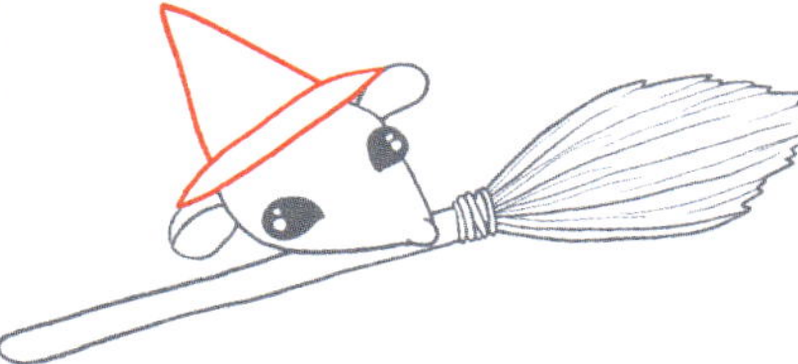

4. Add two sets of pointed fingers wrapped around the broomstick.

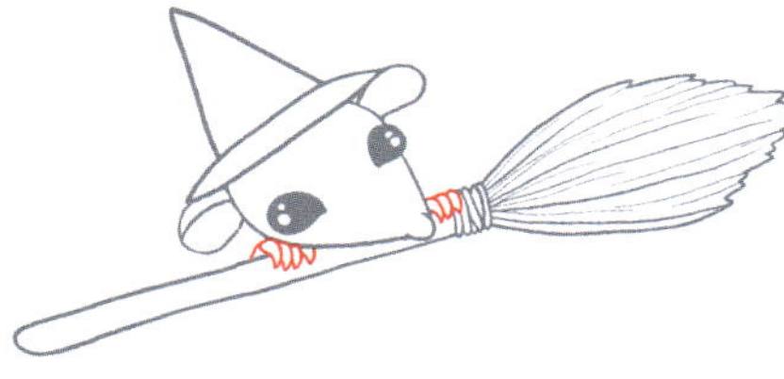

5. Under the stick, draw two feet with long toes. Use curved lines to draw the body and knee.

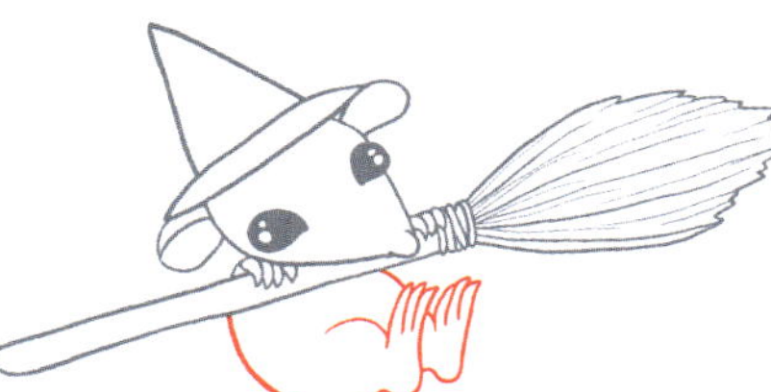

6. Under the body, draw a curled tail in the shape of a crescent.

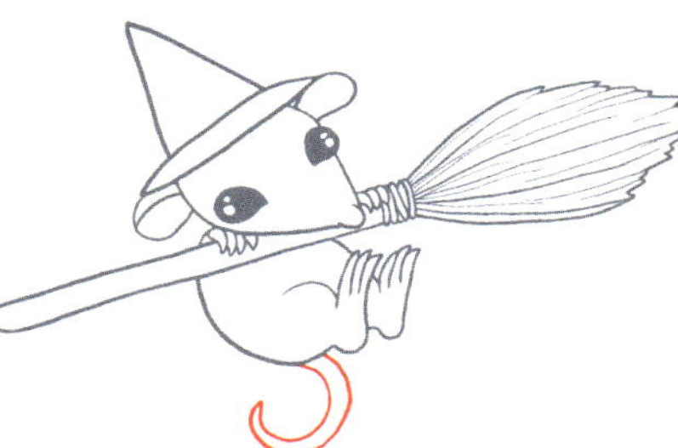
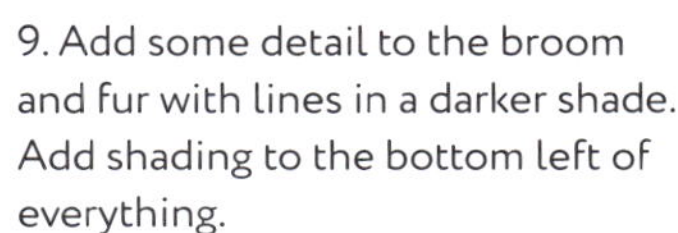

7. Cleanly trace your sketch with pencil on watercolor paper before inking. I used a pencil with a smaller lead point to sketch the inside bristles.

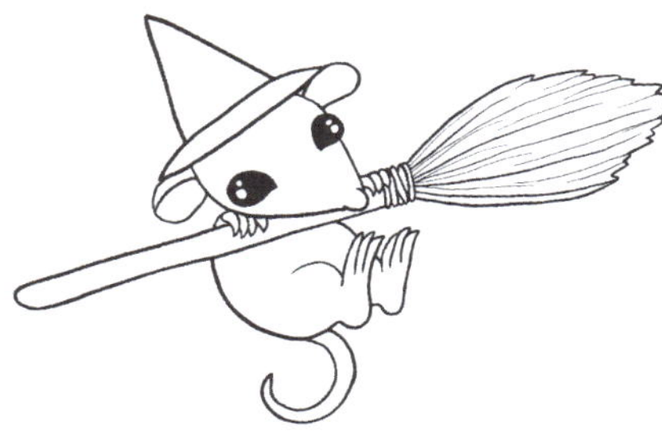

8. I used watercolors to make the opossum a light gray with a pale face and pink nose, claws, and tail. Then I used brown and yellow for the broom, and black for accents of the hat, bindings, and feet.

9. Add some detail to the broom and fur with lines in a darker shade. Add shading to the bottom left of everything.

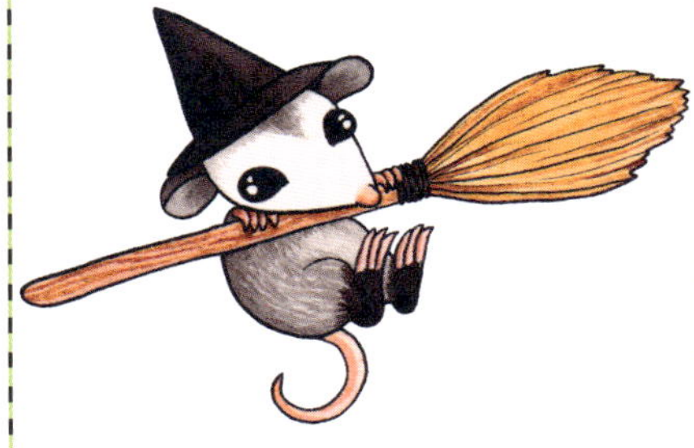

MUSHROOM PARASOL

1. Sketch a teardrop shape for the head. Draw a coat underneath with a rectangle with a line down the left side.

2. Add the arms with two ovals for the left and three ovals for the right. Use a rounded rectangle for the feet and lines for the legs.

3. Draw round and curved ears on the sides of the head. Add a solid circle eye with highlights and round the tip of the head for the nose.

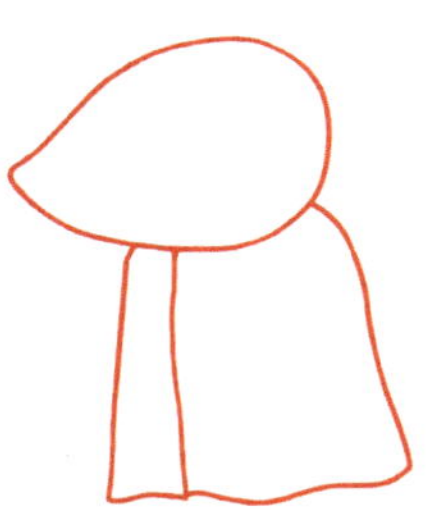

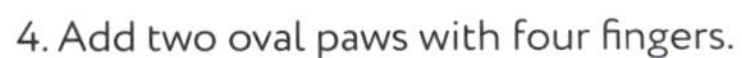

4. Add two oval paws with four fingers.

5. Draw the collar and sleeves of the coat with two drawstrings in the middle.

6. Give the mouse a curved tail and rain boots.

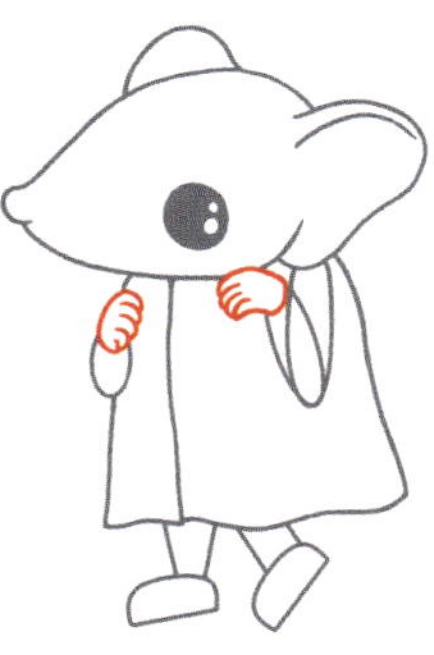

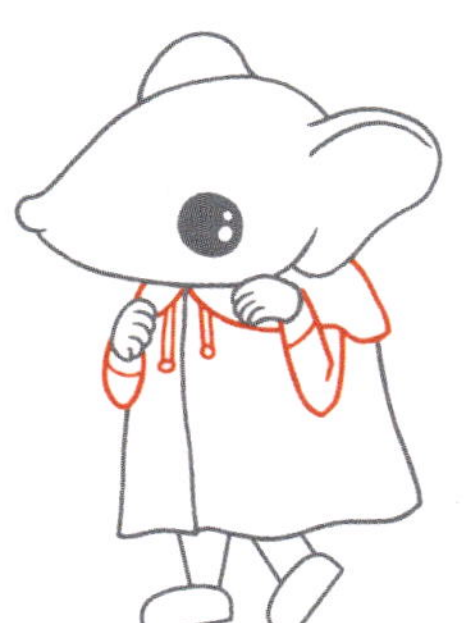

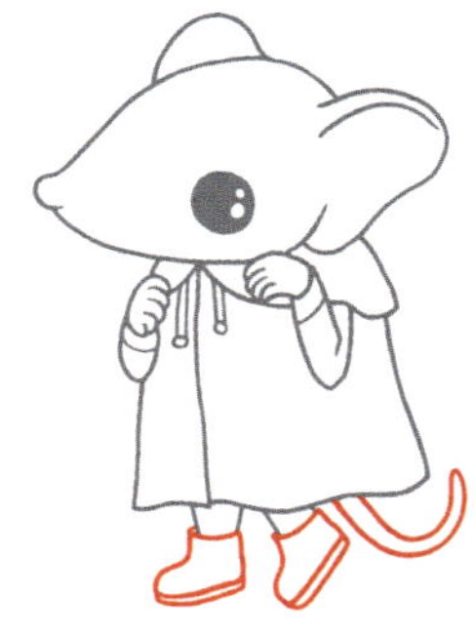

7. In the right hand, place an umbrella in the shape of a mushroom.

8. Cleanly trace your sketch with pencil on watercolor paper before inking.

9. I used watercolors of light brown, cream, pink, and dark yellow. Add striped texture to the underside of the mushroom and the mouse.

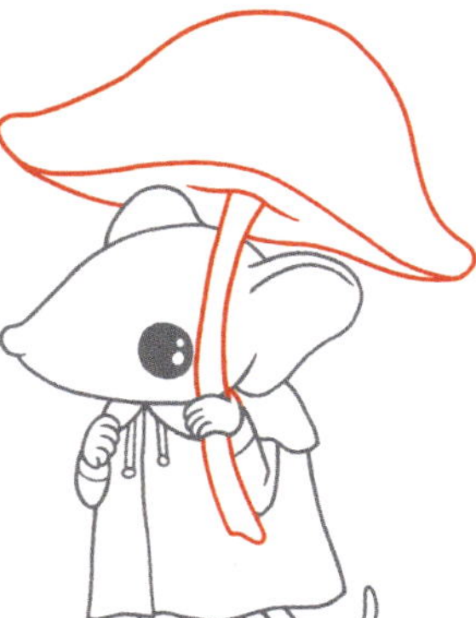

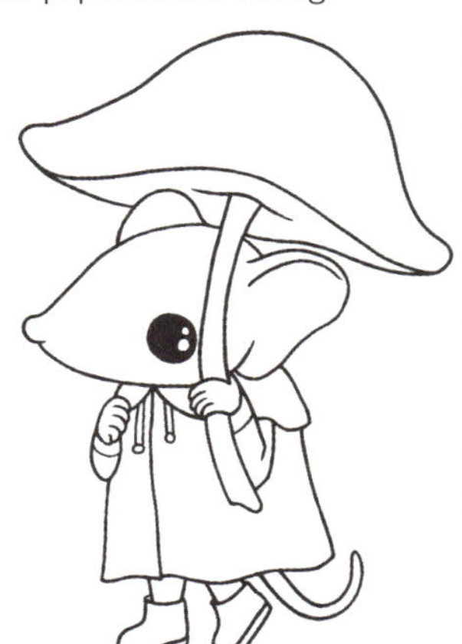

COUNT BUNNY

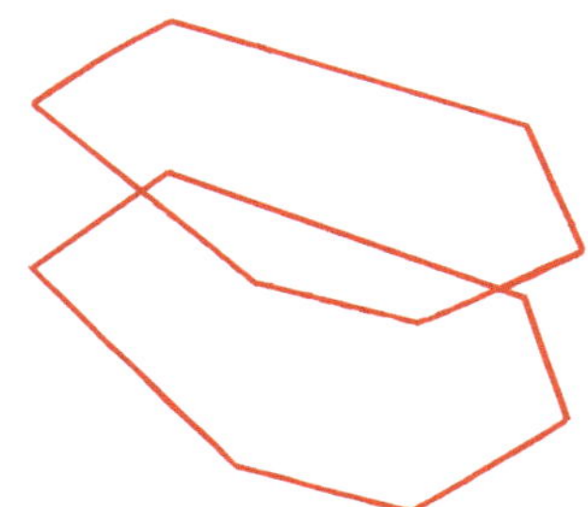

1. Draw two overlapping coffin shapes (long hexagons).

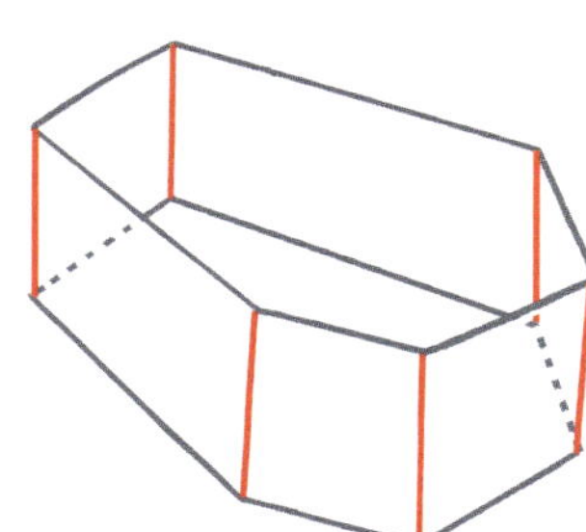

2. Connect the corners with lines and erase any lines that would be hidden.

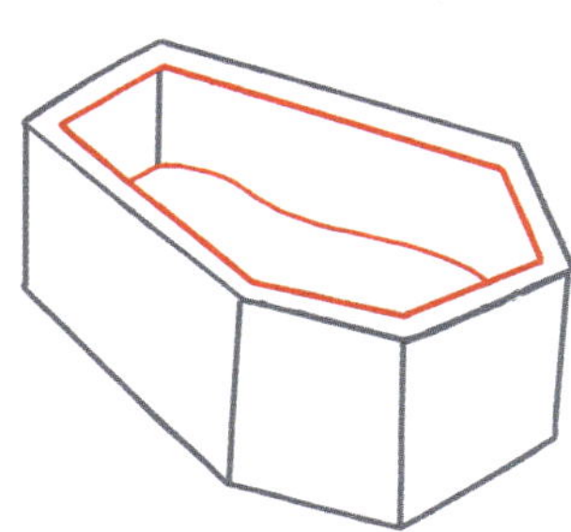

3. Draw a smaller coffin shape inside with a wavy line along the bottom.

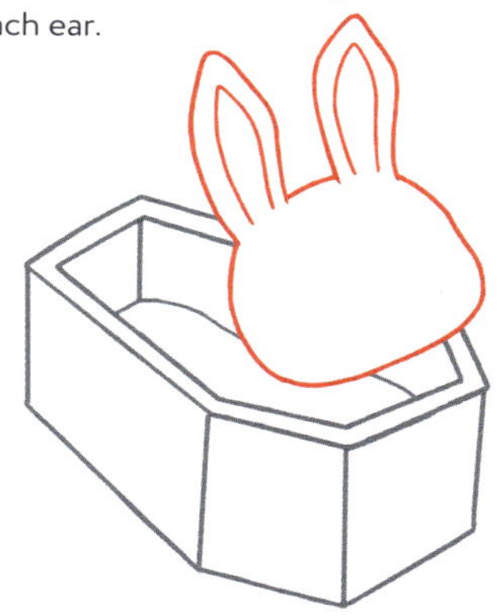

4. Just above the coffin, draw a rabbit's head with an oval and two tall triangle ears. Draw another triangle inside each ear.

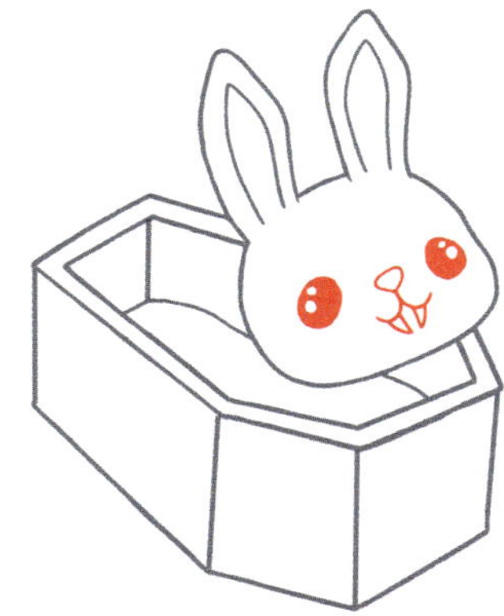

5. Add two solid circle eyes with highlights, a triangle nose, and two curved lines with triangle fangs for the mouth.

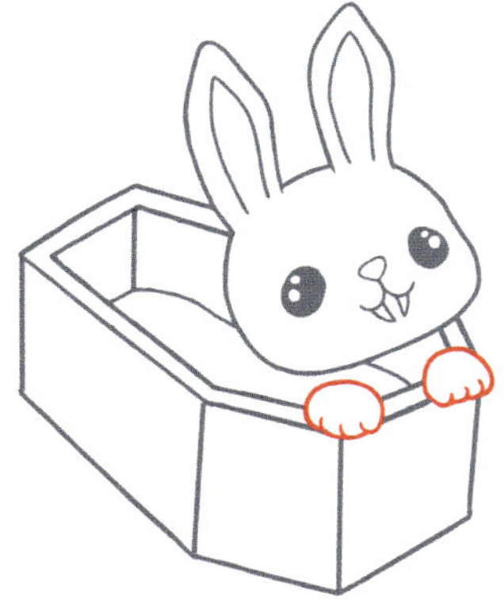

6. Draw two oval paws with four toes on the edge of the coffin.

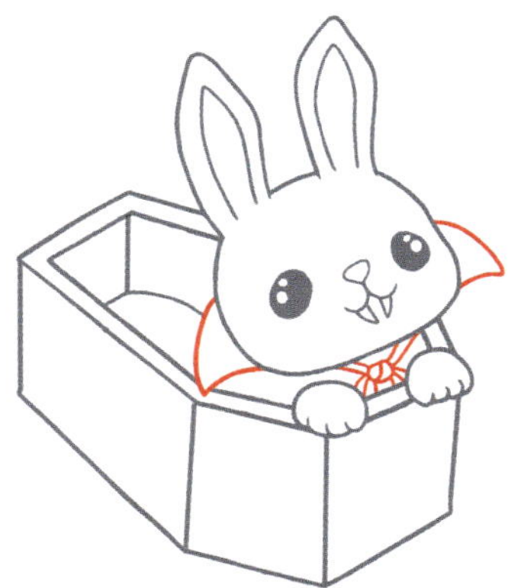

7. Draw the corners of a cape on the sides of the head and a tie under the chin.

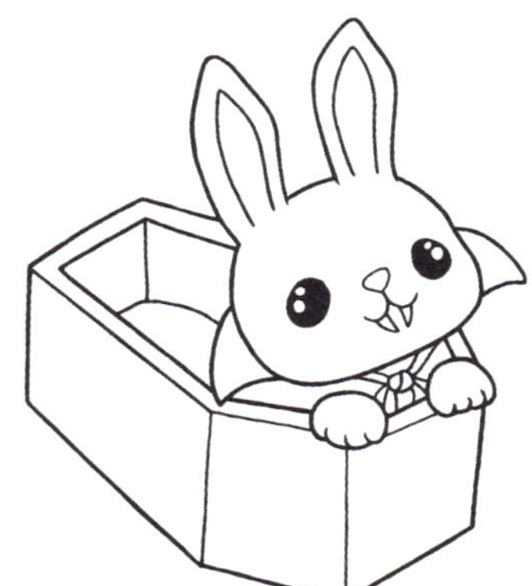

8. Cleanly trace your sketch with pencil on watercolor paper before inking.

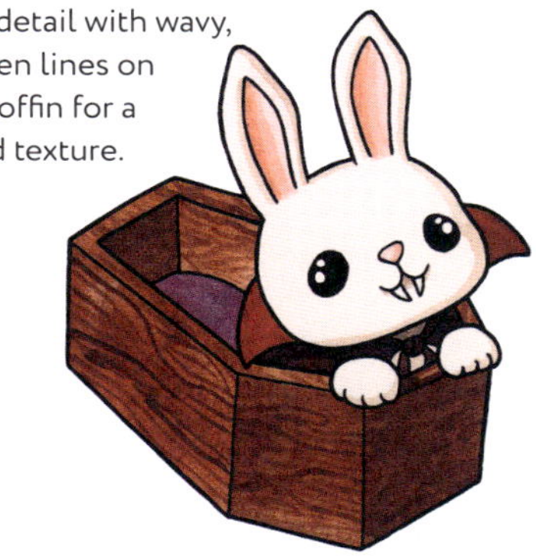

9. I used watercolors to make the coffin brown with purple bedding. I left the rabbit white and added pink accents. The cape is black with red inside. Add detail with wavy, uneven lines on the coffin for a wood texture.

SKELETON CAT TREE

1. Draw an oval for the head and a line for the neck. Add lines for the arms, with the left arm pointing up to the right and the right arm pointing to the left.

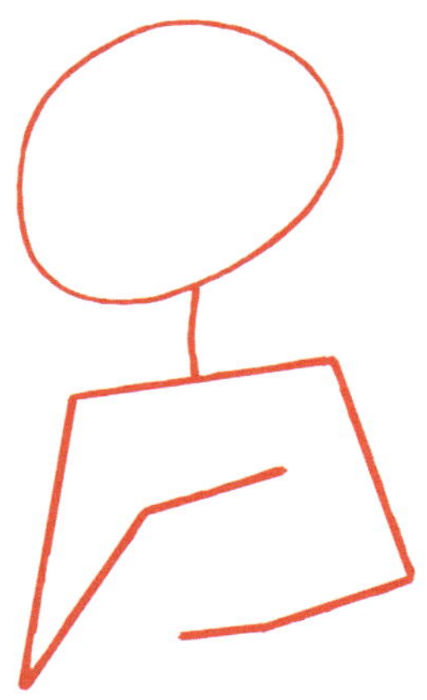

2. Turn the oval into the shape of a mushroom for the skull. Make a happy expression with curved lines for the eyes, an upside-down heart for the nose, and lines for the teeth.

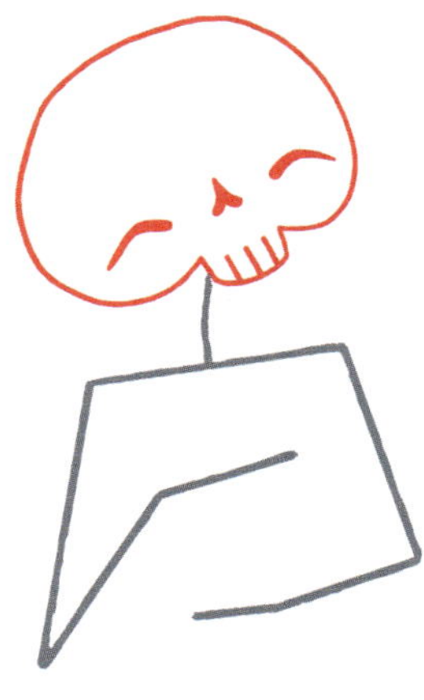

3. Draw a short-sleeved T-shirt with a rounded collar.

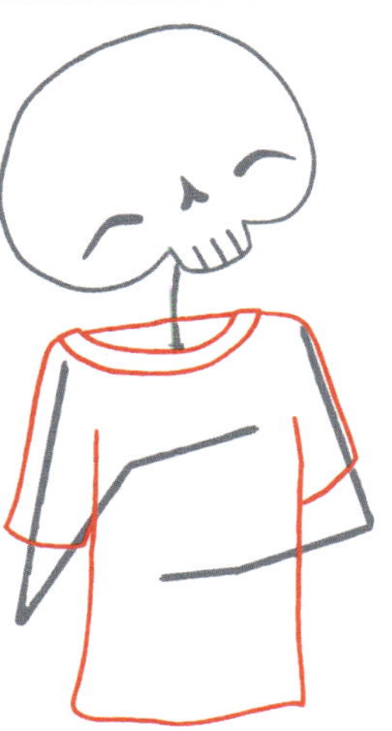

4. Draw the spine between the skull and T-shirt with four stacked rectangles.

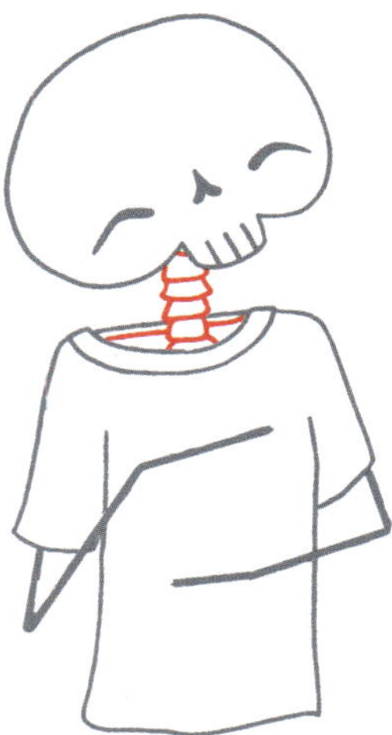

5. Use the sketched lines to draw the skeleton's arms. Separate the fingers into three bones each.

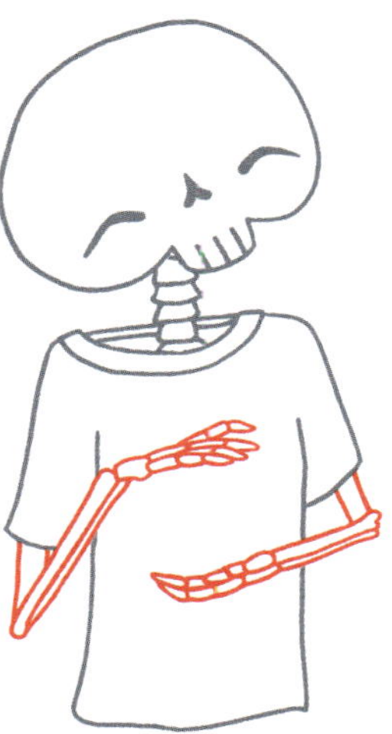

6. Place a sleeping kitten on the right arm. Draw a round head with triangle ears and a sleeping expression. Add a round body with a curved line for the knee and dangling tail.

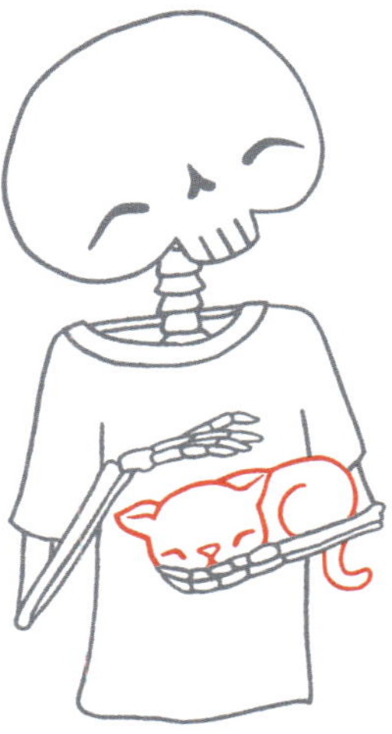

7. Add a second kitten hanging off the right shoulder. Draw only the back of the body with a curved tail and two legs.

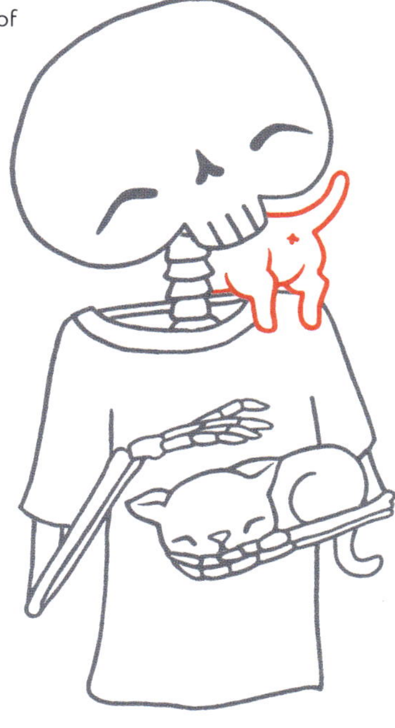

8. Draw a third kitten on top of the head with a rounded head and triangle ears. Add a sweet face and two arms.

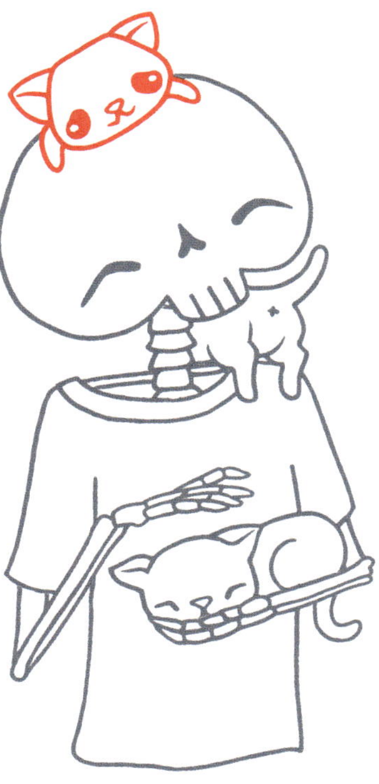

9. Cleanly trace your sketch with pencil on watercolor paper before inking.

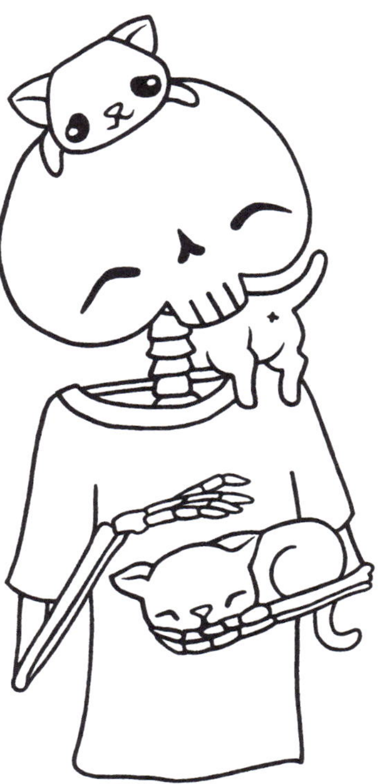

10. I kept the skeleton white and used watercolors to make the shirt black. Then I made each cat a different color using gray, muted orange, and cream. With a thin brush or pen, add detail to the kittens with short lines to make patterns. Add shading with a warm gray color or India ink on the skeleton and underneath the kittens.

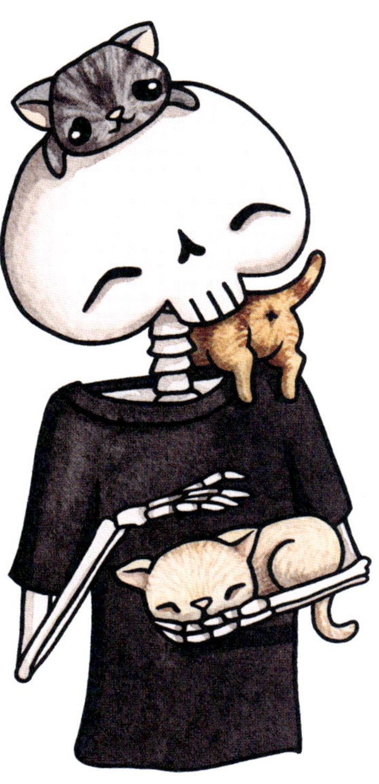

MAGICAL HEDGEHOG

1. Sketch a bean shape.

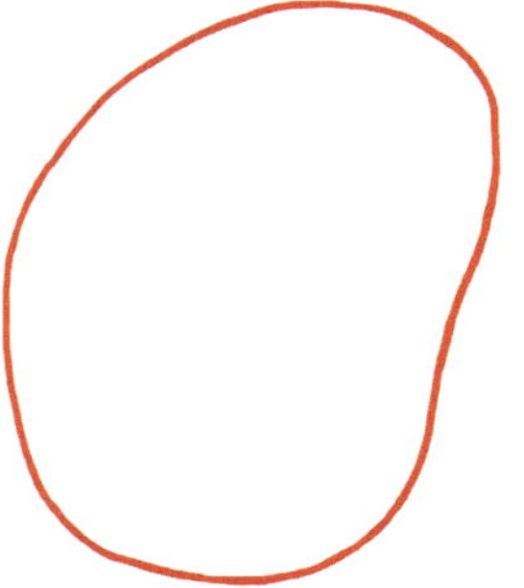

2. Add a rounded ear on the top left. Draw two solid circle eyes with highlights, a triangle nose, and two curved lines for the mouth.

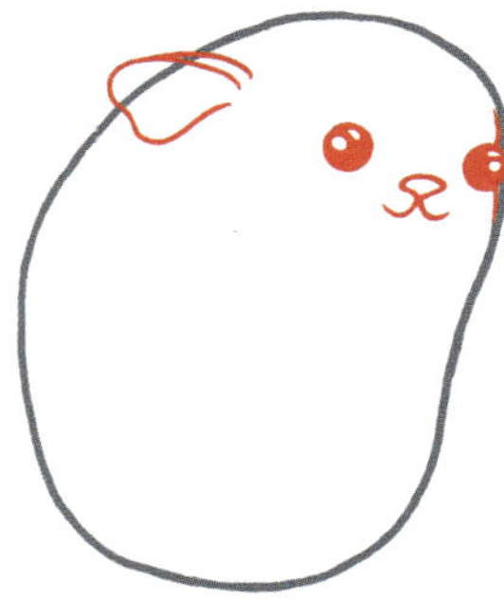

3. Draw a large witch's hat on top of the head with a trapezoid brim and a triangle top.

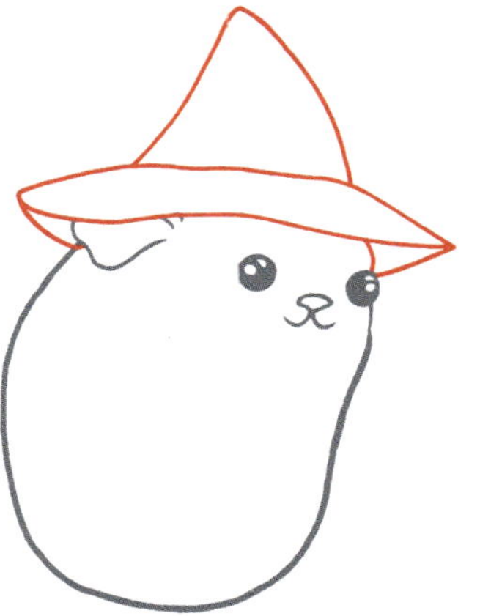

4. Use the bean sketch to draw a round body. Draw two small, short legs with four toes on the feet. Draw a curve between the legs.

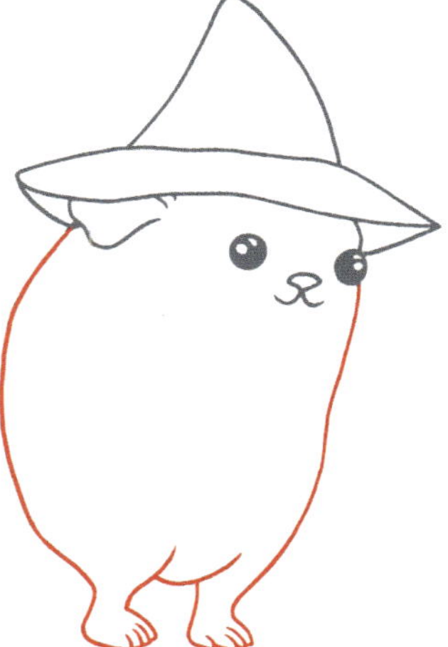

5. Draw the right arm with a mushroom gripped in the hand.

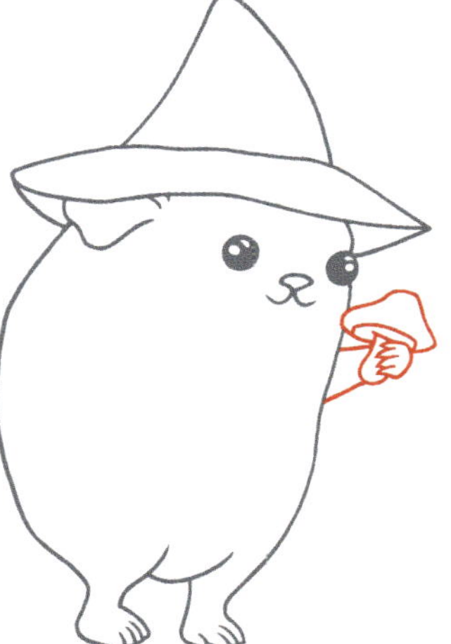

6. Draw the left arm with a basket over the wrist. Add abstract shapes for the mushrooms inside the basket.

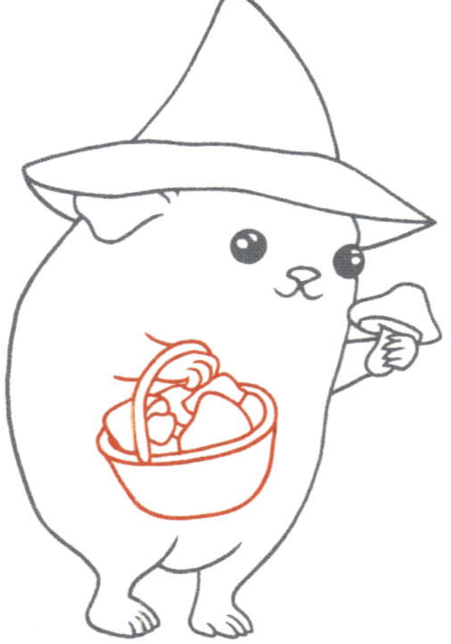

7. Around the body, add a cloak that drapes over the left arm and ties at a bow under the chin.

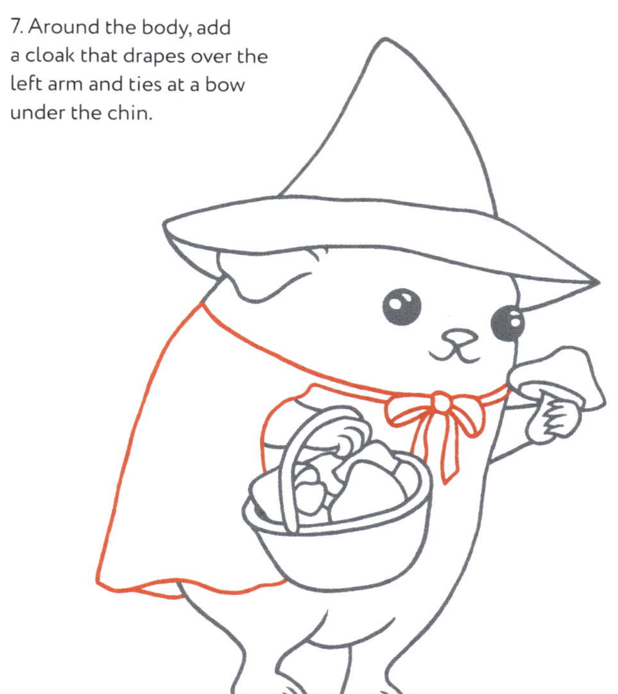

8. Draw spiky quills around the face and add texture along the body.

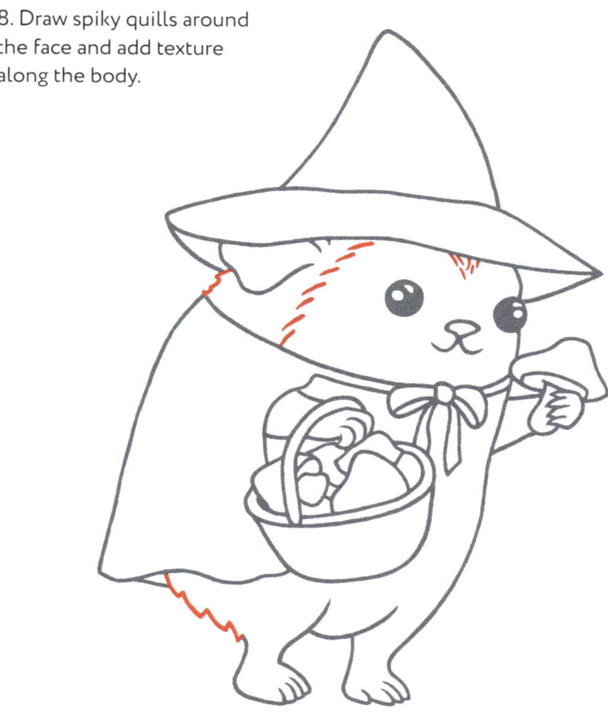

9. Cleanly trace your sketch with pencil on watercolor paper before inking.

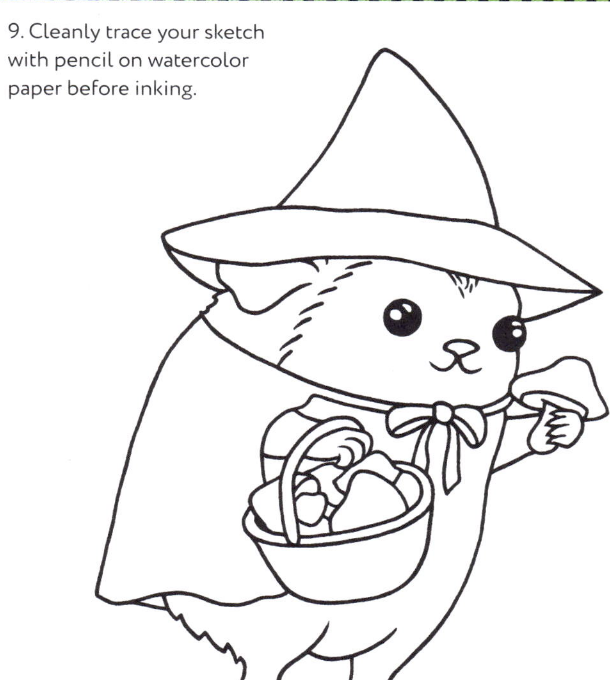

10. I used watercolors to make the hedgehog light brown and the hat and cloak black. The basket is brown with hues of red for the mushrooms. Add the quill texture along the head and back with a dark brown in short lines. Add shading as if the light is coming from the top right.

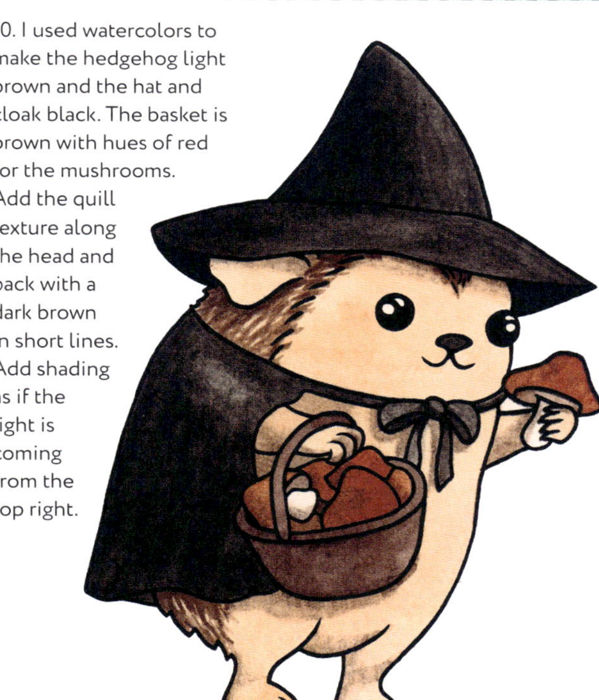

BADGER'S BEWITCHING BATH

1. Sketch two ovals, making the top one thin and the bottom one thicker.

2. Connect the ovals with curved lines on the sides to form a cauldron shape.

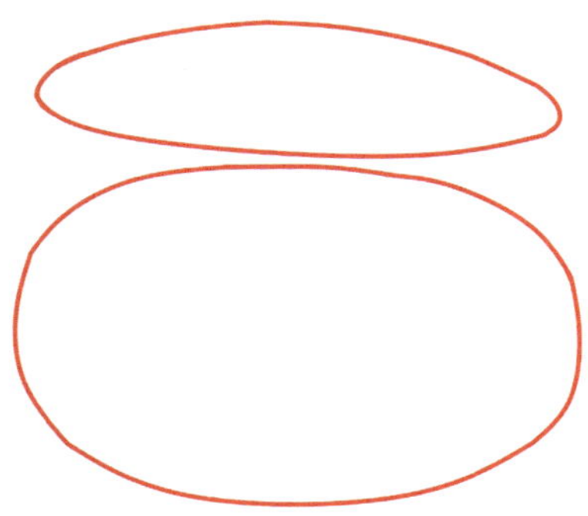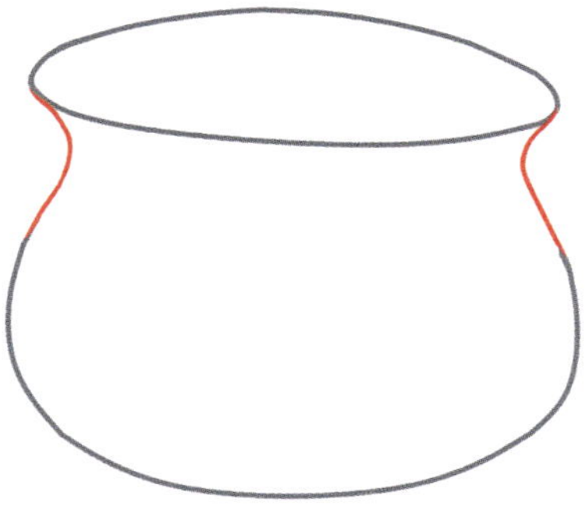

3. Draw two more curved lines to form the rim and liquid inside.

4. Sketch a teardrop shape for the head just above the water.

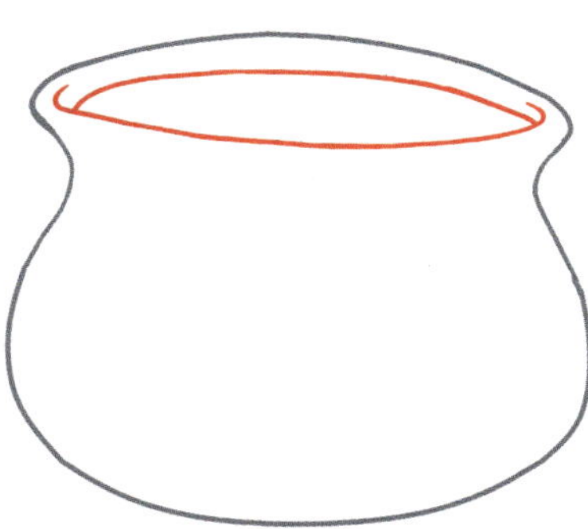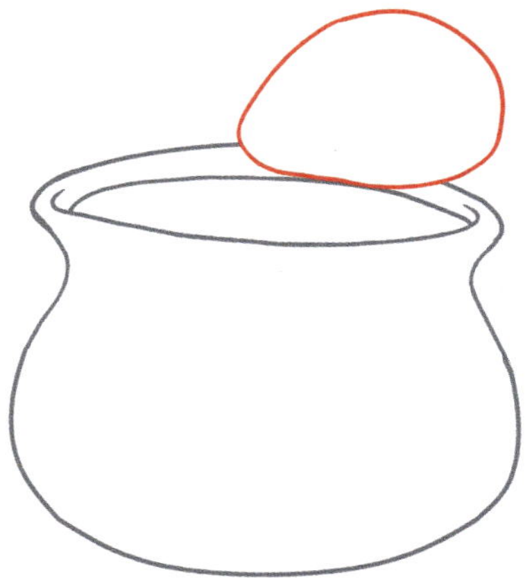

5. Add a droopy witch's hat with a thin oval for the brim and a triangle top that folds over on the right.

6. Add small, rounded ears with a line down the middle, two solid oval eyes with highlights, and an oval nose.

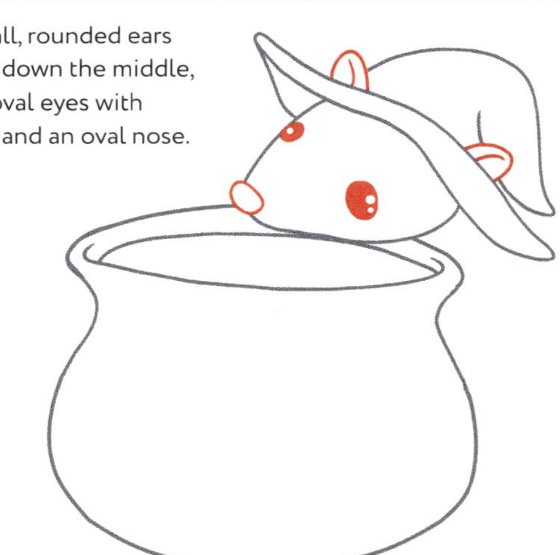

7. Draw a wavy line for the neck at the waterline.

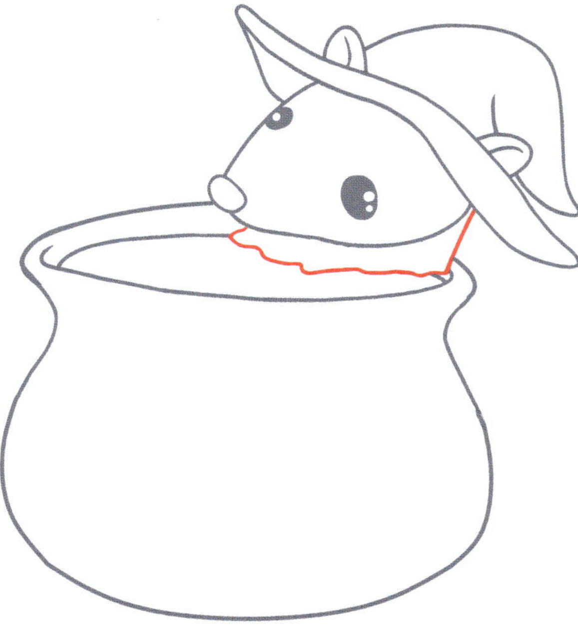

8. Cleanly trace your sketch with pencil on watercolor paper before inking.

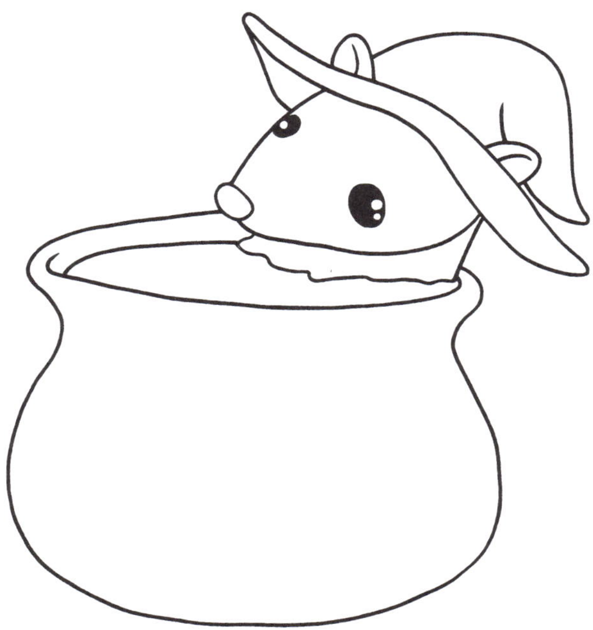

9. Use light shades of gray for the badger and water and dark shades of gray for the hat and cauldron.

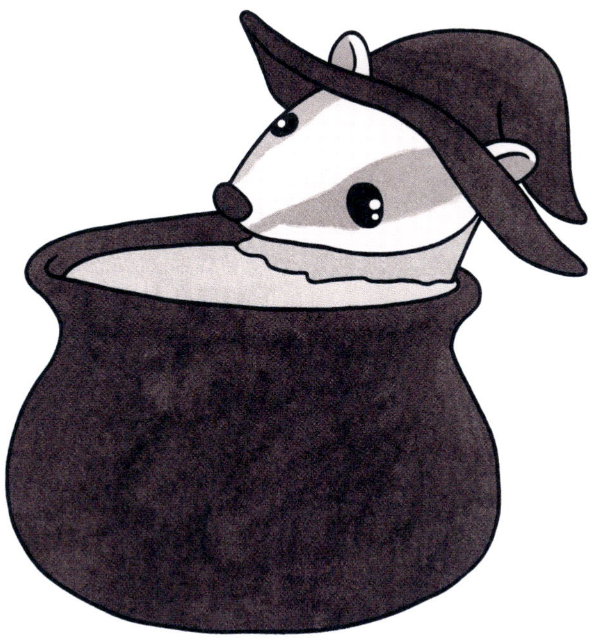

10. With a thin brush or pen, add texture to the badger in the ears and along its stripes and neck. Add detail with wavy lines on the water. Add shading on the hat, under the head, and on the cauldron.

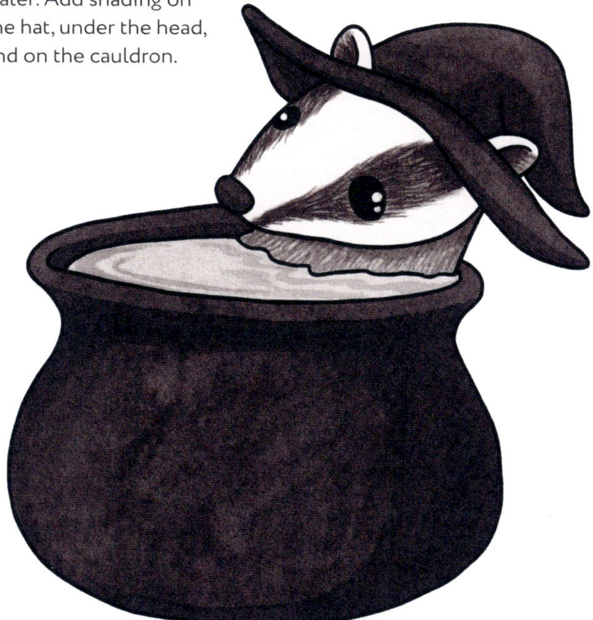

1. Draw a coiled snake with a compact S shape. Add a teardrop-shaped head on the top right and a wavy tail on the bottom.

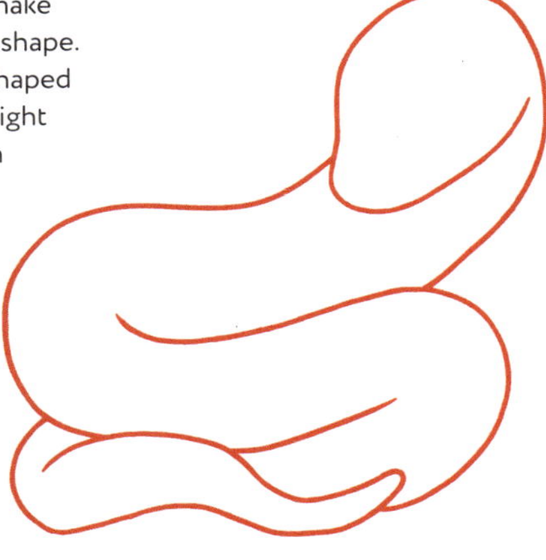

2. Sketch a round head and the top of a torso in the middle of the snake body.

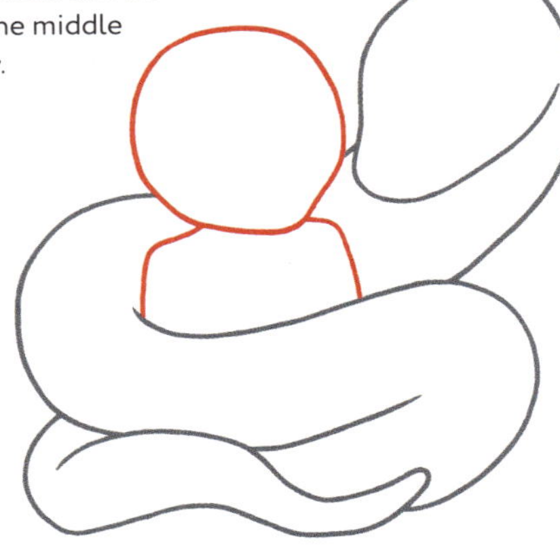

3. Draw straight hair in a short bob with bangs.

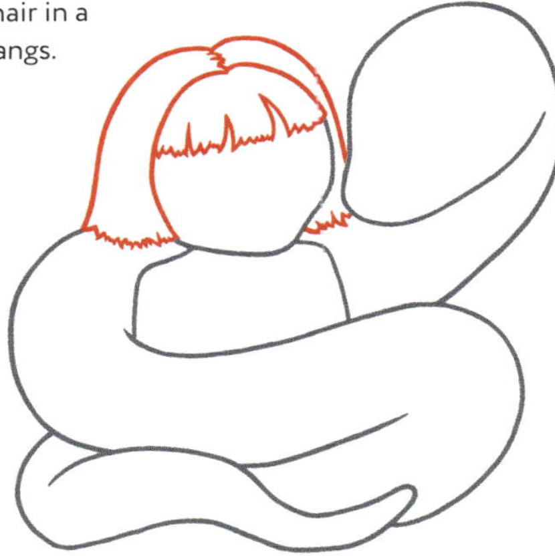

4. Give the human a vampire face with curved lines for eyes and an open mouth with two triangle fangs.

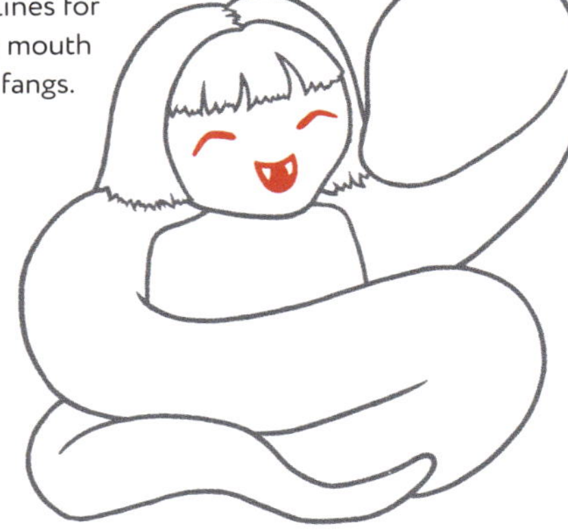

5. Add a shirt with a collar and bow at the middle.

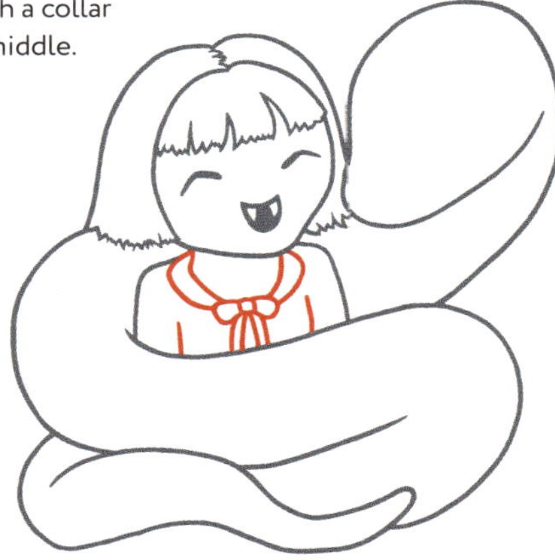

6. Draw two hands resting on top of the snake.

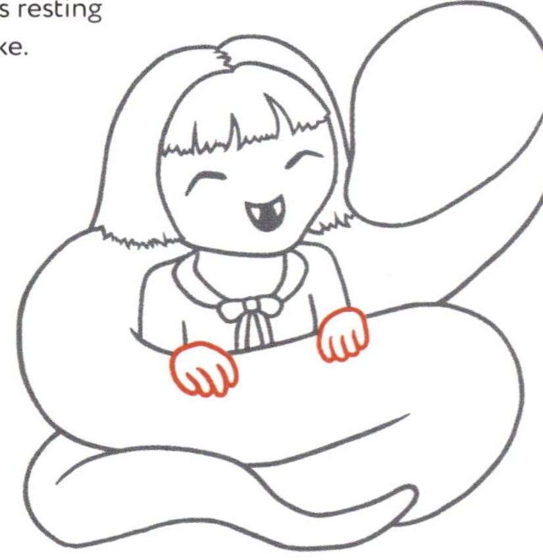

7. Make the legs fold on top of each other with the feet on the left. Draw simple flat shoes. Draw only where it's visible between the snake.

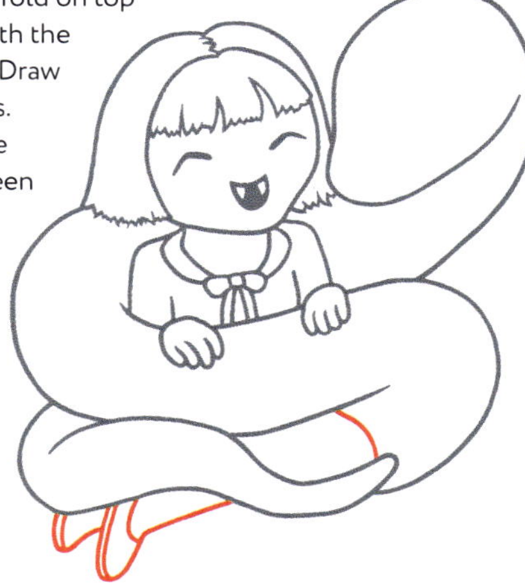

8. Draw the snake's face with an arched line for the eye, two dashes for the nostrils, and a curve for the mouth.

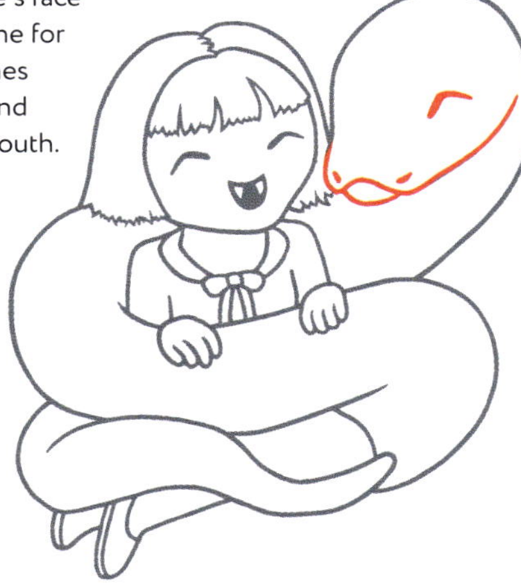

9. Cleanly trace your sketch with pencil on watercolor paper before inking.

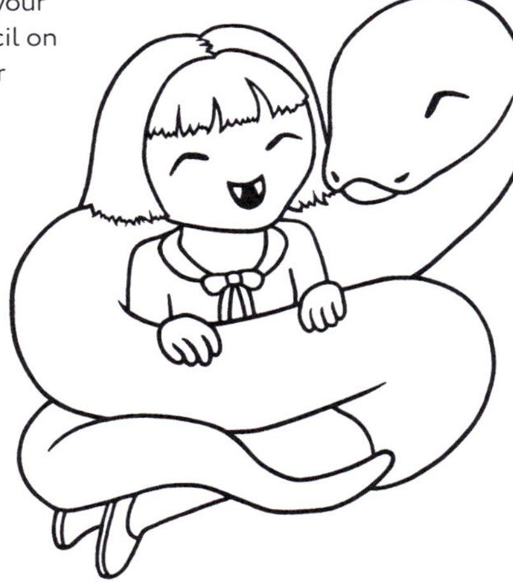

10. I used diluted ink in shades of gray, leaving some white in the hair.

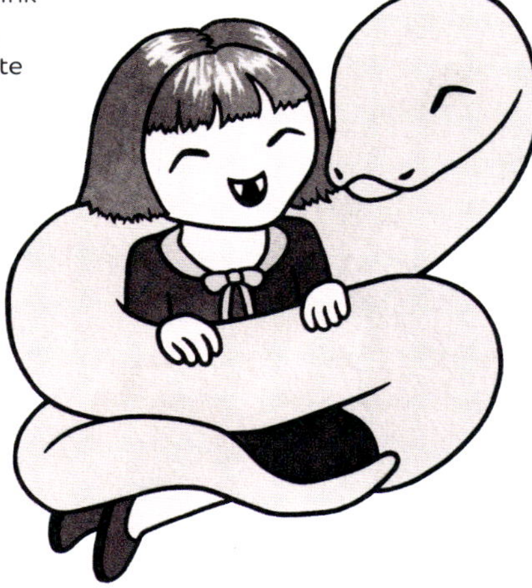

11. Make a pattern on your snake with a slightly darker color. Add a second layer to the pattern with a darker shade than the previous one. Add shading along the underside of the snake body, under her hair and head, and on her clothes.

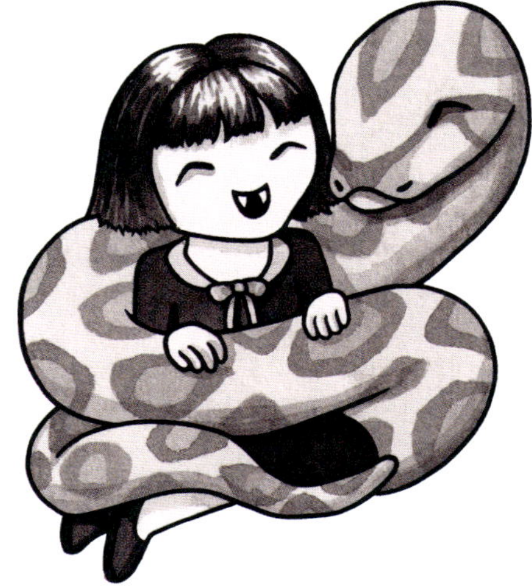

OWL FAMILIAR

1. Draw three ovals to form a frame.

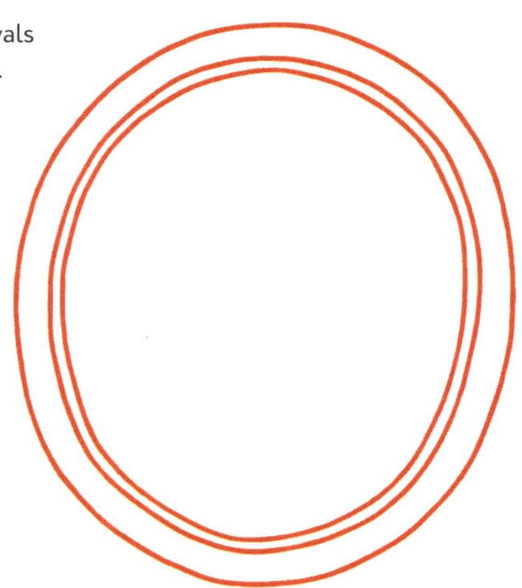

2. Sketch a figure in the right side of the frame. Draw a circle for the head, lines for the neck, and a bent left arm with two long ovals and a circle for the hand.

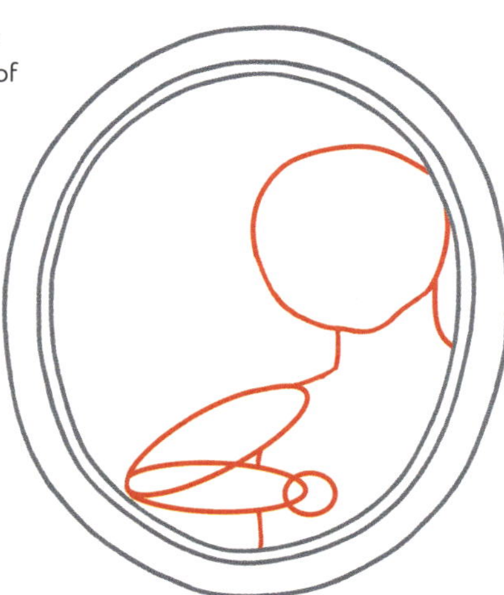

3. Sketch the body of an owl sitting on the arm.

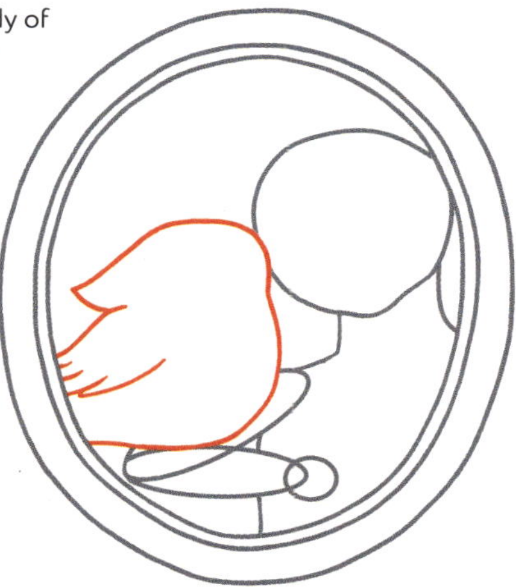

4. Draw the owl's face with arched lines for the eyes and circles around them. Add the beak with a triangle and a curve underneath.

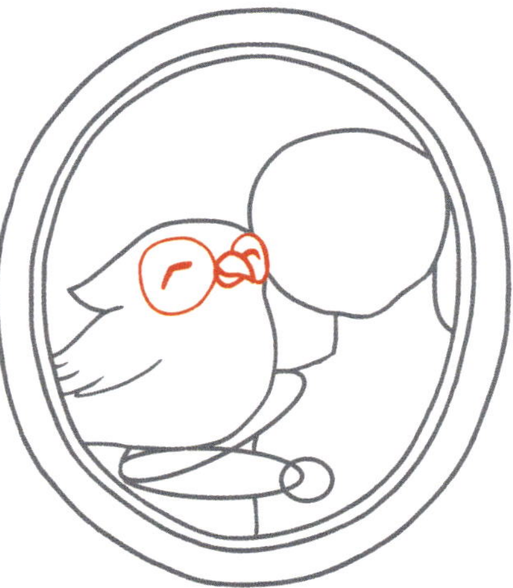

5. Add claws under the body with three talons each.

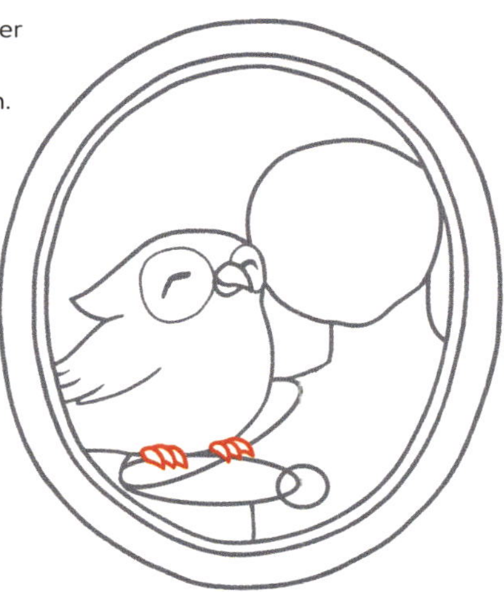

6. Draw the witch's solid oval eyes with highlights and a smiling mouth. Add detail to the neck by extending the line.

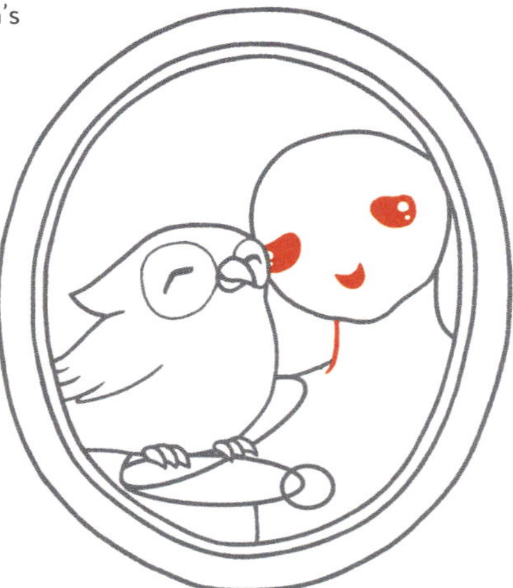

7. Add a simple witch's hat with a curved brim and triangle top. Draw long wavy hair on the right.

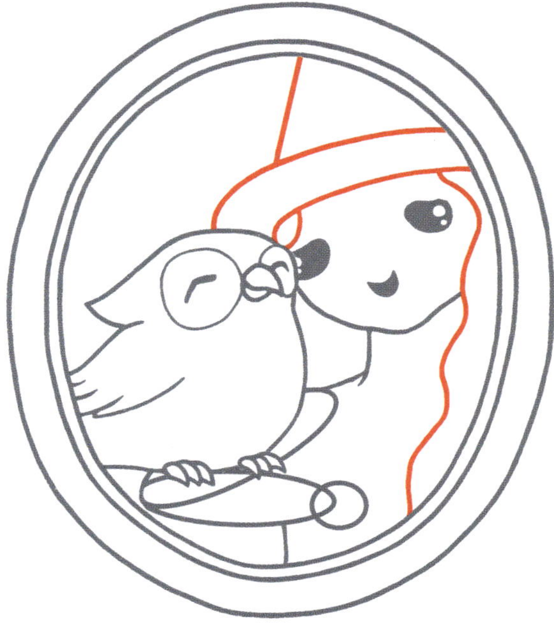

8. Draw a long-sleeved shirt with a rounded neckline and add the hand.

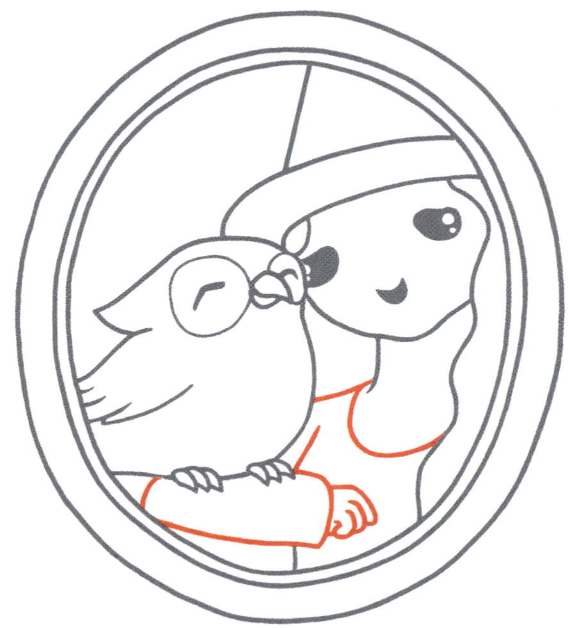

9. Cleanly trace your sketch with pencil on watercolor paper before inking.

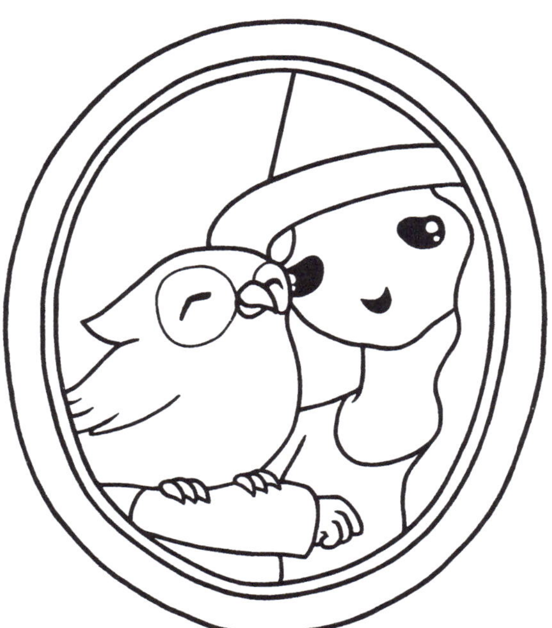

10. Use shades of gray, with the hat, shirt, and outer frame in black. I used diluted ink. Add texture to the owl with a triangle pattern and to the witch's hair with wavy lines. Add shading to the witch and owl.

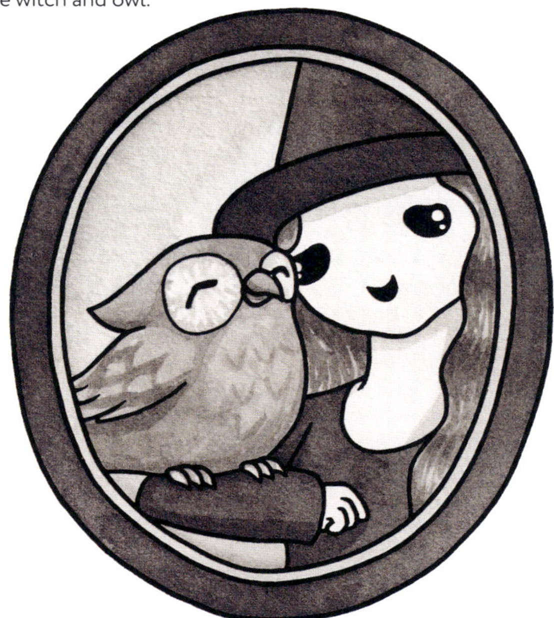

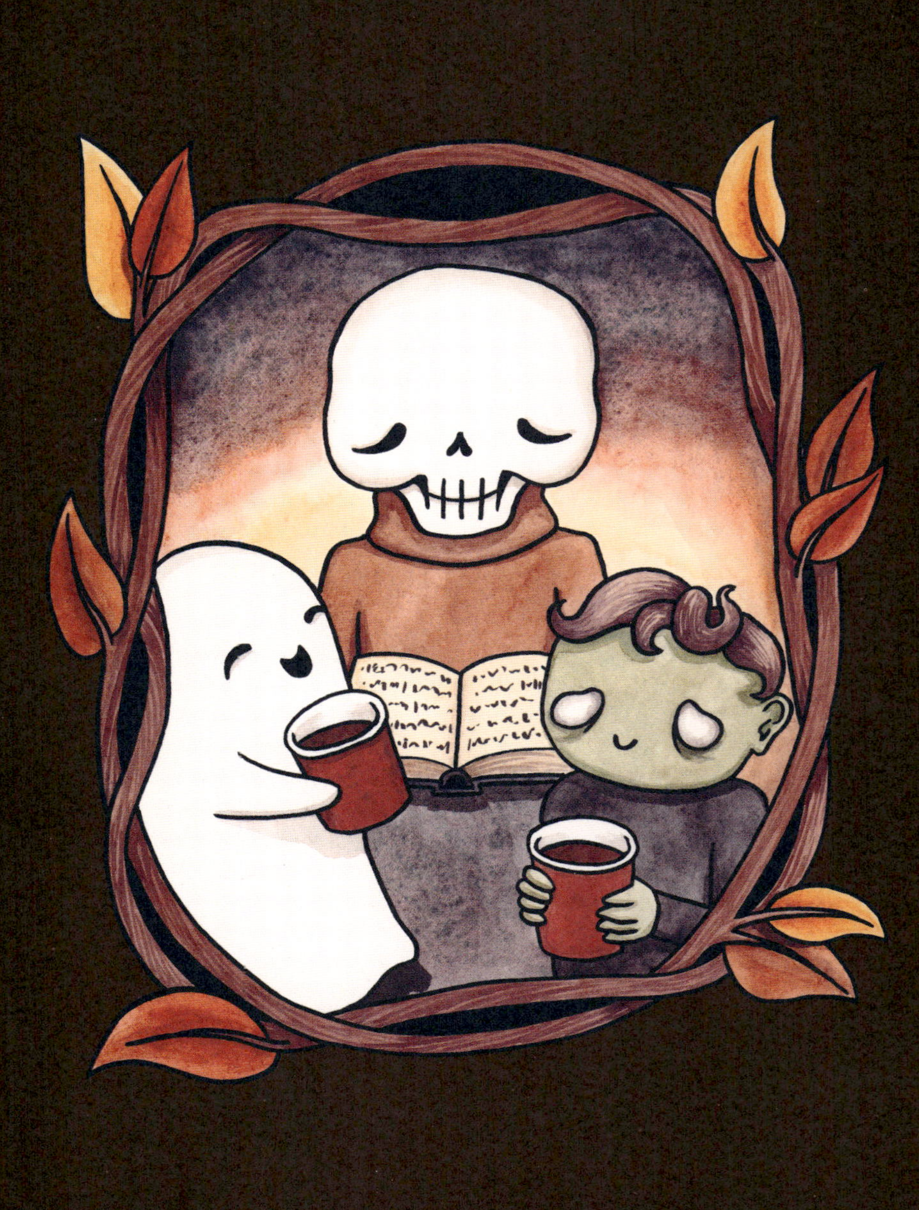

gourd hamlet

GHOSTLY FRIEND

1. Draw a long bell shape.

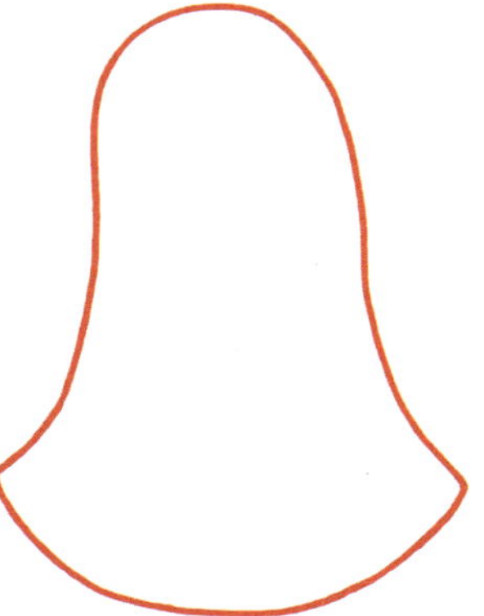

2. Add a happy face.

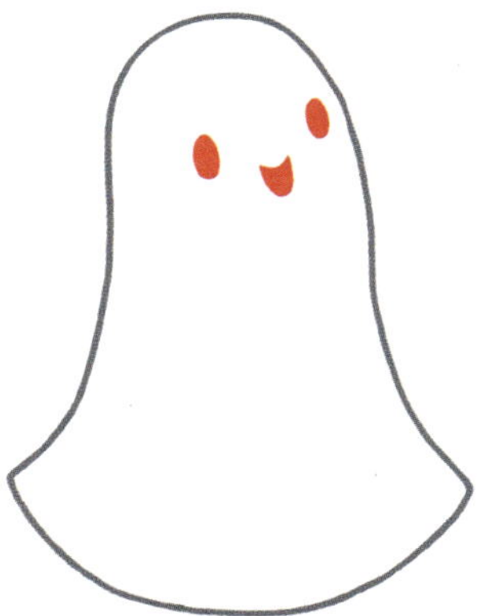

3. Use curved lines to make the bottom of the bell look like pleated fabric.

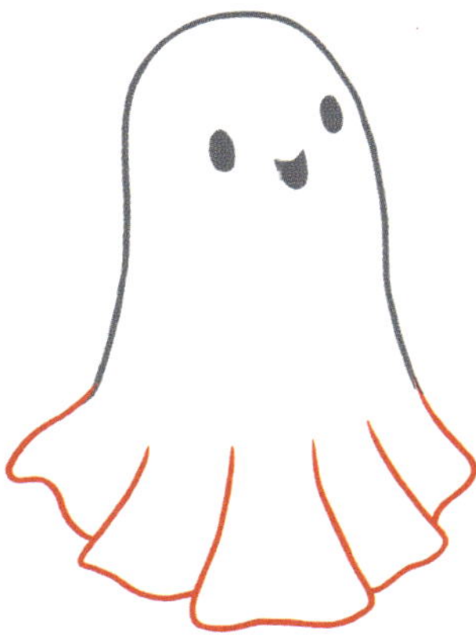

4. Draw bats flying around your ghost with a circle and triangle ears for the head and two pointed arches with a scalloped bottom for the wings.

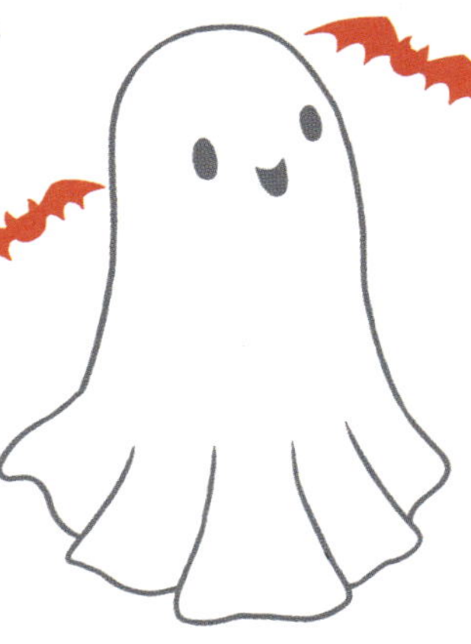

5. Cleanly trace your sketch with pencil on watercolor paper before inking.

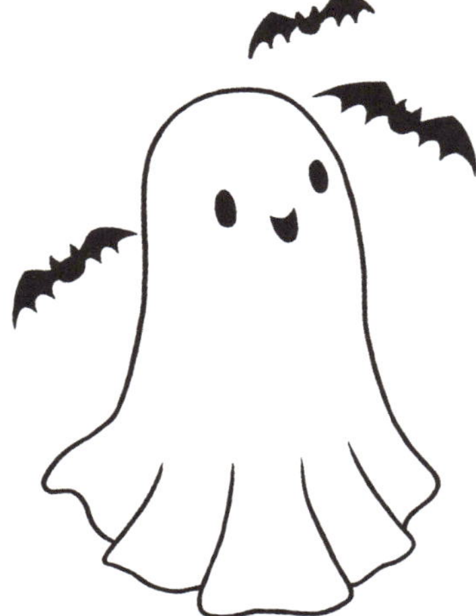

GHOST FAMILY PORTRAIT

1. Sketch two ovals, one within the other.

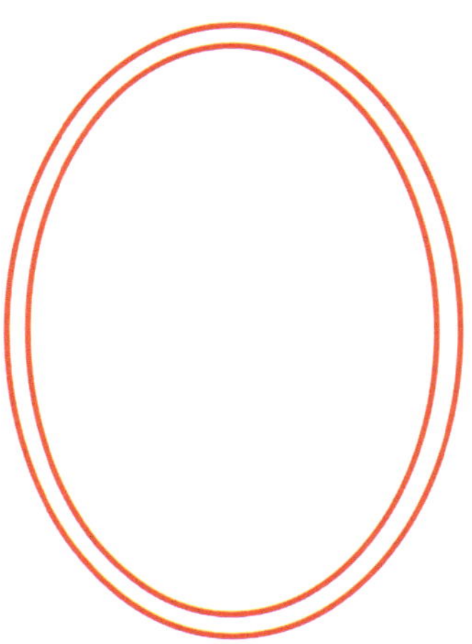

2. Using the ovals, make four curvy ovals that curl at the ends. Add circles at each place the ovals meet.

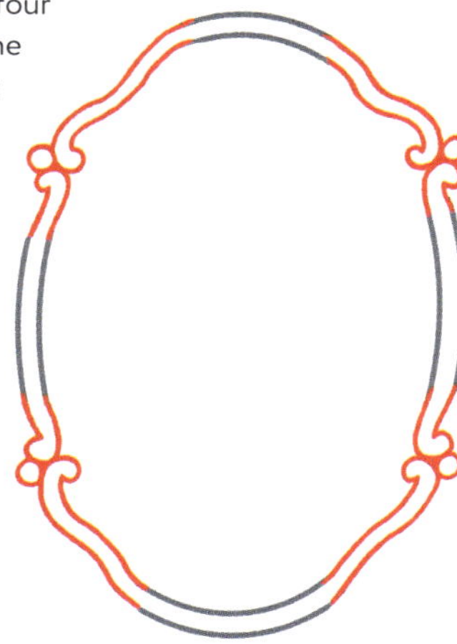

3. Add skulls on the top and bottom of the frame (one right side up, one upside down) with a mushroom-shaped head, two solid circle eyes, and lines for the teeth. Draw two teardrop-shaped leaves on the sides of each skull.

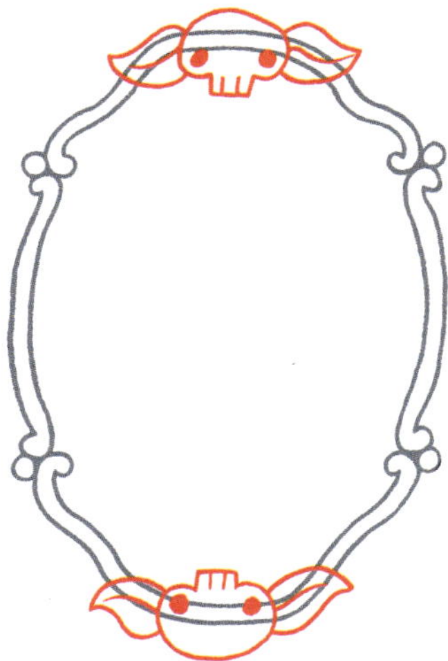

4. Inside the frame, draw four happy ghosts with arches of varying heights. Add an arm for the tallest ghost using a triangle.

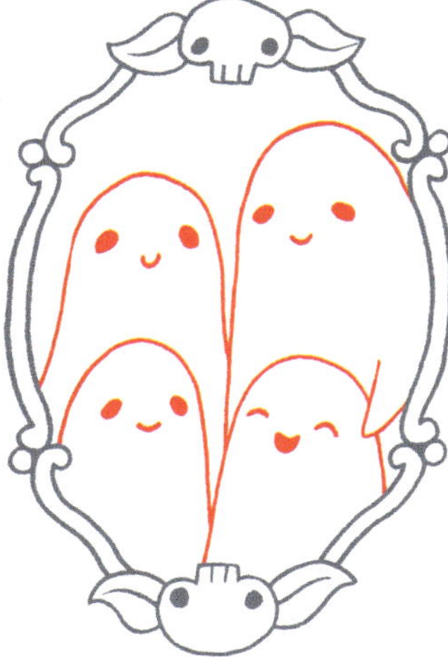

5. Cleanly trace your sketch with pencil on watercolor paper before inking.

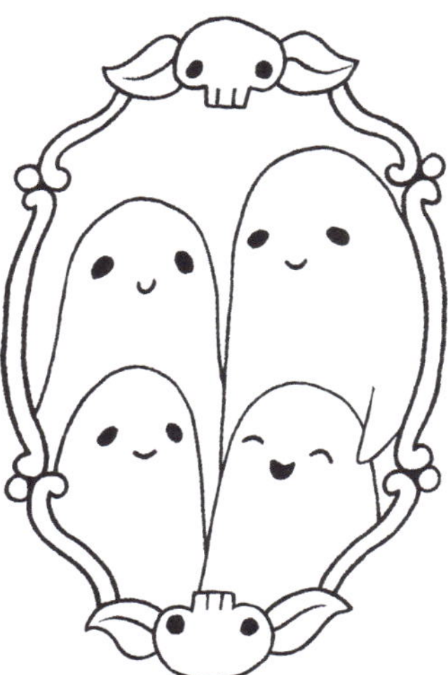

6. Color the frame, except for the skulls, in diluted ink. Then, add shading to the frame with black. For the background, make a pattern like wallpaper.

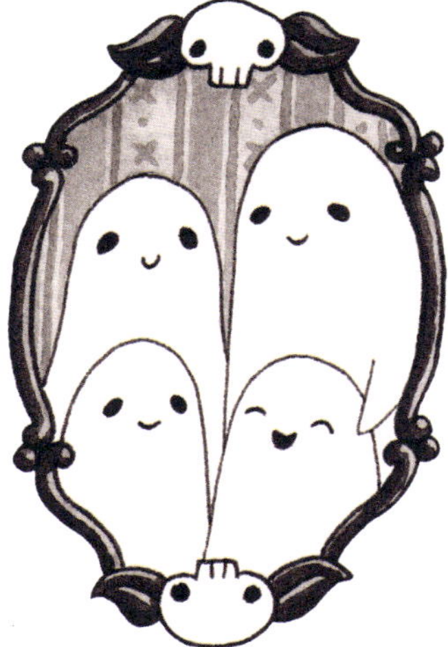

PATCHING BOO-BOOS

1. Draw an arm holding a needle. Make the arm a thin triangle and the needle a thin oval with a pointed enc and a rounded end. Add a dot in the rounded end.

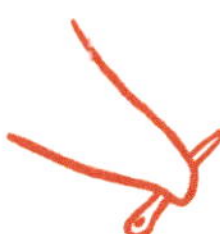

2. Draw the top half of a ghost hunched over the needle using a curved line. Then add a content facial expression.

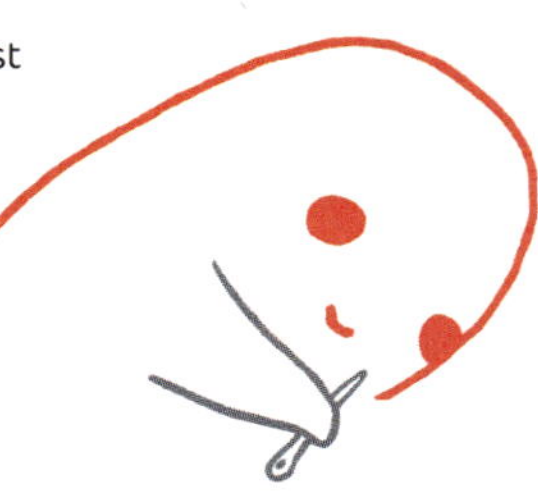

3. Draw the bottom half of the body, or sheet. Make the left side straight and the right side lifted. Add waves along the bottom.

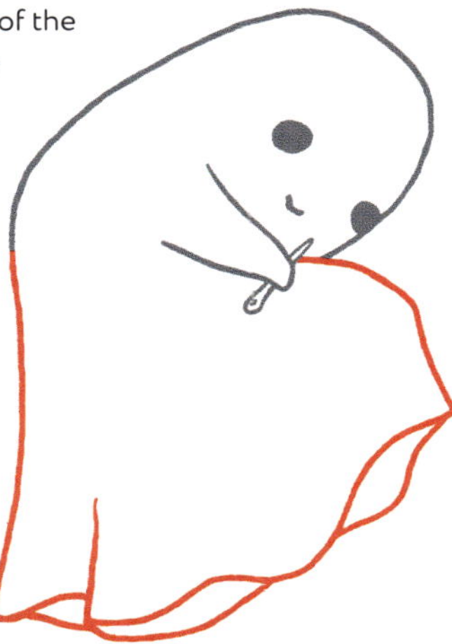

4. Make a wavy line of thread going through the needle and attach it to a square patch with stitching on the sides.

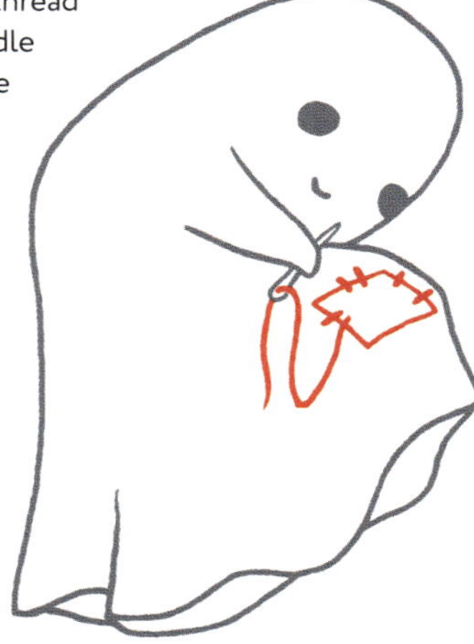

5. Cleanly trace your sketch with pencil on watercolor paper before inking.

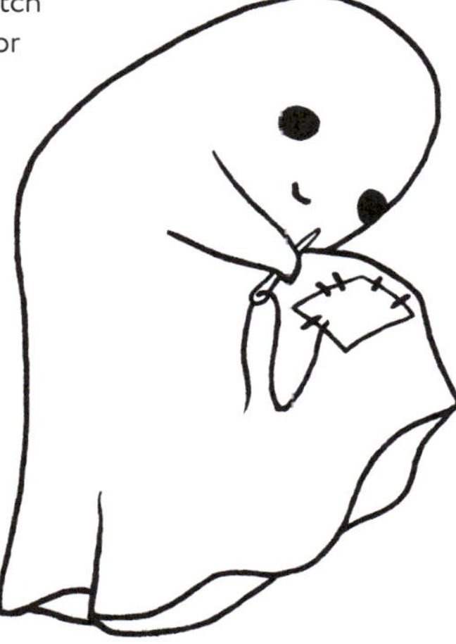

6. Using marker or pencil, color the patch any bright color you'd like and add shading to the ghost's sheet.

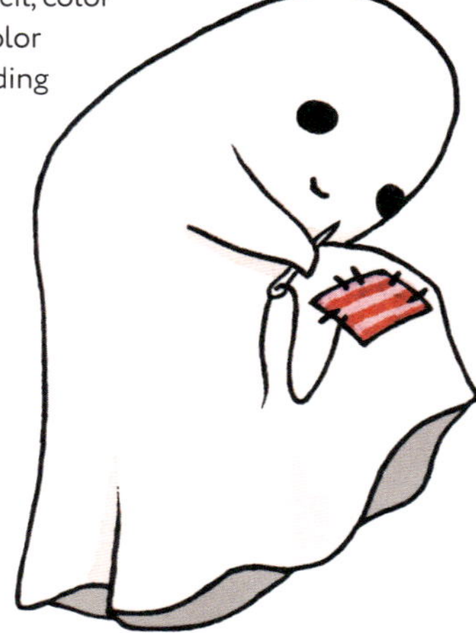

DANCING GHOSTS

1. Draw two bent bell shapes side by side.

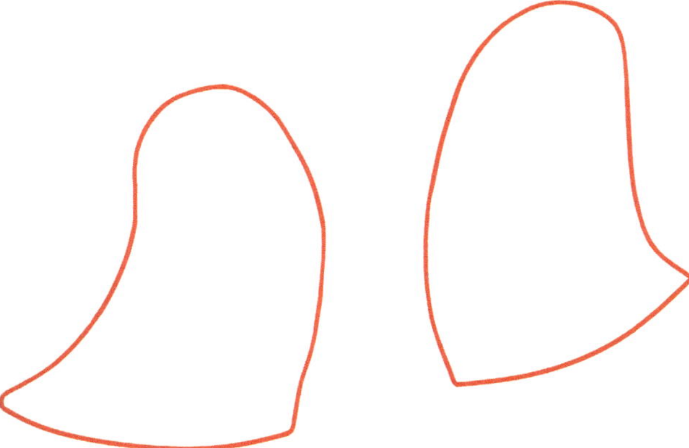

2. Add waves to the bottom edges to show the folds of the sheets.

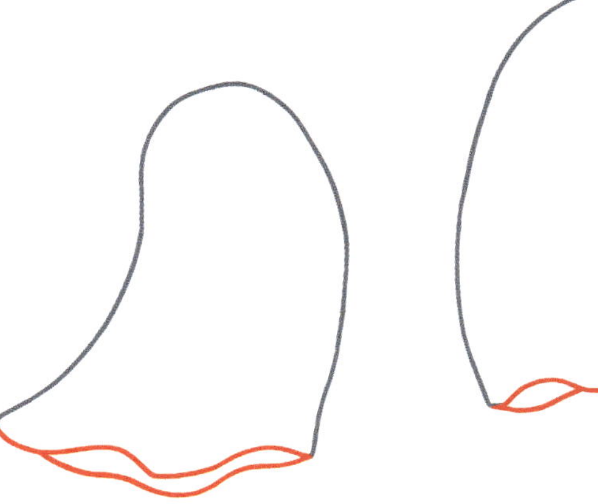

3. Add arms with curved lines on the sides of the bell shapes.

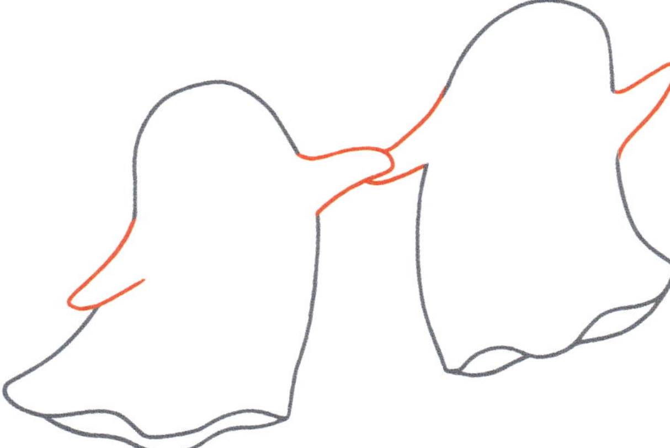

4. Have the ghosts hold hands by curling one oval over and the other under.

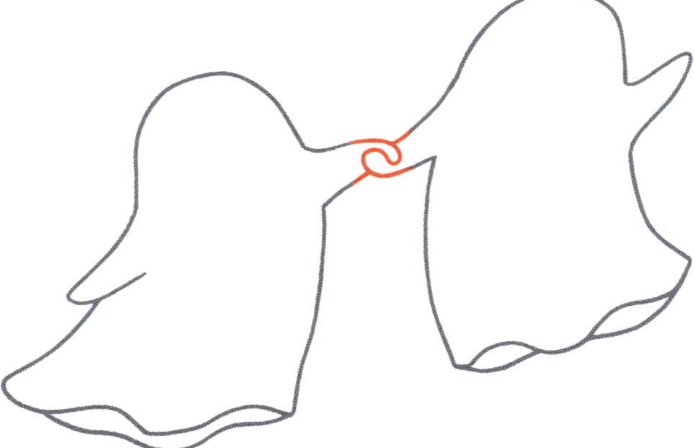

5. Give each ghost a happy face.

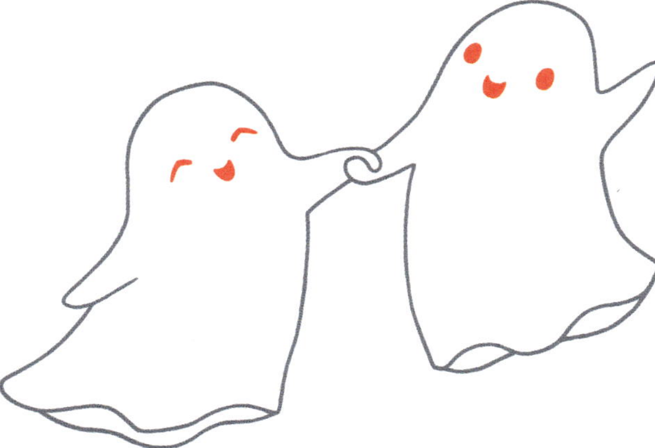

6. Cleanly trace your sketch with pencil on watercolor paper before inking.

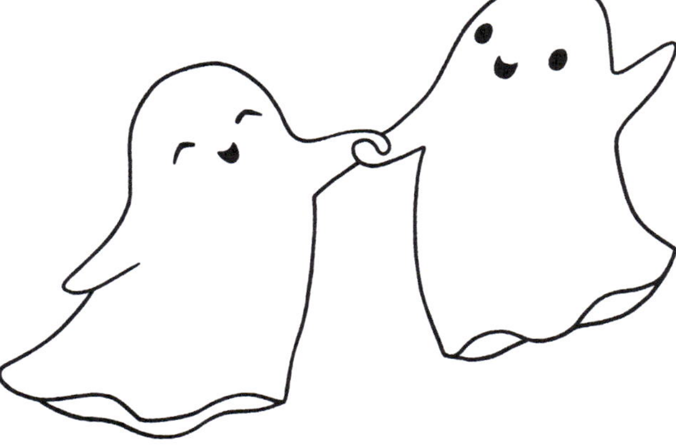

HAUNTED KITE FLIGHT

1. Draw a paper bat at an angle, starting with a rectangle with pointed ears and a pointed bottom. Add eyes and a mouth with fangs.

2. Start the wings with squares on each side. Then add an arrowpoint triangle with a line down the middle.

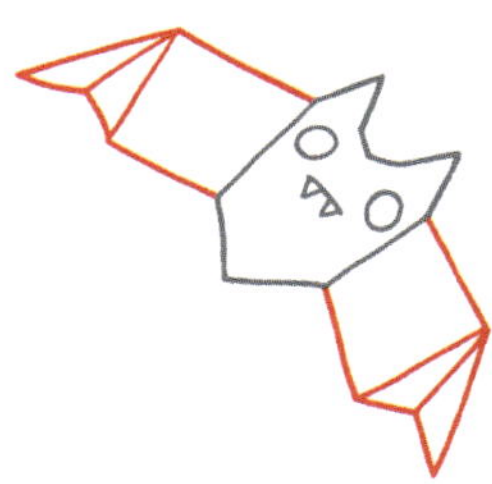

3. Draw a ghost in the bottom left angled to the right. Make a rectangle body with a wavy bottom, a rounded head, and arms stretched up beside the head. Add three circles for the face.

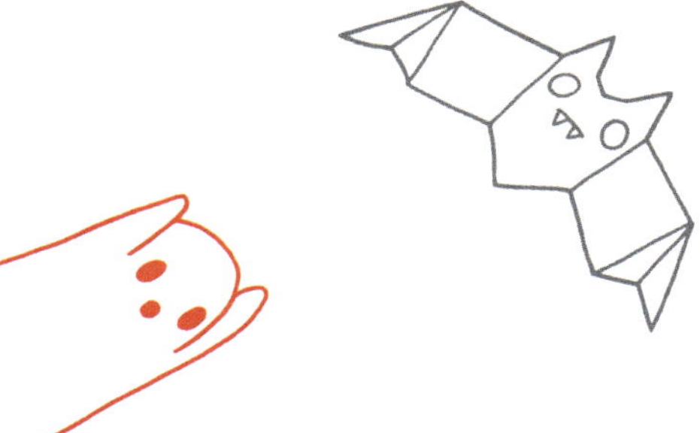

4. Make a rectangle wrapped in string in the ghost's hand. Then draw a line from the rectangle to the bat and attach it to the middle of each wing.

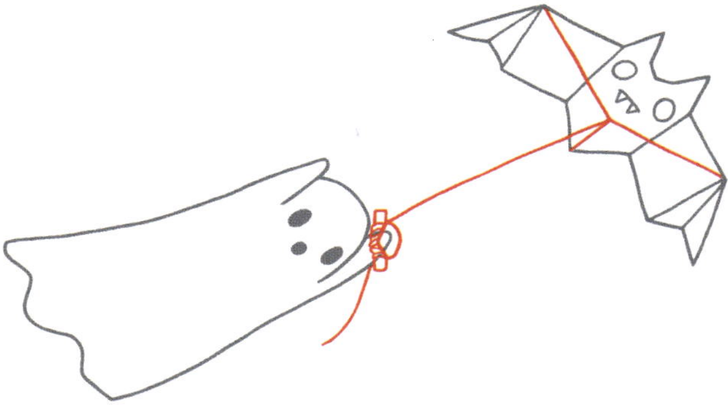

5. Cleanly trace your sketch with pencil on watercolor paper before inking.

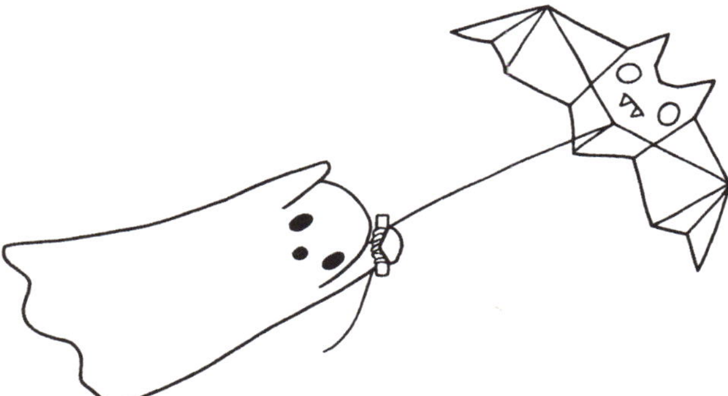

6. Color the bat kite and the string a dark gray. Leave the bat's eyes and fangs white. Add some shading on the bat's wings and next to the ghost's arms.

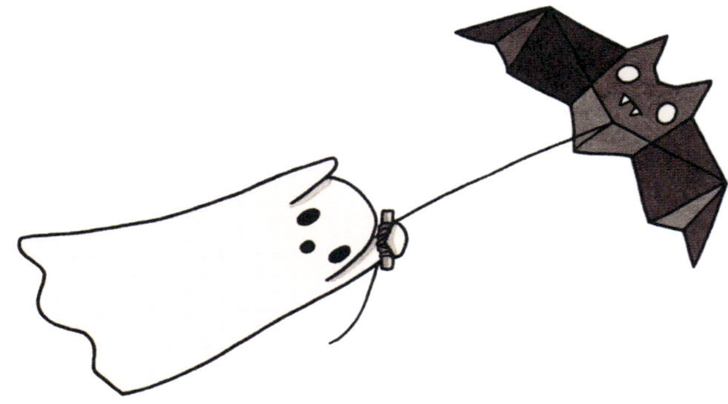

APPARITION PHOTO BOOTH

1. Draw a photo strip with a long rectangle and four squares within it.

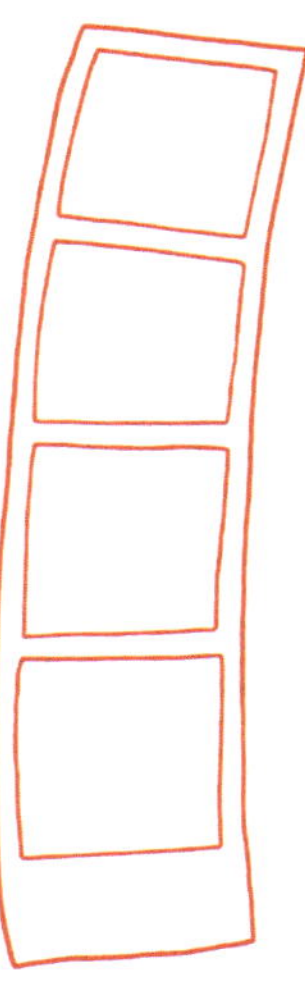

2. In the top frame, draw two arches for two ghosts. Make one smiling and the other with its tongue sticking out.

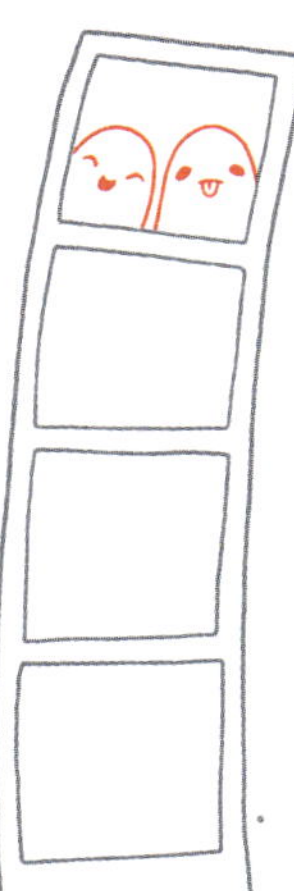

7. Color the background of each frame gray. Add shading around and on the ghosts for depth.

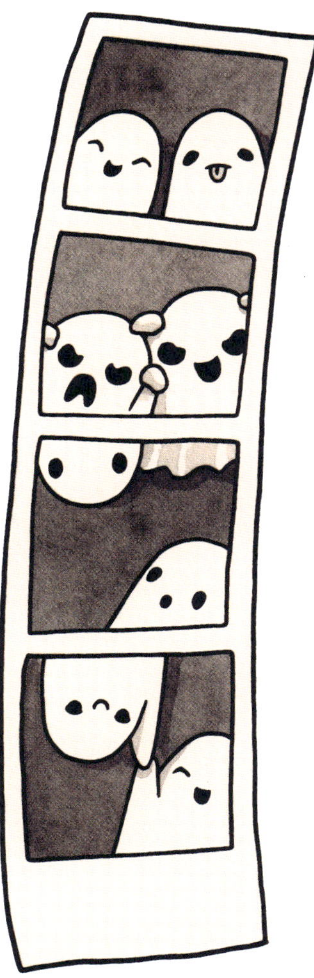

3. In the second frame, draw two arches and give them scary faces. For the arms and hands, add two ovals for each ghost and a rectangle arm in between.

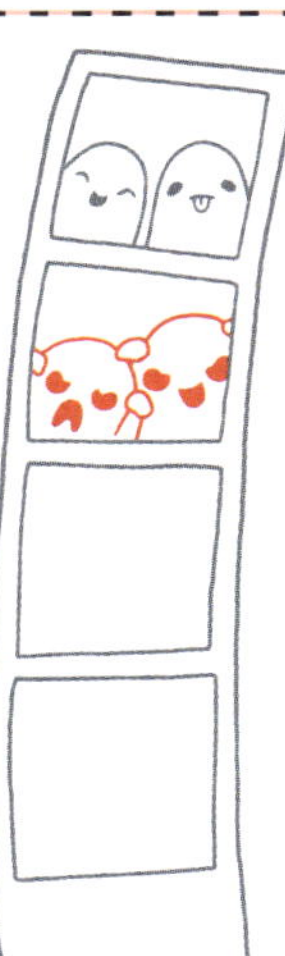

4. In the third frame, draw one upside-down arch at the top left of the square with a wavy line to the right. Draw a curved line on the bottom right for the second ghost. Add the eyes to the top ghost and eyes and a mouth to the bottom ghost.

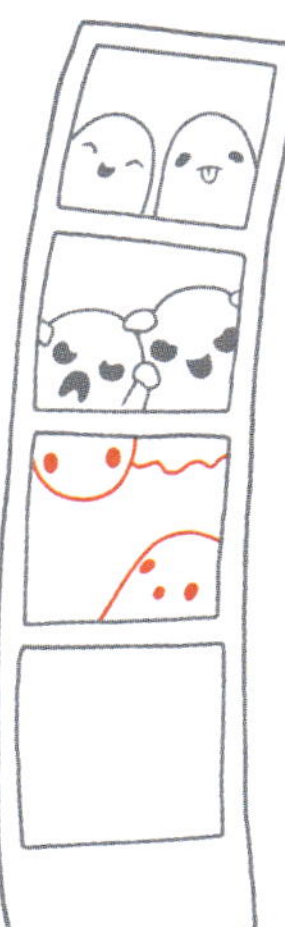

5. In the bottom frame, draw an upside-down arch with a stretched out arm. Do the same for the second ghost in the bottom right corner, making them high-five. Add happy facial expressions.

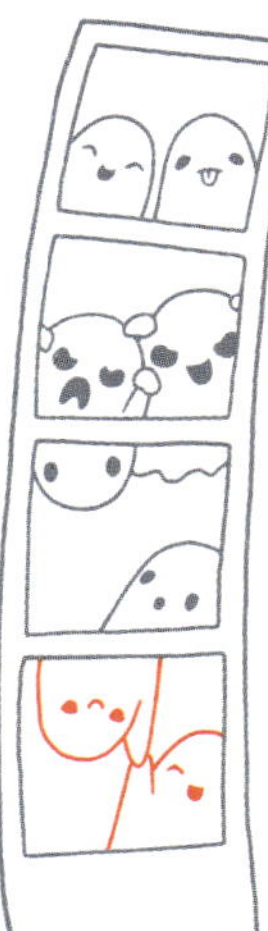

6. Cleanly trace your sketch with pencil on watercolor paper before inking.

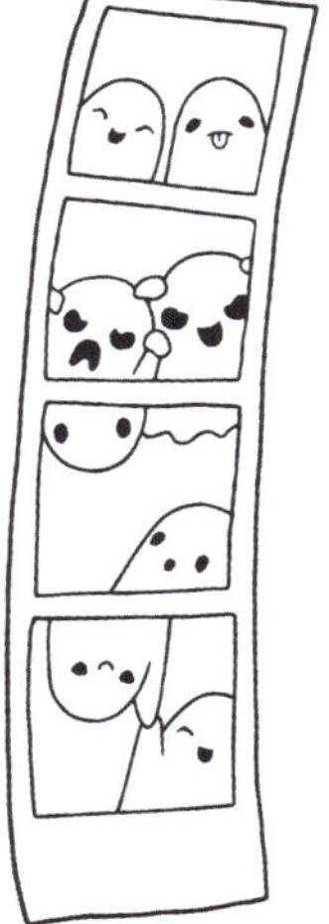

BABY YETI

1. Sketch a rounded body with oval arms on each side.

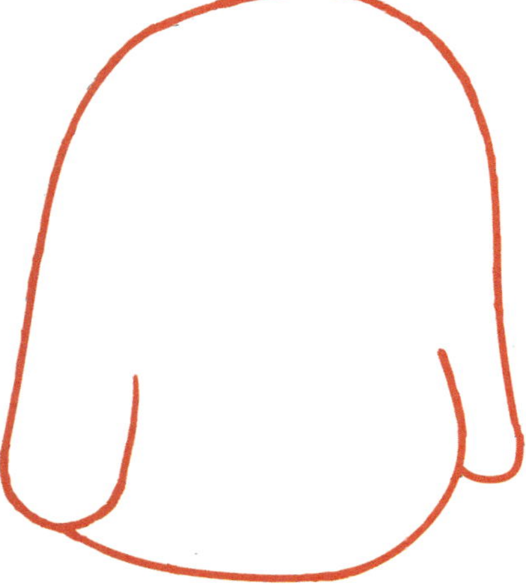

2. Draw a curved line in the top part of the body for the face and add two solid oval eyes with highlights and a mouth with two triangle fangs.

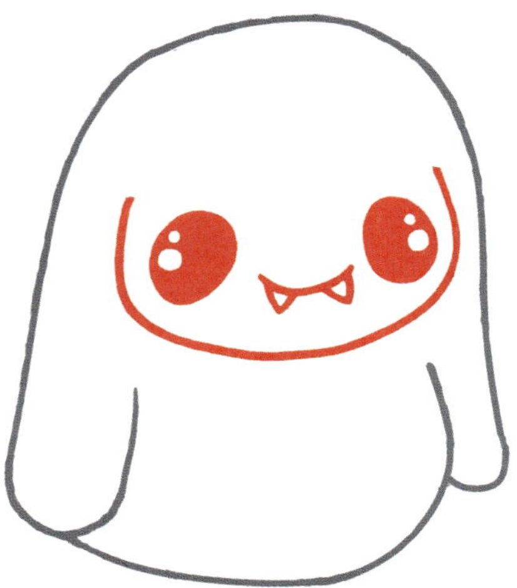

3. Draw locks of fur above the face with sweeping triangles.

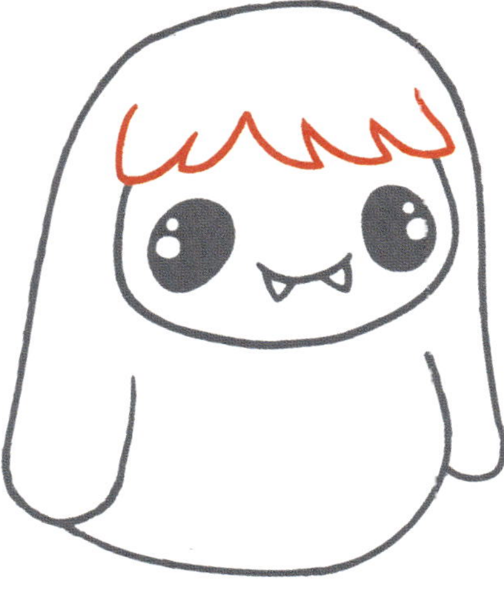

4. Under the body, draw two big feet with an oval and five toes. Draw lines to attach the feet to the body.

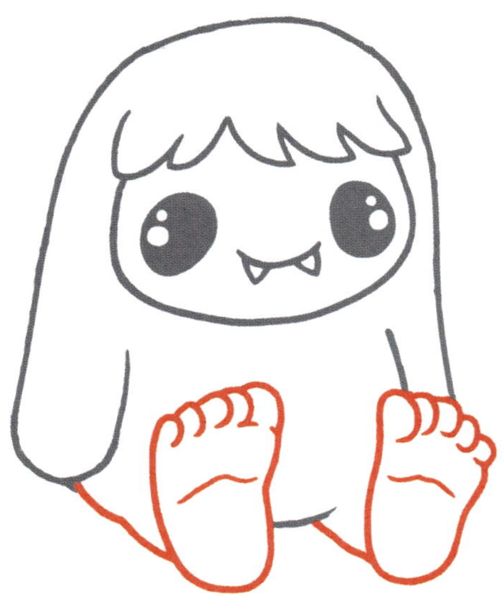

5. Draw a fuzzy outline on the body. Add the left hand.

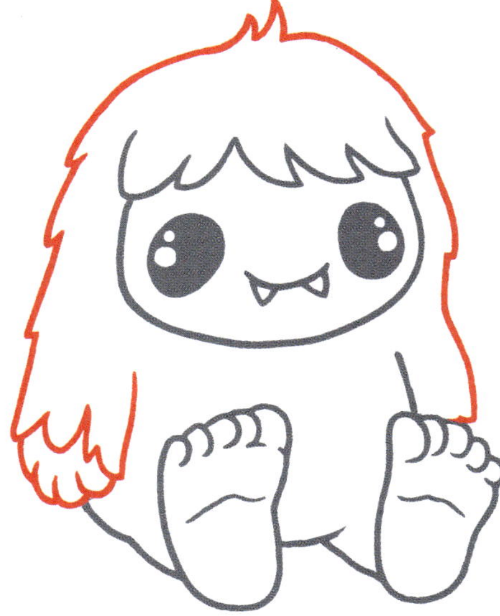

6. Add two pointed horns on top and detail them with some lines.

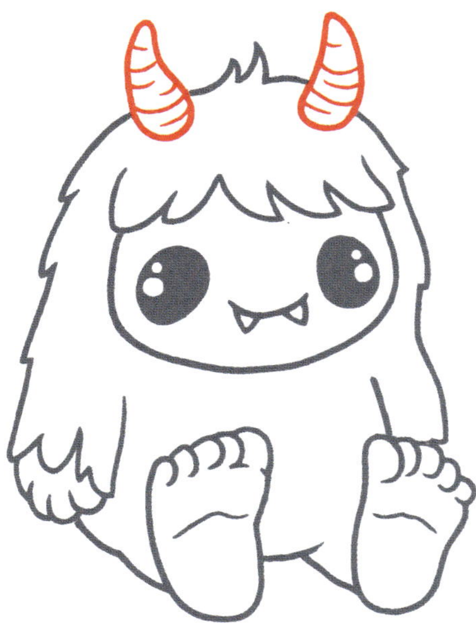

7. Cleanly trace your sketch with pencil on watercolor paper before inking.

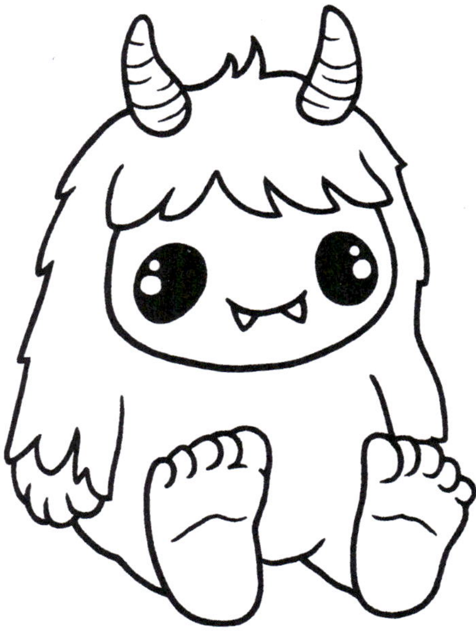

8. For the skin and horns, I used watercolors of light shades of brown. I added depth to the fur by shading it with a muted violet. Add shading to the skin and horns, using a darker shade of brown.

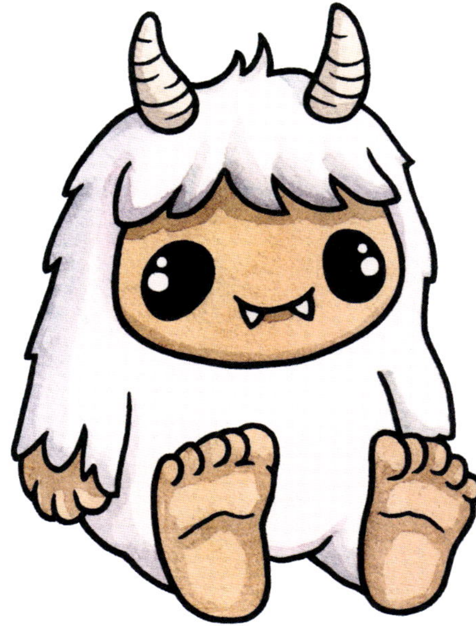

SWINGING SKELETON

1. Draw a twisted branch with spindly ends. Draw the seat of a swing at the bottom of the page with a rectangle and two rectangular sides.

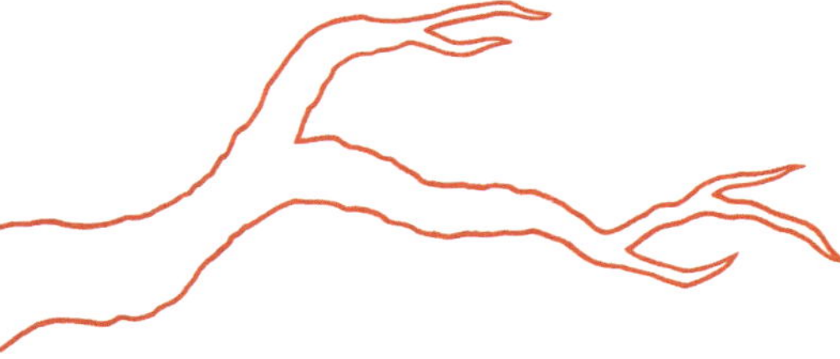

2. Sketch a figure sitting on the seat with a circle head, hands, and feet. Use lines to make a stick figure.

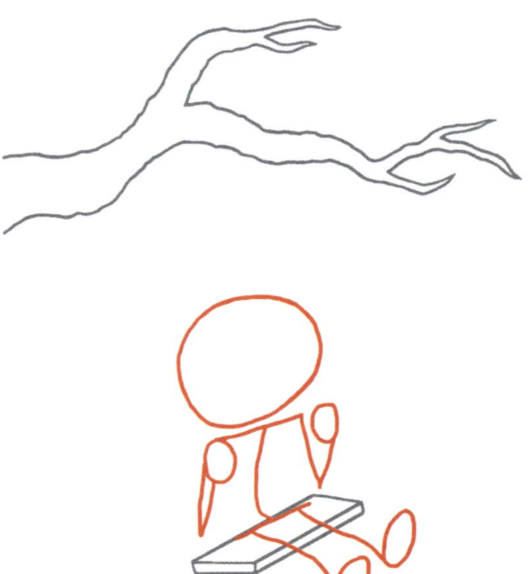

3. Attach two ropes from the branch to the swing seat with ovals. Add the skeletal hands wrapped around the ropes with four fingers each.

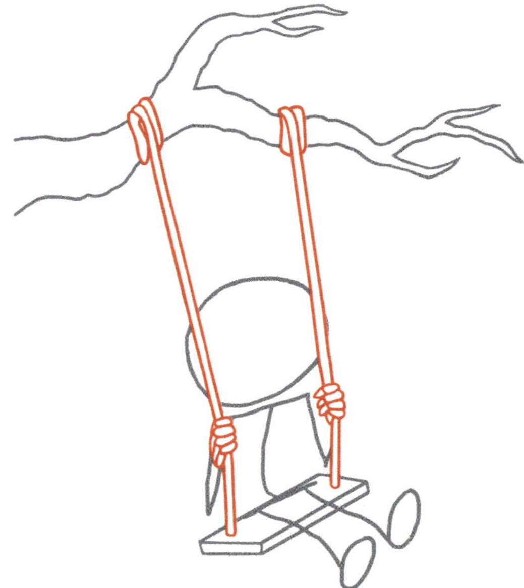

4. Draw the skull in a mushroom shape. Give it a happy expression.

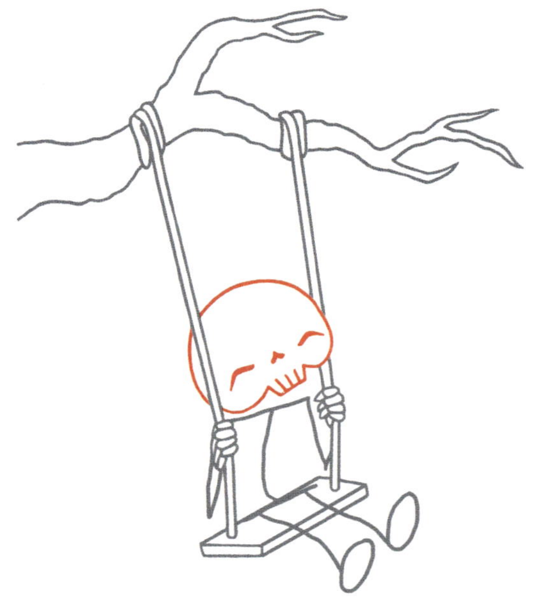

5. Add rectangles for the shorts. Make the bony legs in two sections. Draw the shoes with the soles facing out.

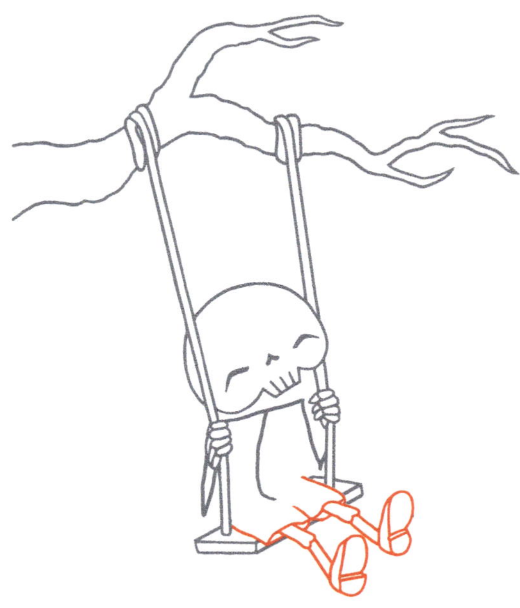

6. Give the skeleton a simple shirt and add the bony arms.

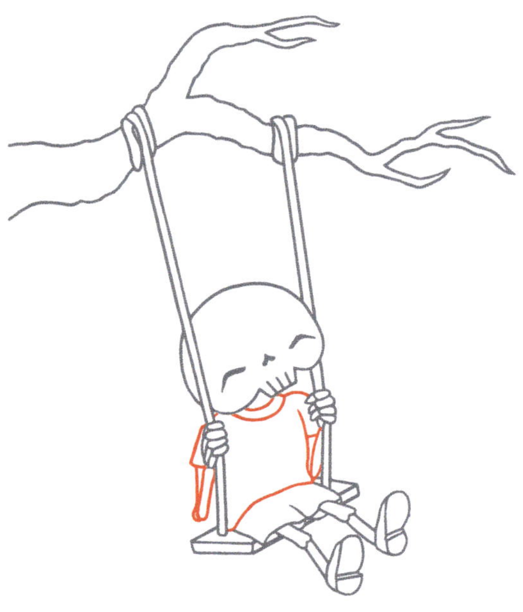

7. Cleanly trace your sketch with pencil on watercolor paper before inking.

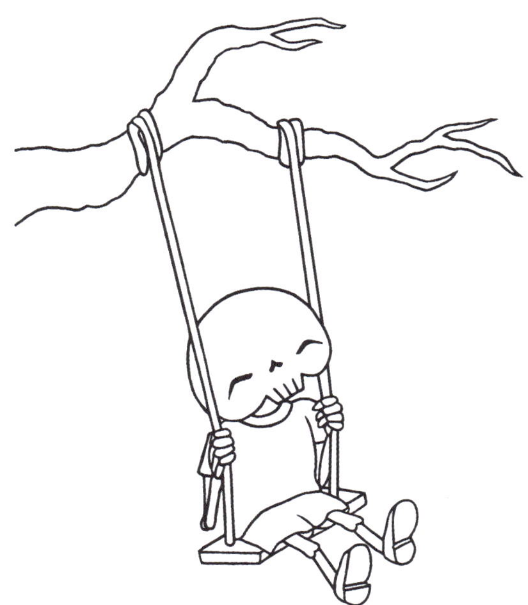

8. For the branch, shirt, shorts, and shoes, use shades of gray. Using a thin brush or pen, detail the branch and ropes with lines. Add the shading to the branch, skeleton, and swing.

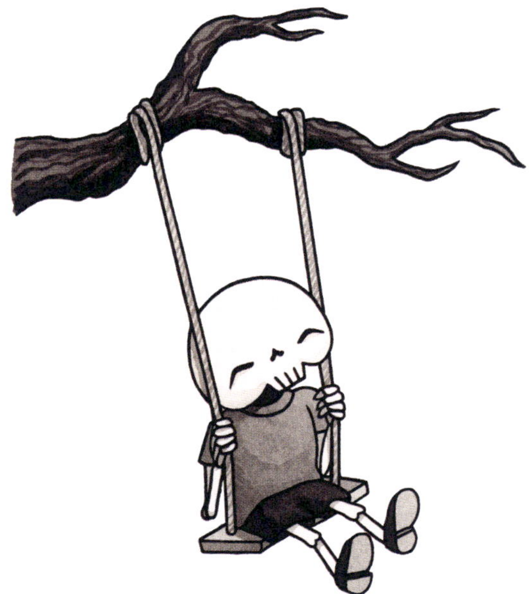

VINCENT VAN PLAGUE

1. Draw a rectangle with a thin rectangle on the right side.

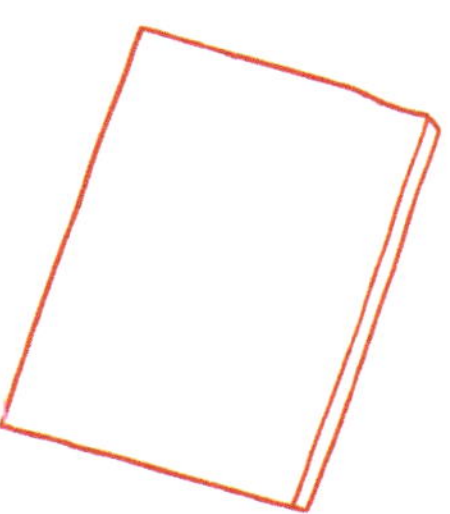

2. Add two short rectangles on top and a long rectangle on the bottom. Add three rectangle legs below and one rectangle extending from the top.

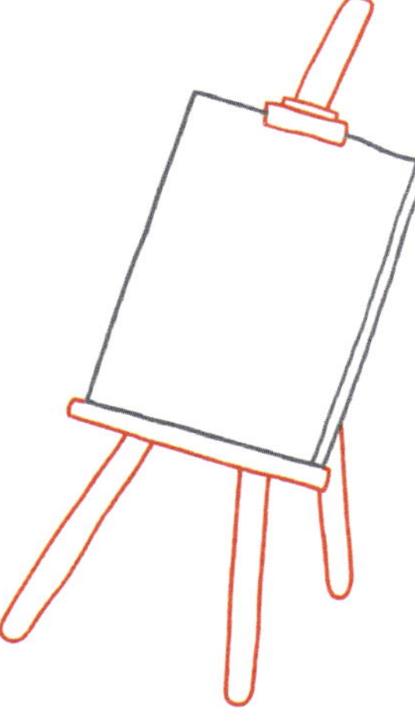

3. Draw a teardrop shape with a pointed tip for the head and a bell shape for the body.

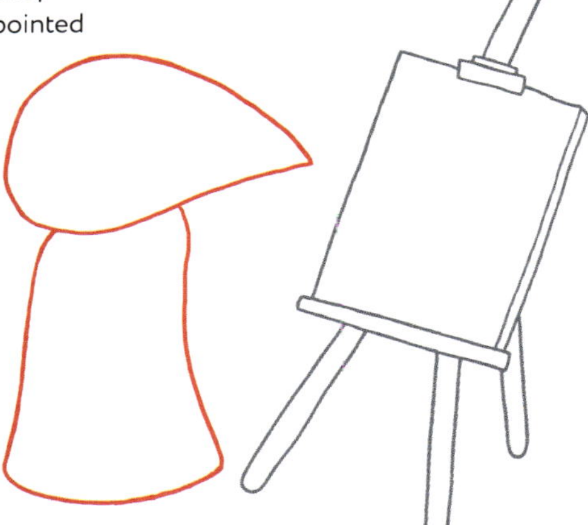

4. Around the left side of the head, draw a hood. Then add a solid oval eye and a dot for the nostril.

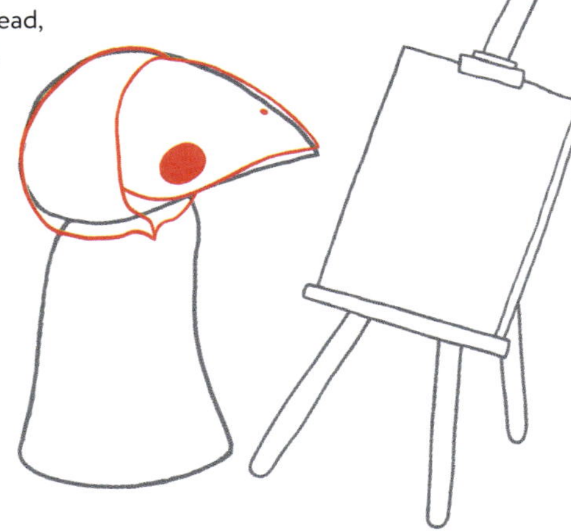

5. Draw the left arm with a rectangle sleeve and a triangle hand. Then add a paintbrush with a teardrop-shaped brush.

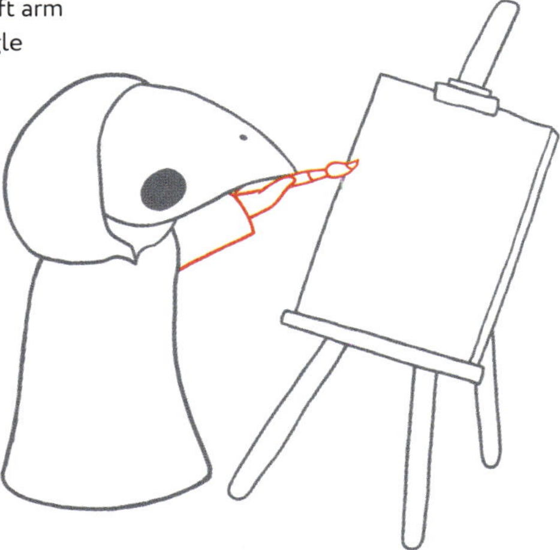

6. Draw the right arm with a bent rectangle sleeve and a curved hand. Then add a painter's palette with a circle and splotches around the edge.

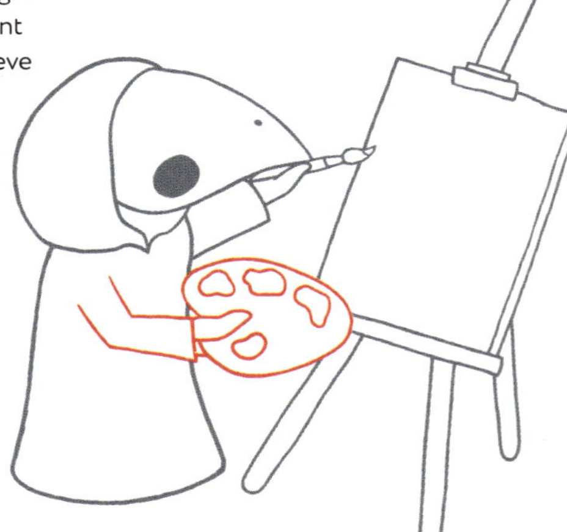

7. Using the outline of the body, make a robe with wavy lines. Add the front of a cape with buttons down the middle.

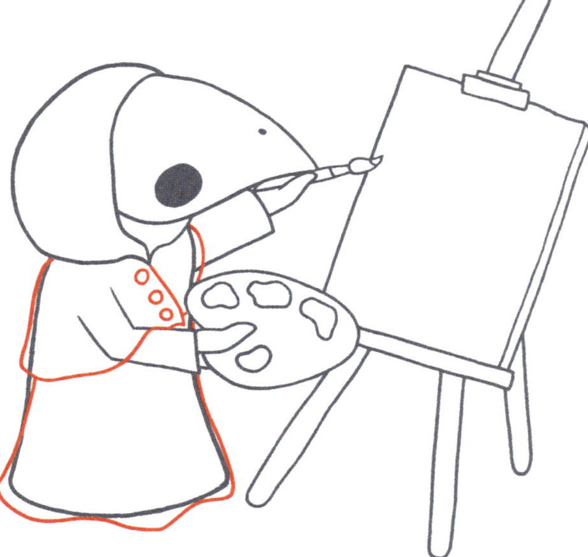

8. Draw a cute cat on the canvas with a rounded square head, rounded triangle ears, and a splayed-out body. Give it a happy facial expression and add some stars around it.

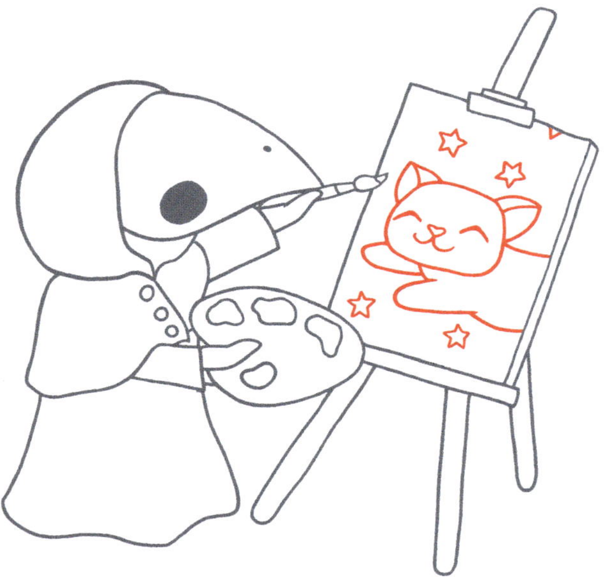

9. Cleanly trace your sketch with pencil on watercolor paper before inking.

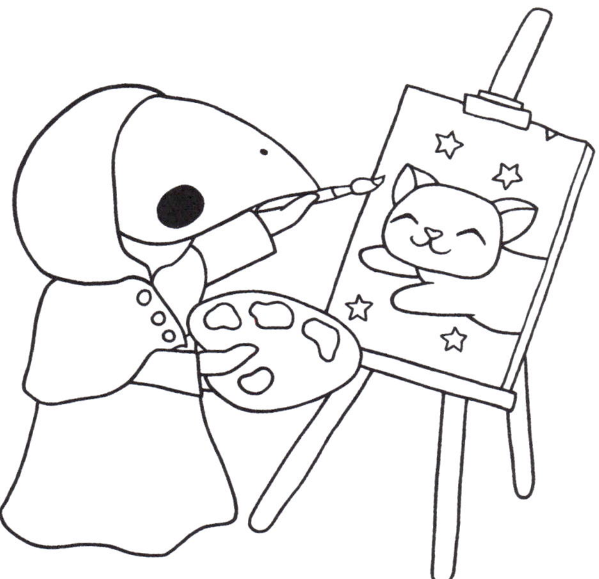

10. Color the robe, some splotches of paint, and the canvas background black. Use gray for the cape, paintbrush, cat, and easel. Add shading to the plague doctor, canvas, and easel.

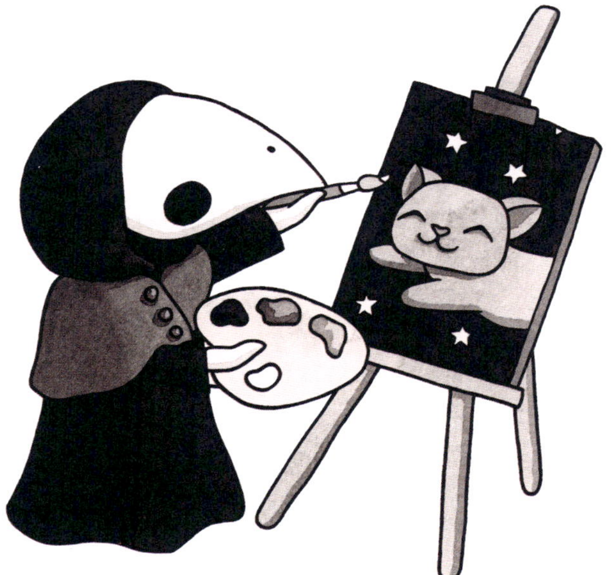

CHASING THE MOON

1. Sketch a long oval head and a smaller round body.

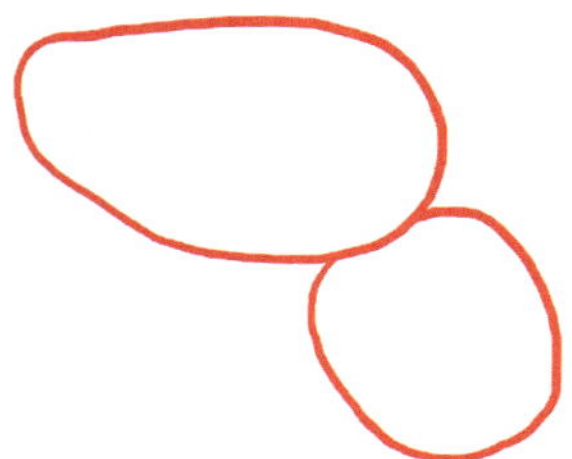

2. Add lines on each side for the arms. Draw one bent leg and one straight leg with lines. Draw a curved line for the tail. Add ovals for the feet.

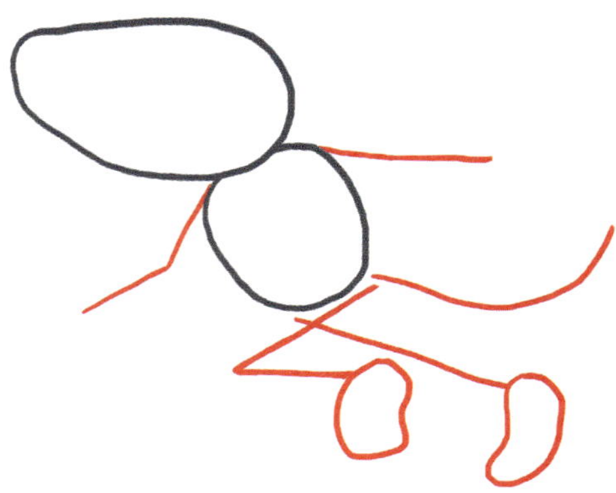

3. Add detail to the face with a round nose, a solid circle eye with highlights, and a curving mouth. Add a tooth in the mouth and fluffy details along the edges of the head.

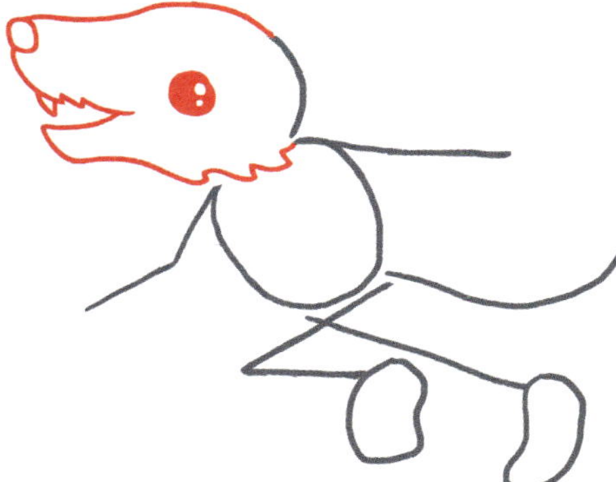

4. Add triangle ears on the right of the head with fluffy details.

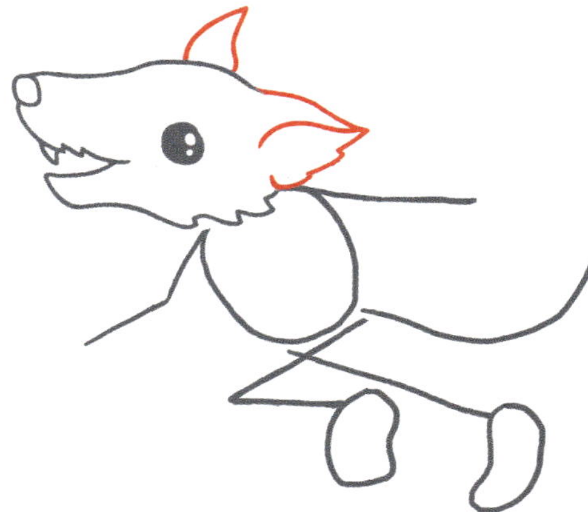

5. On the body, draw a simple bodice with short sleeves and a poofy skirt with a wavy bottom lining.

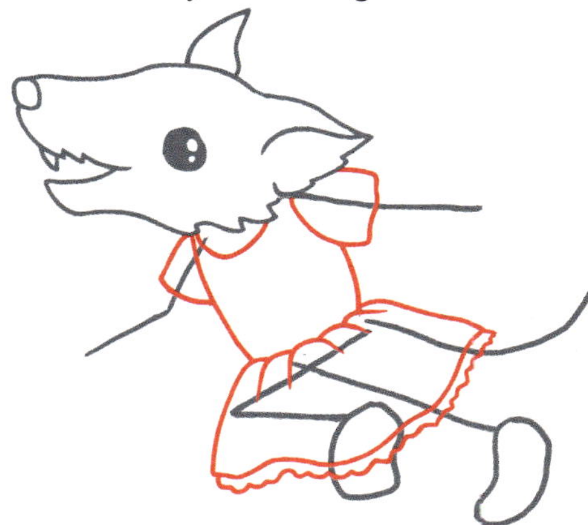

6. Add arms with large hands. Draw one on the left and one behind her on the right.

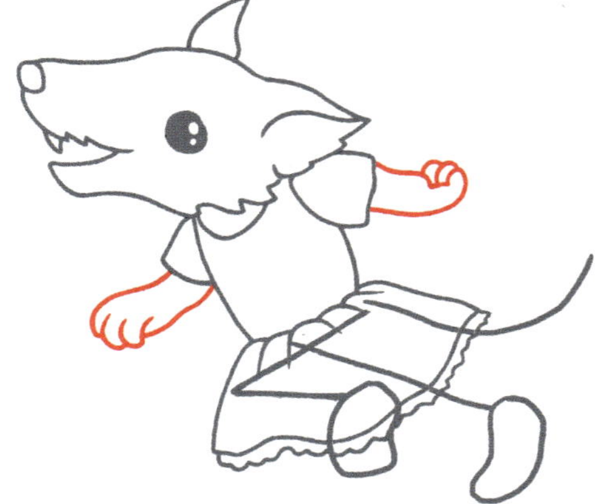

7. Add the legs and feet below the skirt of the dress. Add a fluffy, curved tail.

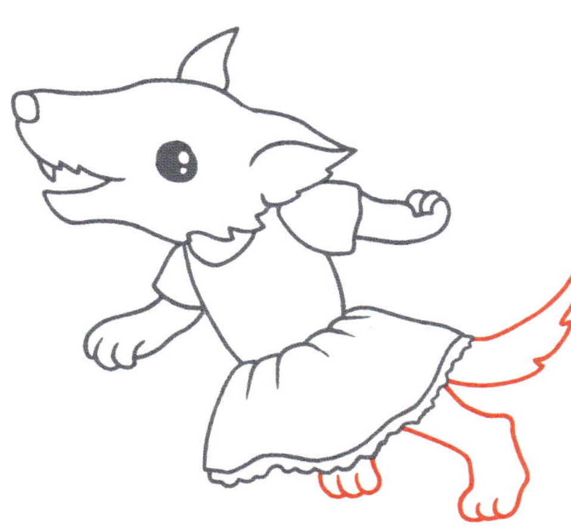

8. Draw a ball in the top left corner with long movement lines behind it.

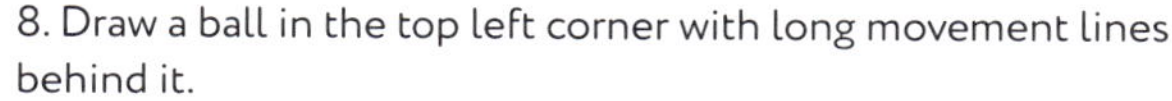
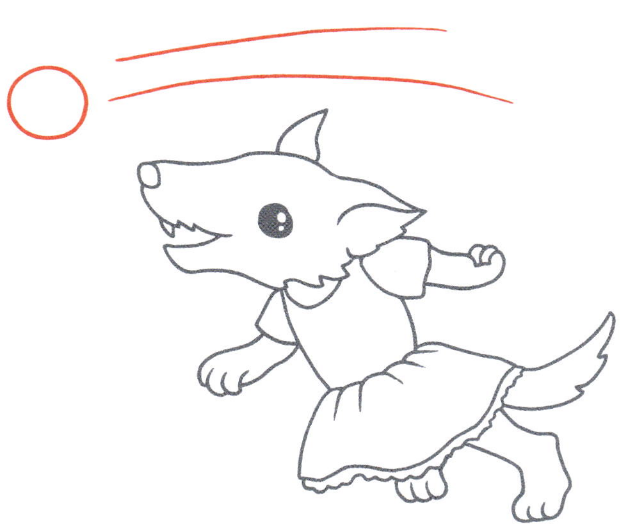

9. Cleanly trace your sketch with pencil on watercolor paper before inking.

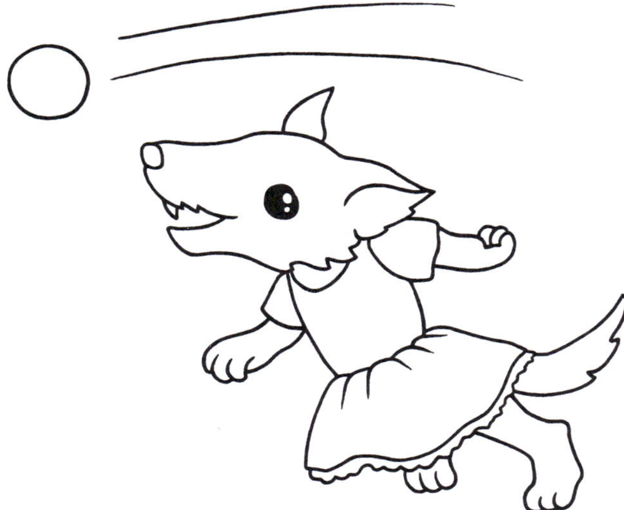

10. I used watercolors to make the ball purple, the wolf brown, and the dress pink with a yellow lining. Using a thin brush or pen, add detail to the fur with dark lines. Add shading to the ball, fur, and dress.

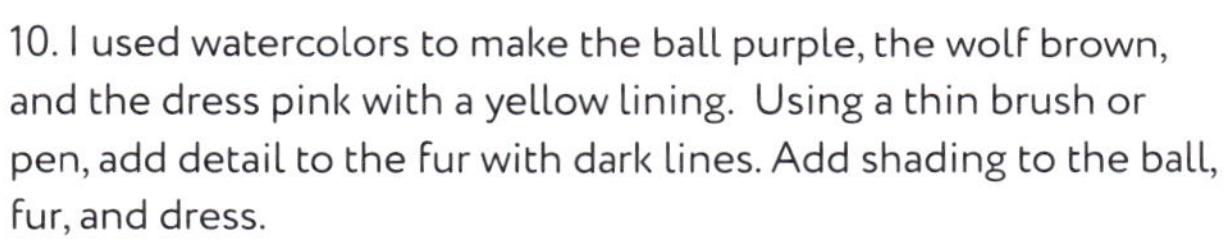
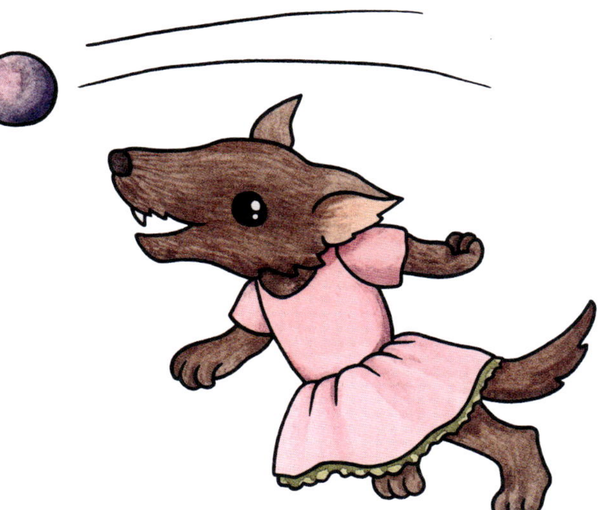

ZOMBIE LEMONADE STAND

1. Sketch a big rectangle with a line across the middle.

2. Turn the bottom half of the rectangle into a wooden counter with a smooth rectangle top and three rectangles down the front with rough edges.

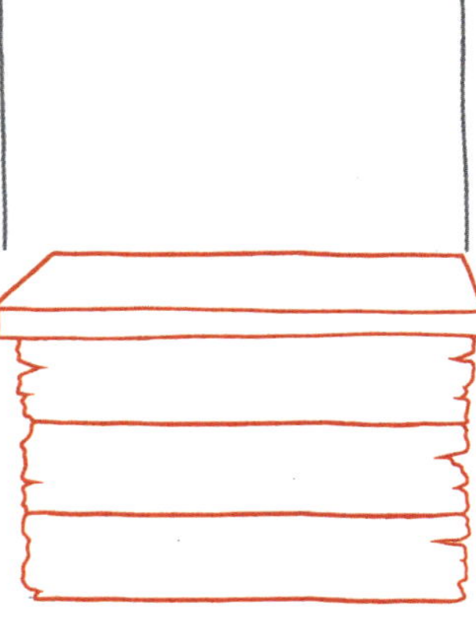

3. Make a striped canopy of five rectangles and triangles supported by oval beams.

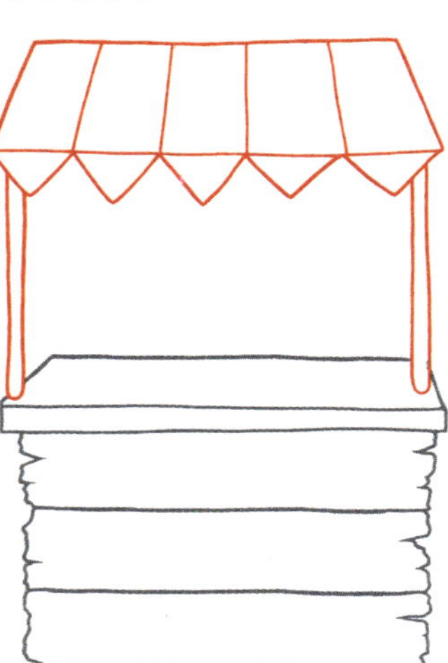

4. Draw a boy behind the stand with a rounded face. Place his hands on the counter and give him curly hair and a content facial expression.

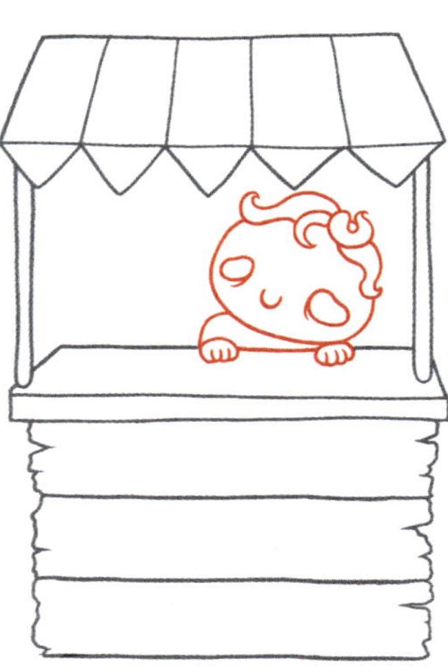

5. Draw a pitcher of lemonade with a U-shaped vase and a curved handle. Add an oval inside the vase and three lemons. Then draw some cups around the boy with a rectangle and an oval

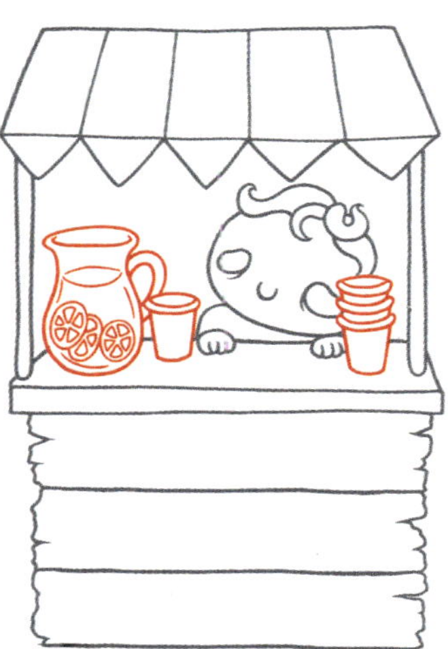

6. Add a rectangle sign in front of the stand. Write "Lemonade 25¢" inside.

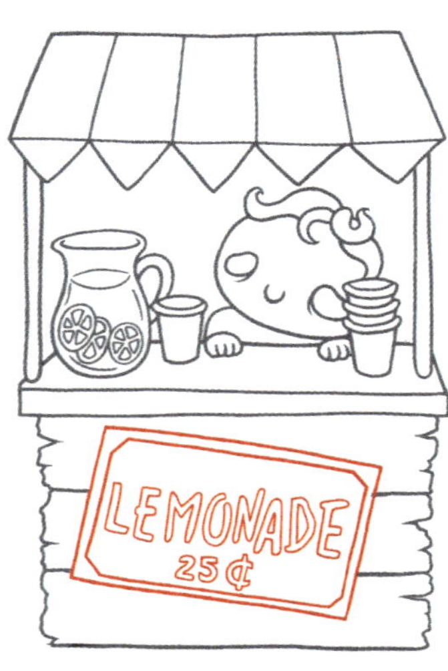

7. Cleanly trace your sketch with pencil on watercolor paper before inking. I used a pencil with a smaller lead point to trace the lemons and the words on the sign.

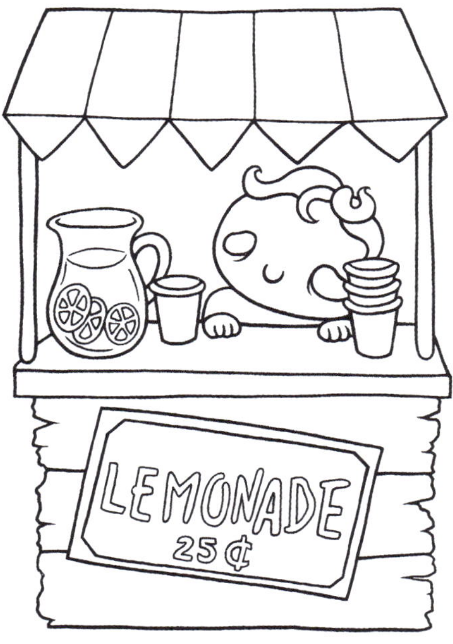

8. Make two sections of the canopy, the cups, the boy's shirt, and the lemonade sign black. Use gray for the posts, the boy's hair, lemons, and wooden counter.

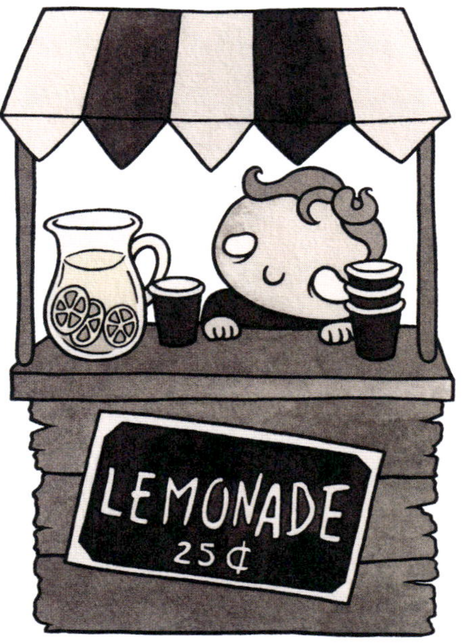

9. Add a lot of shading on and around the boy's eyes. With a thin brush or pen, add texture to the wooden planks and the boy's hair. Add shading to the boy, the counter, and the wooden planks.

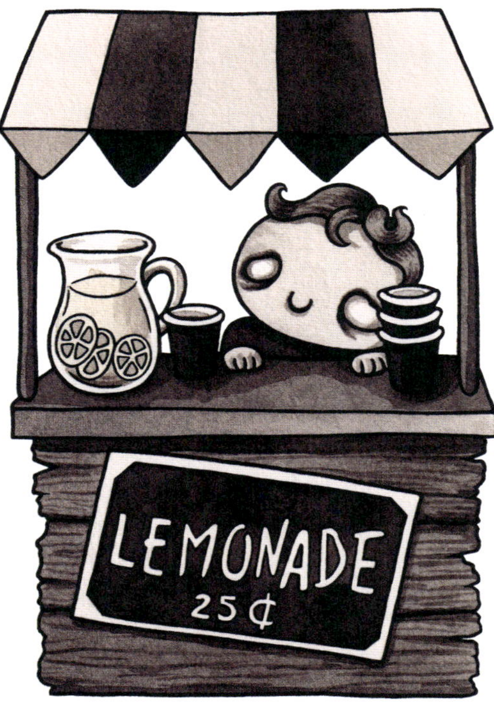

CREEPY CART

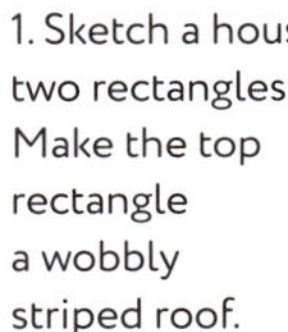

1. Sketch a house with two rectangles. Make the top rectangle a wobbly striped roof.

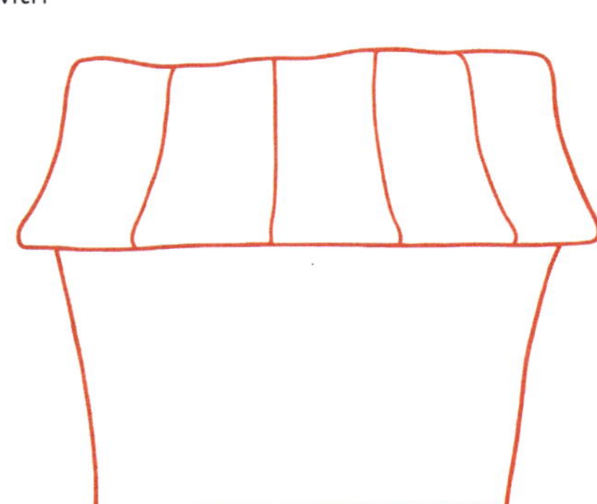

2. Draw a rectangle underneath with two circles for wheels. Inside the wheel draw two more circles and horizontal lines.

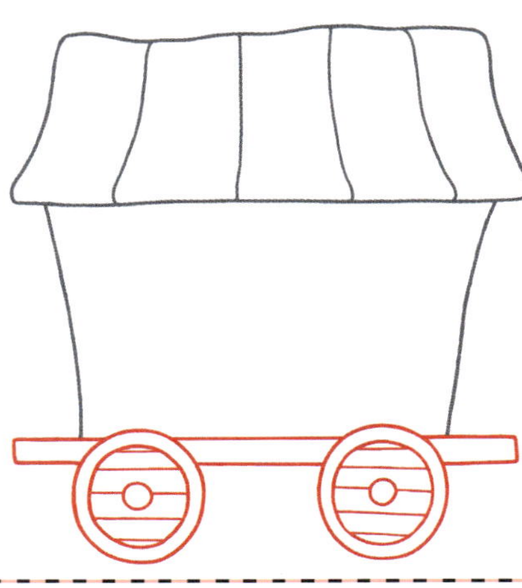

3. Add two coffin-shaped windows. Draw a rectangle on the bottom of the window and a cross inside.

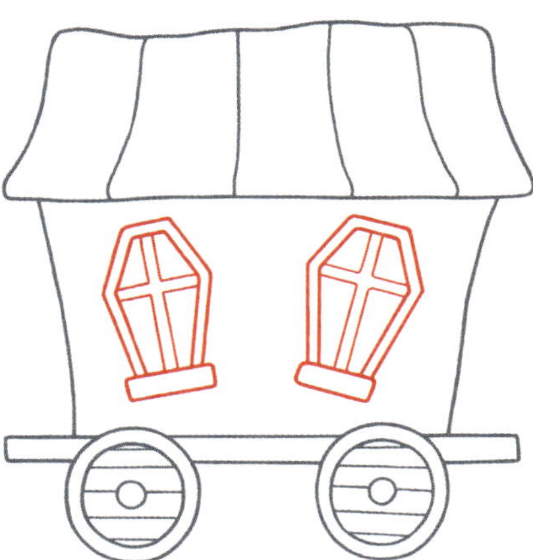

4. Draw a branch on each side of the roof.

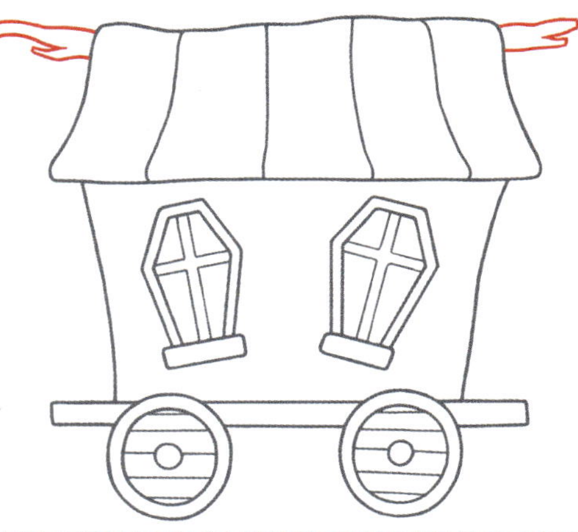

5. Hang a lantern on the left with a string attached to a loop. For the lantern, draw a semicircle with pointed sides and a curve underneath.

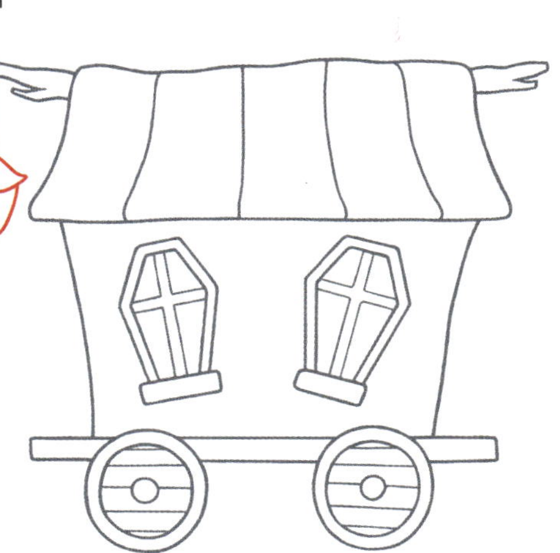

6. Underneath the lantern, draw the profile of a skull with a circle and a square mouth. Add the eyes and an arch for the arm.

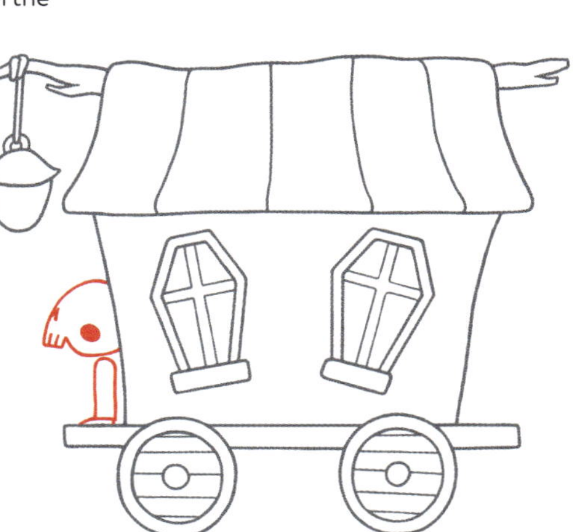

7. Draw a robe with a hood and a wavy bottom.

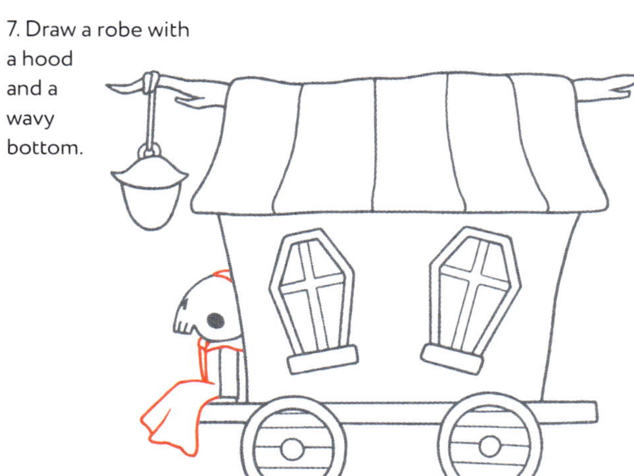

8. Add an open chest partially visible on the right with a rectangle lid and two sides of a square.

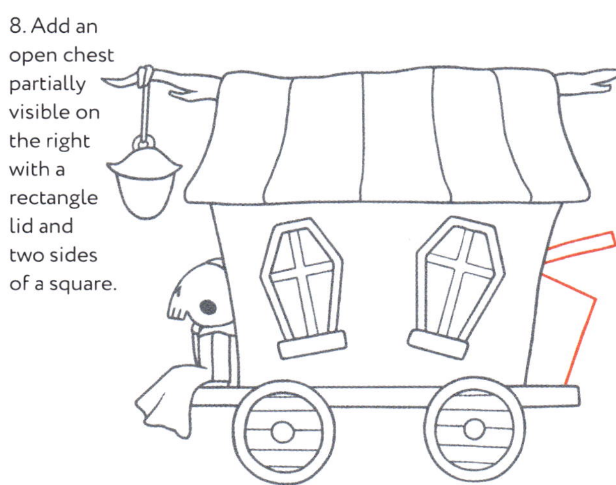

9. Draw a creature inside the chest. Make the body round and draw two wavy tentacles.

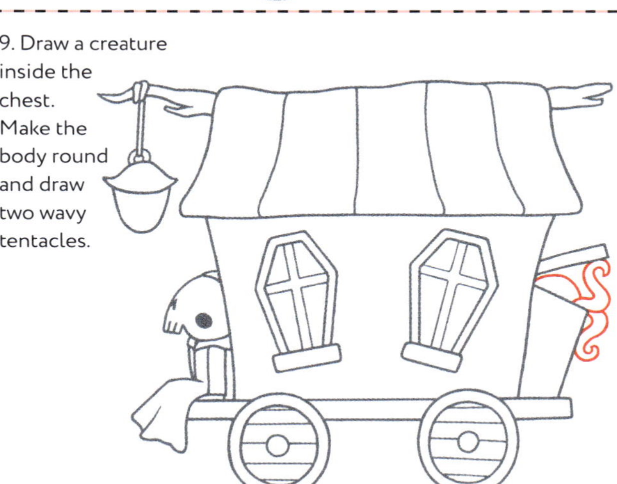

10. Cleanly trace your sketch with pencil on watercolor paper before inking.

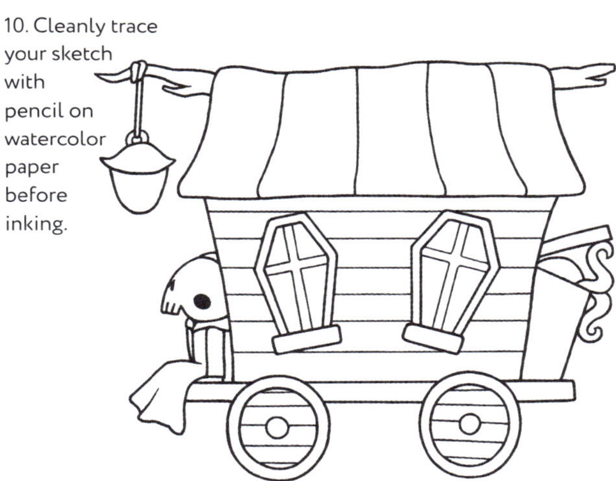

11. Make sections of the roof, the top of the lantern, the windows, and the skeleton's robe black. Use shades of gray to color the rest of the illustration. Add shading under the roof and windows, and on the lantern, skeleton, and chest.

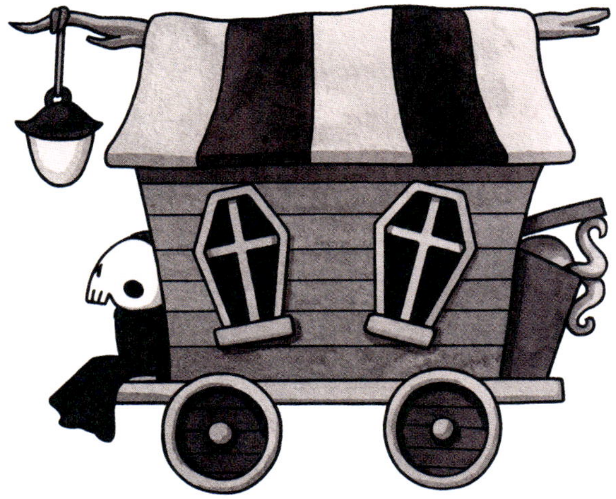

GHOUL SCOUT

1. Sketch the body with a circle head, hands, and feet. Use lines for the neck, shoulders, torso, arms, hips, and legs.

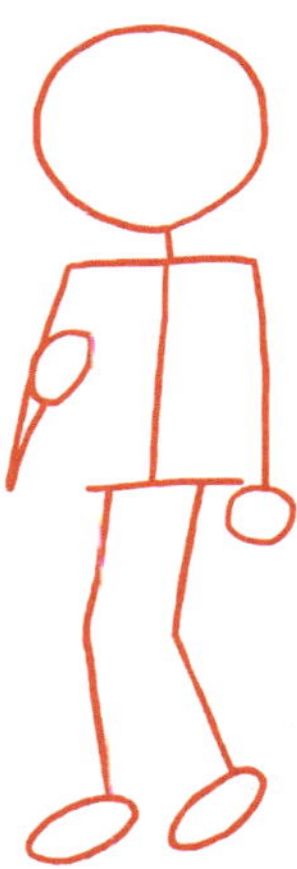

2. Draw a Girl Scout's outfit with a simple collared top and skirt. Add a sash with some badges.

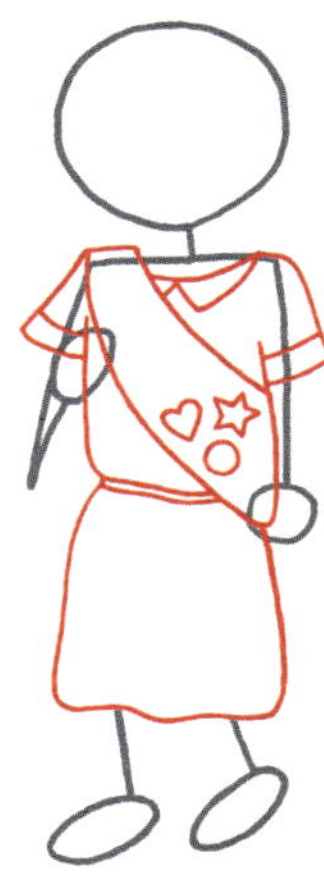

3. Draw a beret on her head with a dollop shape.

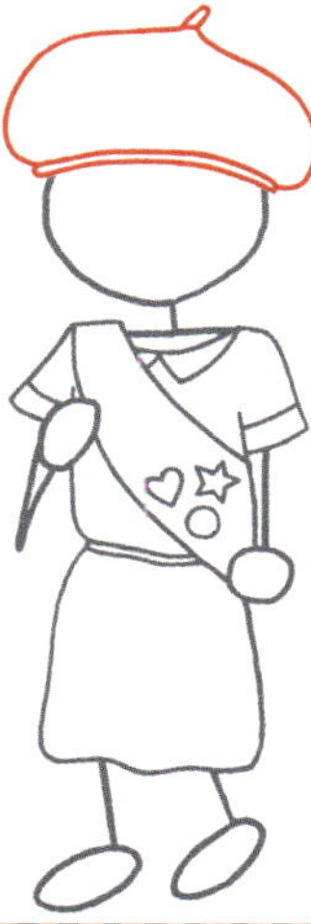

4. Give her pigtails and a happy facial expression.

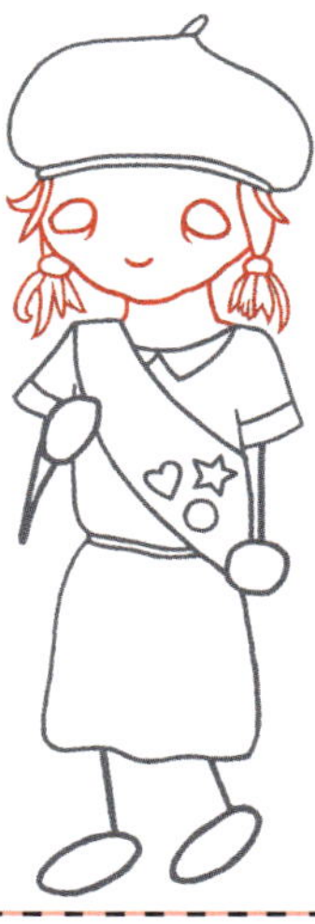

5. Draw the left hand holding a bone-shaped cookie.

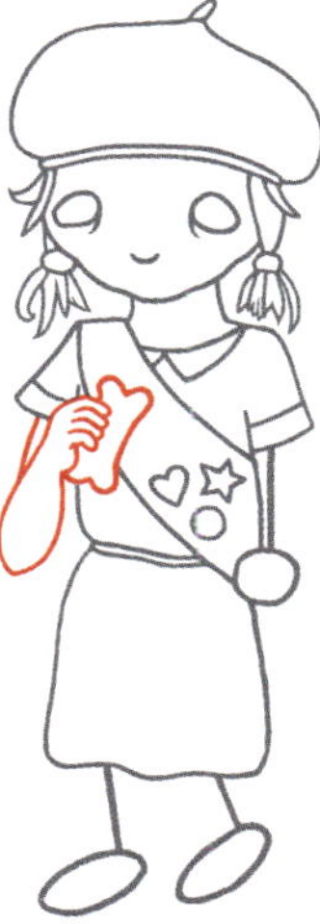

6. Draw the right hand holding a cookie box. Make the box with a rectangle and two rectangle sides. Add the bone-shaped cookie inside a burst.

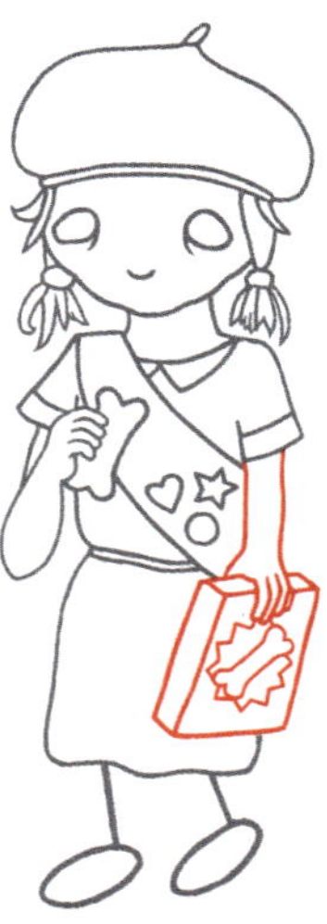

7. Draw the legs and Mary Jane shoes with a short heel and a cutout on top. Make the socks uneven heights.

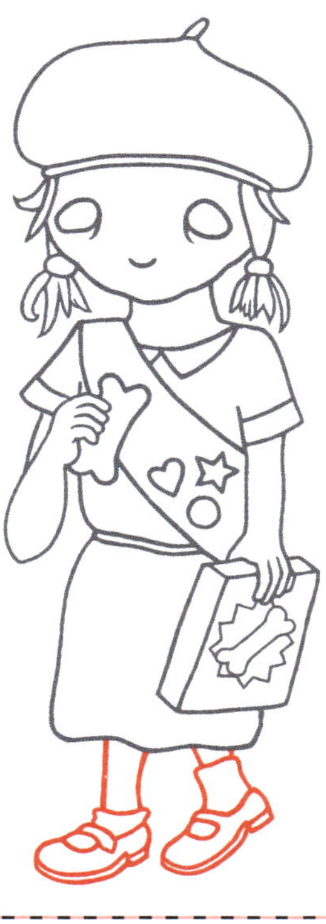

8. Cleanly trace your sketch with pencil on watercolor paper before inking.

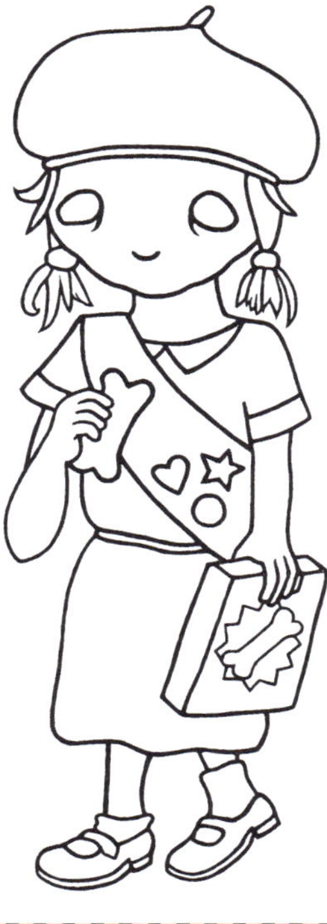

9. I used watercolor to make her skin green and her outfit pink. The cookies are pale brown, the cookie box is black, and her hair and shoes are dark brown.

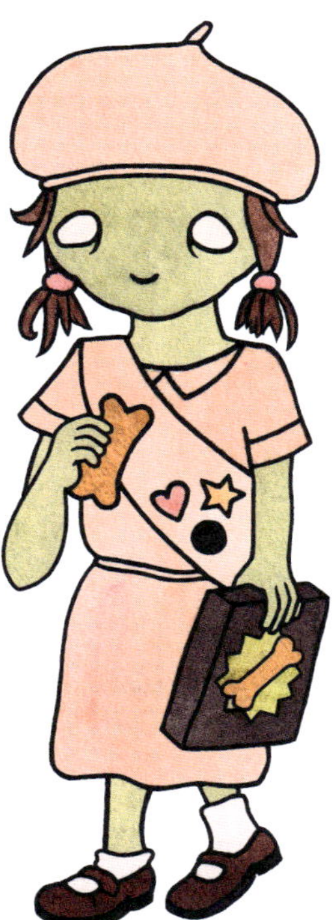

10. With a thin brush or pen, add lines to her hair and texture to the cookies. Add thick shading to the eyes. I used warm gray. Use the same color to shade the rest of the character.

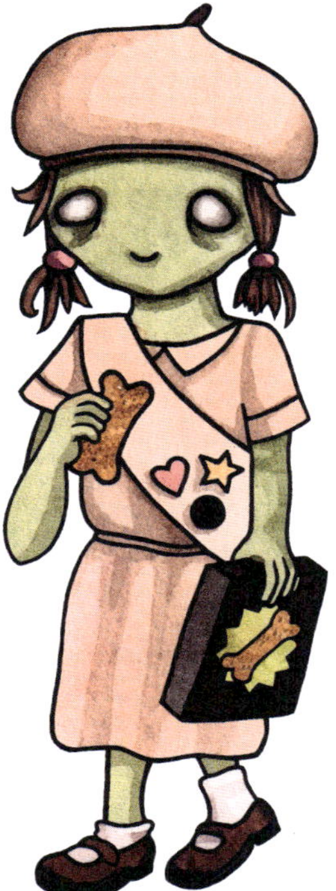

GARDEN UNDERWRAPS

1. Draw a simple figure with a round head, rectangle body that continues into rounded legs, and oval arms. Draw two oval eyes and a small mouth.

2. Have the mummy hold hedge clippers. Use rectangles for the handles and cross the semicircle blades.

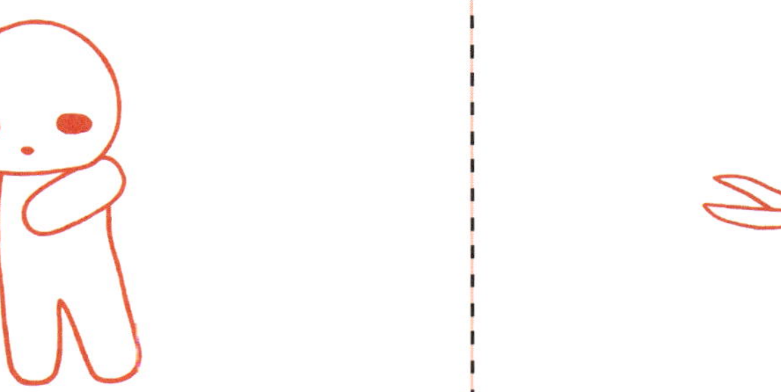

3. Draw bandages crossing all over the mummy. Add the bandages one section at a time.

4. Add a row of plants and bushes in front with abstract shapes and flowers and leaves.

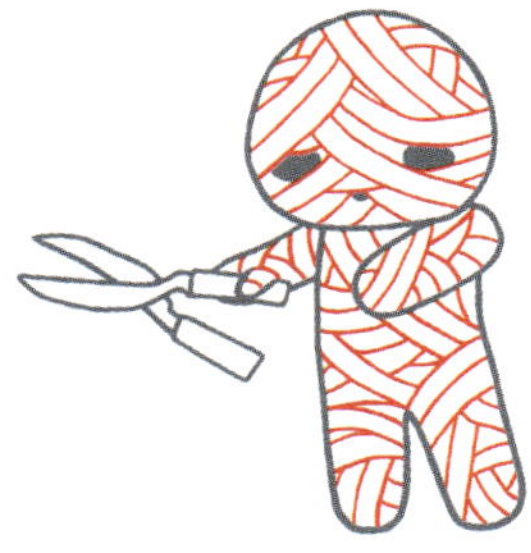

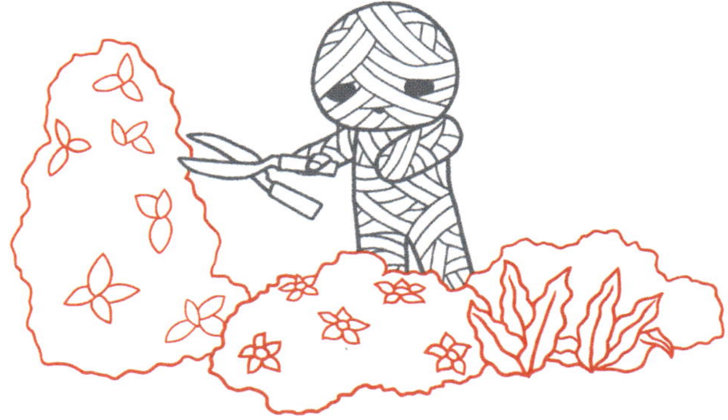

5. Draw a spiky fence to the right with three arrowhead posts.

6. Extend a loose strip of bandage from one of the fence posts to the mummy.

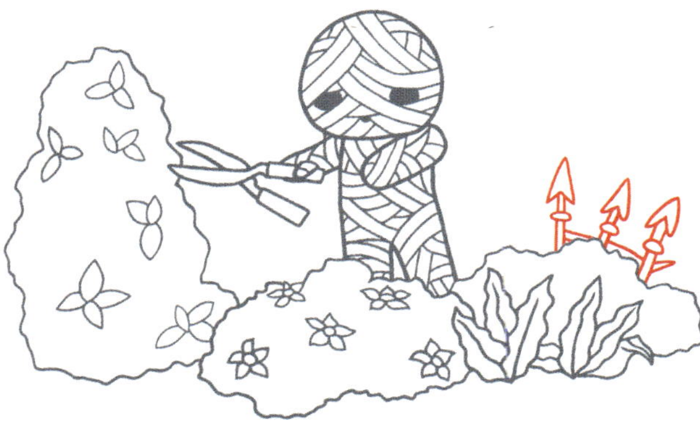

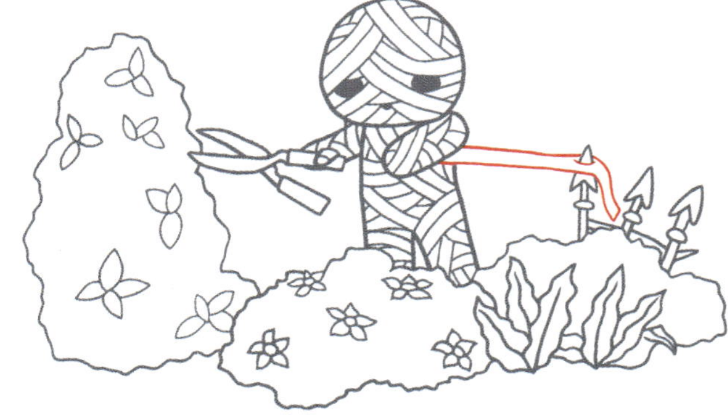

7. Draw a picket fence and some more bushes in the back.

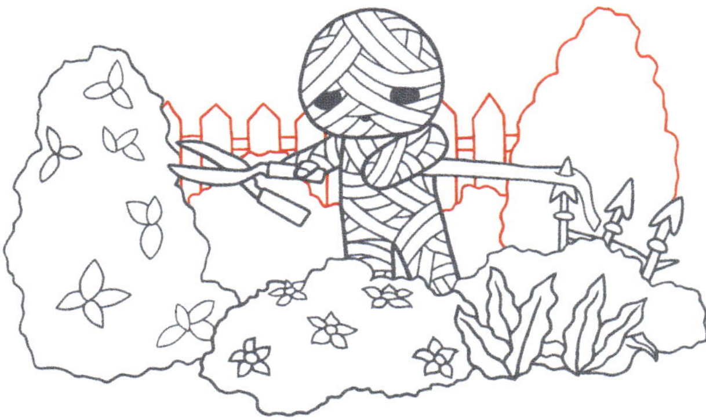

8. Add some trees with full leaves in the back, one on the left and one on the right.

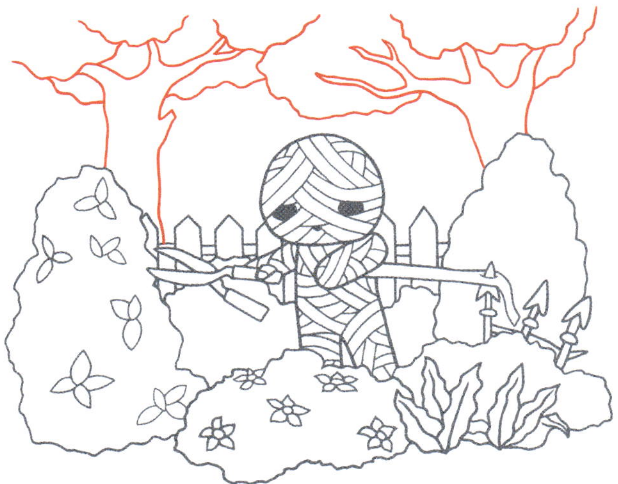

9. Cleanly trace your sketch with pencil on watercolor paper before inking. I used a pencil with a smaller lead point when tracing the mummy's bandages.

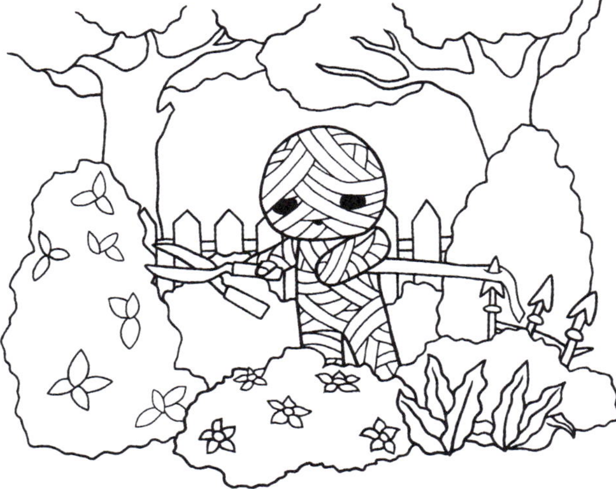

10. I used watercolors to make the background purple and used varying shades of green for the trees and bushes. The fences are brown, the handles of the hedge clippers are black, the flowers are pink, and the mummy is beige. Detail the tree trunks with wavy lines. Add shading on the bottom left side of everything.

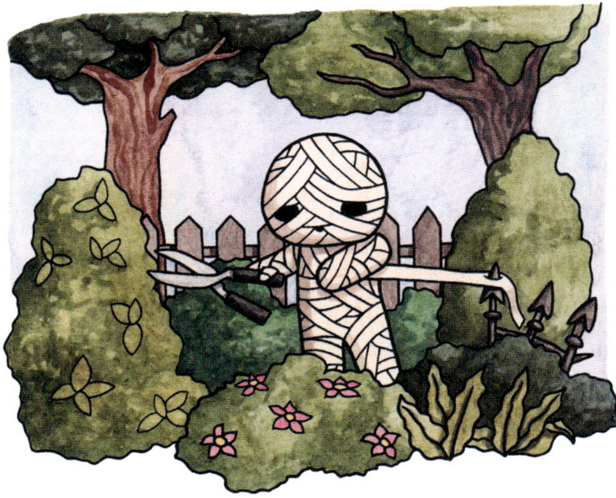

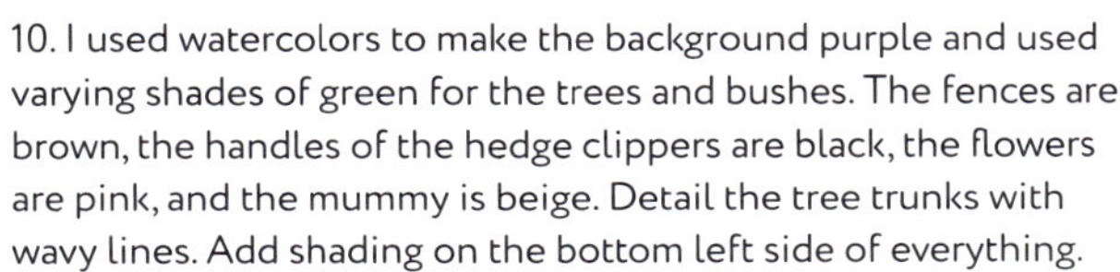

CREEPY CAMPFIRE TALES

1. Draw a campfire with two flames, one inside the other, and three cylinders underneath for the logs.

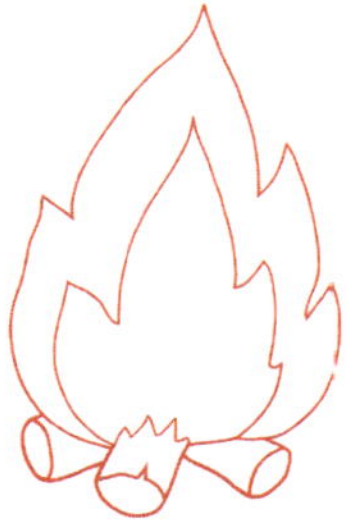

2. Draw a big log behind the campfire with a long rectangle and an oval on the end. Add a branch coming off the top with a little leaf.

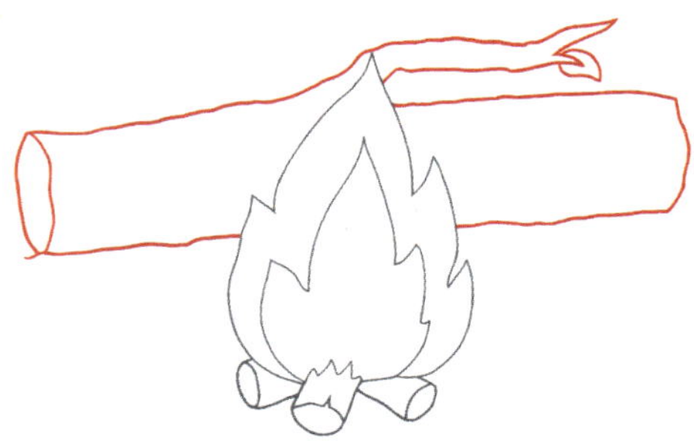

3. On the bottom left, draw a ghost in a curved oval sitting on a lumpy shape. Draw a small branch in its outstretched hand with a round marshmallow at the end.

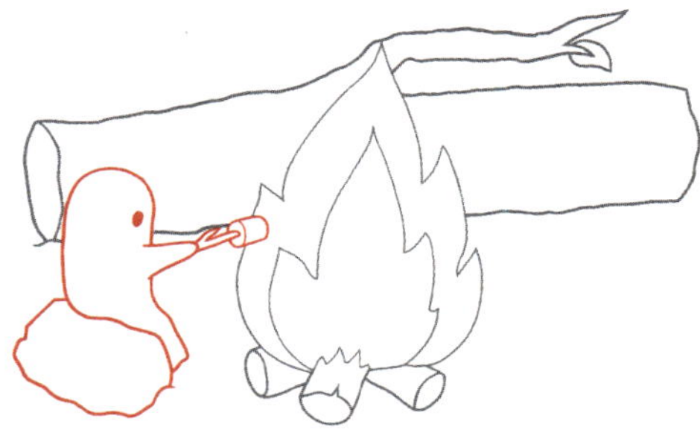

4. Draw another ghost on the right with a wavy bottom. Add arms and a happy facial expression. Extend a thin oval from the left arm and attach a round marshmallow.

5. Draw a third ghost sitting on top of the branch. Add two triangle hands holding a U-shaped mug. Give the ghost a happy facial expression.

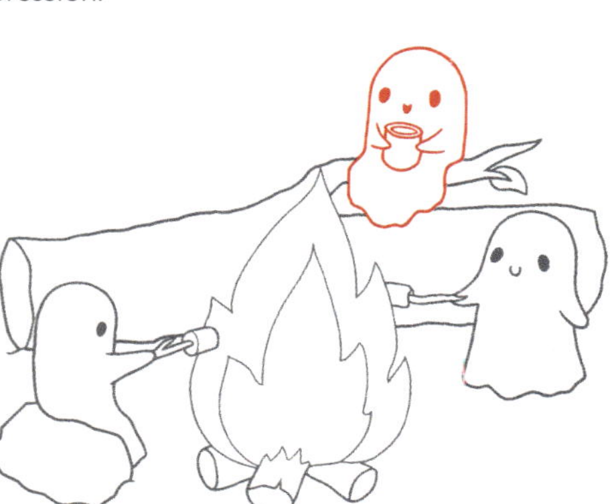

6. Add a skeleton sitting on the log with a mushroom-shaped head with a curve for the lower jaw. Add a collared sweater over a robe. Draw the arms and bony hands holding an opened book on its lap.

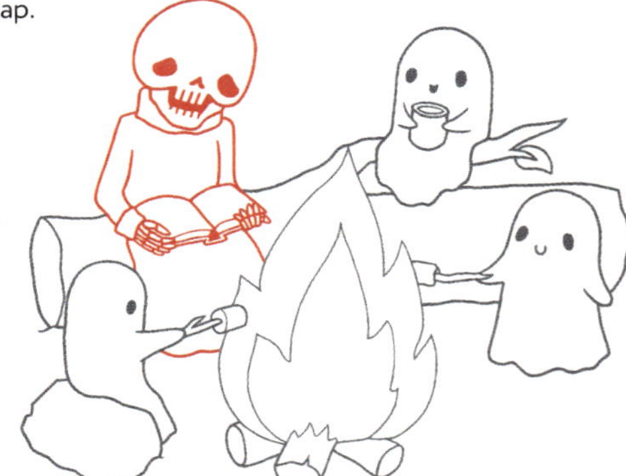

7. Finish the scene with a backpack in the bottom right corner and lines for trees in the background.

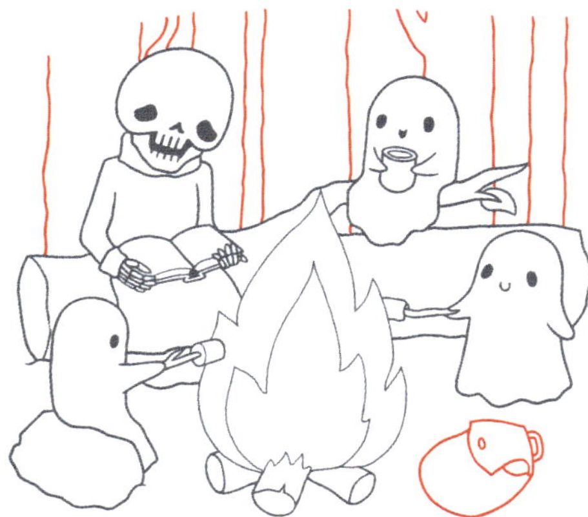

8. Cleanly trace your sketch with pencils of varying lead point sizes on watercolor paper before inking.

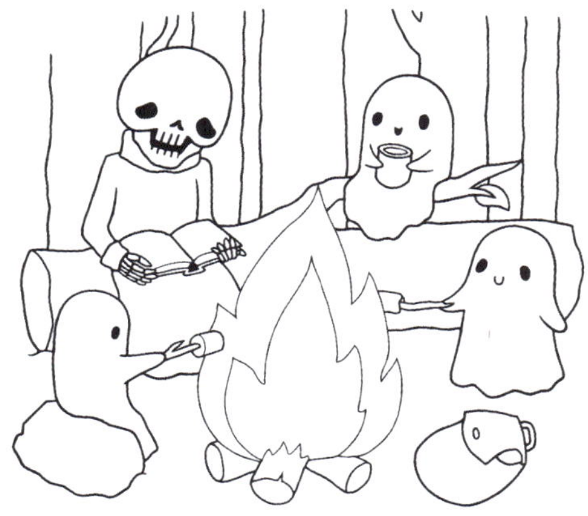

9. Color the campfire first. I used watercolors in light orange for the inner flame and a darker orange for the outer flame.

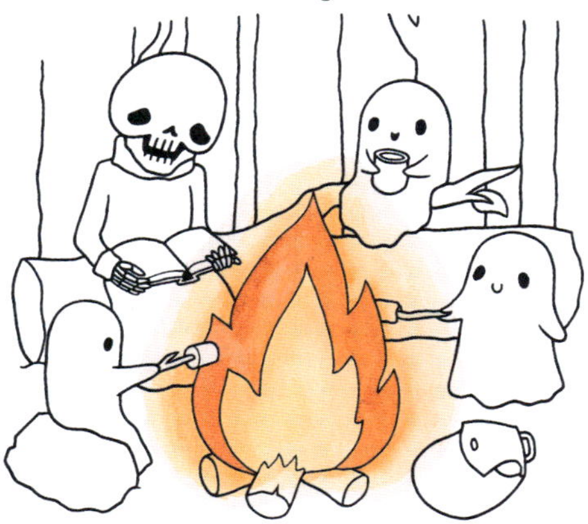

10. I used black for the background, brown for the trees and logs, red for the skeleton's top and the backpack, and green for the leaf.

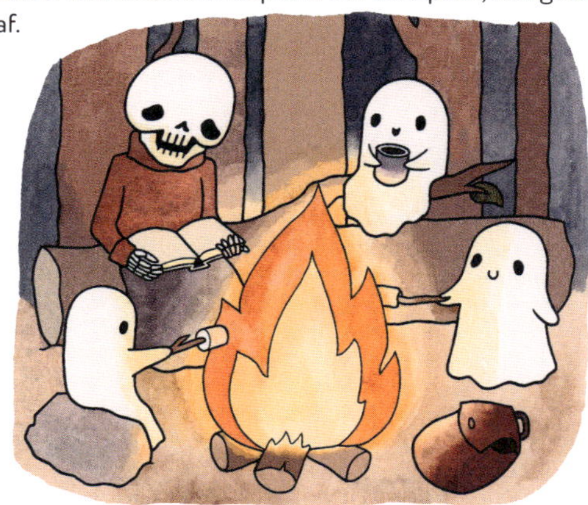

11. With a thin brush or pen, add wavy lines to the trees and some scribbles of text on the book. Add shading to the background and on the back of everything, as the light is coming from the campfire. With black ink, put trees and plant silhouettes around the edges of the illustration like a border.

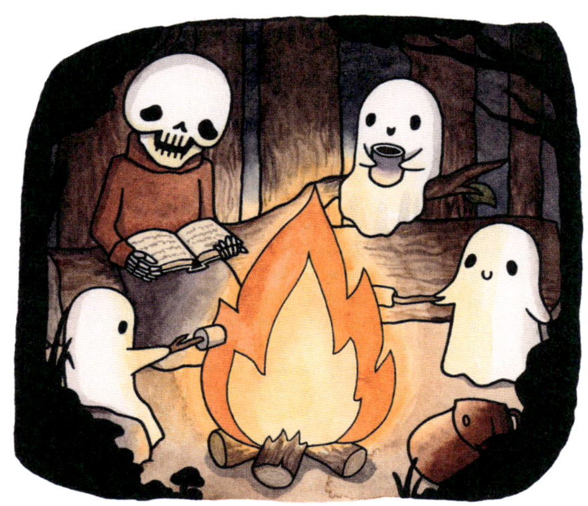

GHOSTMADE COOKIES

1. Sketch a table with a rectangle and a wavy tablecloth down the front.

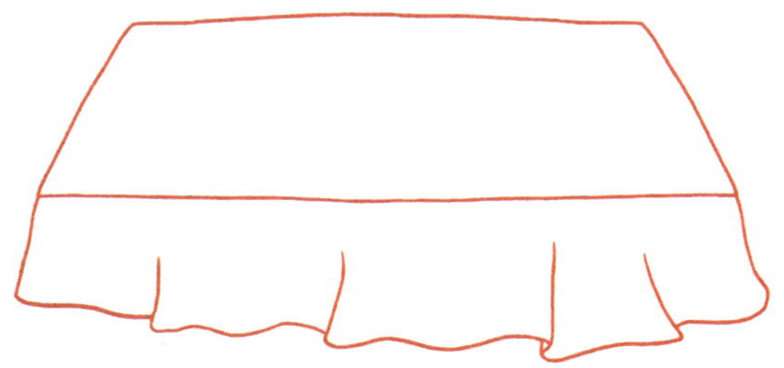

2. Draw a small ghost peeking above the table with an arch for the head and two rounded hands. Give it a happy facial expression.

3. Give the ghost a chef's hat with a rectangle band and an oval top with a curve in the middle.

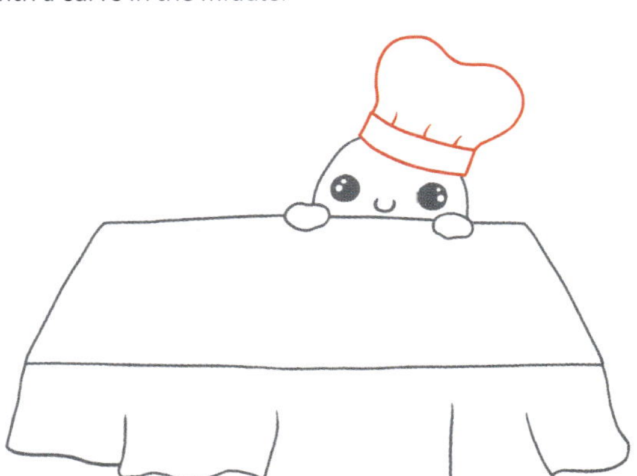

4. Draw another ghost in front of the table. Make an arch for the body with a wavy bottom. Add oval arms and a happy facial expression.

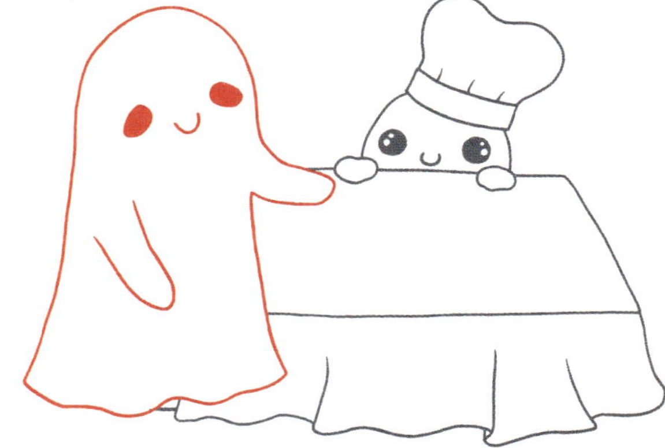

5. Have the ghost hold a rectangular tray with rectangle edges to give it depth. Add oven mitts on the hands.

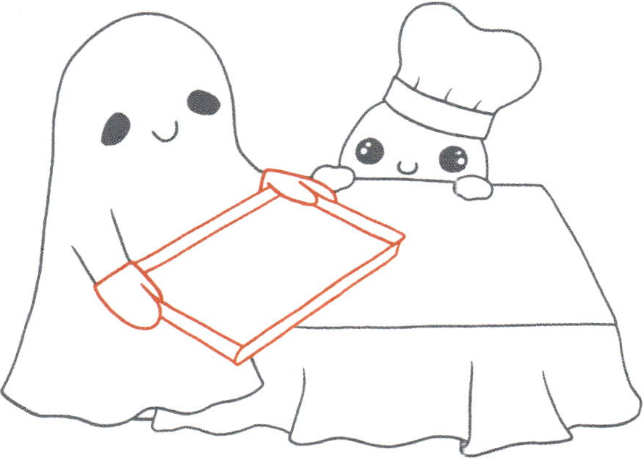

6. Draw an outline on the tray for the parchment paper, then draw rows of cookies in the shape of crescents, bones, and stars.

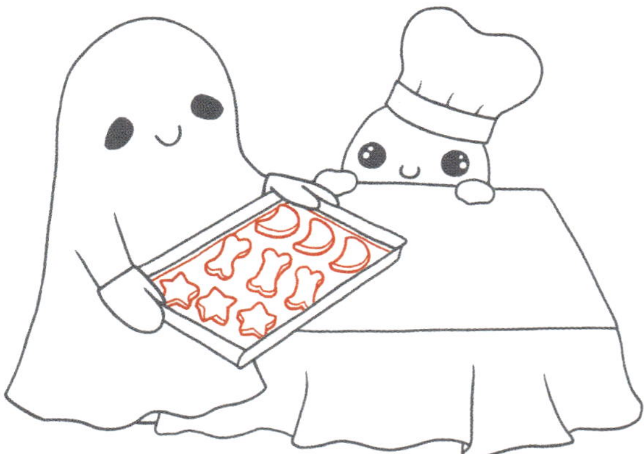

7. Add a rolling pin on the table with a cylinder with a knob on each end.

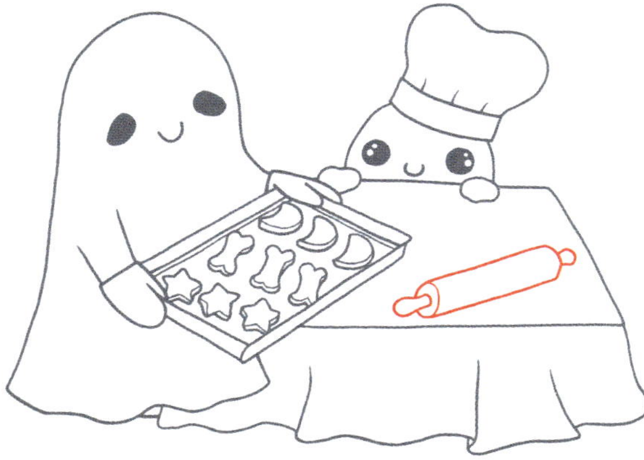

8. Cleanly trace your sketch with pencil on watercolor paper before inking. I used a pencil with a smaller lead point to trace the details on the cookies and rolling pin.

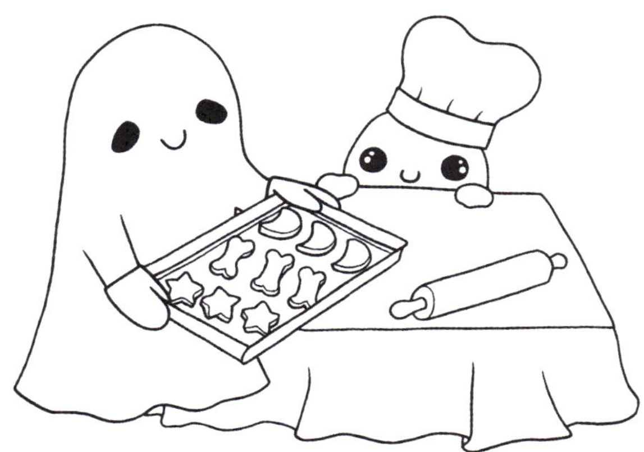

9. I used watercolors to make the background and parchment paper yellow, the tablecloth purple, and the oven mitts, cookies, and rolling pin shades of brown.

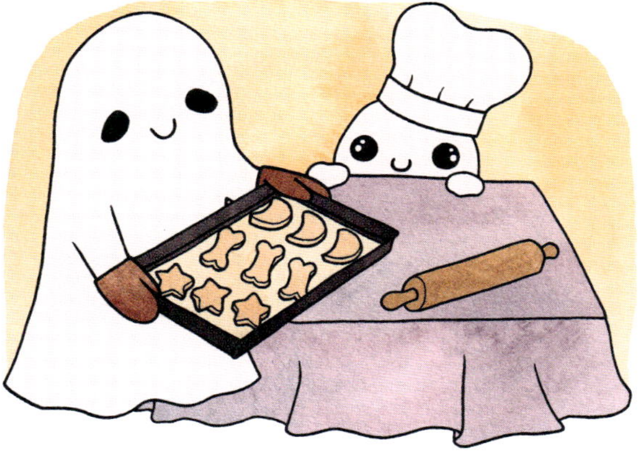

10. Using orange, I made a pattern in the background for wallpaper. With brown paint and a smaller brush, I added more detail to the wallpaper. Use a thin brush or pen to add details to the cookies and rolling pin.

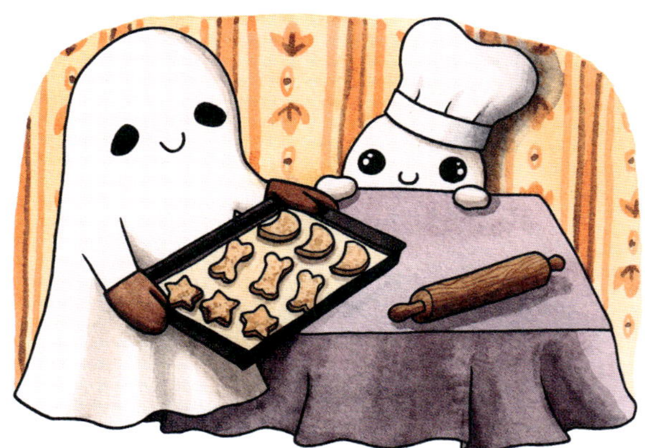

GHOSTLY GAME ROOM

1. Sketch a table with a rectangle and a wavy tablecloth down the front.

2. Make the boardgame with two rectangles. Draw a Ouija pointer with an upside-down heart with a circle cutout.

3. Sketch a figure on the left with a circle head, one arm pointed to the right, and the other hand above the first arm. Make the figure kneeling with short legs and oval feet on the left. Draw another figure to the right with its back facing us.

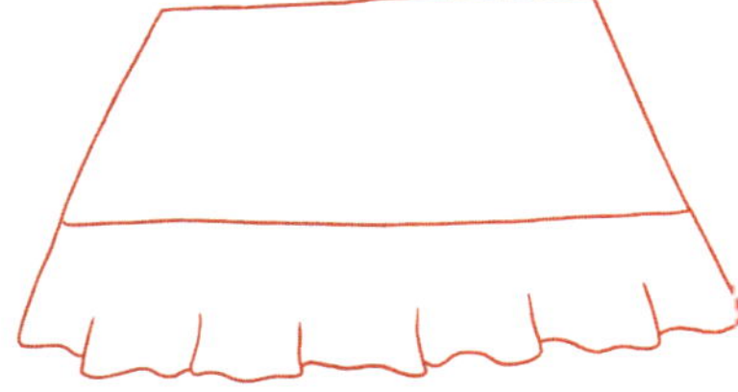

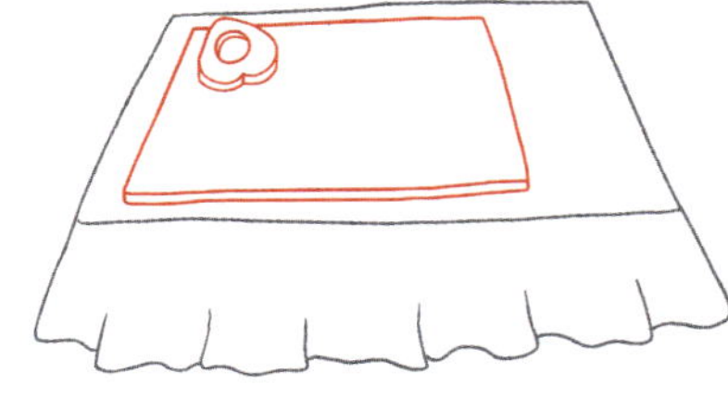

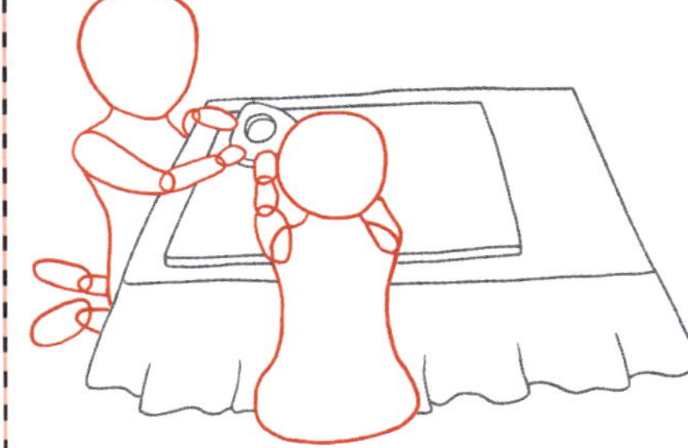

4. Give the left figure short, straight hair, a startled expression, and glasses.

5. Draw a simple short-sleeved dress and shoes.

6. Add detail to the arms and hands using the outline you previously sketched.

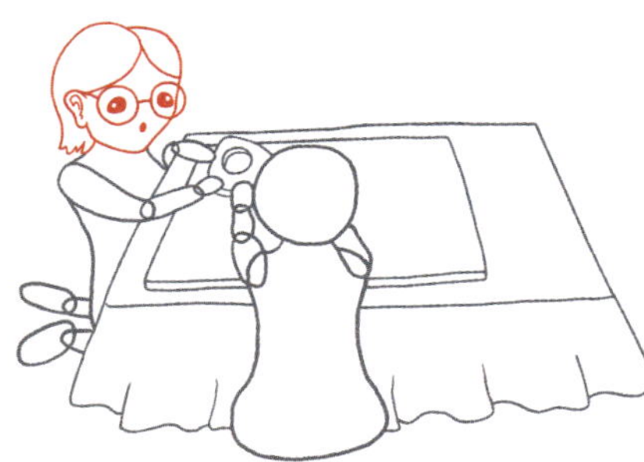

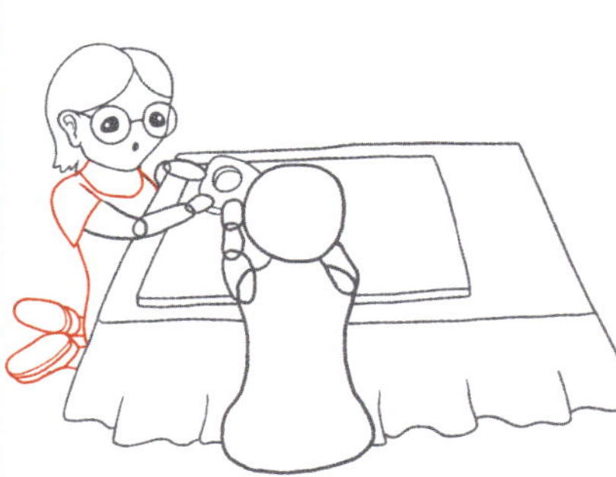

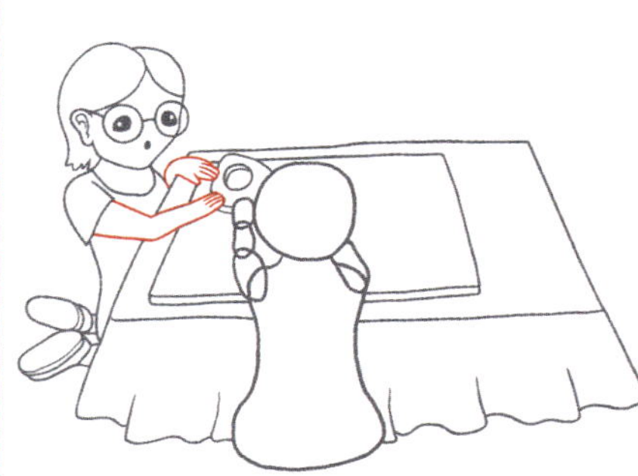

7. Add detail to the figure in the front with two low buns, a short-sleeved shirt, and a skirt.

8. Draw a laughing ghost holding the Ouija pointer with a rounded body and oval arms.

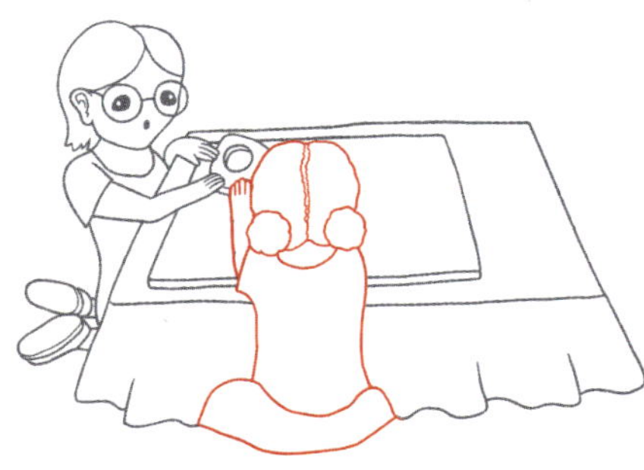

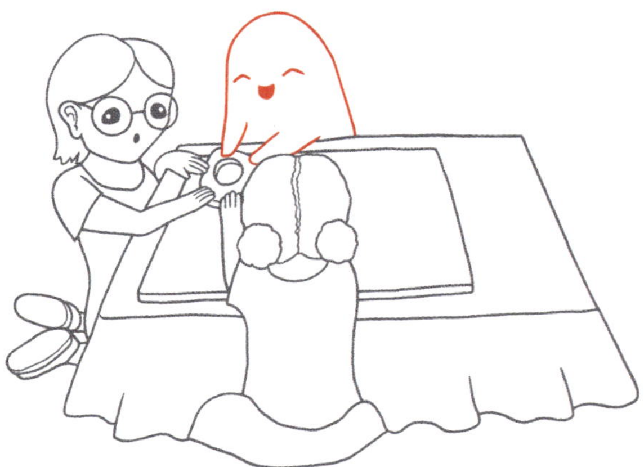

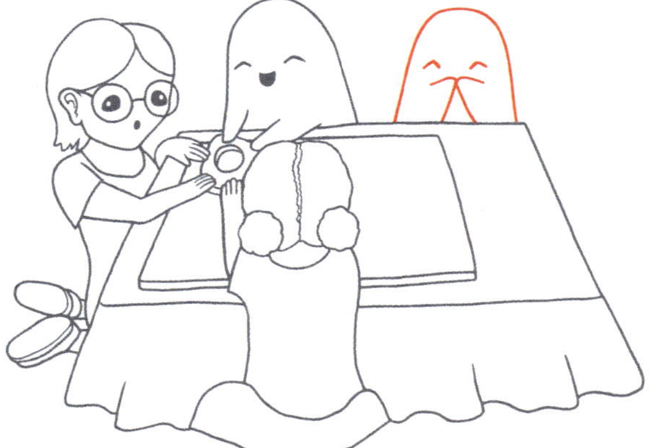

9. Draw a second ghost on the right with a rounded body. Make the arms meet at the mouth, like it's trying to stifle a laugh.

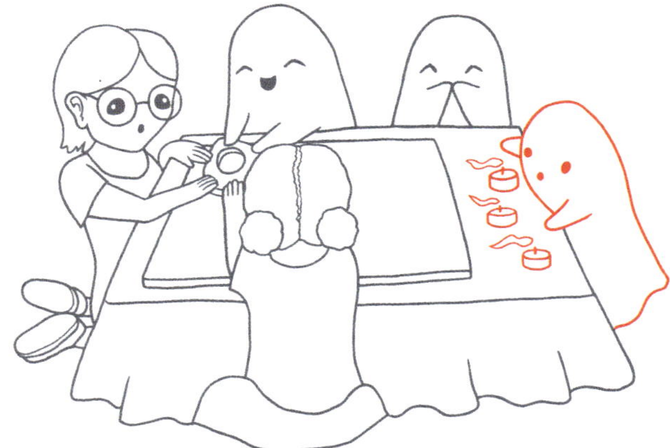

10. Draw a third ghost on the right side of the table with three candles in front of it. Make the flames blow to the left.

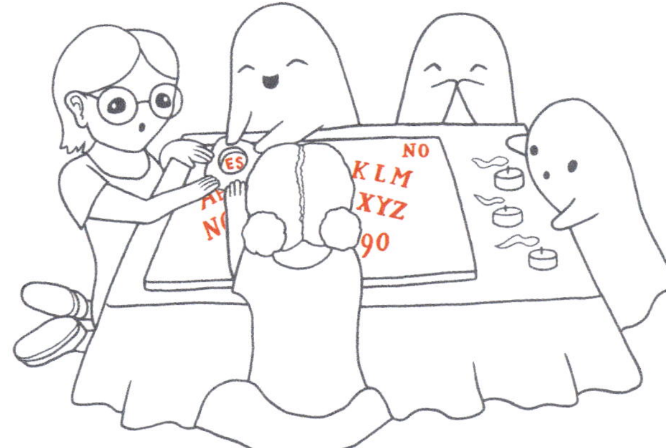

11. Add the letters and numbers that are visible parts of the Ouija board.

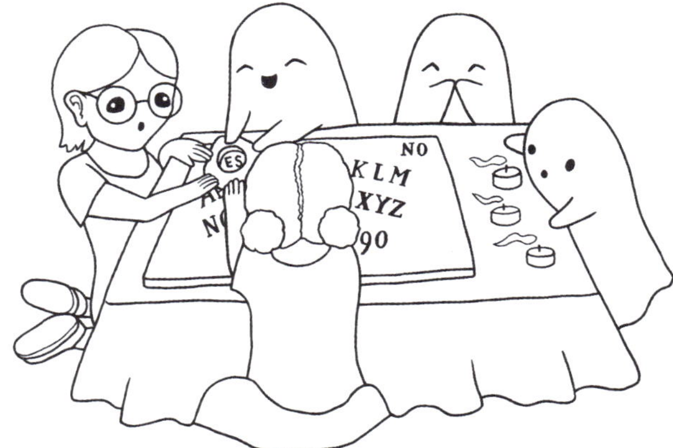

12. Cleanly trace your sketch with pencils of varying lead point sizes on watercolor paper before inking.

13. Make the girl's shoes, the girl in the front's hair, and the tablecloth black. Use various shades of gray to color everything except the ghosts. Add texture to the board and the girls' hair with thin lines in a darker shade. Add shading for depth.

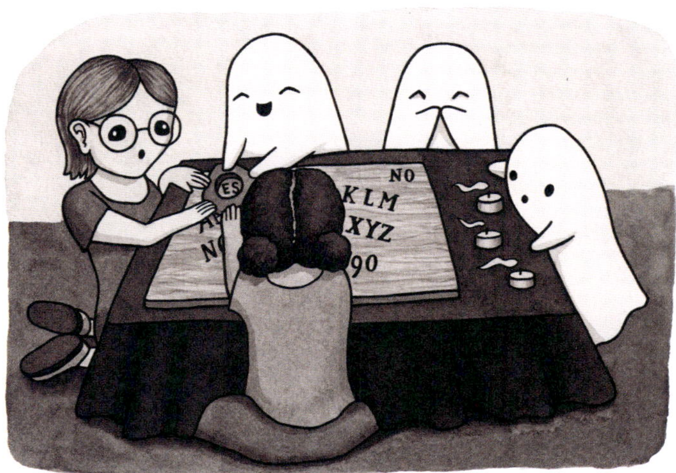

BEDTIME SCARY STORIES

1. Sketch a big rectangle with two lines across the middle.

2. Draw a bed on the left with a rounded headboard and baseboard, half of a rectangle pillow, and a rectangle for the folded blanket below.

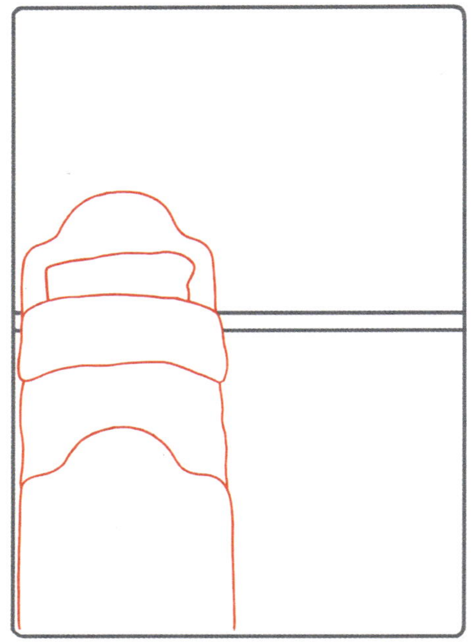

3. Turn each board into a wrought iron design with a smiling pumpkin in the middle.

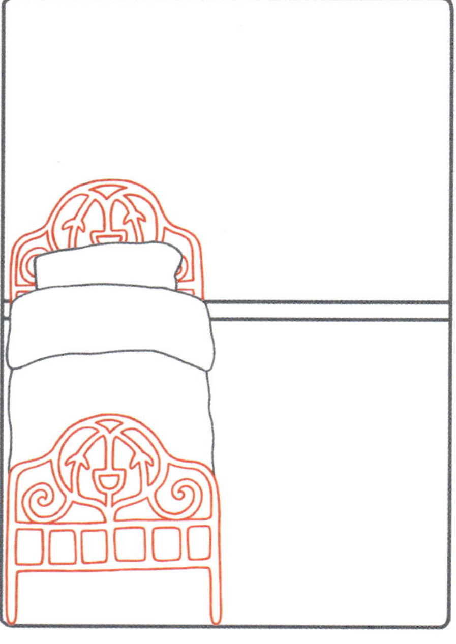

4. On the bed, sketch a child with a rounded head and hands, legs, and feet. Place an open book between their hands with their eyes peeking over it.

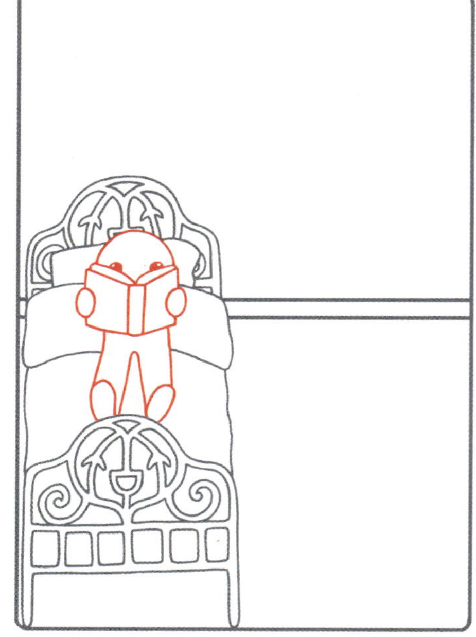

5. Give the child hair, add detail to the hands, and draw a shirt and pants.

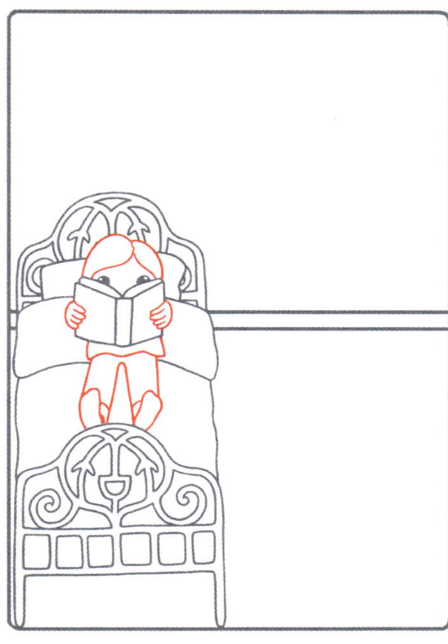

6. Draw a ghost's head and hands peeking around the left side of the headboard.

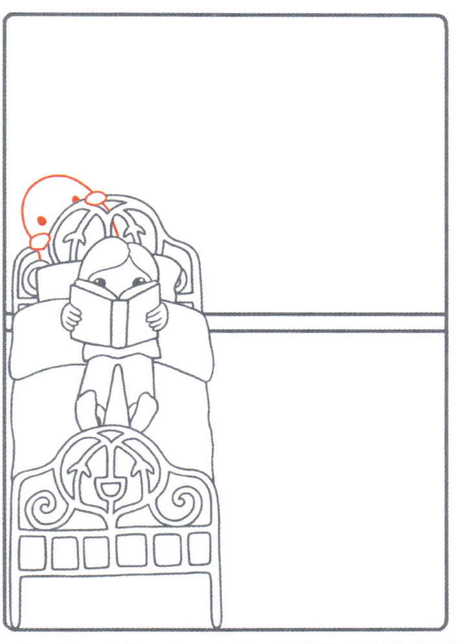

7. Draw a second ghost underneath the bed, making a rounded head with two arms.

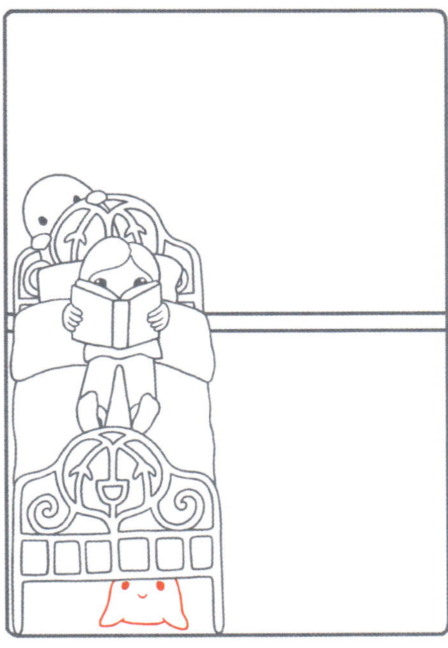

8. Draw a poster on the wall with a rectangle and small rectangle strips of tape at three corners.

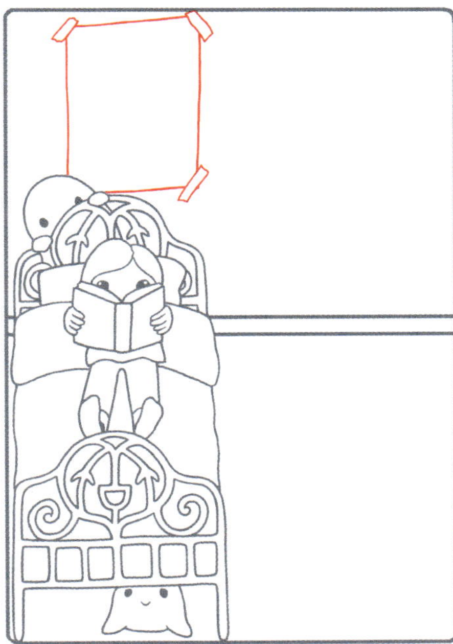

9. Draw a sleeping bat with a teardrop-shaped body, an oval head, and triangle ears on the poster. Draw lines across the body to show its wings wrapped around itself and some stars.

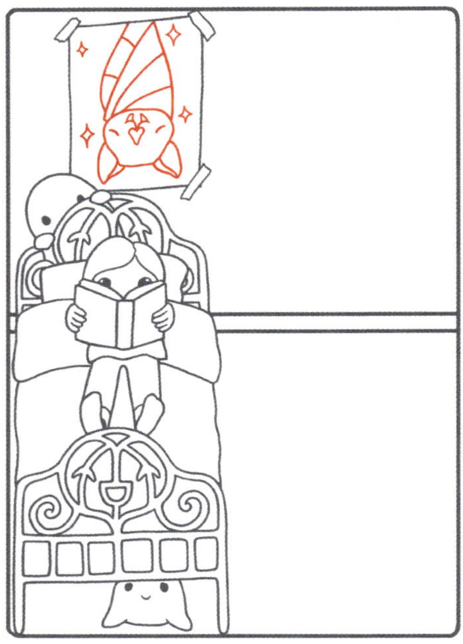

10. On the right, draw a square nightstand with two doors on the front and small curves for the feet.

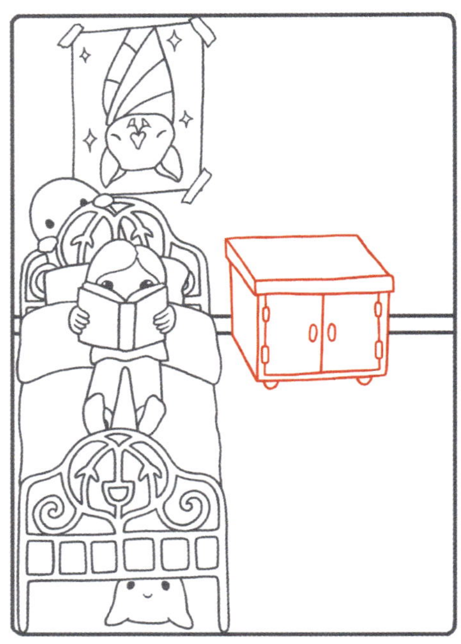

11. Open one of the doors of the nightstand and draw the head and arm of a ghost peeking out.

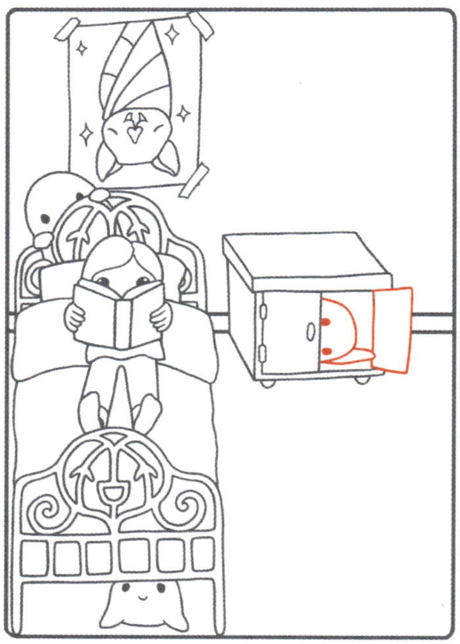

12. Add a mushroom lamp on the nightstand. Don't forget the cord!

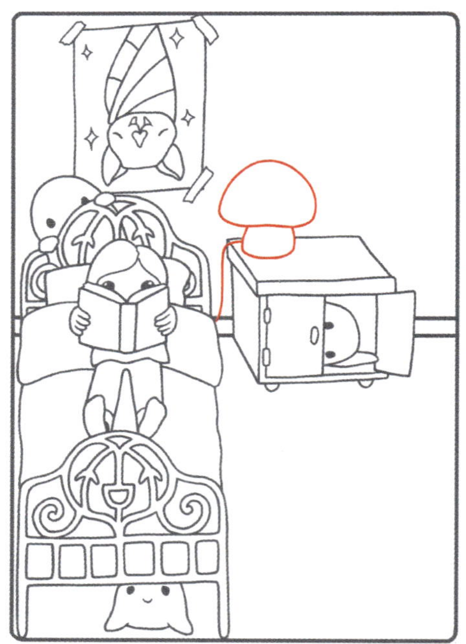

13. In the top right, draw a curtain and windowsill. Make another ghost's head and hands peek out from behind the curtain.

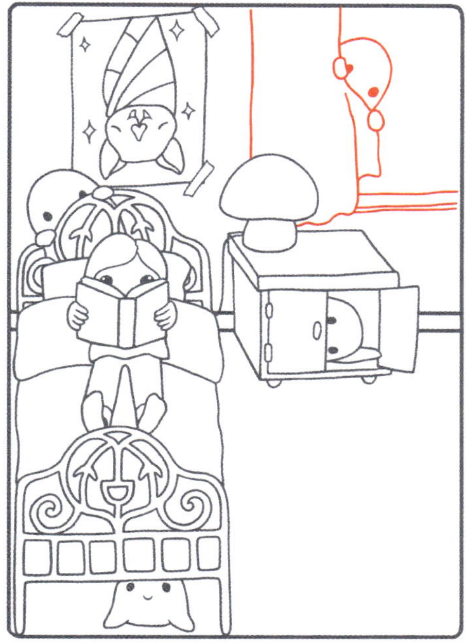

14. In the bottom right, draw a pumpkin pouf chair with another ghost hiding behind it.

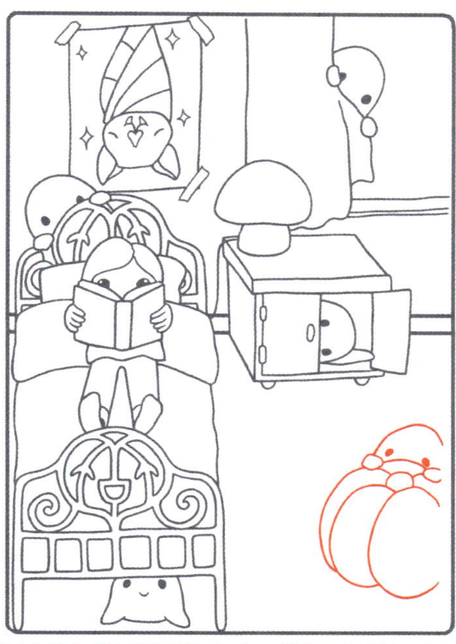

15. Cleanly trace your sketch with pencil on watercolor paper before inking.

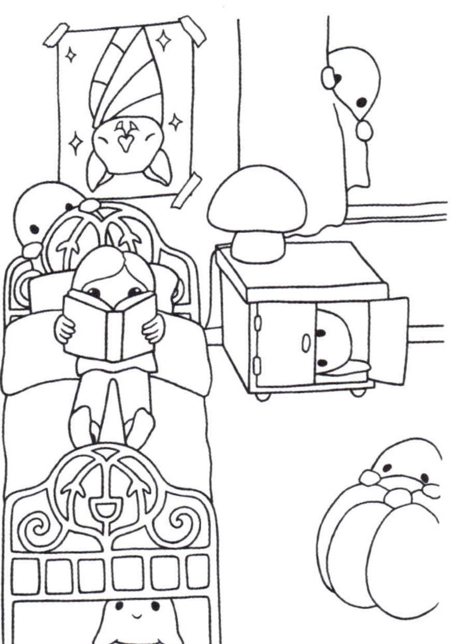

16. Color the scene in shades of black and gray, making sure to leave a light area around the lamp. Add shading, remembering that the lamp is where the light comes from.

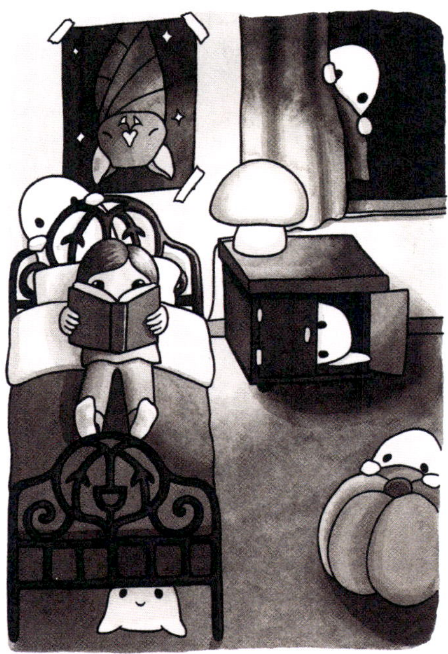

SUPERNATURAL SLEEPOVER

1. Sketch three sitting figures. Draw the left one with a round head and oval body. Draw the middle one with a teardrop-shaped head and a trapezoid body. Then draw the right one with a round head, square torso, and a wavy diamond shape underneath.

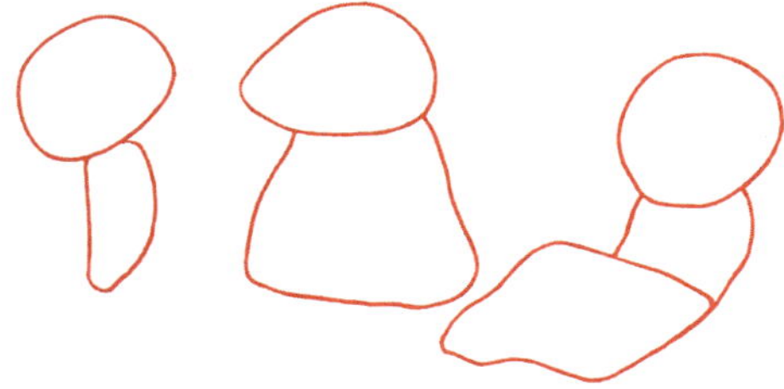

2. Draw the left person's arm and crossed legs and the right person's arms with ovals and circles.

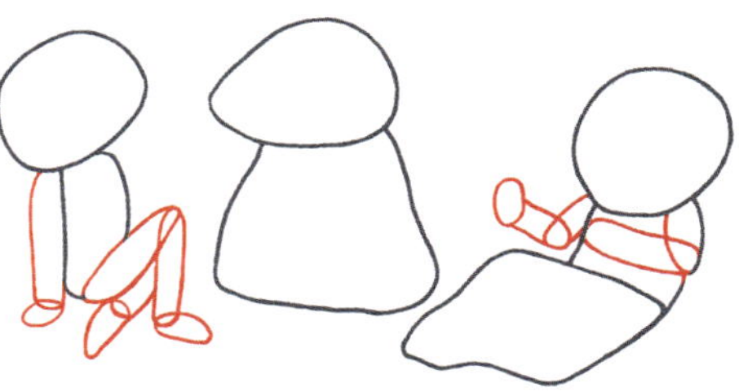

3. Draw three sides of a rectangular tent around the figures. Drape the fabric on the top and sides and add a clothespin at the top.

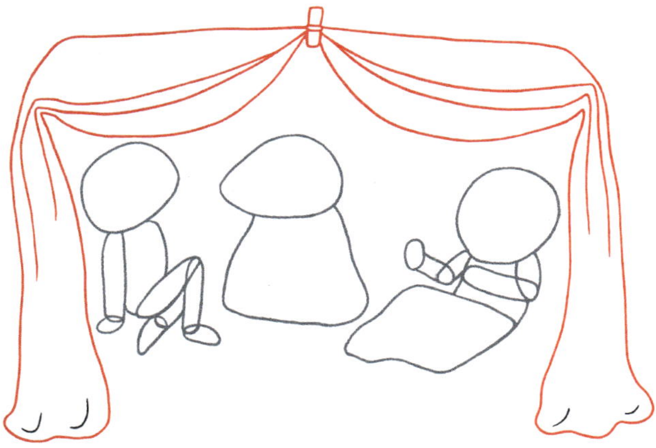

4. Add a string of lights across the top with small circles for the lights. Draw a pumpkin decoration at each end.

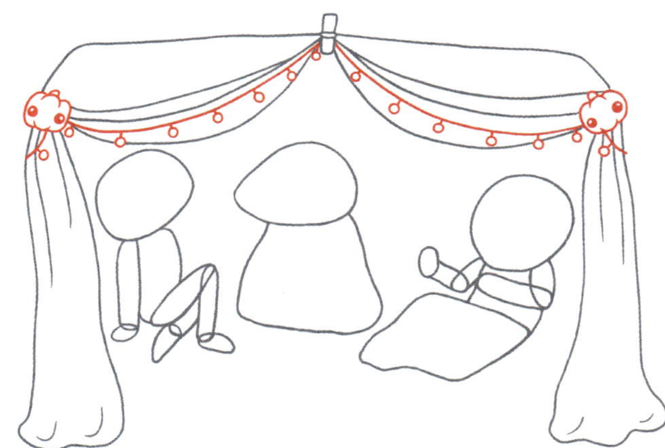

5. The character on the left is a skeleton. Draw a mushroom-shaped head and a skeletal hand.

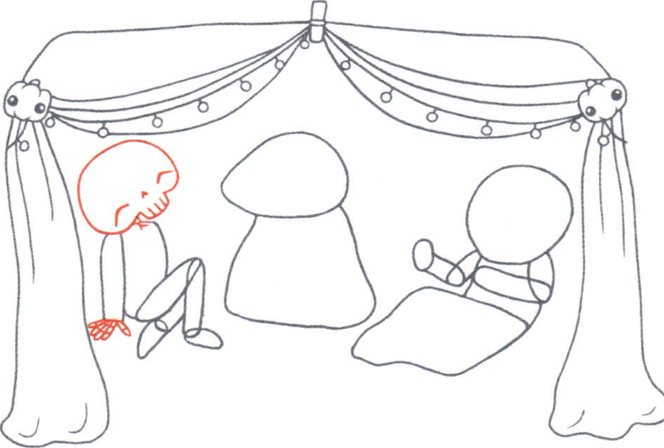

6. Draw the skeleton's sweater with a ghost pattern, then add the pants and socks.

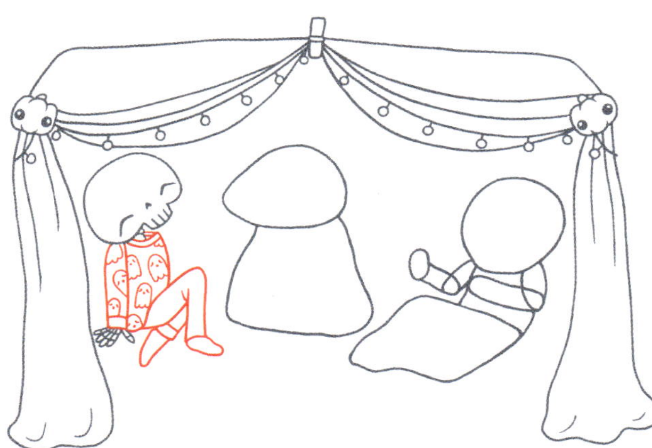

7. Add details to the werewolf with pointed ears, a rounded nose, and a fang. Wrap a blanket around the body that crosses in the middle.

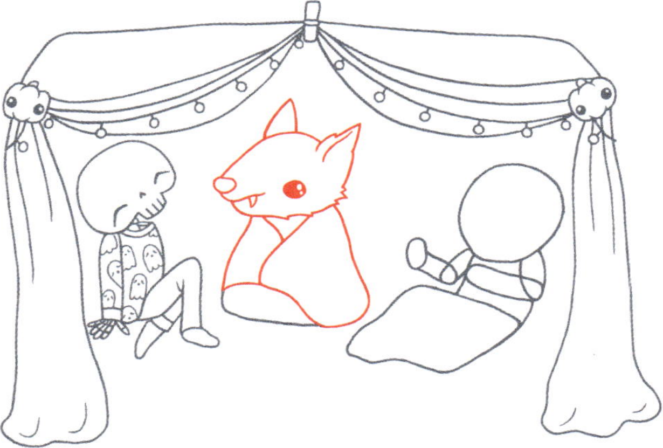

8. Draw the werewolf wearing an old-fashioned nightgown with a collar peeking out from under the blanket.

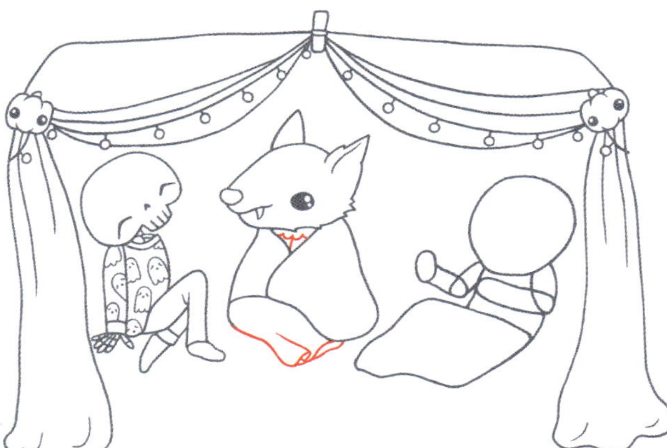

SUPERNATURAL SLEEPOVER continued

9. The character on the right is a vampire. Draw slicked-back hair and a fanged smile.

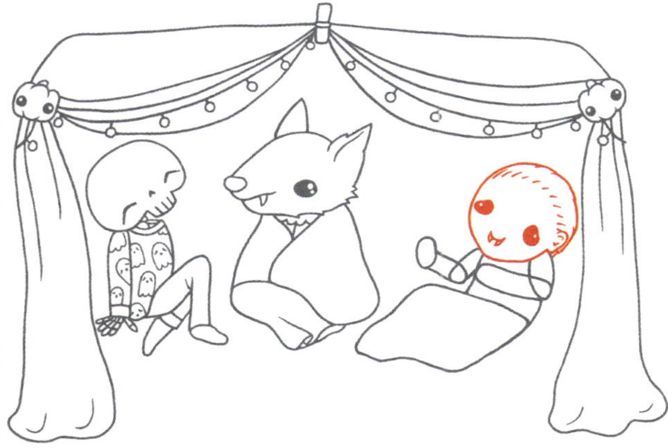

10. Draw the vampire's arms and hands with a magazine held between. Detail the magazine with a moon and bats.

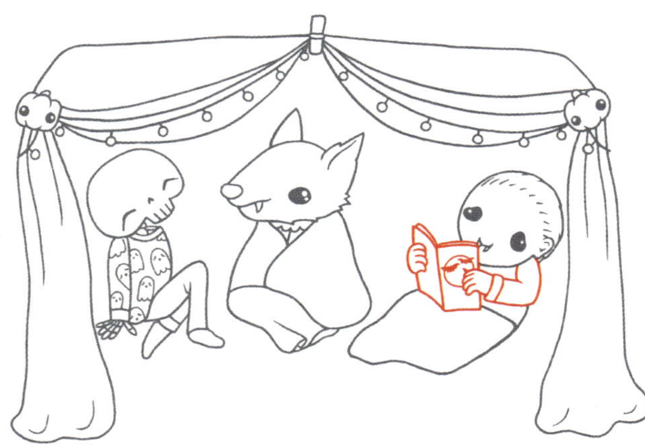

11. Place a blanket over the vampire's lap and a pillow under its elbow.

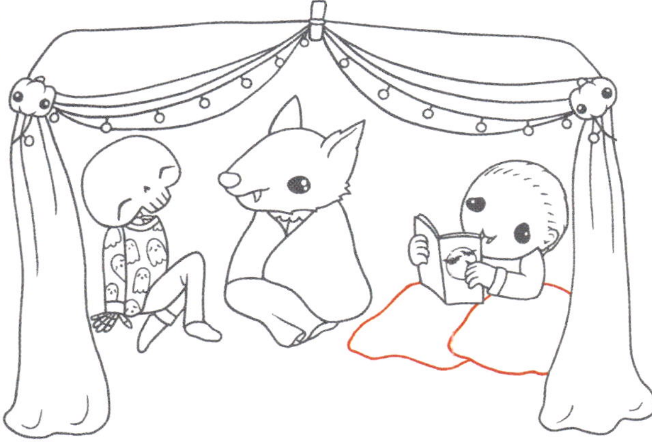

12. On the left, make a striped, square bucket of popcorn. Add the lumpy popcorn inside with a bone sticking out. Next to the vampire, draw a rectangular IV bag of blood.

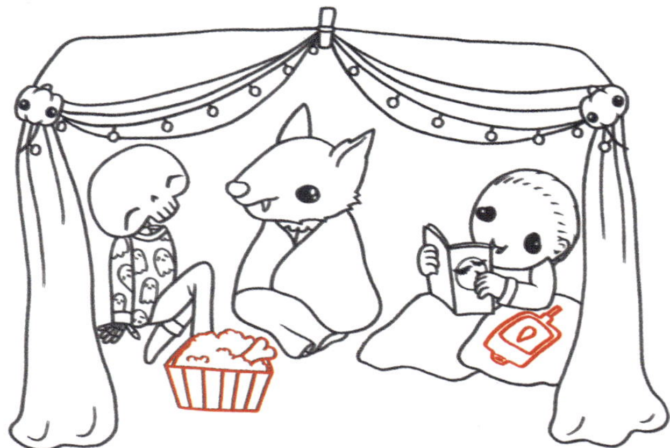

13. Draw some square pillows behind the characters.

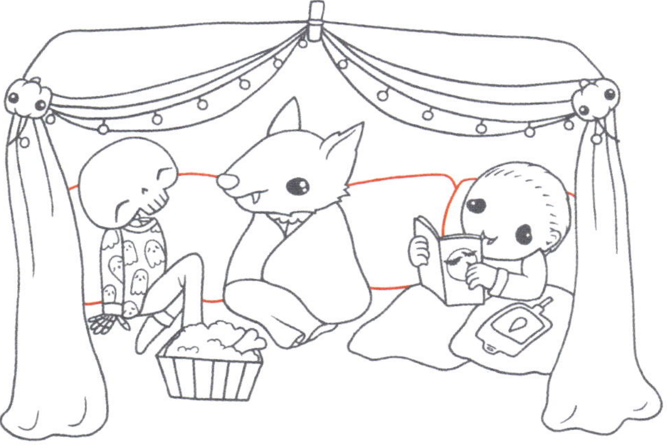

14. Add rugs on the floor where visible. Make the one on the right a moon-and-star pattern.

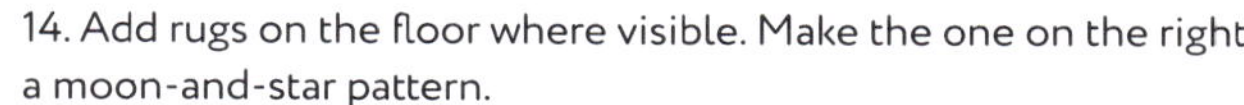
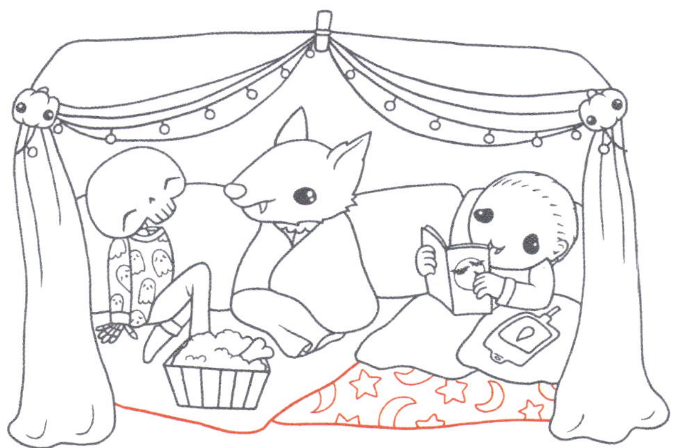

15. Cleanly trace your sketch with pencils of varying lead point sizes on watercolor paper before inking.

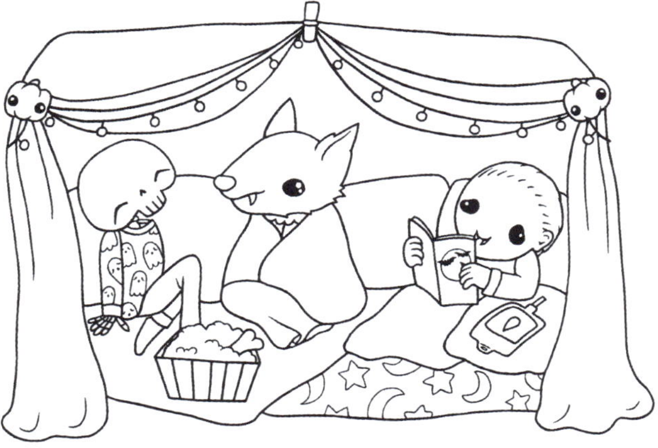

16. Color the scene in various shades of black and gray. With a thin brush or pen, add texture to the popcorn and the characters' hair or fur. Add shading, making sure the back of the tent is darkest.

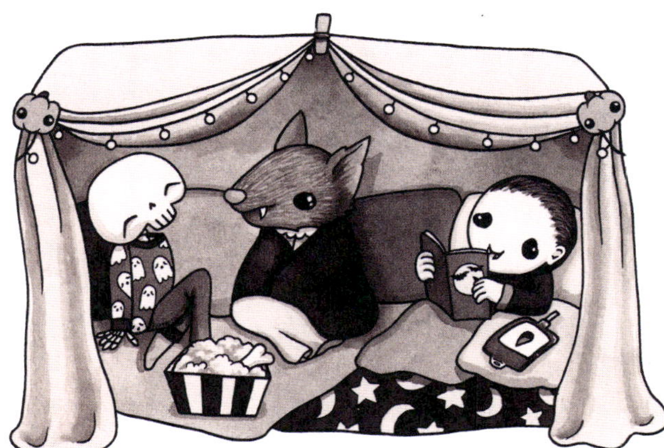

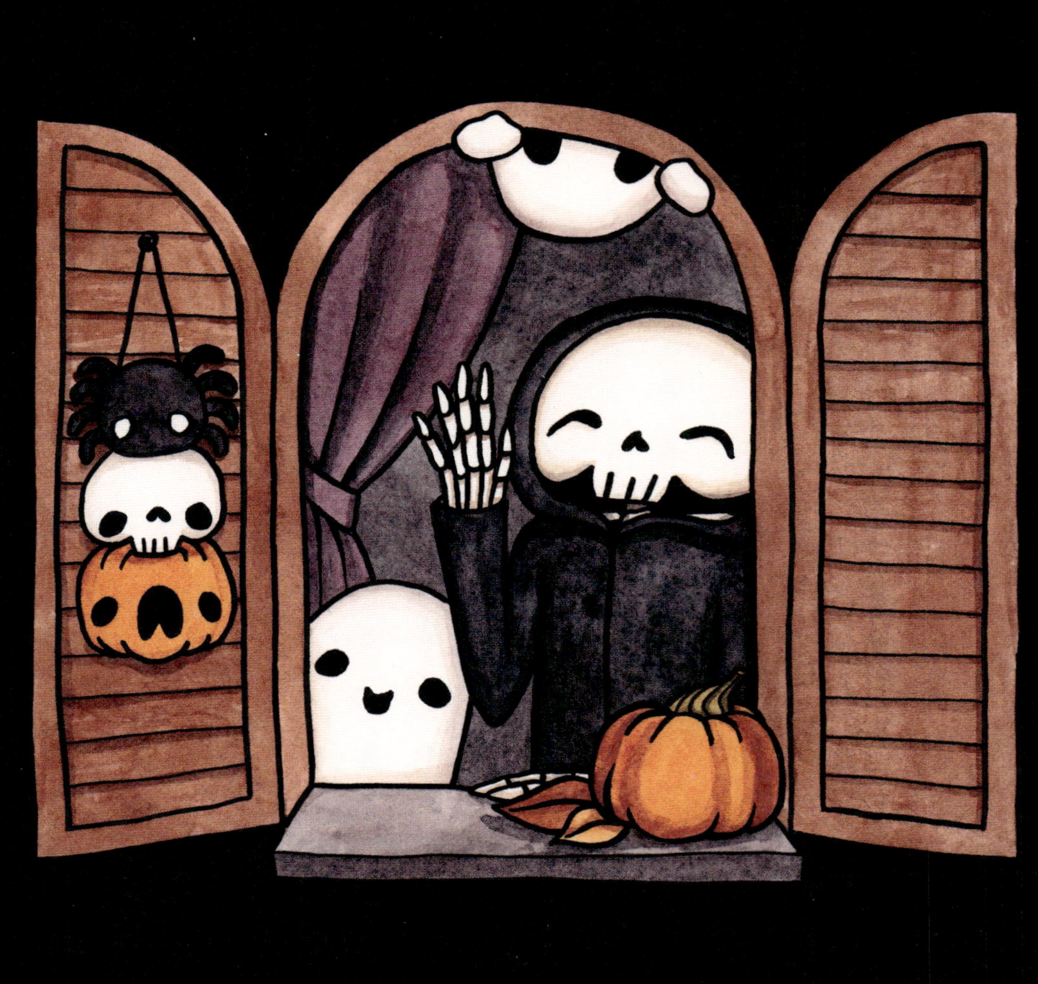

hollow lanes

OLD MULBERRY HOUSE

1. Draw a simple house with a pentagon and an oval outlining the roof.

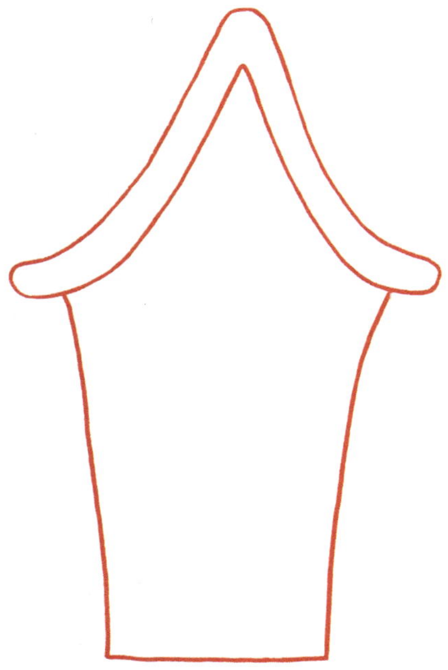

2. Extend the house to the right with two more rectangles.

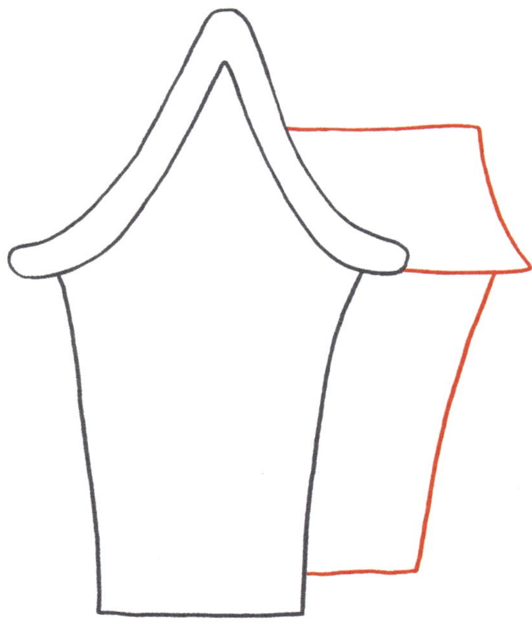

3. Add an arched door with a semicircle window and a circle for the doorknob. Then add one circle window and two arched windows with oval windowsills.

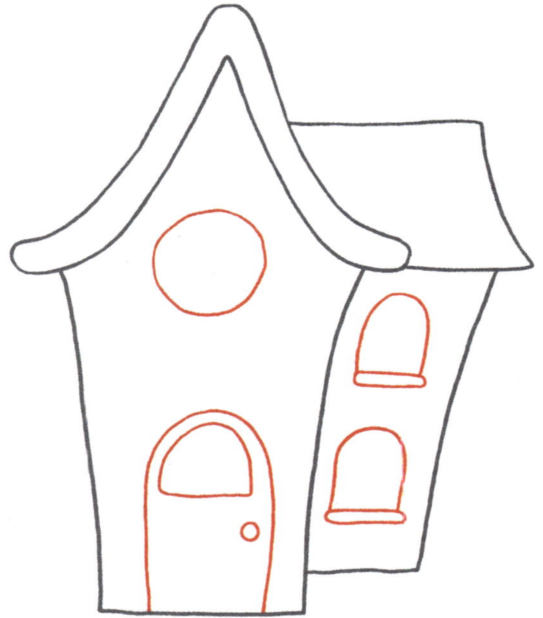

4. Draw three wispy ghosts flying out of the windows. Give them varying facial expressions.

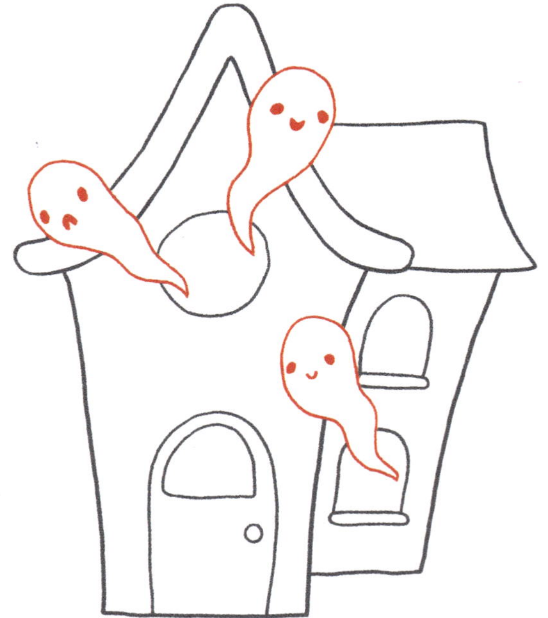

5. Add details with lines on the roof, door, and windows.

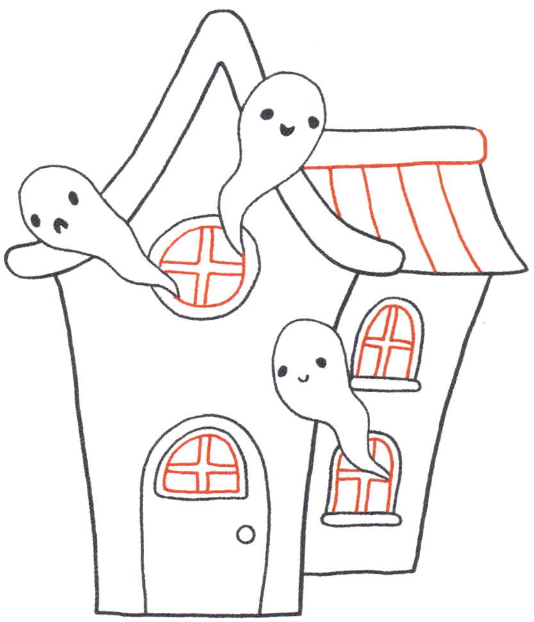

6. Cleanly trace your sketch with pencil on watercolor paper before inking.

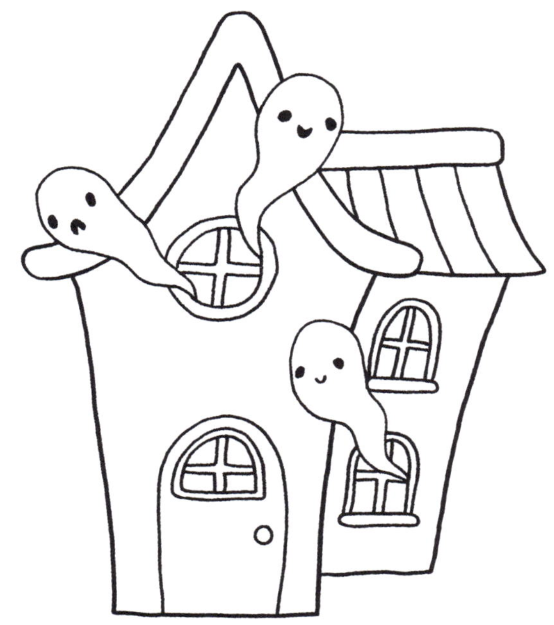

7. I used different shades of gray to color the house. Add shading to the underside of the roof, windowsills, and doorknob.

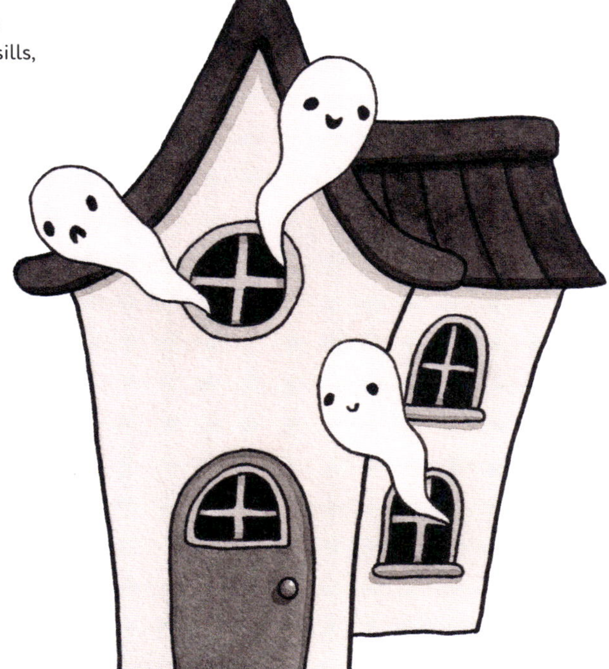

PUMPKIN COTTAGE

1. Sketch a large, rounded trapezoid.

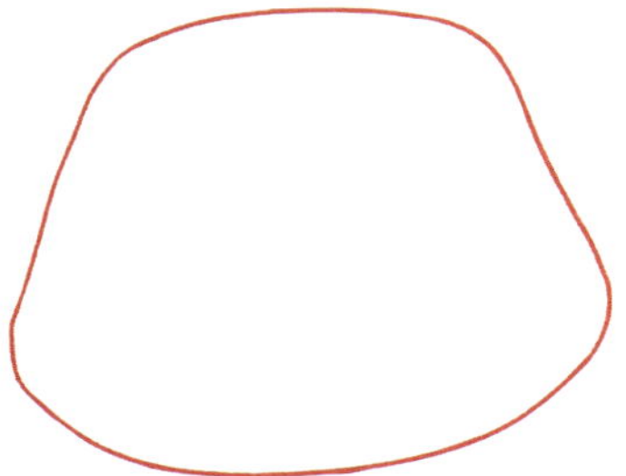

2. Draw curves on the top and bottom of the trapezoid to make the ridges of a pumpkin.

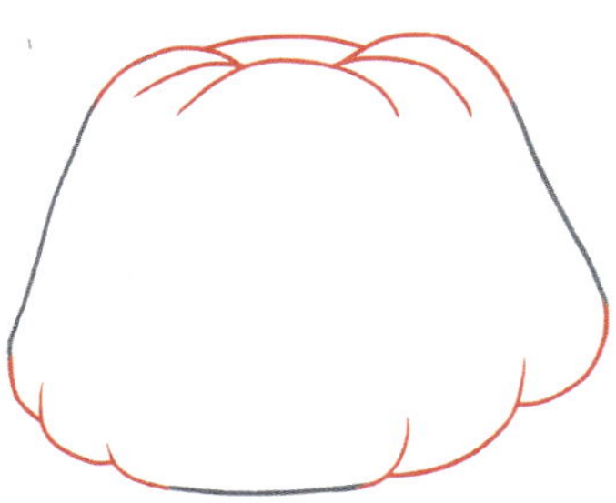

3. Add a curved stem on top with a leaf behind it.

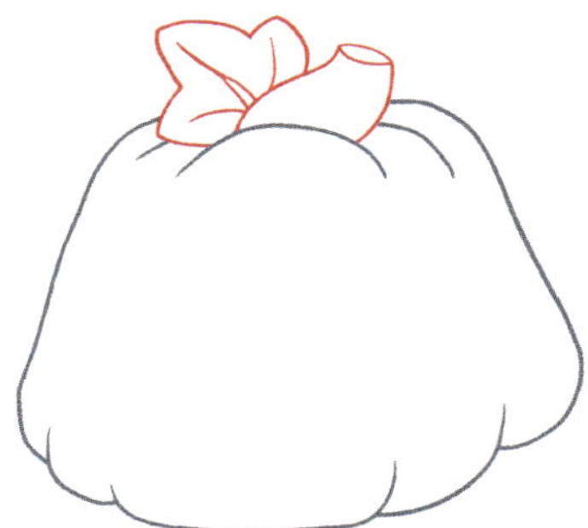

4. Draw a smoke cloud in a curving, lumpy shape coming from the stem.

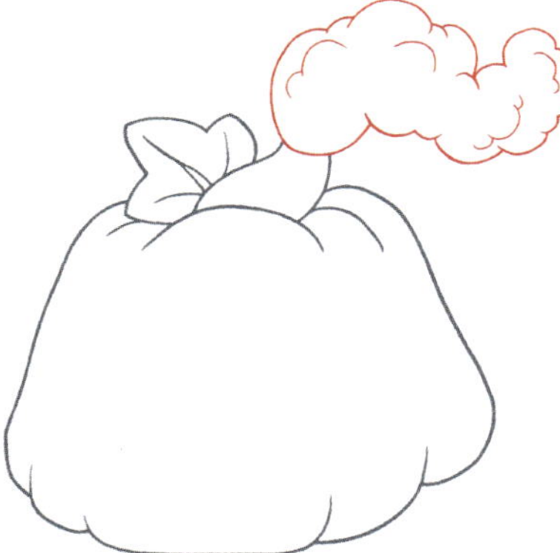

5. Add an arched door and two oval windows with lines crossing in the middle.

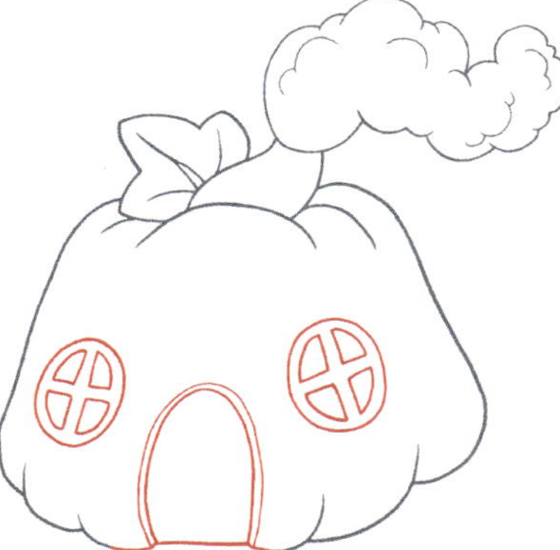

6. Cleanly trace your sketch with pencil on watercolor paper before inking.

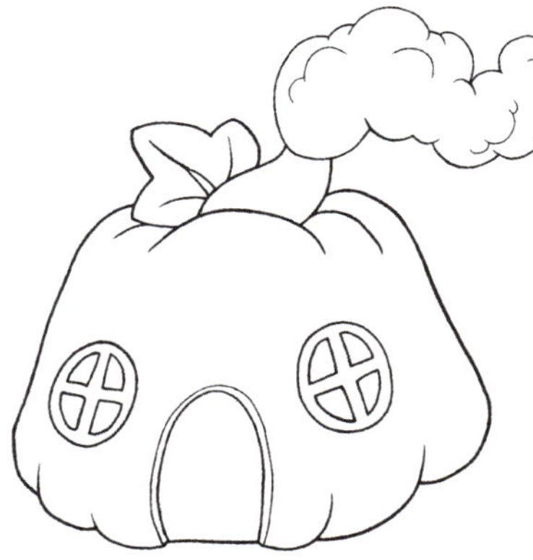

7. I used markers in orange for the pumpkin, brown for the windows and doors, green for the stem and leaf, and beige for the smoke. Add shading on everything except for the smoke.

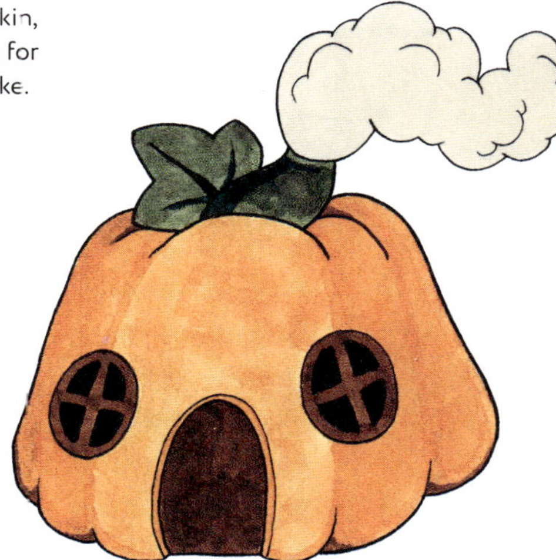

MUSHROOM LODGE

1. Draw a chunky mushroom. Add lines underneath the top.

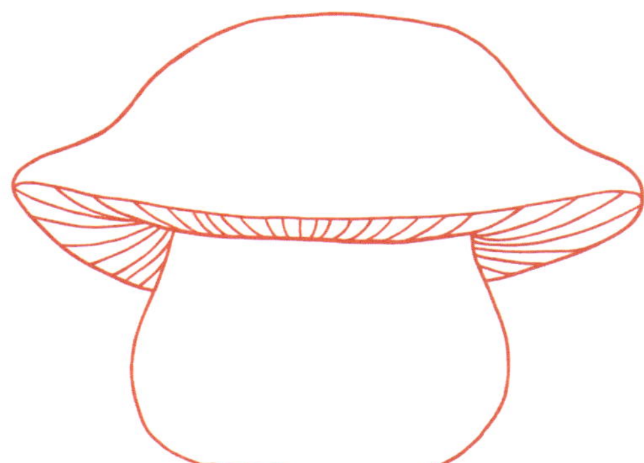

2. On the stem, add an arched doorway with squares around the edge. Draw two arched windows with crosses. On top of the mushroom, add a smaller mushroom chimney with a wavy stem.

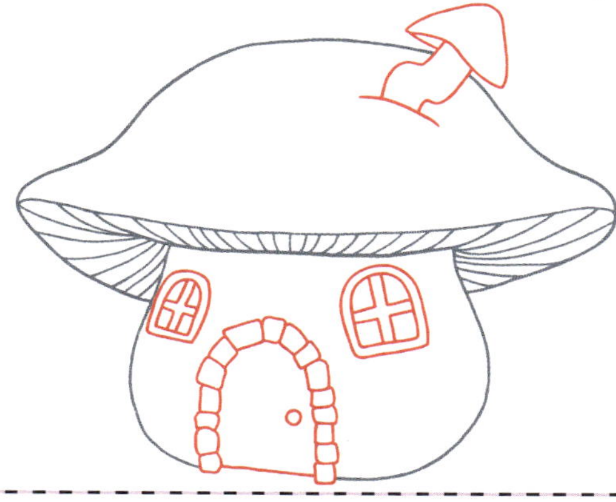

3. Place smaller mushrooms and bushes around the sides of the mushroom house.

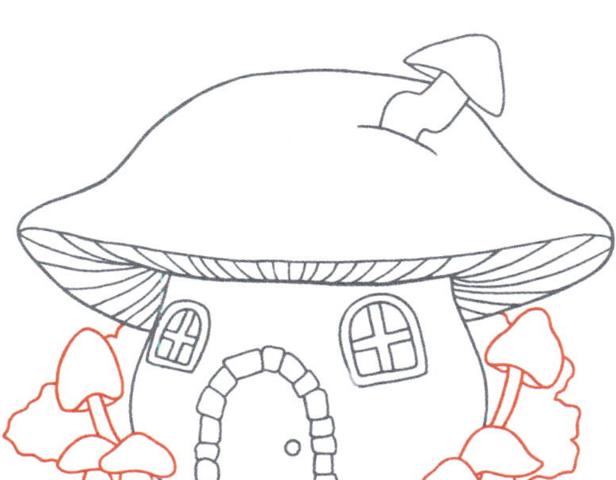

4. Cleanly trace your sketch with pencil on watercolor paper before inking.

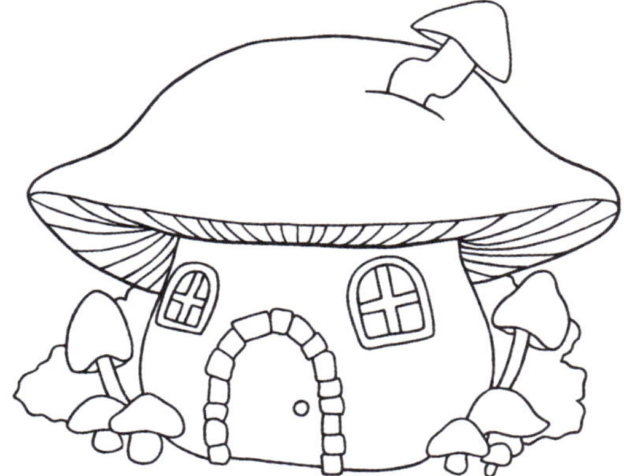

5. I used shades of brown for the mushroom tops, doors, and windows; gray for the stones of the chimney and around the door, and green for the bushes. Add shading underneath the mushroom roof, windows, and bushes, and on the right of the door.

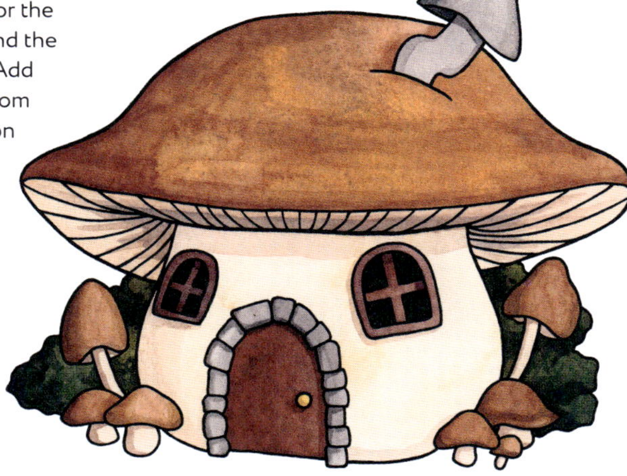

BABA YAGA'S PLACE

1. Sketch a pentagon-shaped house with a rectangle on the right of the roof and a square underneath for depth. Draw angled lines under the house.

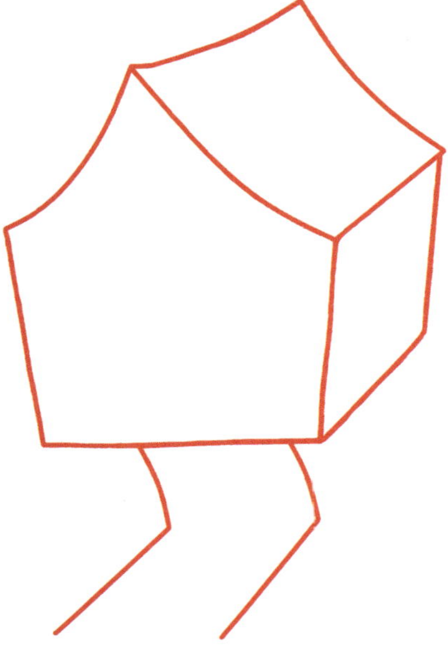

2. Add a door with a curved top and porch. Draw two arched windows with oval windowsills.

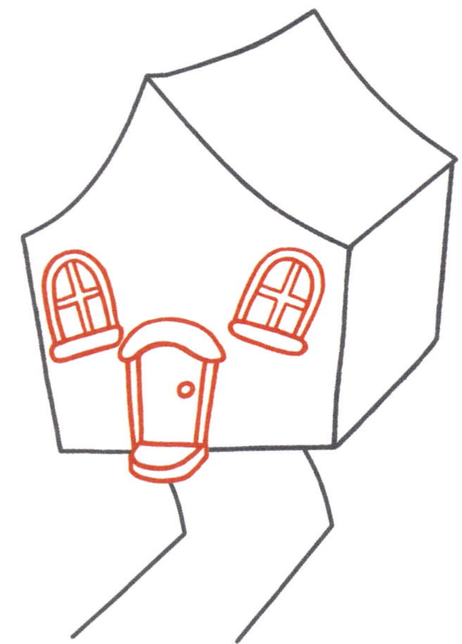

3. Draw a skull on the roof with a teardrop-shaped head and two pointed horns.

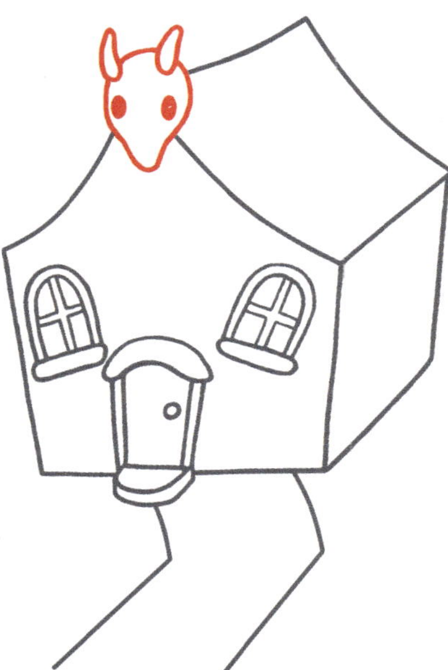

4. Add layered U-shaped tiles. Draw a thin rectangle across the top and down the front of the left side.

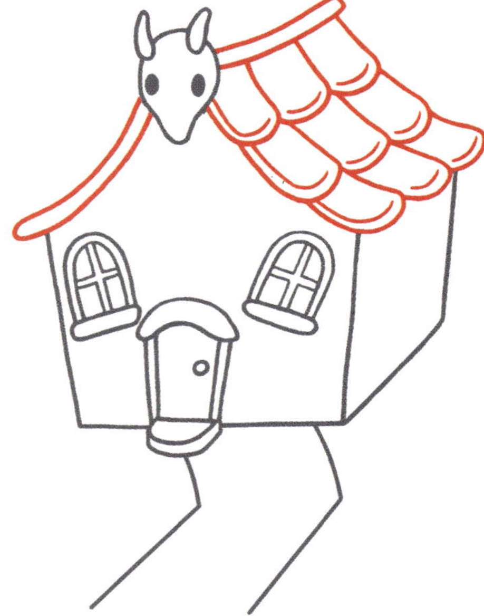

5. Draw horizontal lines on each wall.

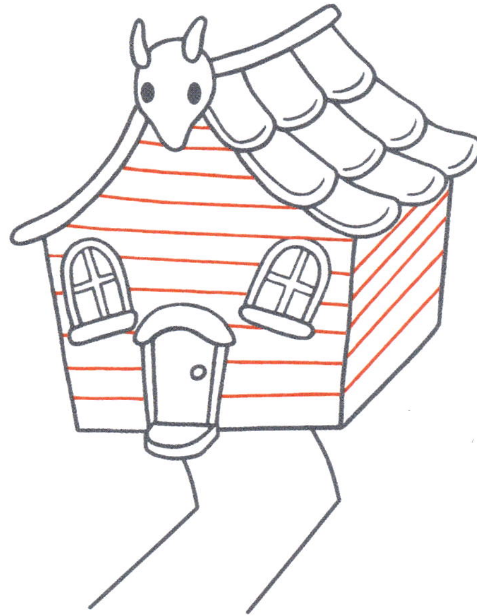

6. Turn the angled lines under the house into bird legs. Add fluffy detail at the top, thicken the lines into legs, and make feet with four talons.

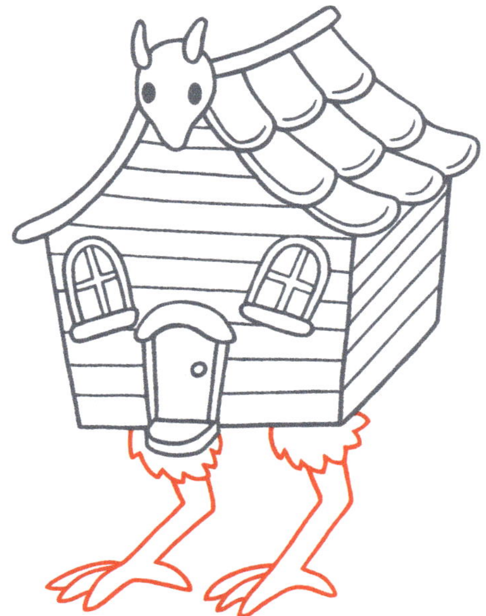

7. Cleanly trace your sketch with pencil on watercolor paper before inking.

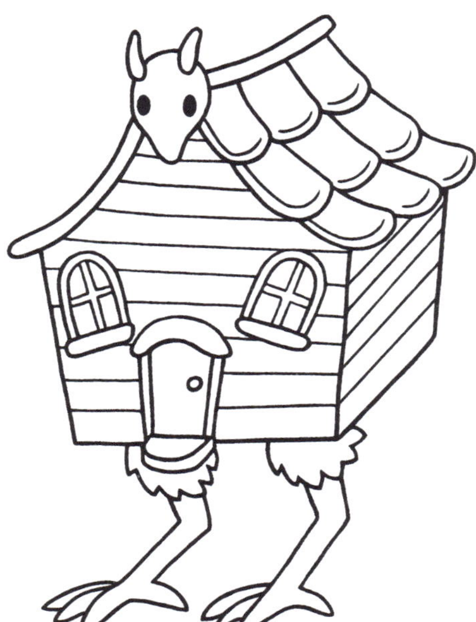

8. I made the house brown with a dark brown roof, windows, and door. Then I made the fur of the bird legs black and the legs yellow. Add shading to the lower right side of everything.

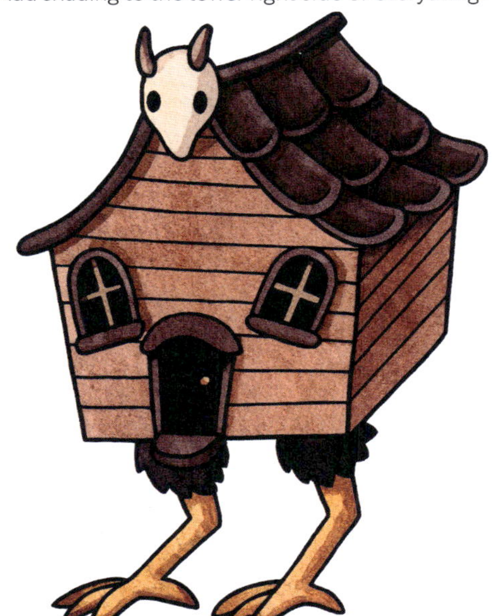

BOOTIQUE

1. Draw an arched window with a wide trim around it. Add rectangle details on each side.

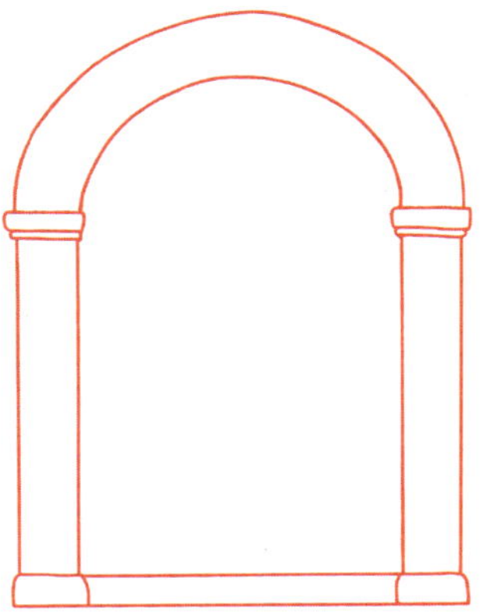

2. Add decorative details to the window and molding.

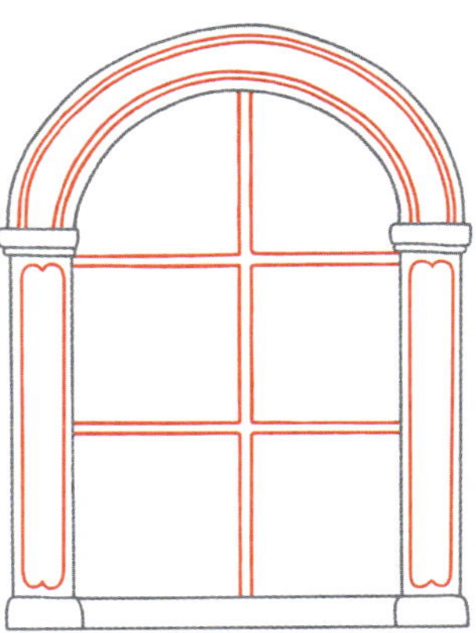

3. Inside the window, draw a line across the bottom and add scalloped bunting at the top angled on each side.

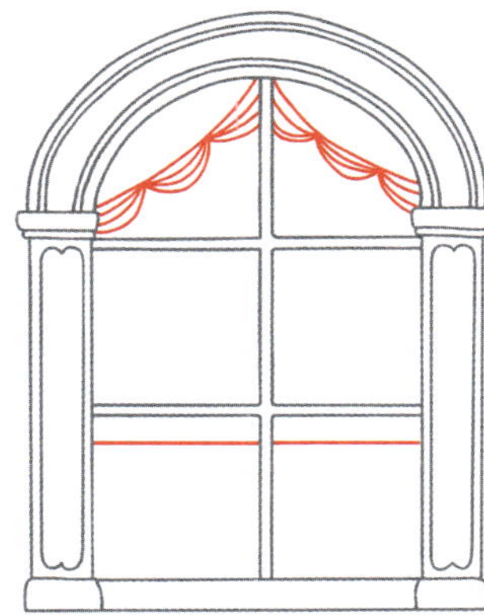

4. On the left, draw a happy ghost with a stand underneath it.

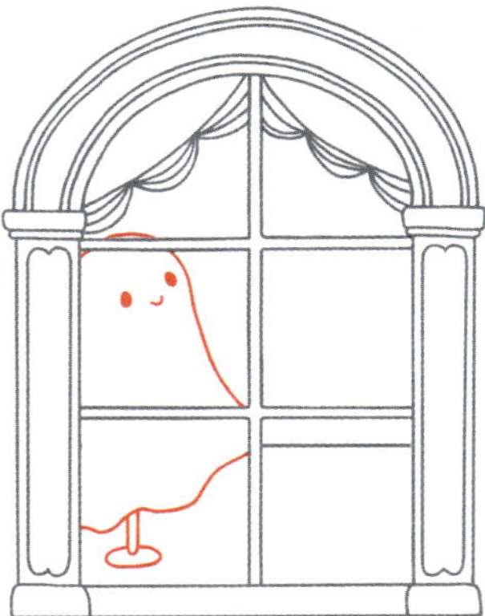

5. On the right, draw a second ghost facing the first.

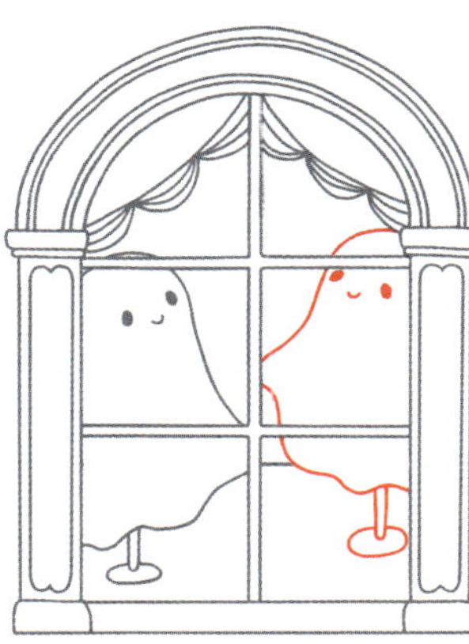

6. Write "BOOTIQUE" above the window, replacing the Os with little ghosts.

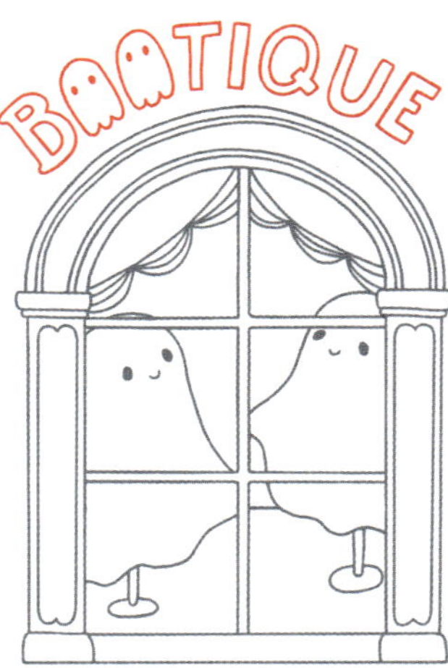

7. Cleanly trace your sketch with pencil on watercolor paper before inking.

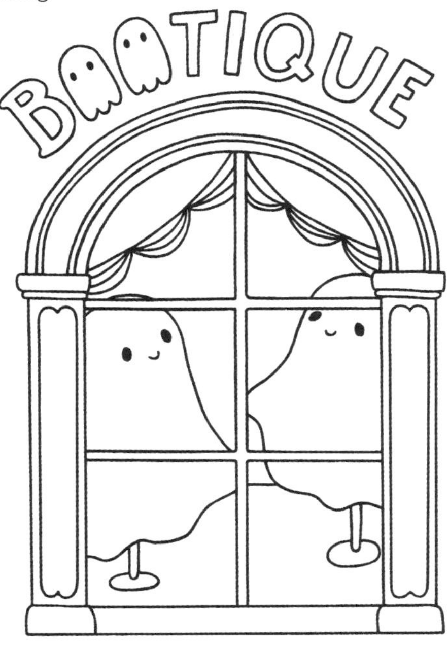

8. Color with shades of gray and black in and around the window.

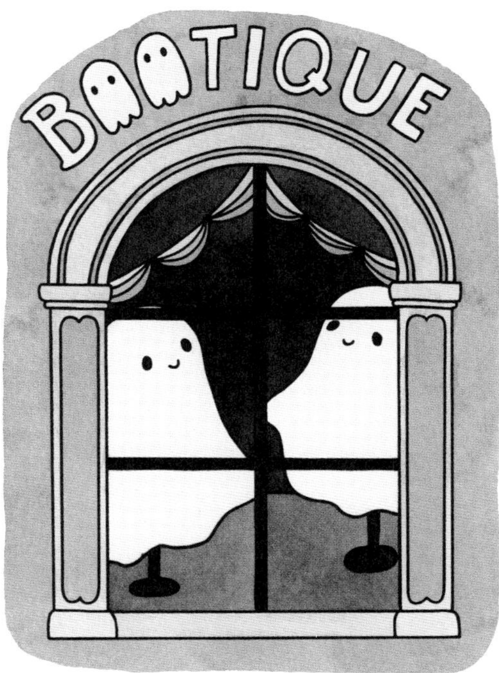

9. Add textures with diagonal lines on the sign and make the wall around the window a brick pattern. Use a thin brush or pen to draw patterns on the ghosts. Add shading, making sure the shadows are all on the same side.

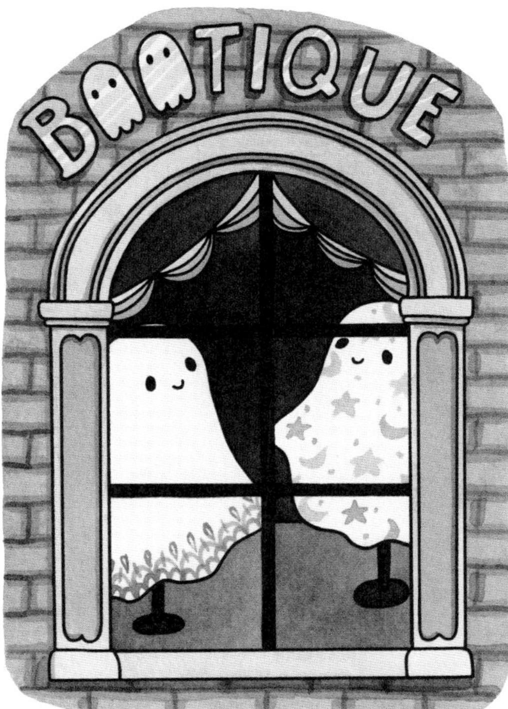

GHOST ROAST CAFÉ

1. Draw the simple shape of the front of the truck with a rectangle back.

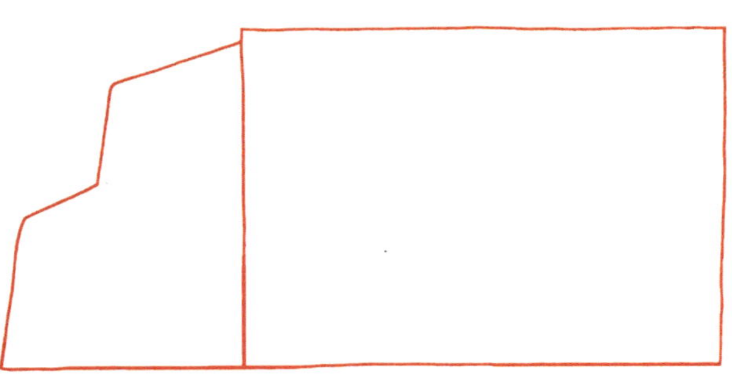

2. Add two wheels with three concentric circles. Connect the wheels with a curved line on top that extends across the middle and out at the sides.

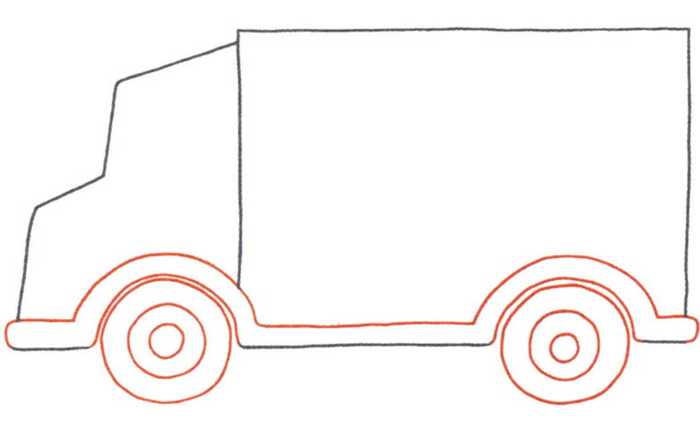

3. Add a window in the front of the truck and a headlight with a semicircle cut in half.

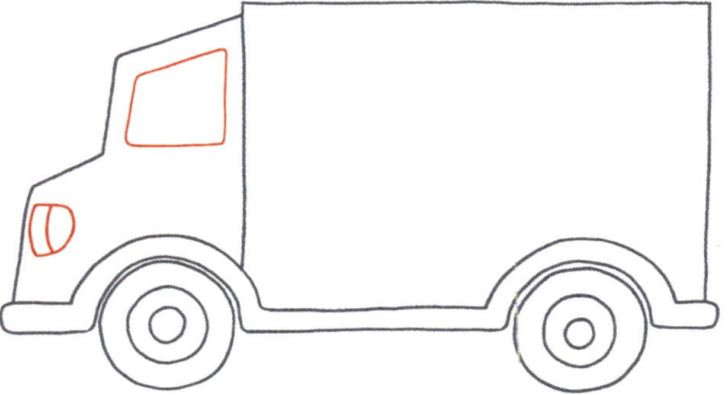

4. On the back of the truck, draw a big rectangle window with a scalloped awning. Draw two rectangles along the bottom for a countertop.

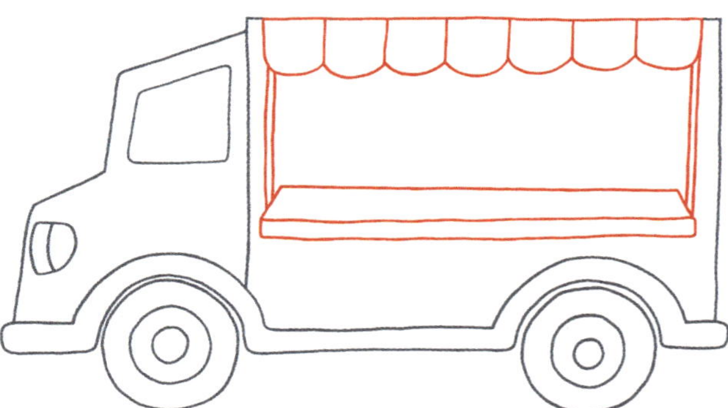

5. Hang a headstone-shaped menu to the right of the window. Add text here.

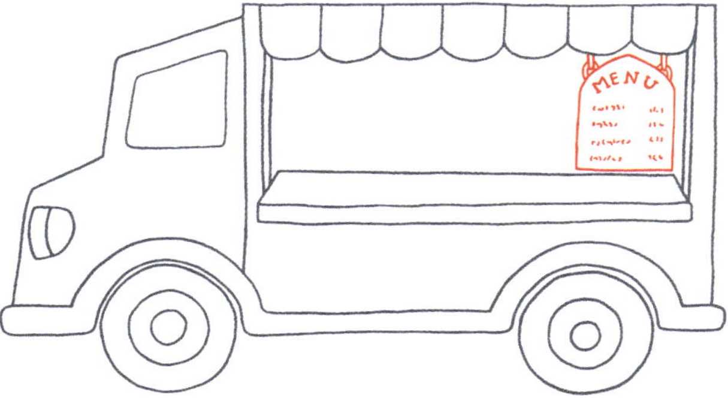

6. Add details to the truck's door like the frame and handle and some bolts to the wheels.

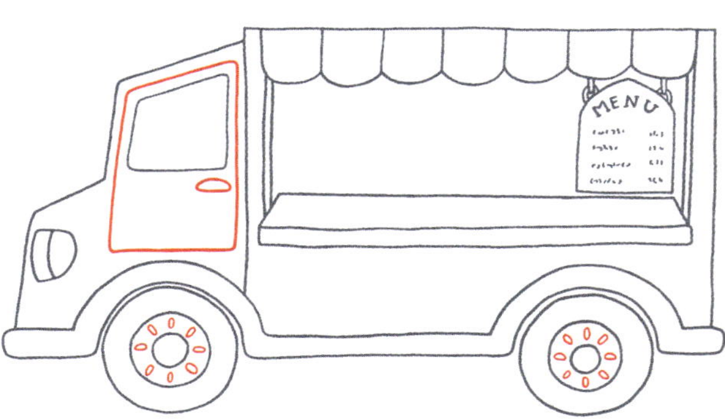

7. Make a sign on top of the truck and write "COFFEE."

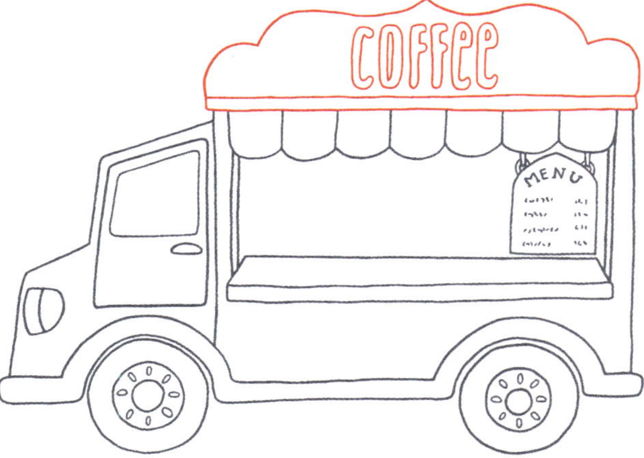

8. Decorate the sign with ghosts and flourishes.

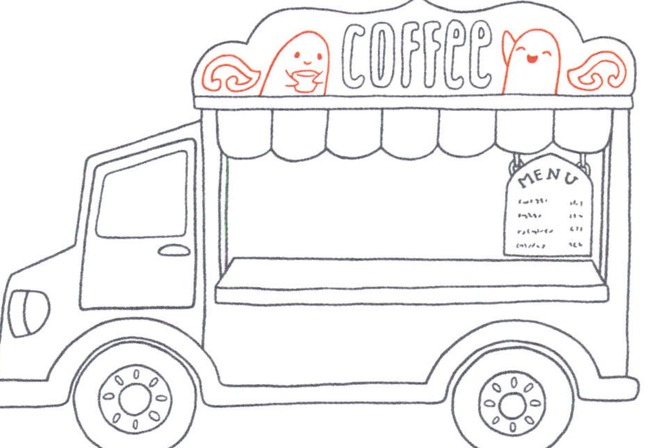

GHOST ROAST CAFÉ continued

9. Draw a ghost inside the window with its arm on the counter.

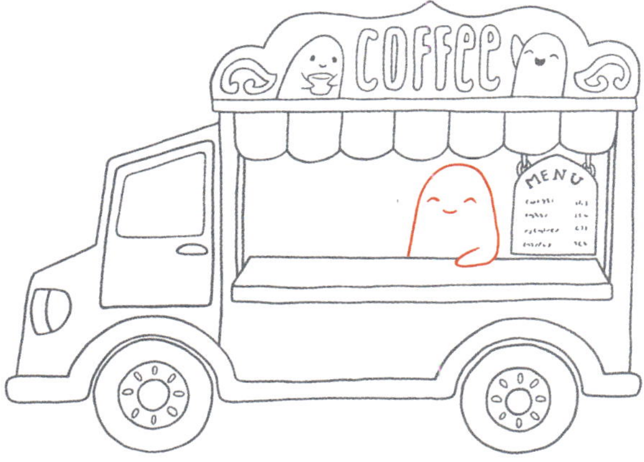

10. Add a coffee machine on the counter using rectangles. Then add a stack of cups and a container for straws.

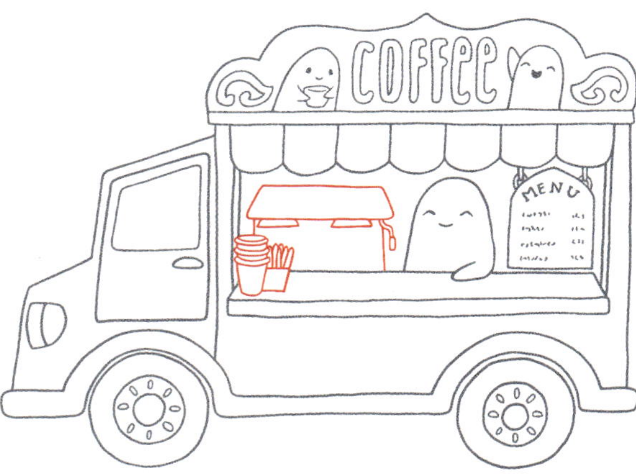

11. Draw a ghost standing in front of the window holding a coffee.

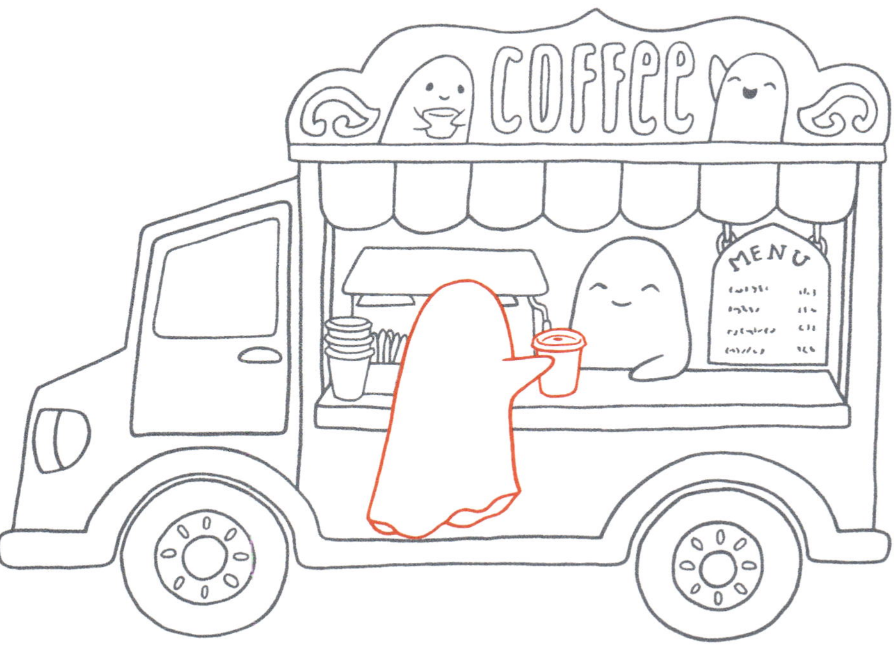

12. Cleanly trace your sketch with pencil on watercolor paper before inking.

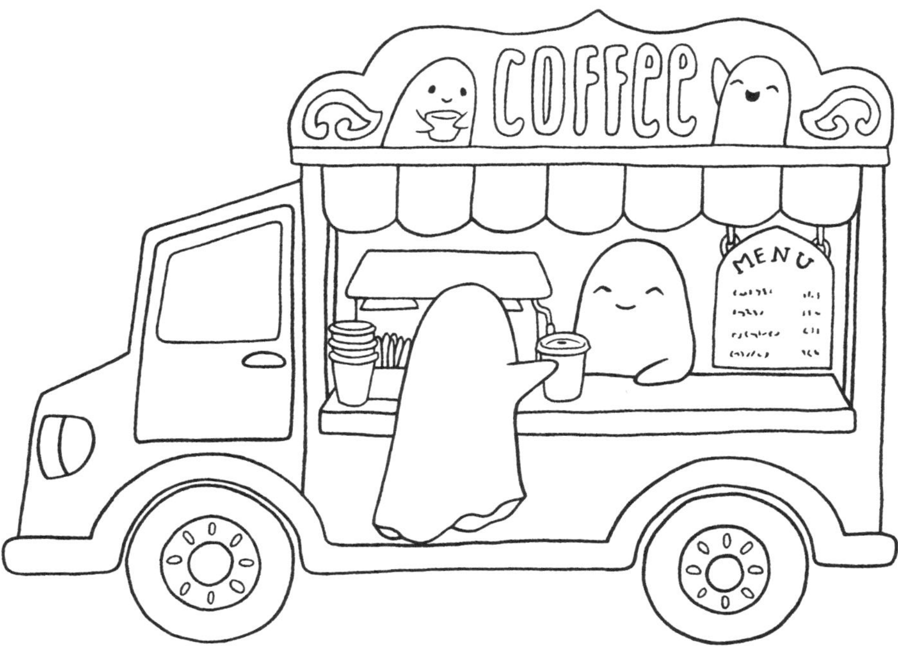

13. Color the illustration with shades of gray and black, leaving the ghosts white. Add shading underneath and to the left of everything.

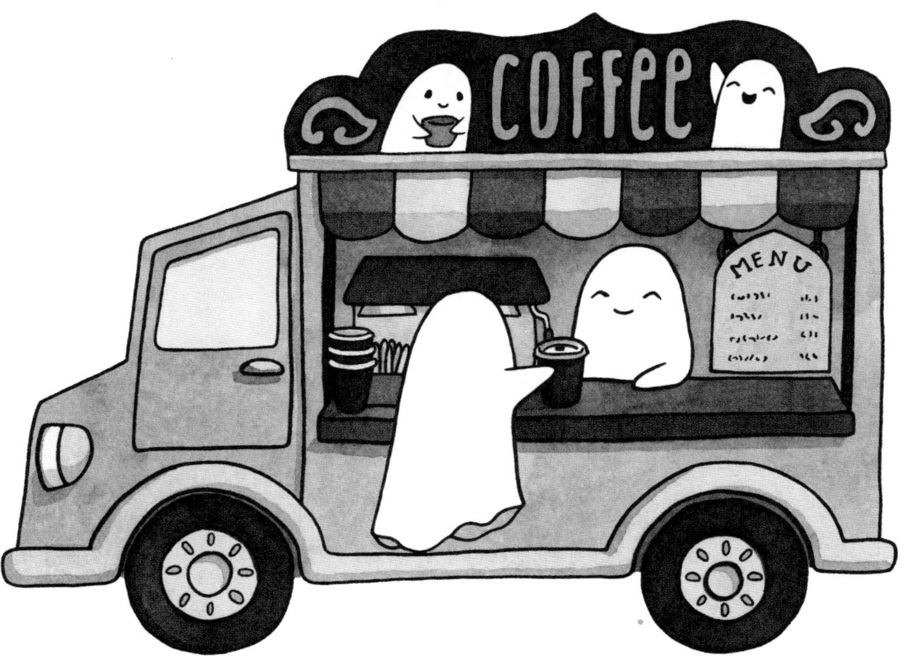

HAUNTED HIDEAWAY

1. Draw a 3D rectangular box.

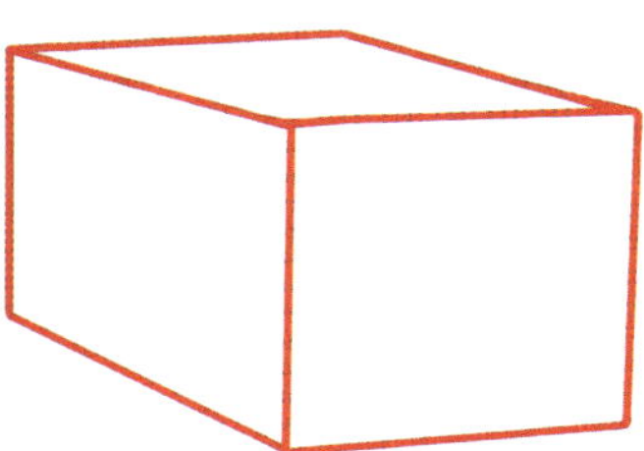

2. Add a curved roof with four long rectangles. Draw a thin rectangle for the top and two thin, curved rectangles for the front of the right side. Add two rectangle pillars on the left.

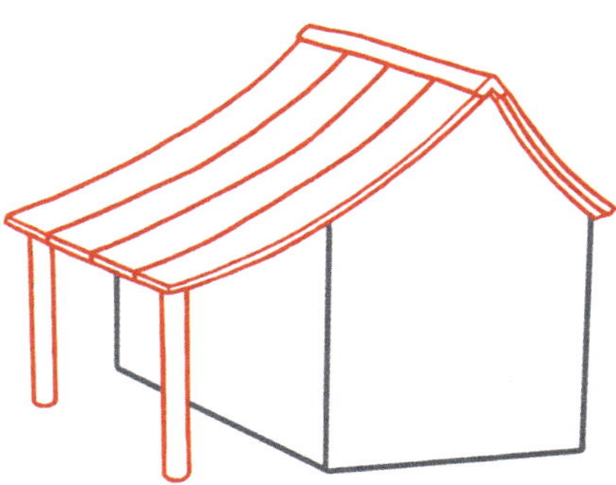

3. On the front side of the box, add a square window with opened shutters, curtains, and a windowsill. Above the window, add a curved embellishment and a crescent moon.

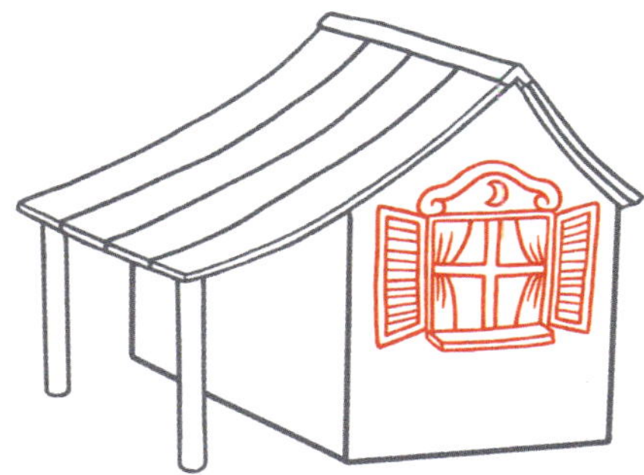

4. On the left side of the box, draw an arched door with a window and doorknob. Next to it, draw the sides of a square window.

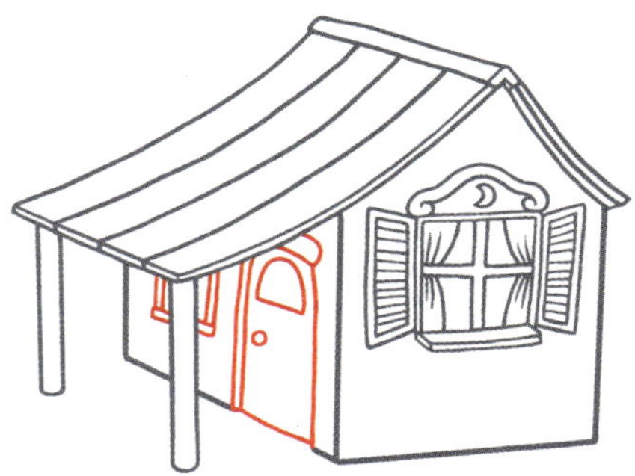

5. Add pumpkins in various sizes and some leaves around the house.

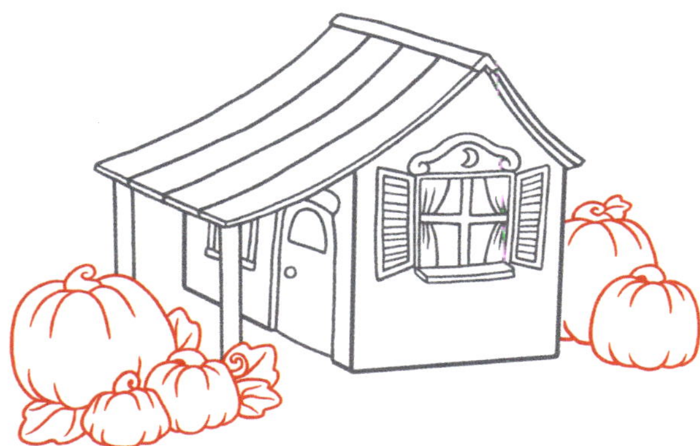

6. Place pine trees behind the cottage on both sides, in varying heights.

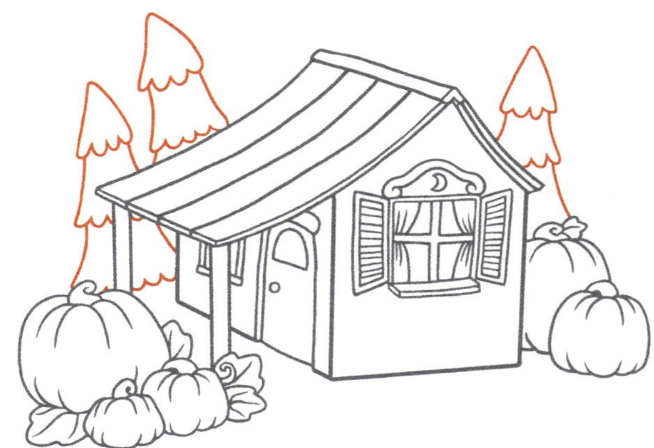

7. Draw a jagged line in front of the cottage for the ground and add a spiky bush.

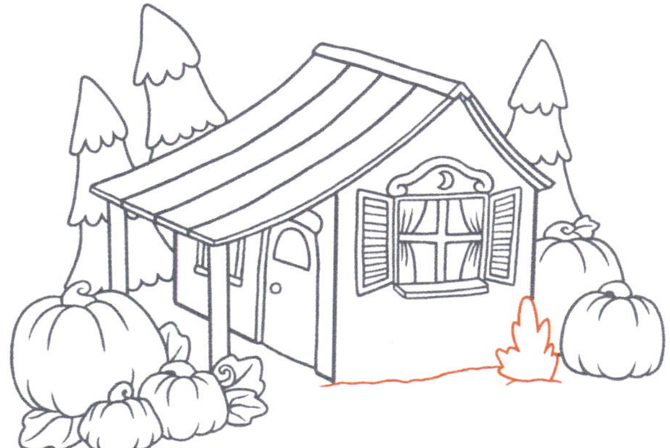

8. Hide ghosts inside the house with two heads in the front window and one in the door window.

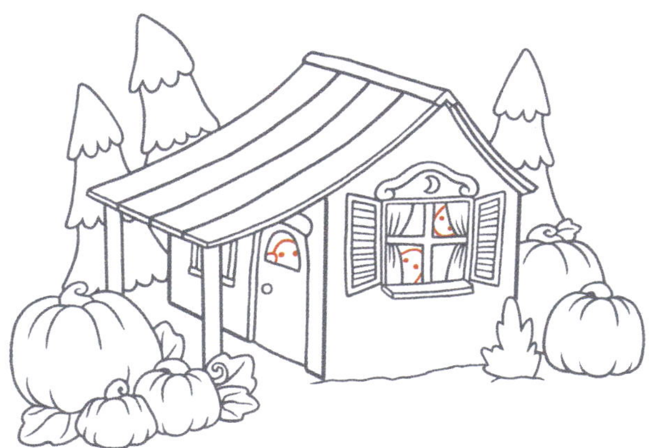

9. Cleanly trace your sketch with pencil on watercolor paper before inking.

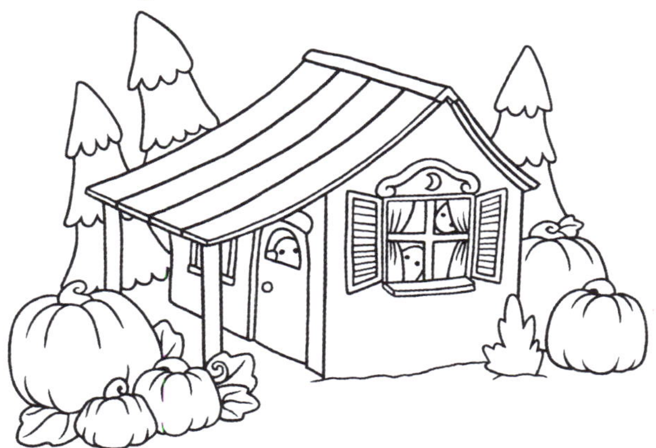

10. I used markers to color in shades of black and gray, leaving the ghosts white.

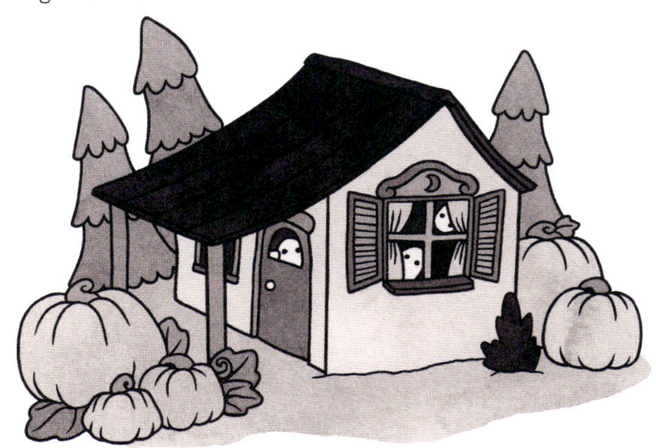

11. Using diluted ink with a thin brush or pen, add stripes to the trees, roof, and the stems of the pumpkins. Add dotted texture on the ground around the cottage. Add shading to the scene. Don't forget the shadow under the awning!

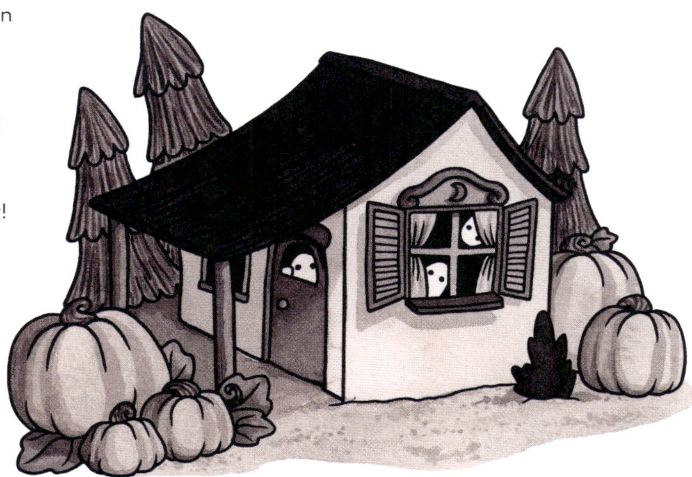

PUMPKIN PATCH

1. Sketch one large oval and four overlapping ovals around it. Draw an overlapping rectangle on the top right.

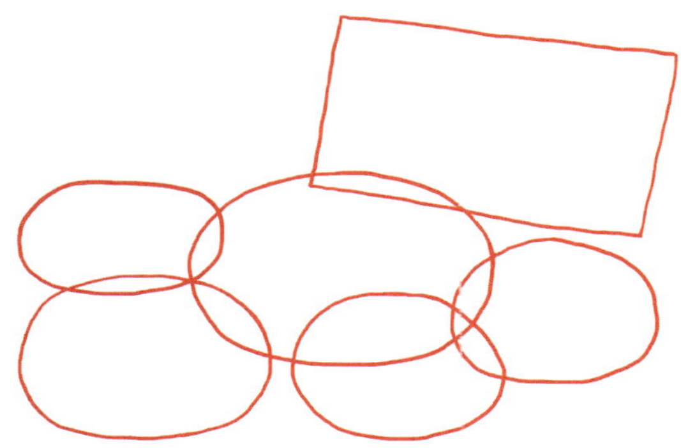

2. Turn all the ovals into pumpkins of varying sizes. Draw the stems only on two of them.

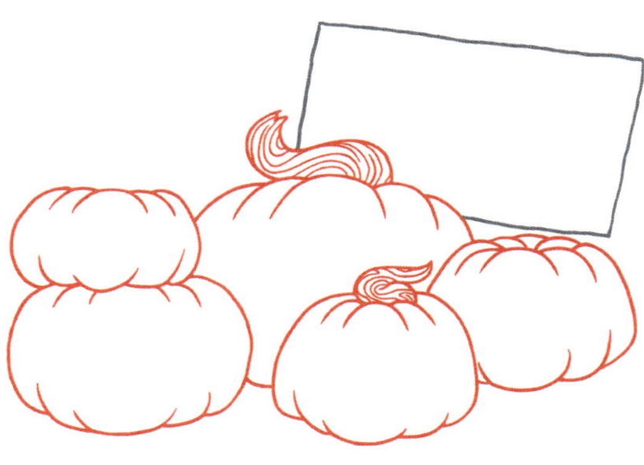

3. Add leaves around the pumpkins.

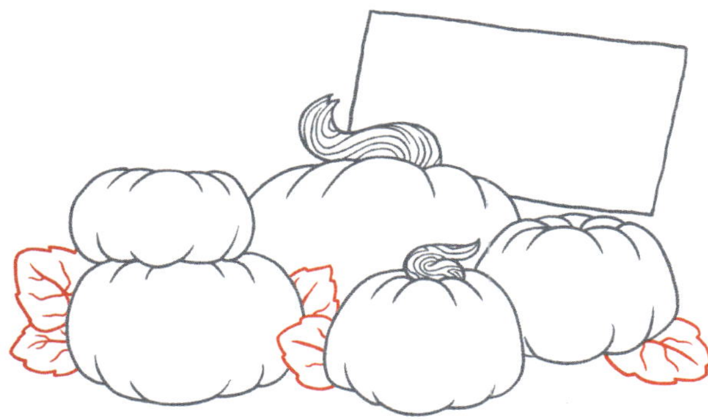

4. On the top left, draw the profile of a crow with two triangles for the beak and an outstretched wing with scalloped detail for the feathers.

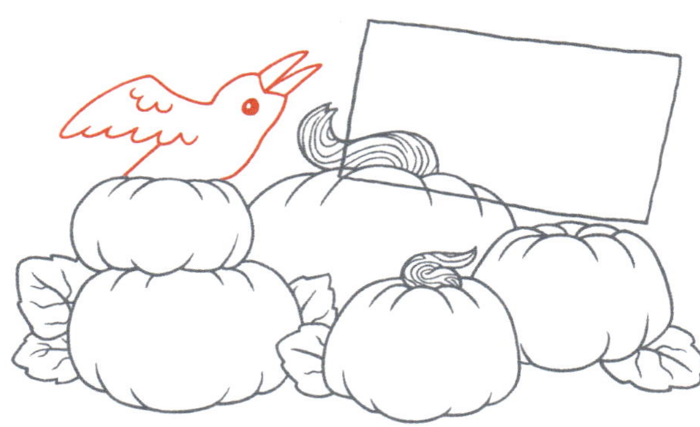

5. On top of the right pumpkin, draw a crow sitting comfortably. Make a diamond beak and divide it into two triangles. Draw a round head, chest, and top of a wing.

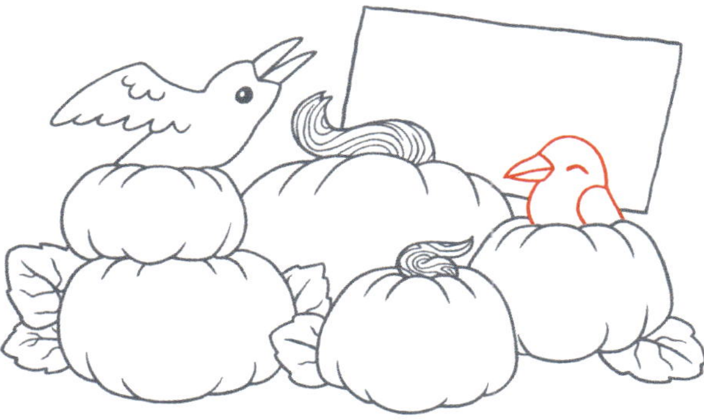

6. Draw horizontal lines across the rectangle to start the sign. Make some of the edges uneven.

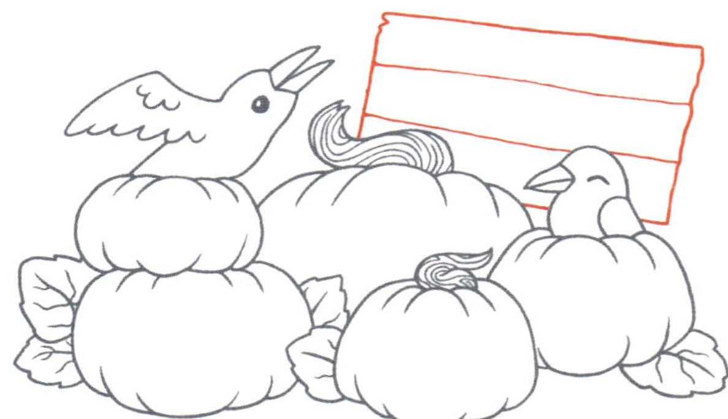

7. Write the words "PUMPKIN PATCH" on the sign where visible.

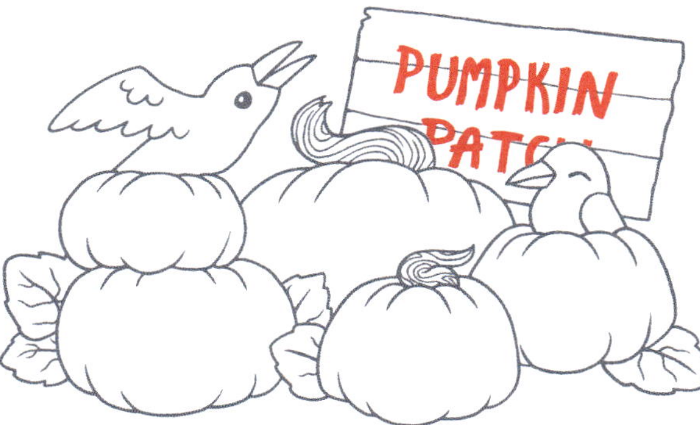

8. Draw three small crows on top of the sign. Draw rounded heads and long, pointy beaks. Give them each teardrop-shaped wings and circle feet.

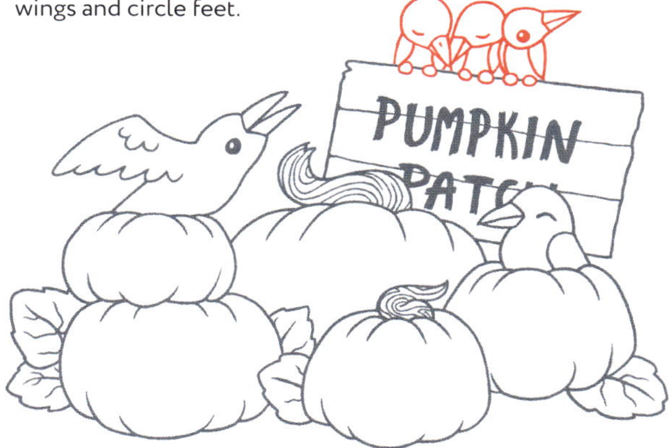

9. Add some bushes behind and around the pumpkins with squiggly lines.

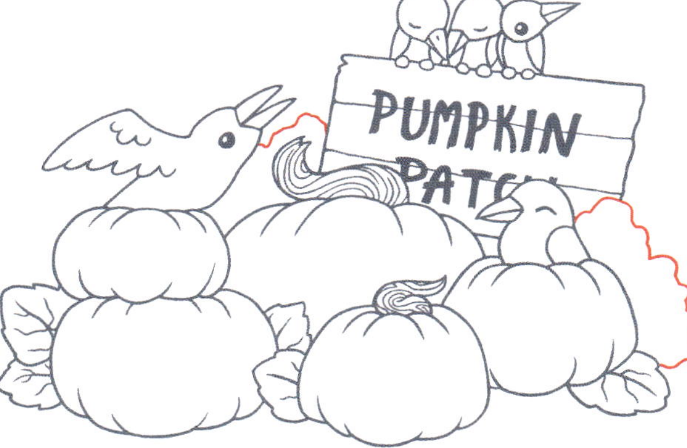

10. Cleanly trace your sketch with pencil on watercolor paper before inking.

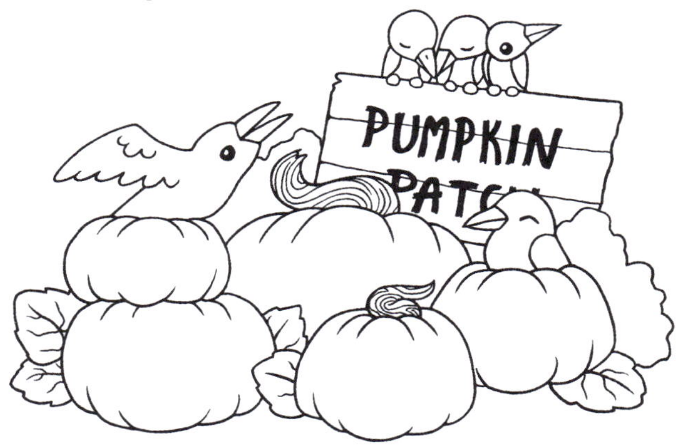

11. I used watercolors to make the pumpkins orange, the sign a light brown, the crows a dark gray, and the leaves and stems green. With a thin brush or pen, add texture using lines on the birds and sign. Give the bushes a cloudy texture using dark gray. Add shading on the crows and pumpkins for depth.

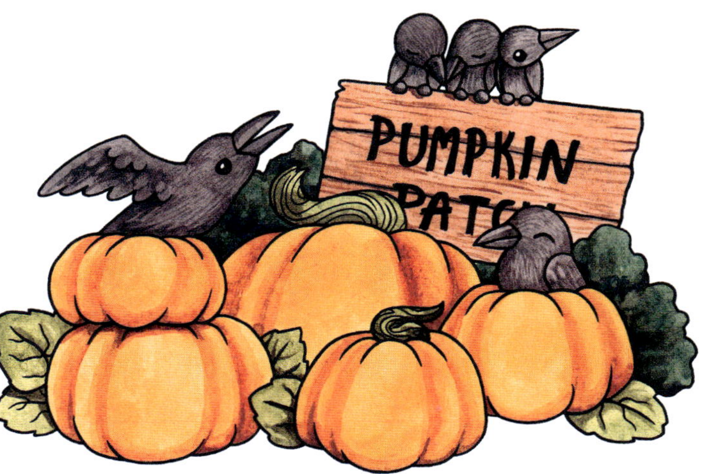

PUMPKIN SAILORS

1. Sketch a U shape with a curved top.

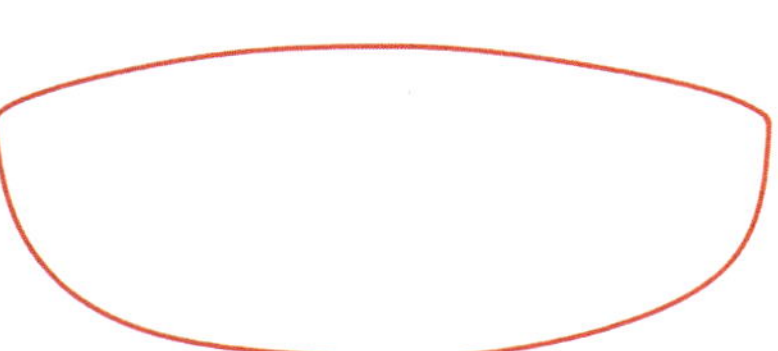

2. Add a pointed oval in the top part of the shape.

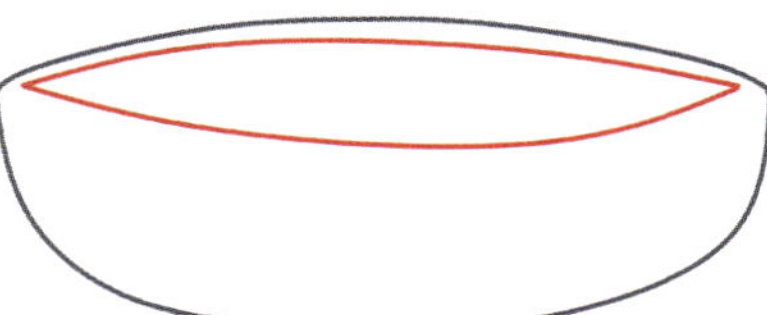

3. Turn the shape into the bottom half of a pumpkin. Draw the ridges with curved lines and make the top edge slightly ragged.

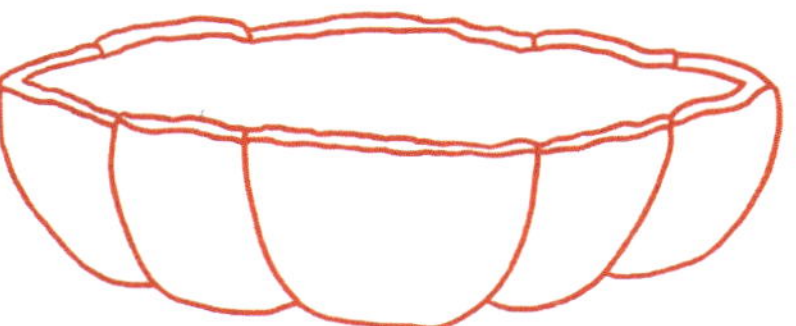

4. Add oars to the middle of the pumpkin. Draw two arches with an oval going through them. Add a wavy line at the end of one oar for the water.

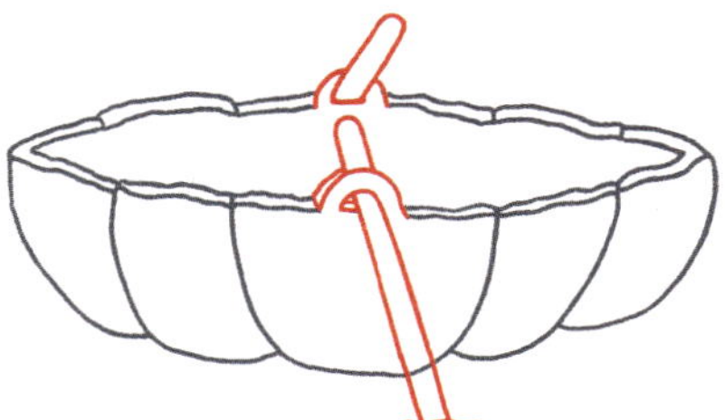

5. Draw a lantern on the left using the shape of an acorn. Attach it to a curved pole in the shape of a question mark. Draw water around the bottom of the pumpkin with wavy lines. Add some heart-shaped lily pads.

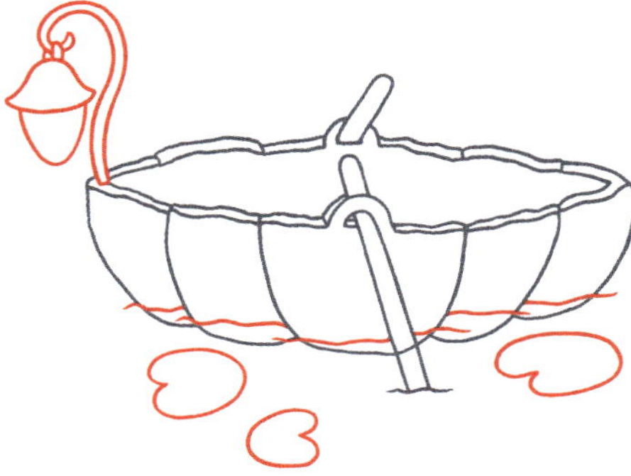

6. Add a ghost inside the pumpkin on the left with an arch and two round hands on top of the edge. Give it a shocked facial expression with three dots.

7. Add a ghost on the right with an arch and a triangle arm. Have it leaning back and staring slightly up.

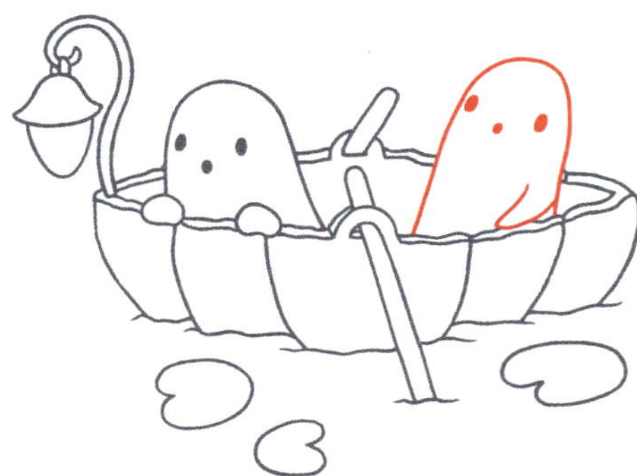

8. Draw five starburst circles around the scene using short dashes. These will be fireflies.

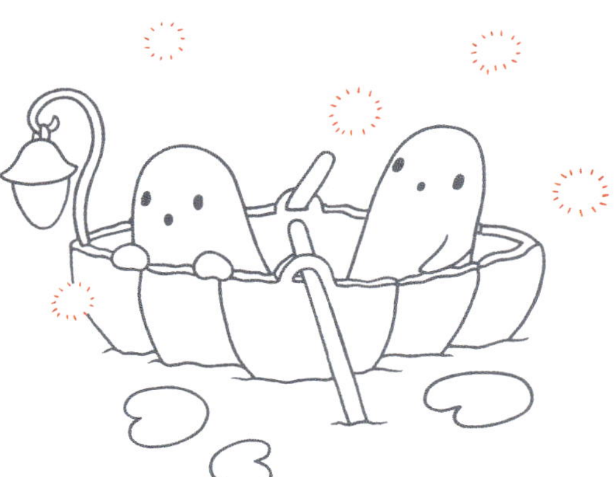

9. Cleanly trace your sketch with pencil on watercolor paper before inking.

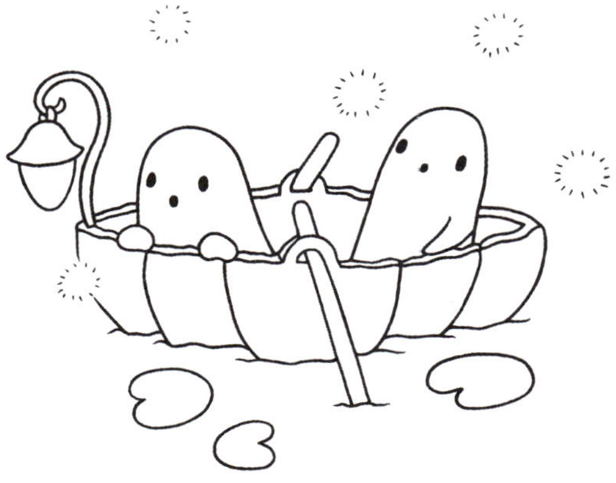

10. Using yellow and orange watercolors, I colored the starbursts and lantern in a gradient that gets darker as you move out. Extend the color around it.

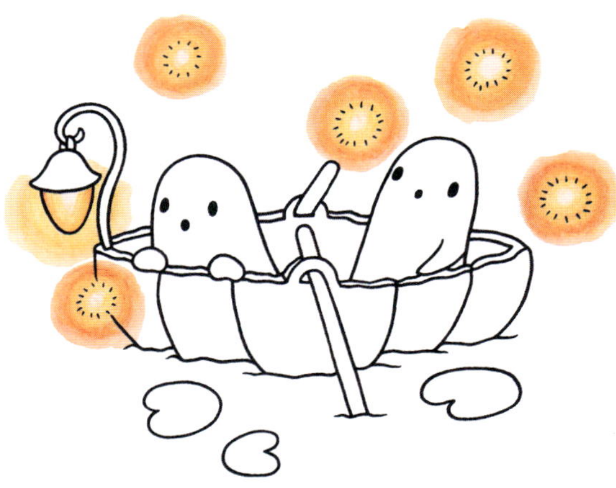

11. Color around everything with black ink, keeping an eye on the gradient around the lights.

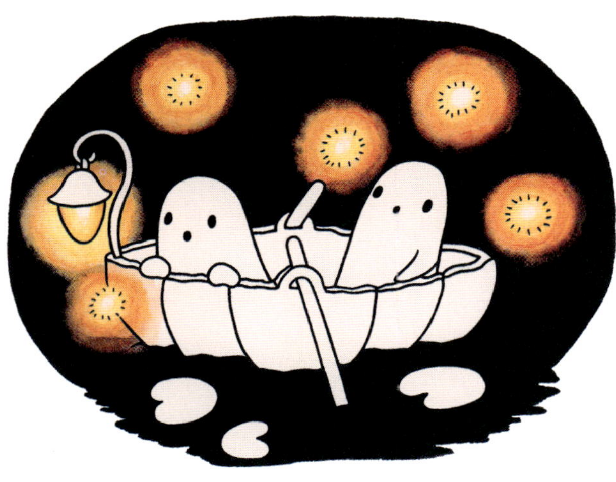

12. Color the boat orange and the lily pads green. Add shading to the boat with brown and color the oars brown. With cool gray, add shading to the bottom of the ghosts. Add a yellow glow to the parts of the ghosts near the light sources. With white ink or acrylic paint, make some wavy lines on the water.

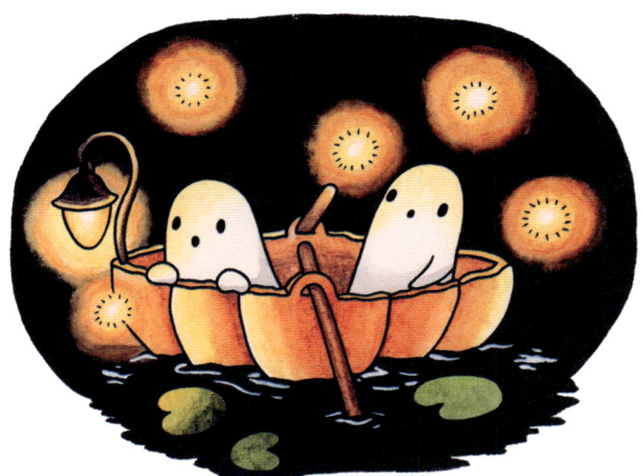

EERIE EATS CONFECTIONERY

1. Draw a rectangle with a thin rectangle in front. Add an arch on top with one thin line and one thick line inside it.

2. Sketch a figure leaning on the counter. Draw a rounded head and two ovals for the bent arms. Curve the hands underneath the chin.

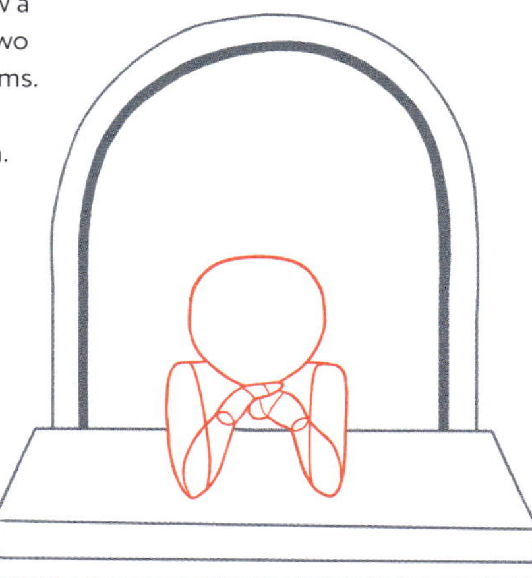

3. Add a witch's hat with a curved brim and a triangle top. Draw a happy facial expression.

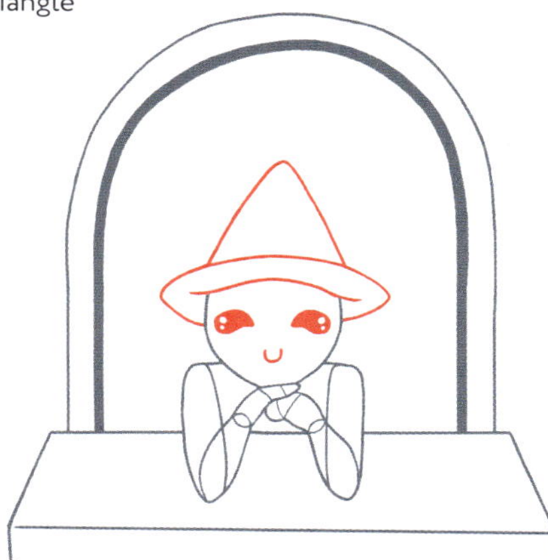

4. Draw a short-sleeved shirt on the torso. Use the guidelines to thicken the arms and make the hands.

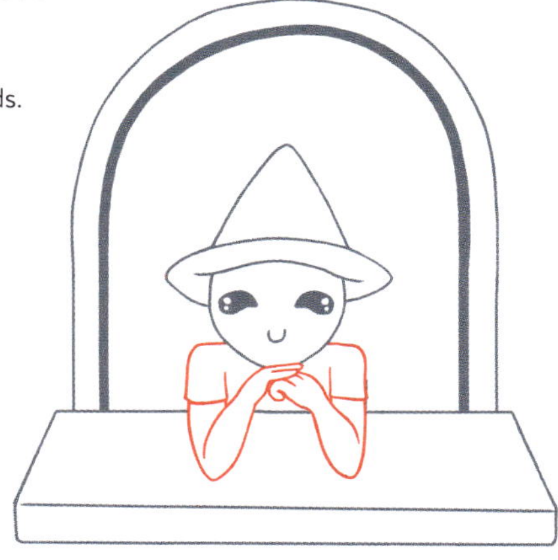

5. Draw braided pigtails with curved lines. Use ovals for hair ties. Make the ends of the bangs and pigtails teardrop shapes.

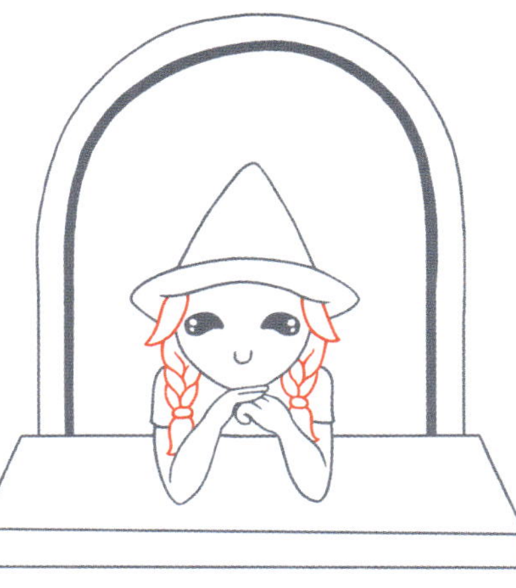

6. Draw a striped bowl on the left using a U shape with a curve inside the top.

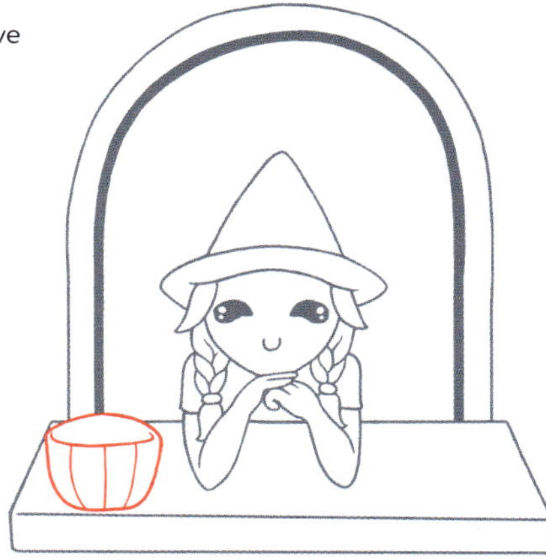

EERIE EATS CONFECTIONERY continued

7. Add skulls on sticks inside the bowl. Draw mushroom-shaped skulls with dots for eyes and lines for the mouth.

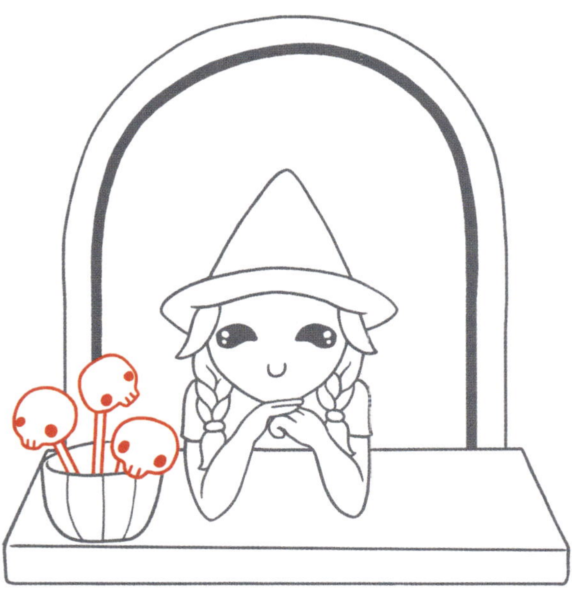

8. On the right, draw another striped bowl. This time add tentacles on sticks inside using curving ovals.

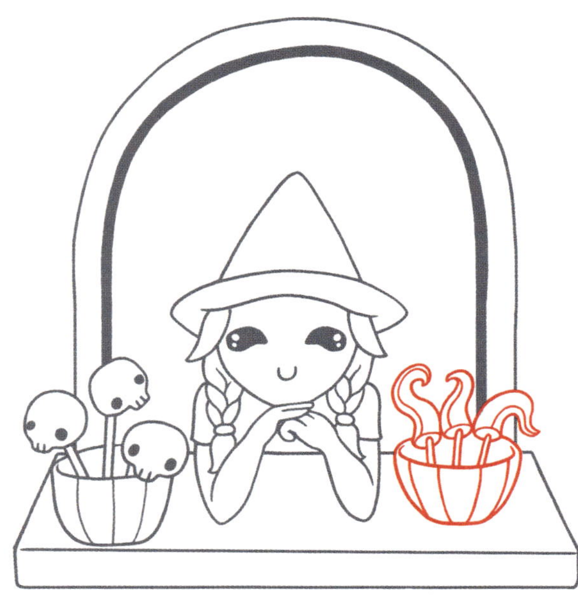

9. Draw a jar with a lid behind each bowl. Make the jars with a rectangle body and a bell-shaped lid.

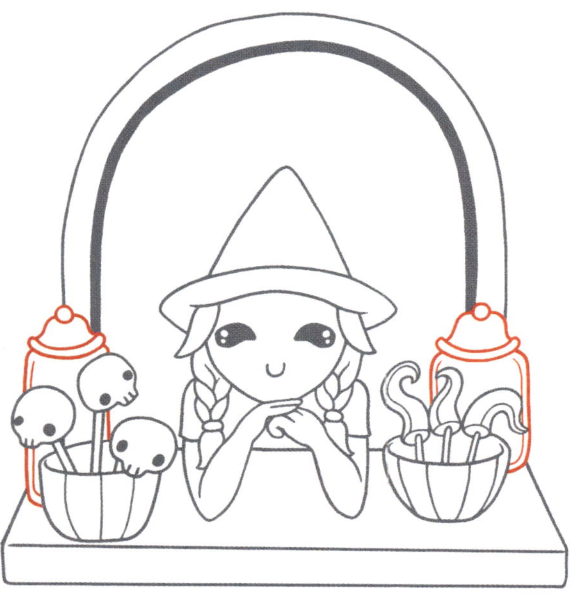

10. Add gumballs inside the jars with circles and scalloped lines.

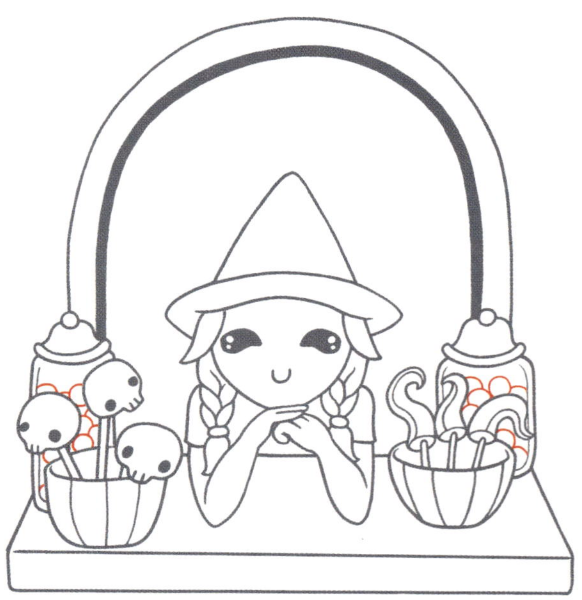

11. In the arch, draw half of a large spiderweb pattern with thick lines. Use straight lines in the directions of a clock and connect with curved lines.

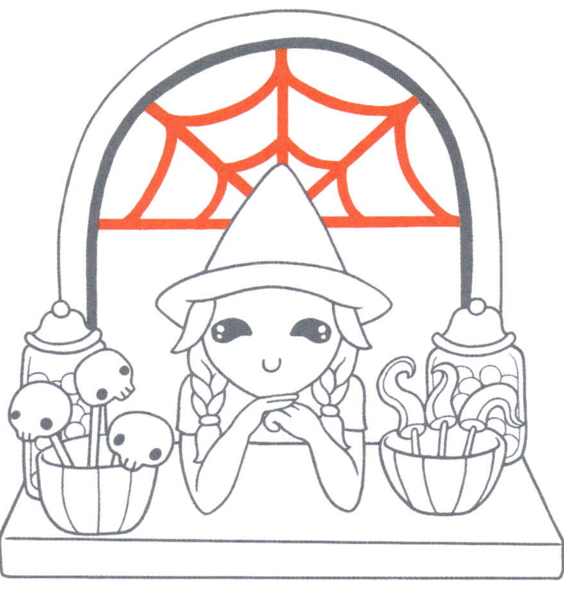

12. Finish the stained glass window with some Gothic arch shapes.

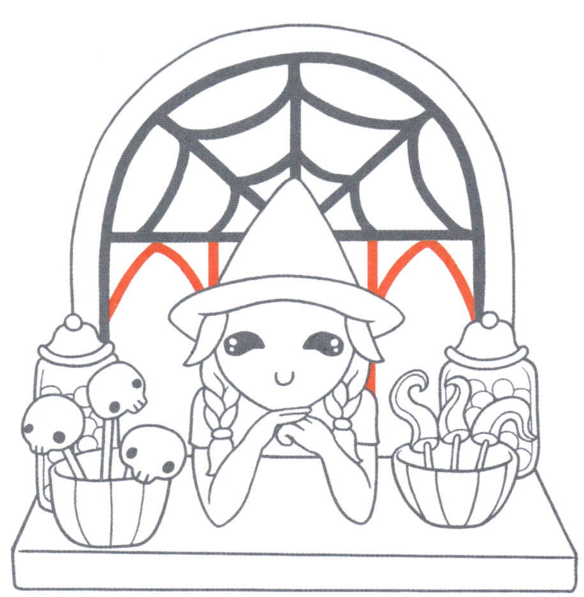

13. Cleanly trace your sketch with pencil on watercolor paper before inking.

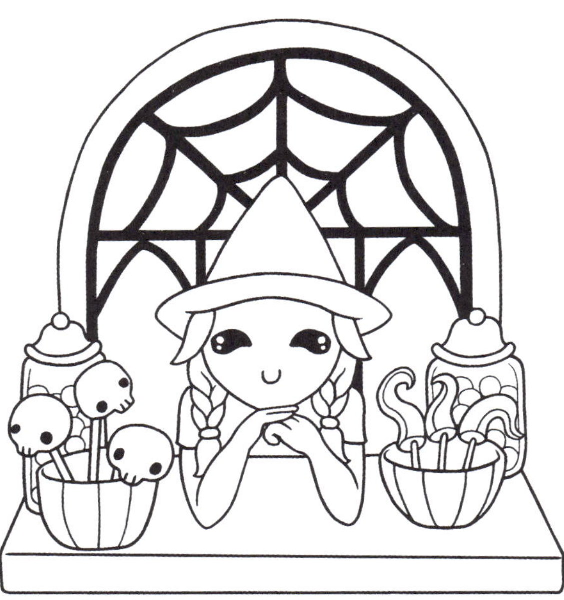

14. I used a combination of yellow, orange, and purple for the stained glass arch. Then, adding green, I colored my drawing with these Halloween colors. Add a striped texture to the wood and the witch's hair. Add shading, keeping in mind that the window is a light source.

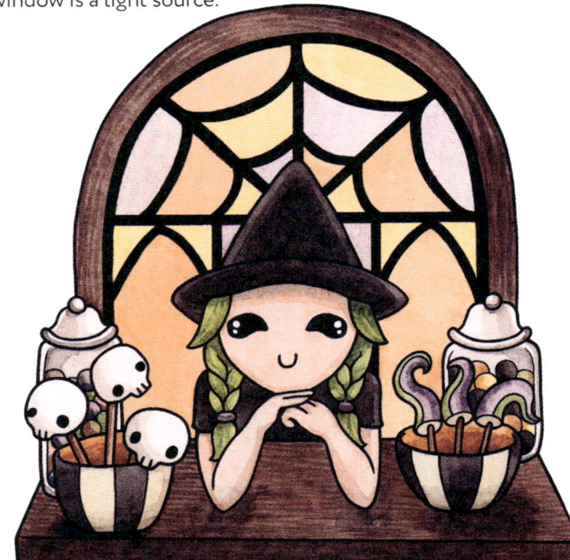

GRAVEYARD PICNIC

1. Draw a slanted rectangle with ragged edges.

2. Sketch two sitting figures on the blanket. Use a circle for the head, a square for the torso, and ovals for the limbs, hands, and feet.

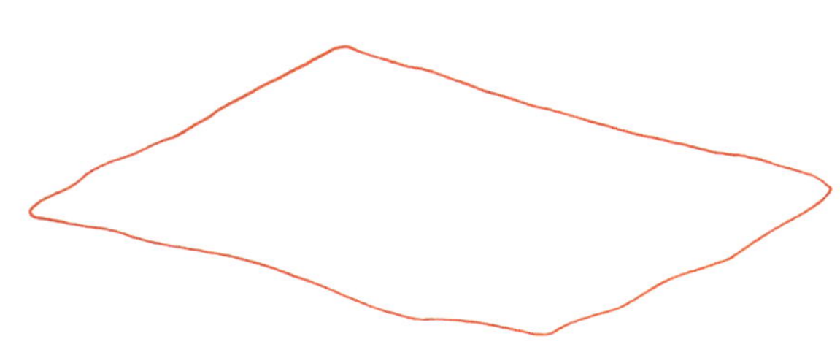

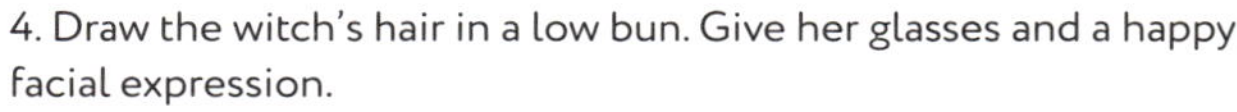

3. The figure on the left is a witch. Draw a witch's hat with a curved brim and a triangle top that curves at the point.

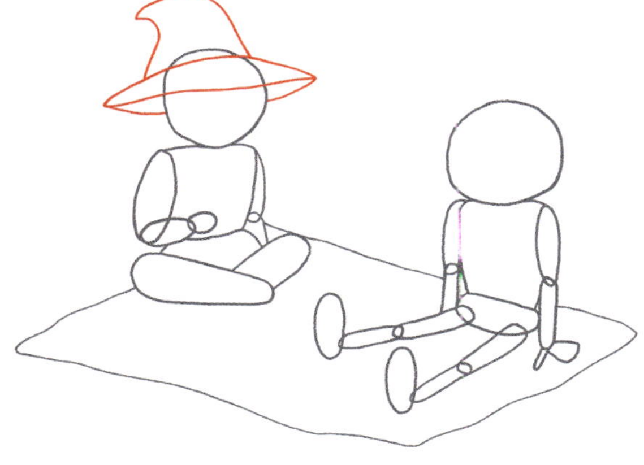

4. Draw the witch's hair in a low bun. Give her glasses and a happy facial expression.

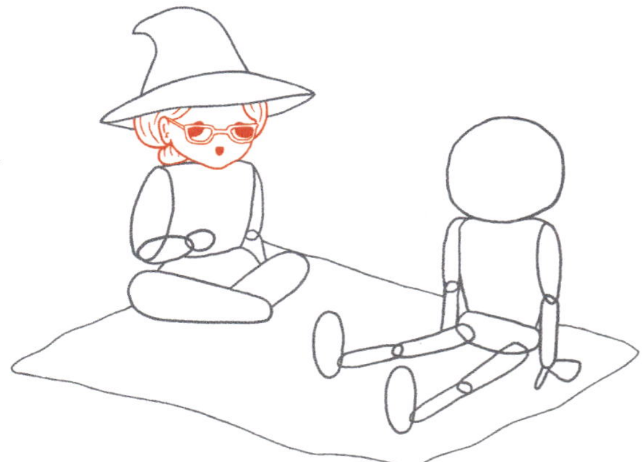

5. Add the long sleeve of her left arm. Draw the hand holding a bitten cookie.

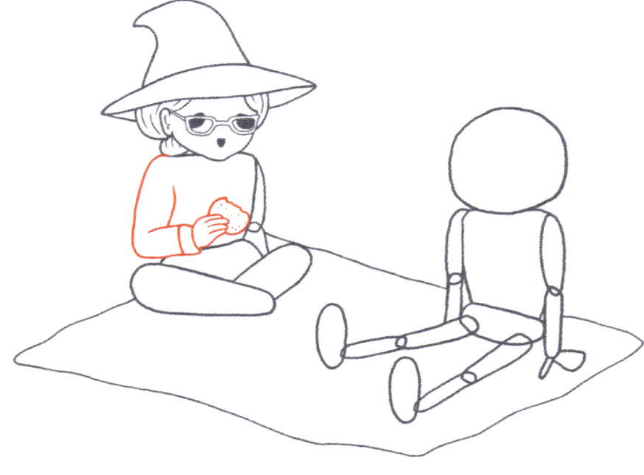

6. Draw the rest of the witch's body. Give her overalls on top of a long-sleeved shirt and drape a skirt over her crossed legs.

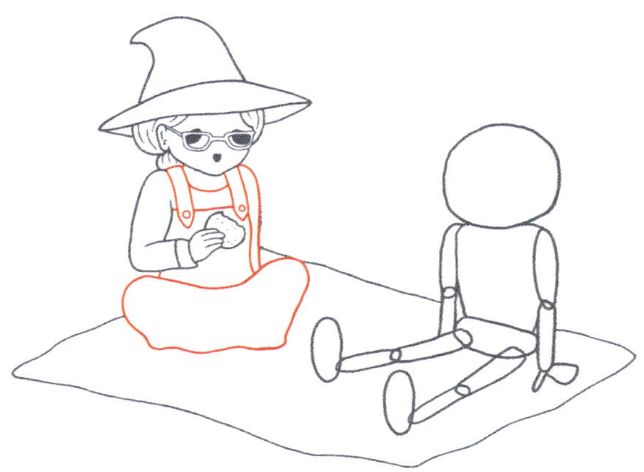

7. Draw a picnic basket in the middle of the blanket. Start with a U-shaped basket with an oval lid cut in half. Add an arched handle in the middle.

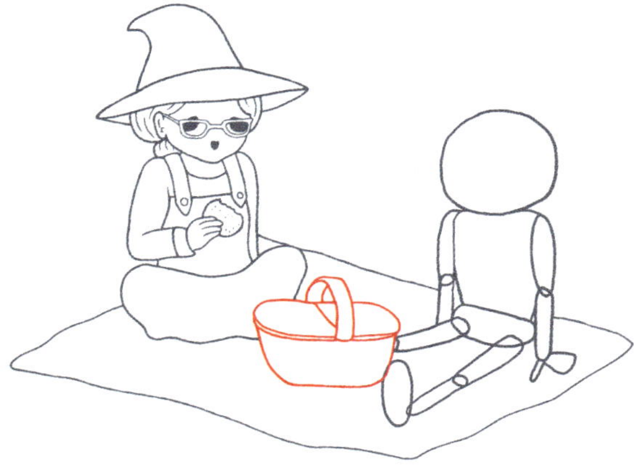

8. The figure on the right is a skeleton. Make a mushroom-shaped head with a smiling facial expression.

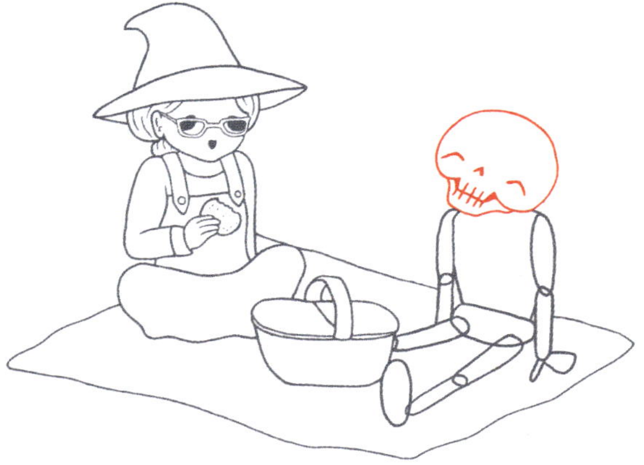

GRAVEYARD PICNIC continued

9. Add detail to the skeleton's body with a long-sleeved shirt and buttons. Draw a skirt and boots. Make the skeletal hand splay on the ground.

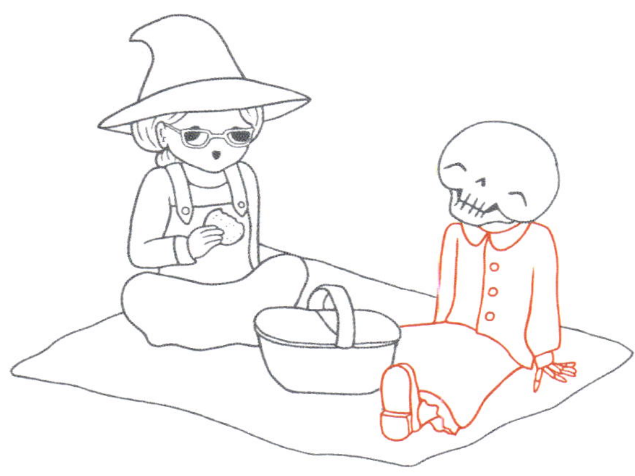

10. Draw a freshly dug grave behind the skeleton with a squiggly rectangle and a mound of dirt. Add a shovel stuck in the ground and a headstone with writing on it.

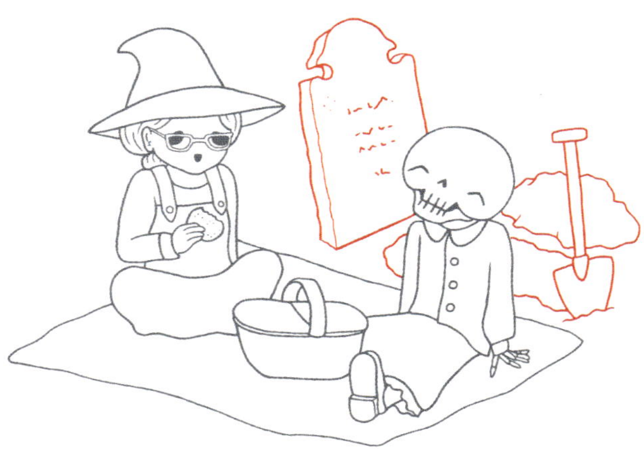

11. Place a pot of flowers on the grave with a U-shaped pot and two flowers with leaves around them.

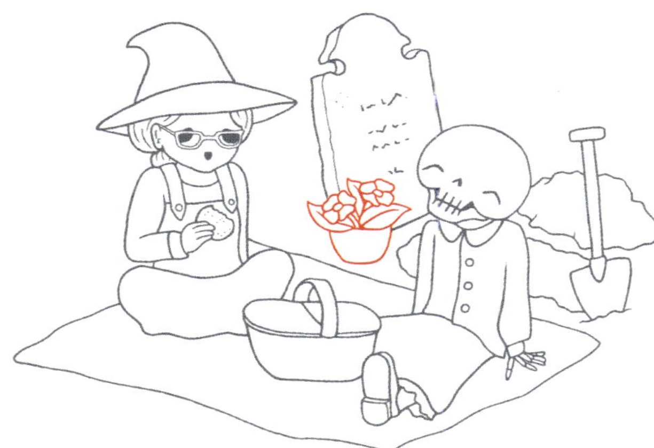

12. Add bushes in the back with squiggly, abstract shapes.

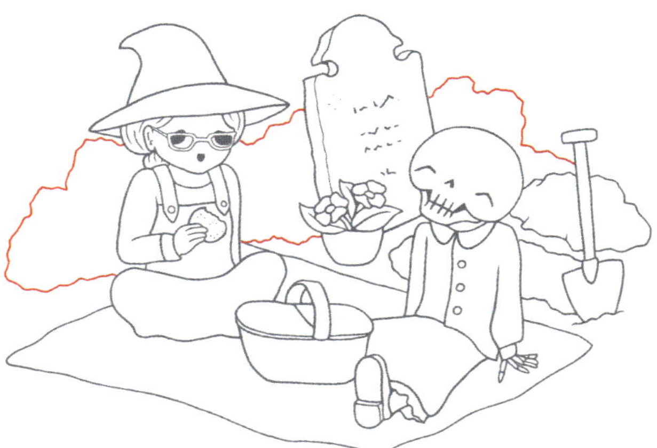

13. Draw the tops of more gravestones behind the bushes with arches and curved lines.

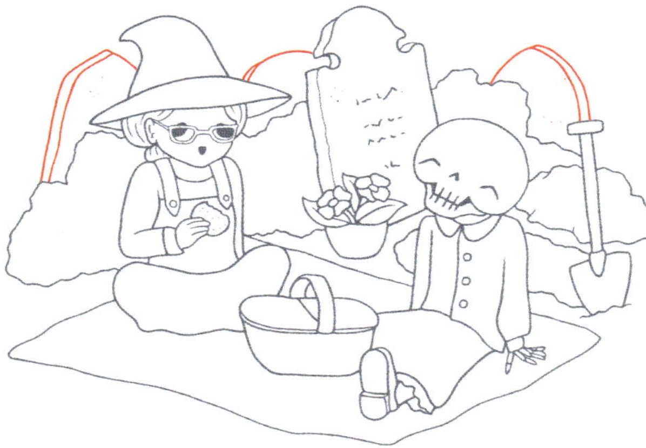

14. Cleanly trace your sketch with pencil on watercolor paper before inking.

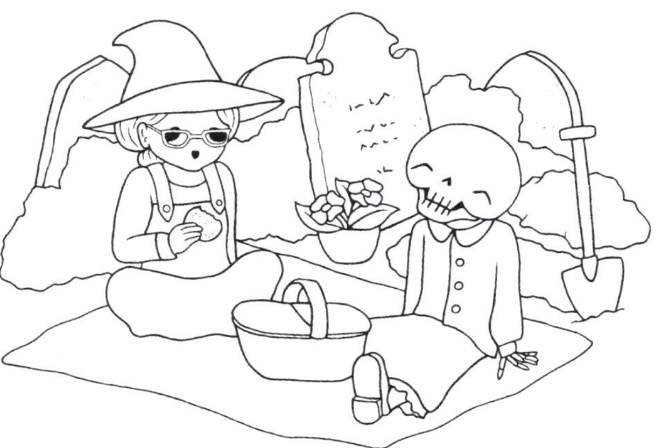

15. Color everything in shades of black and gray, leaving the skeleton's bones white. Create shadows with a darker hue on the bushes, clothes, and blanket.

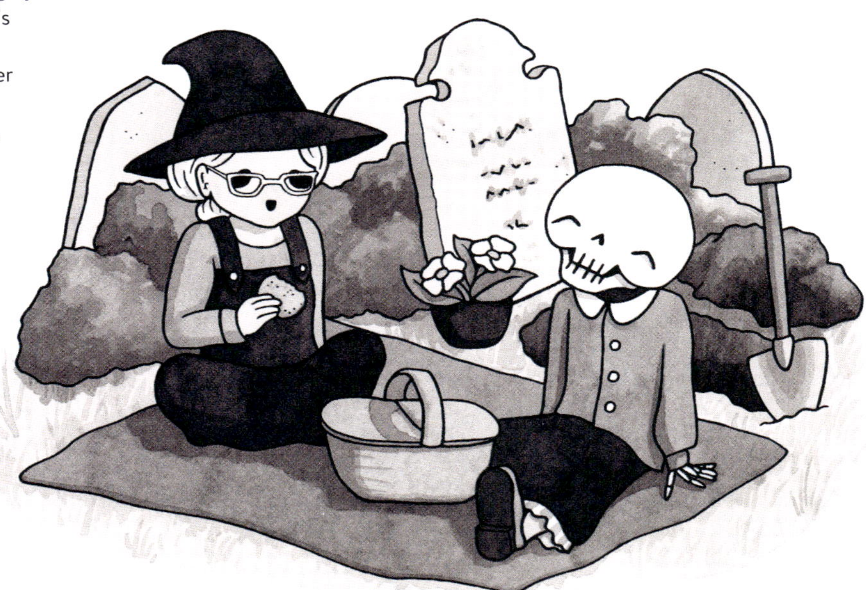

SKULL CHALET

1. Draw a large mushroom-shaped skull with circles for the eyes, an upside-down heart for the nose, and lines for the teeth.

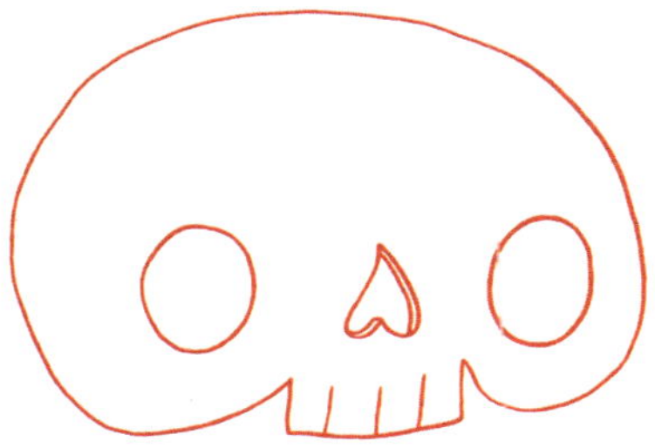

2. Add a witch hat on top. Curve the top of the triangle to the left and make the brim with wavy lines.

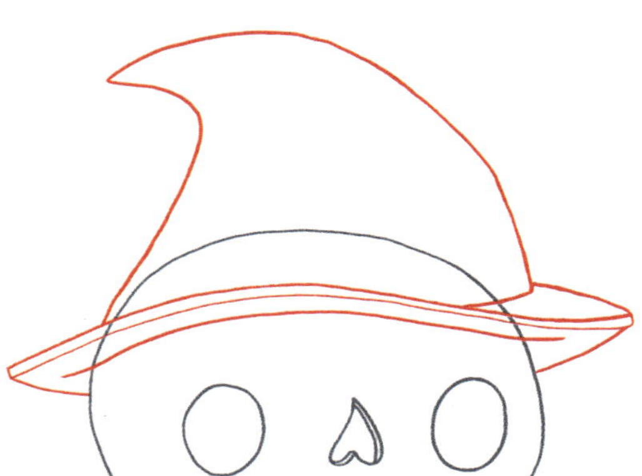

3. Turn the eyes into arched windows with crosses. On the hat, draw an arched door with a knob. Above and to the right, draw a chimney with a rectangle and two lines connecting it to the hat.

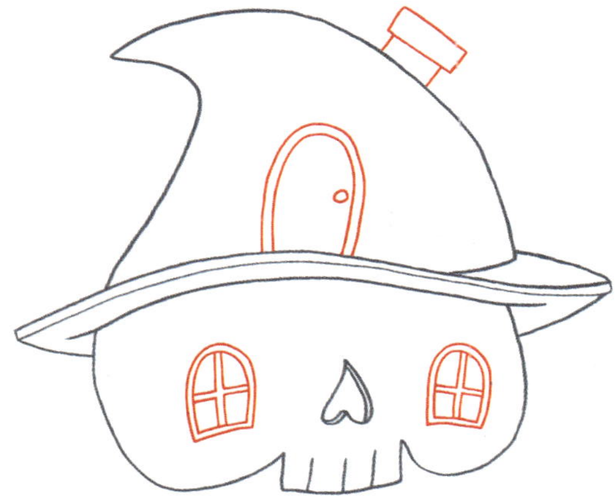

4. Draw a railing on the brim of the hat with a long curved rail and lots of vertical bars.

5. Add a back layer to the railing to create depth.

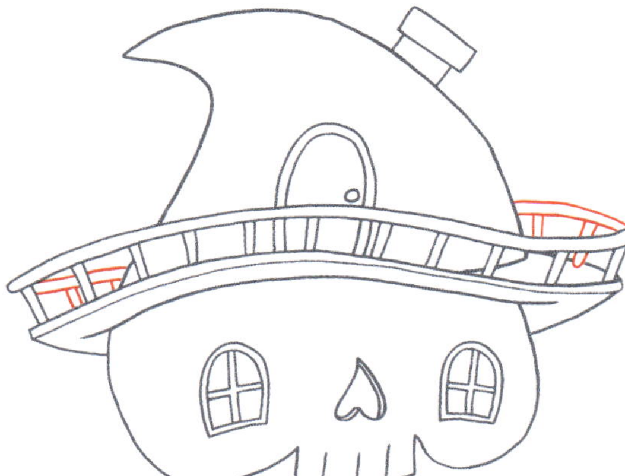

6. Add some rocks and plants around the skull house with abstract shapes.

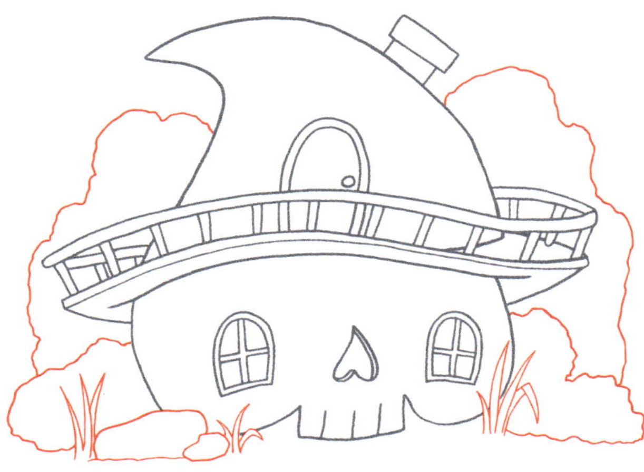

7. Draw a sleeping mouse on the bottom left. Make a teardrop-shaped head, large ears, and a curled tail. Draw its hands and feet close together.

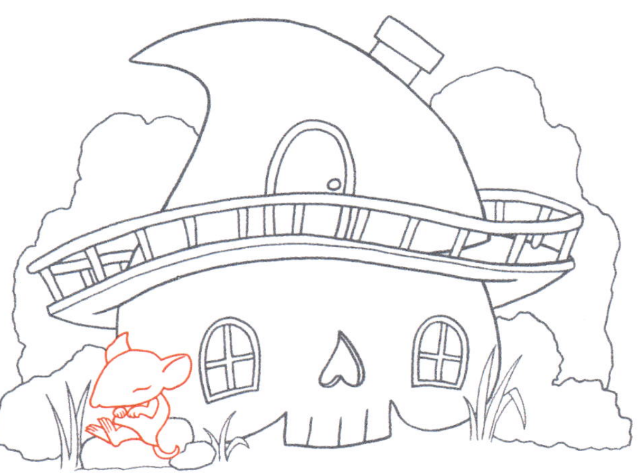

8. Draw another mouse head peeking over the top of the roof. Use a teardrop-shaped head, large ears, and three fingers for each hand.

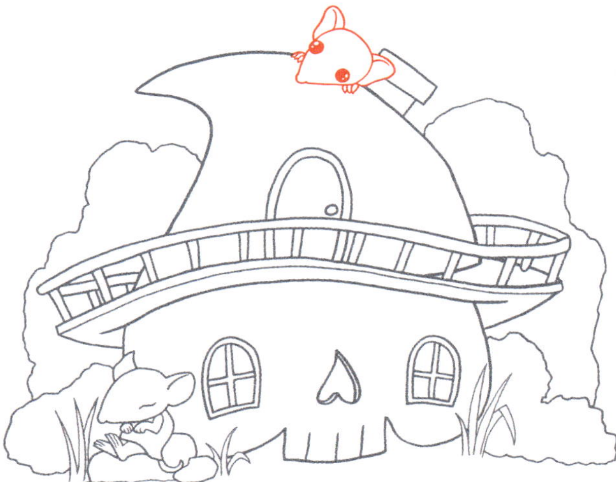

9. Draw a third mouse looking away on the right side of the railing. This one is wearing a simple dress.

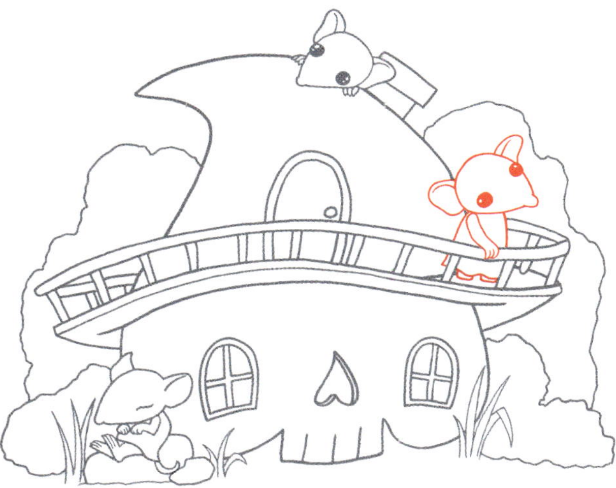

10. Cleanly trace your sketch with pencils of varying lead point sizes on watercolor paper before inking.

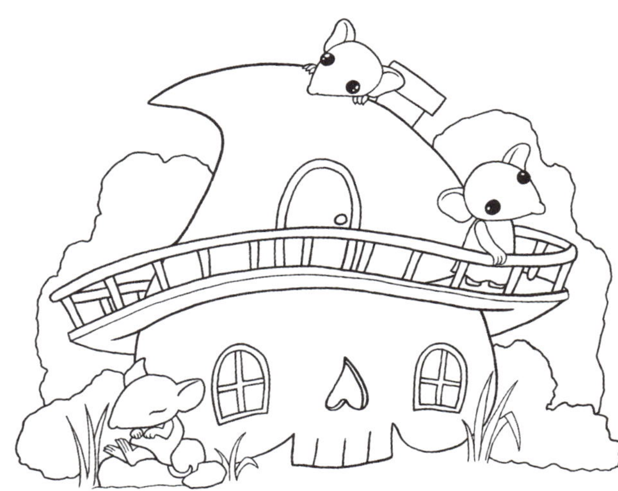

11. I used watercolors in shades of black and gray, leaving the skull part of the house white.

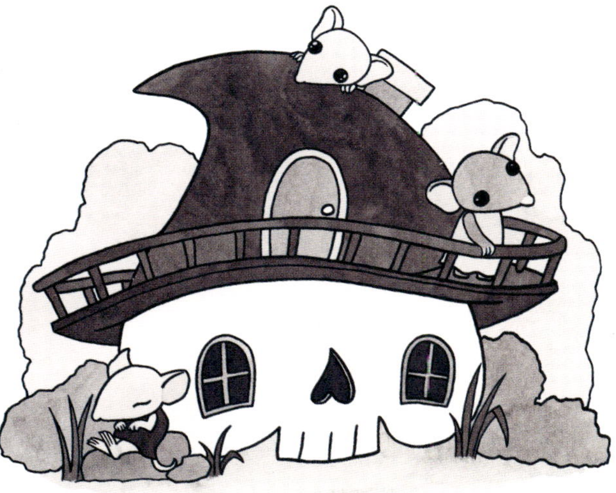

12. Use thin, short lines to make your mice look furry. Add lots of small dots to make the rocks and ground look grainy. Scribble with a medium brush or pen to add texture to the bushes. Add shading as if the light is coming from the top right.

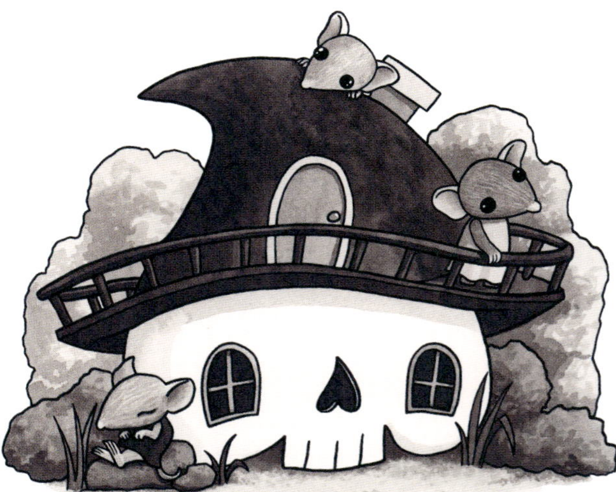

THE FRIENDLY REAPER

1. Lightly sketch a rounded triangle in pencil.

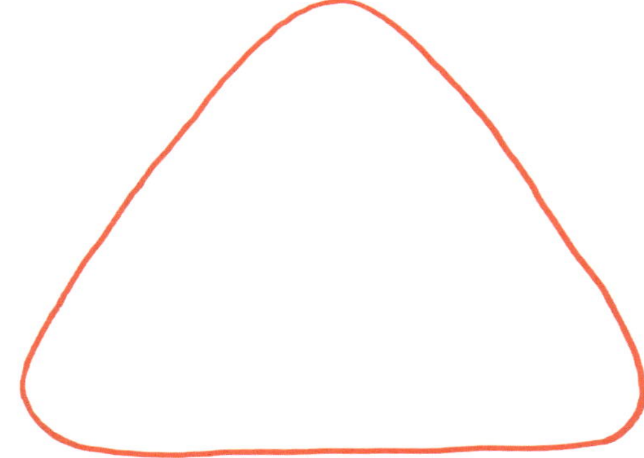

2. On the right side of the triangle, start the reaper with an oval head and a cone-shaped body with a pointed base.

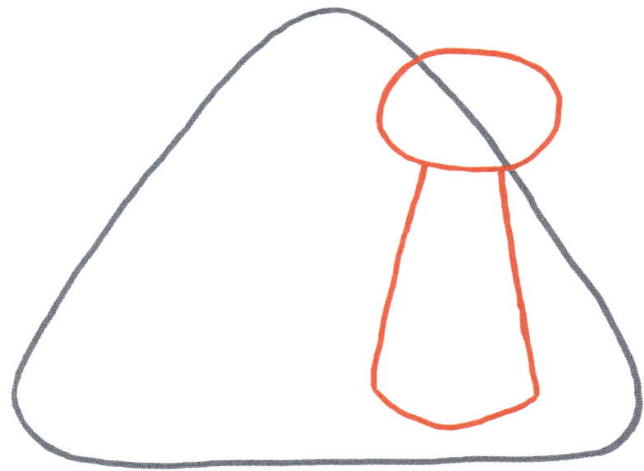

3. Draw the reaper's cloak with a round hood, two curved arms bent at the elbows, and some folds at the bottom.

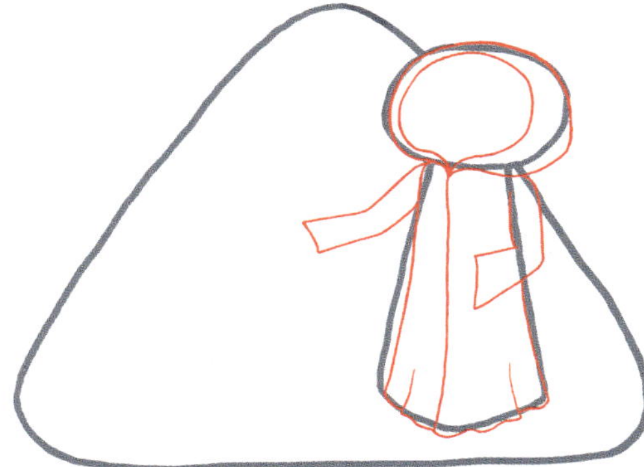

4. Draw a mushroom shape for the reaper's face with lines for the teeth and curves for the eyes.

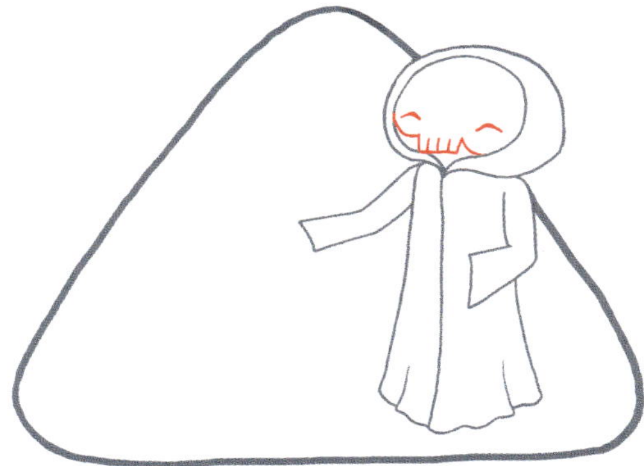

5. Draw skeletal hands with simple curved and pointy fingers. The left hand is splayed out, and the right hand is curved to hold a sack of seeds. Divide each finger into two or three segments.

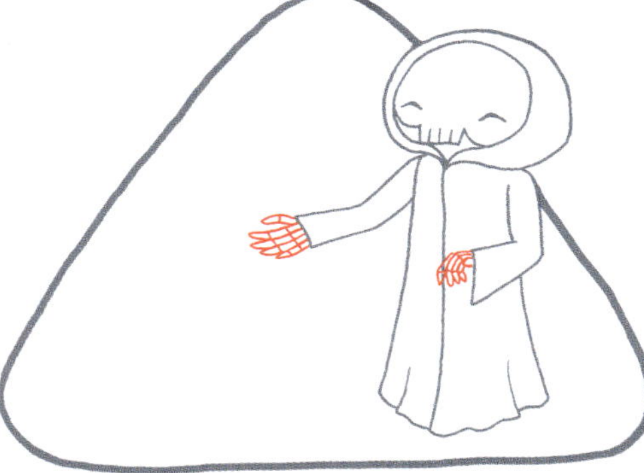

6. Draw an open sack of seeds in the grip of the right hand with a curved U shape and an oval in the top. Add a wavy line of seeds.

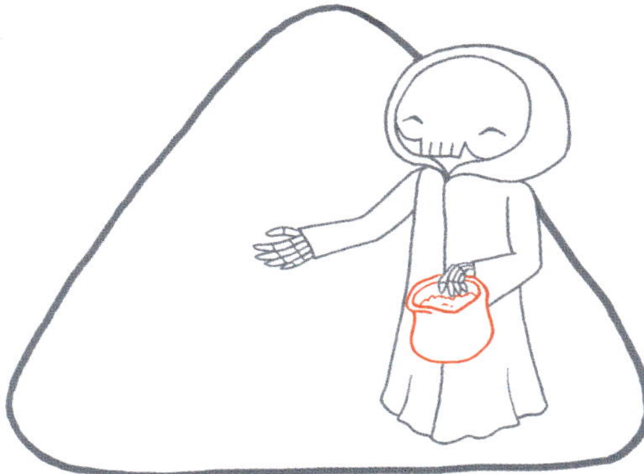

THE FRIENDLY REAPER continued

7. In the background, start a curvy tree that bends to the left with some pointy branches.

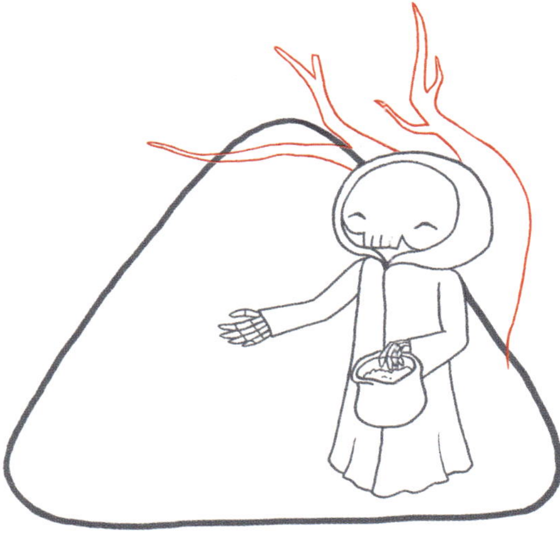

8. Add three gravestones in different shapes around the reaper. Draw the sides of the left and right stones to add depth. Add wavy lines along the bottom edges for the gravel.

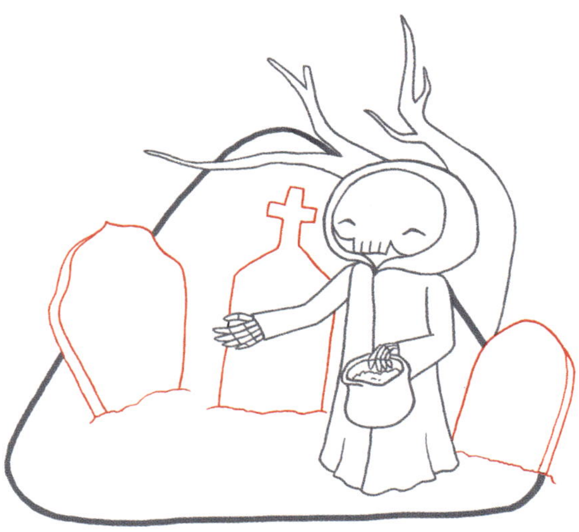

9. Draw three birds, two on the ground and one perched on a branch, using simple teardrop shapes for the heads, bodies, and wings. Give them solid eyes and taloned feet.

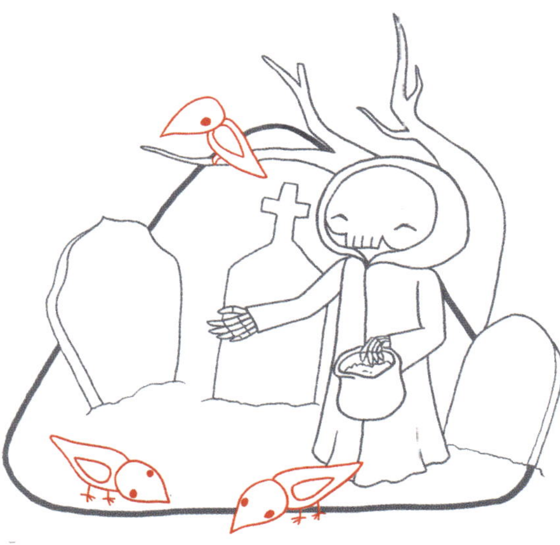

10. Add some bushes on the sides of the drawing and between the gravestones with abstract shapes.

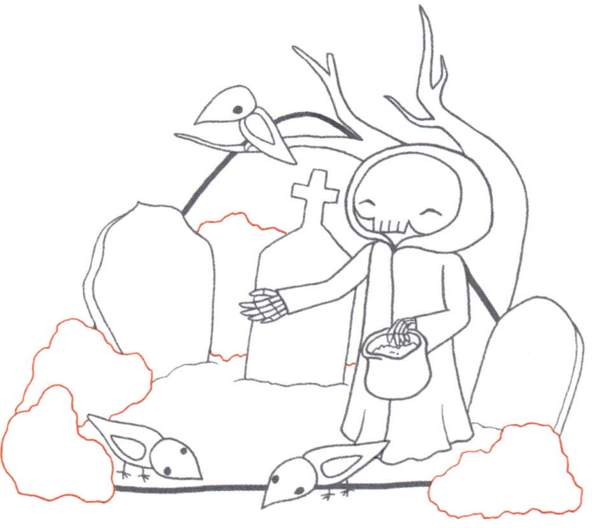

11. Cleanly trace your sketch with pencil on watercolor paper before inking.

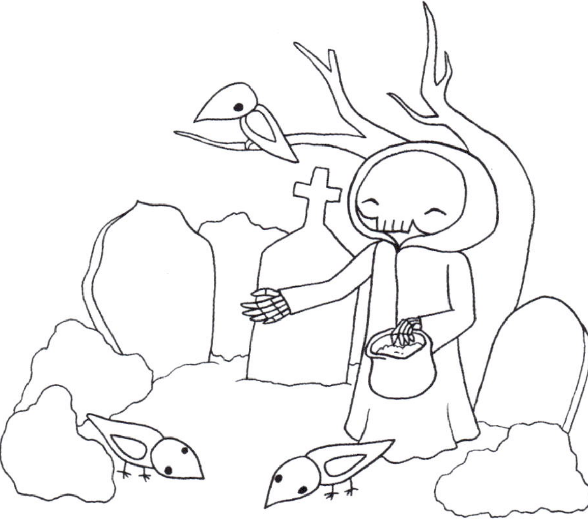

12. Add fine detail to the tree and gravestones using lines. Draw some bird seed on the ground and falling from the reaper's hand with small circles.

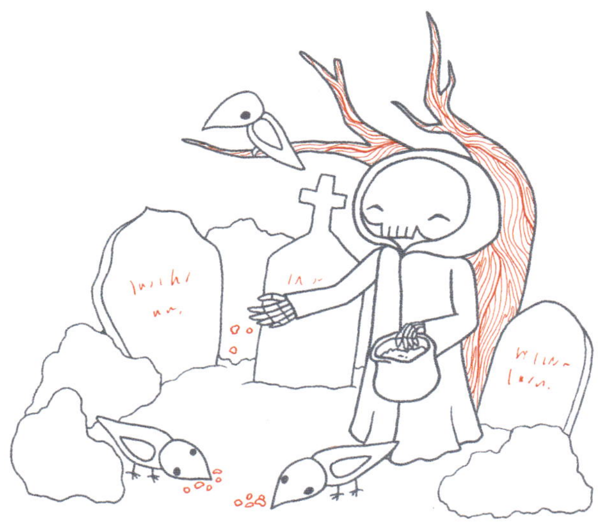

13. I used watercolors in shades of black and gray to color. Leave the reaper, bird heads, and birdseed white.

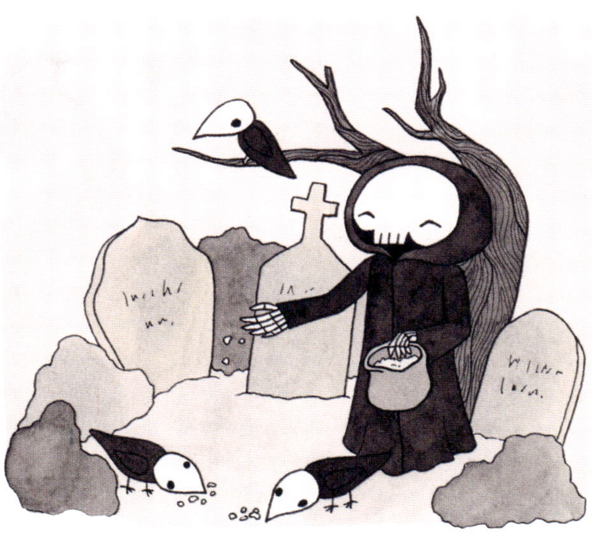

14. Use the technique of stippling to add a grainy texture to the ground and gravestones. Add shading. Remember that the light is in the top right, so shade mostly on the left. Don't forget to shade inside the reaper's hood.

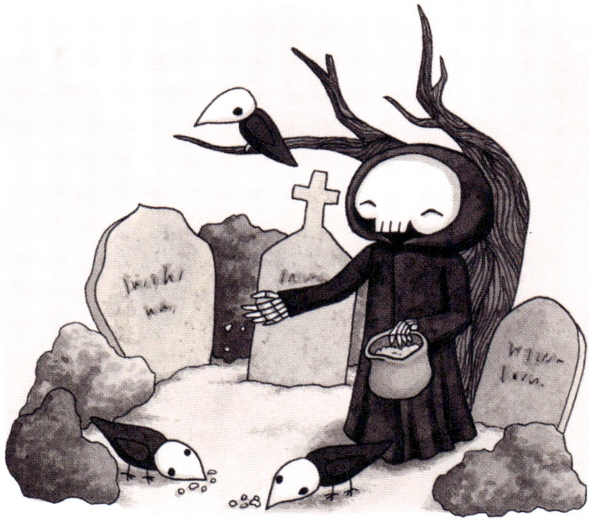

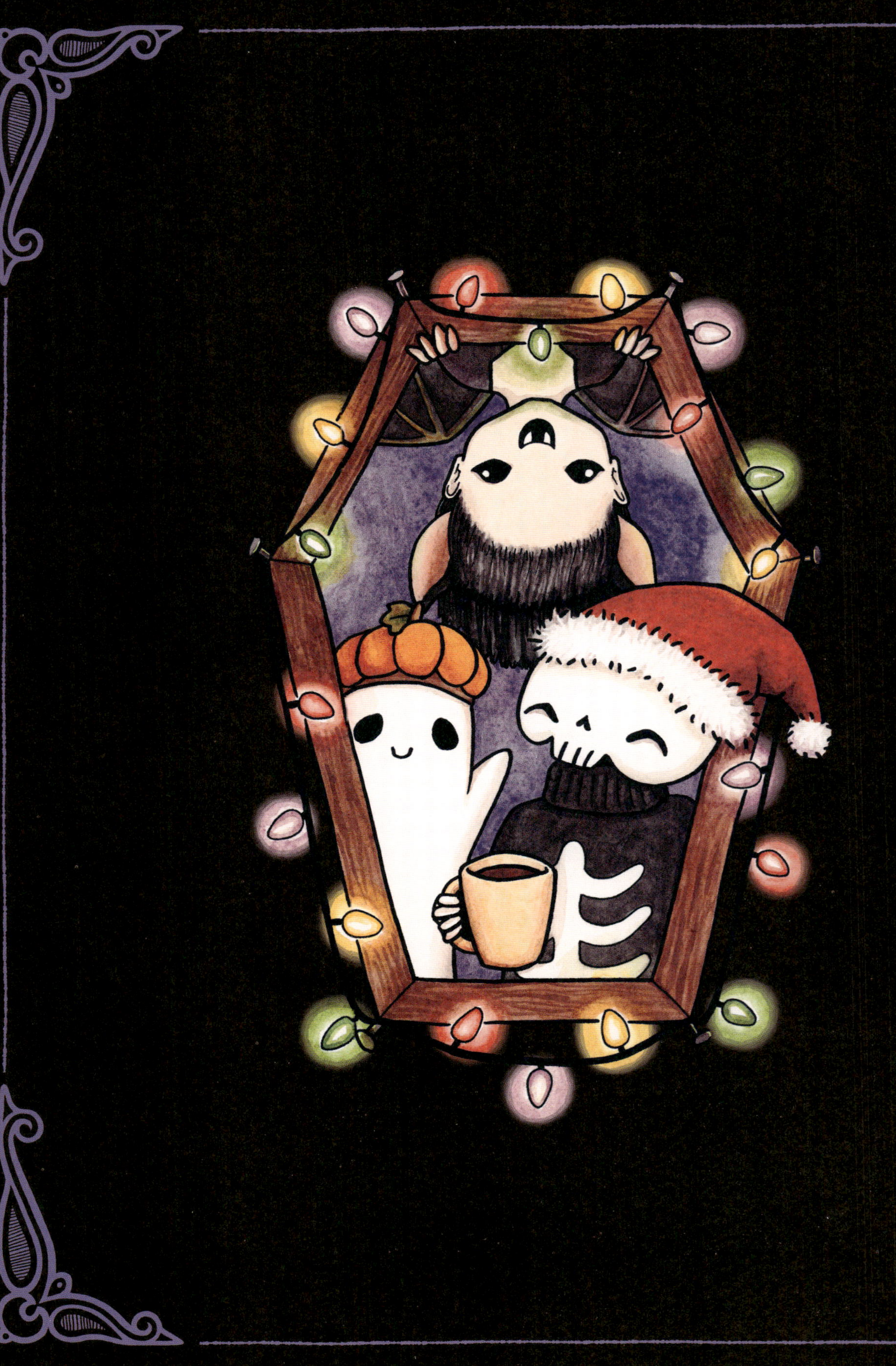

spooky celebrations

LUMINOUS SKULL

1. Draw a large, mushroom-shaped skull with solid eyes, an upside-down heart for the nose, and lines for the teeth.

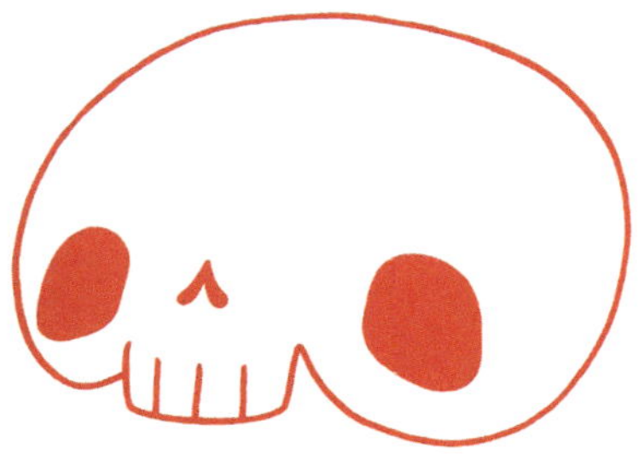

2. Draw five melting candles on top with curved lines and teardrop-shaped flames.

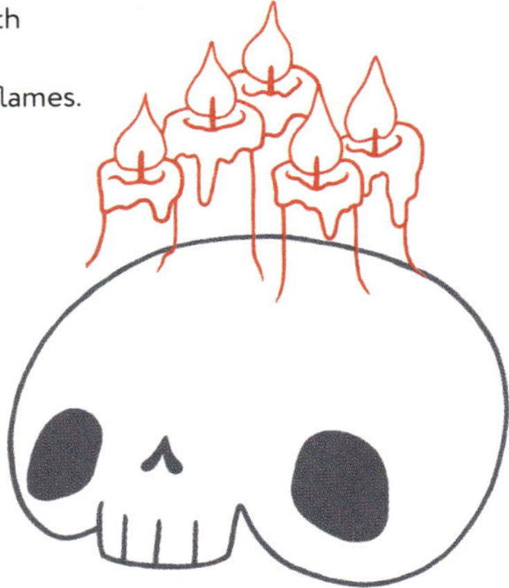

3. With a long wavy line, draw the wax dripping around the candles and oozing down the skull.

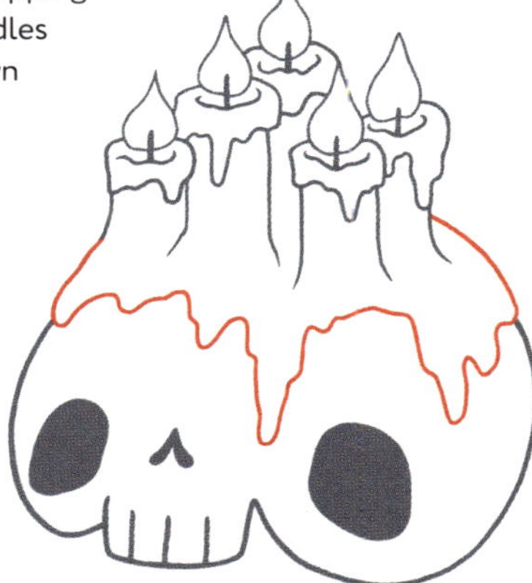

4. Cleanly trace your sketch with pencil on watercolor paper before inking.

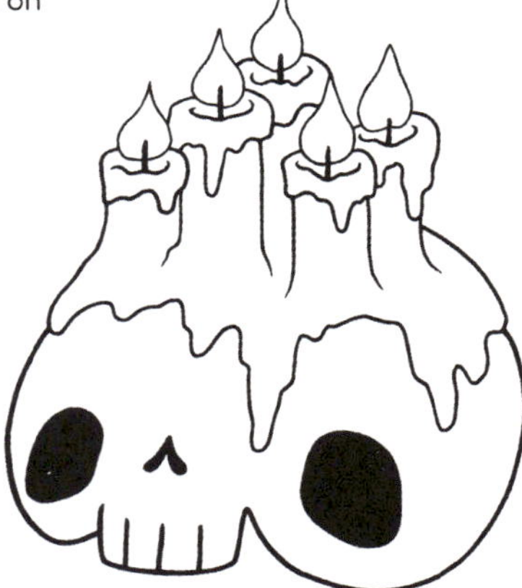

5. I used watercolors to make the candles orange, but I left the skull white. Leave a bright gradient around the flames. Add shading on the lower right side of everything.

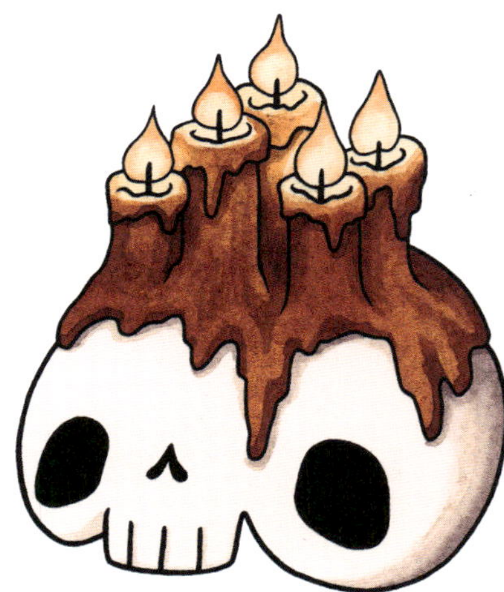

PHANTOM CHEERS

1. Sketch an arch with a wavy bottom edge for a ghost. Add a content facial expression.

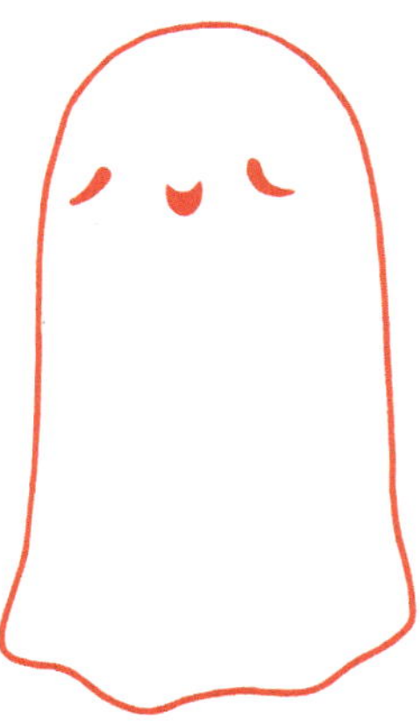

2. Draw two triangle arms pointed toward the middle of the body. Add a mug with a rolled cinnamon stick between the hands.

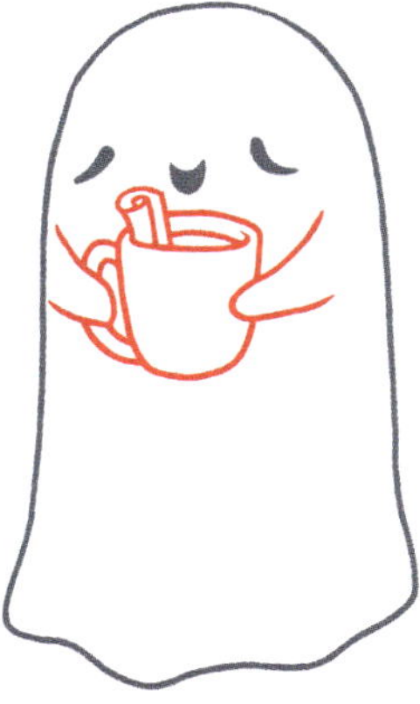

3. Add a beret on top of the head in the shape of a pumpkin. Draw a leaf stem on top.

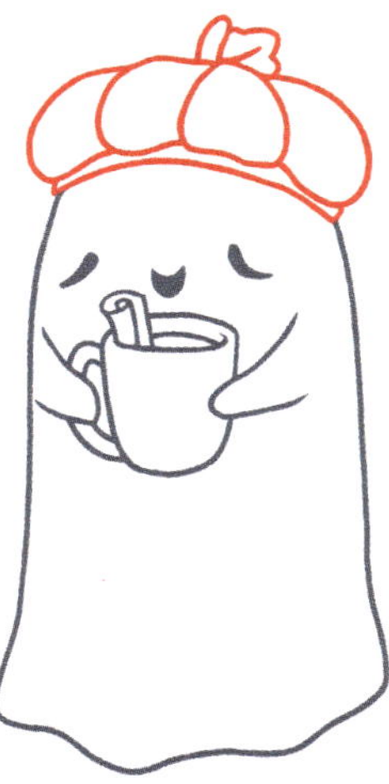

4. Cleanly trace your sketch with pencil on watercolor paper before inking.

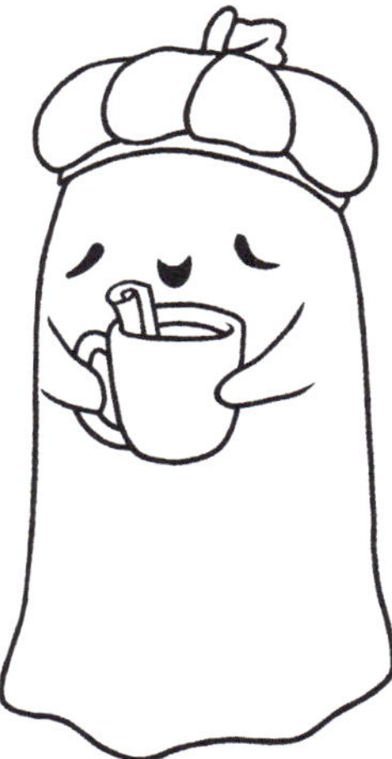

5. Add color in warm shades. I used oranges, browns, and green. Add shading on the beret and around the mug and arms.

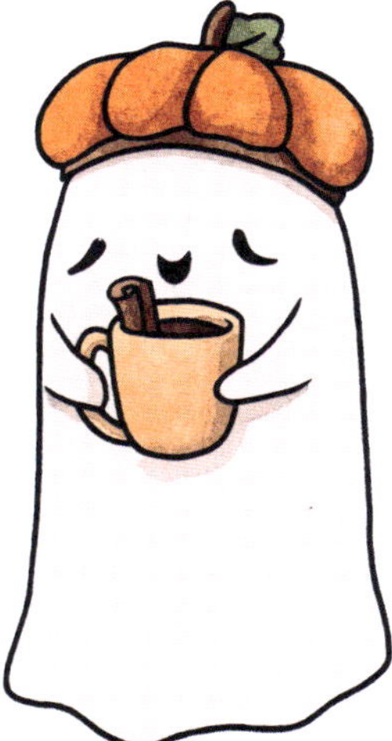

HALLOWEEN STAMP

1. Sketch a rectangle. Add a patterned border with little curves, then draw a price inside the bottom right corner.

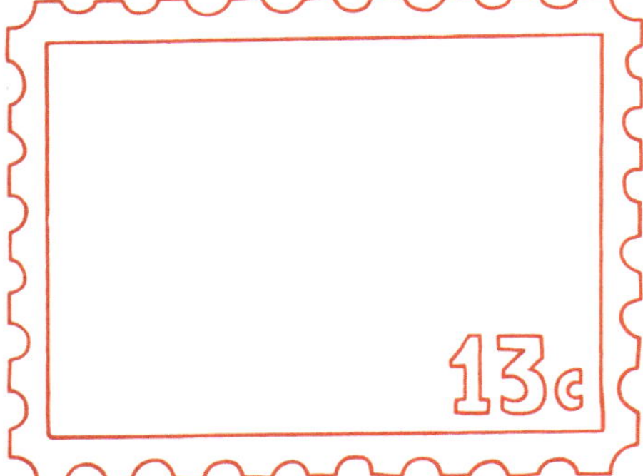

2. Draw a broom inside the frame with an oval stick and a wider oval for the bristles. Add bindings at the neck and lines where it cinches.

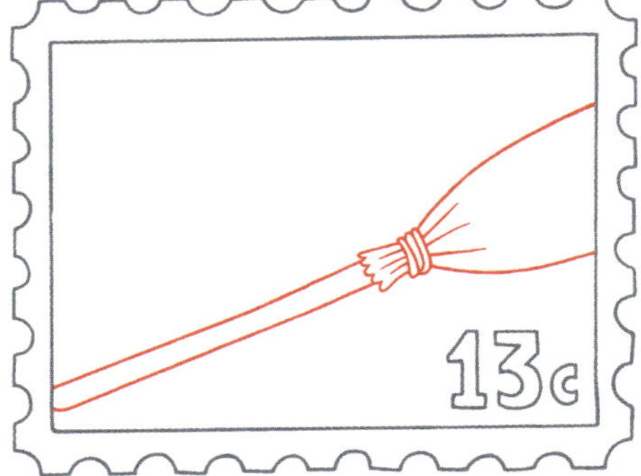

3. Draw a cat sitting on the stick. Use an oval for the head, triangles for the ears, and a curved oval for the tail. Draw two triangle arms and one back leg. Give it a happy facial expression.

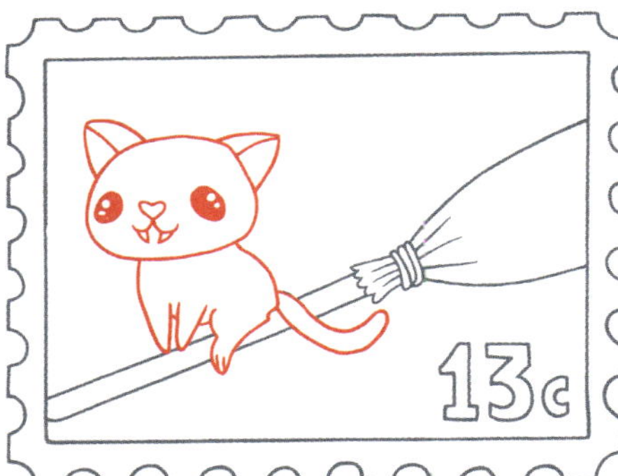

4. Dress the cat in a pointed hat, bow tie, and flowing cape.

5. Cleanly trace your sketch with pencil on watercolor paper before inking.

6. I used markers in purple for the background, pink for the bowtie and broom bindings, pale yellow for the cat, and black for the hat and cape. The broom's stick is brown, the bristles are yellow, and the stamp's price is orange.

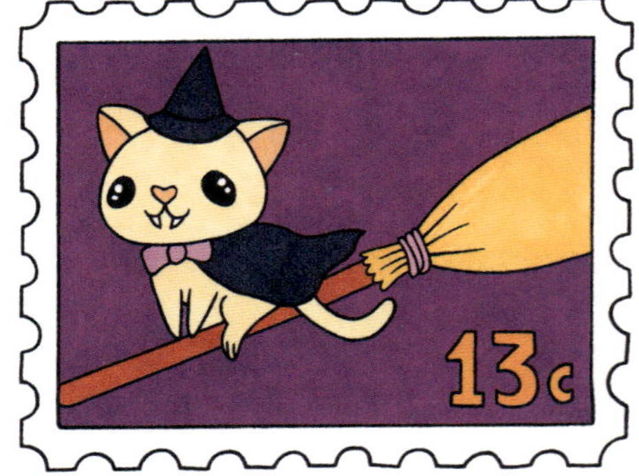

CLOAK AND FANGS

1. Draw a ghost with its arms spread out. Make a rounded head, pointed oval arms, and a wavy bottom edge.

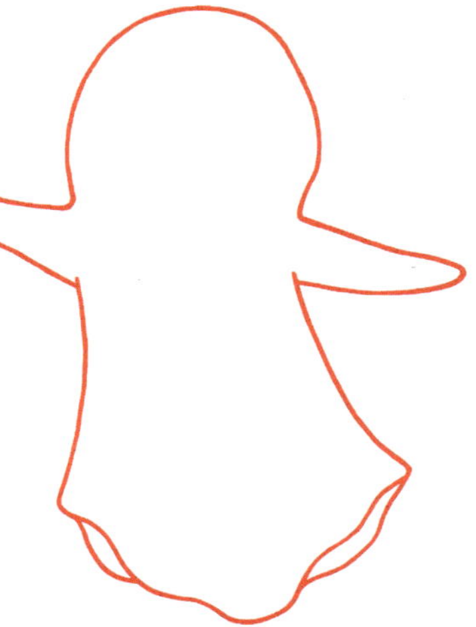

2. Add a mischievous face and fanged smile.

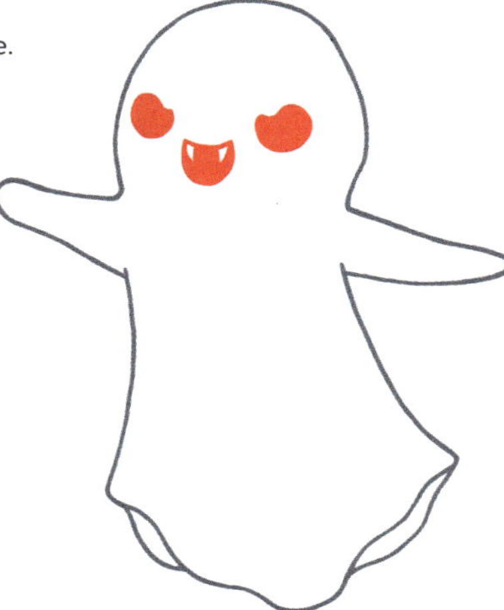

3. Add a tall collar with a pointed oval around the neck. Draw a bow dangling at the center.

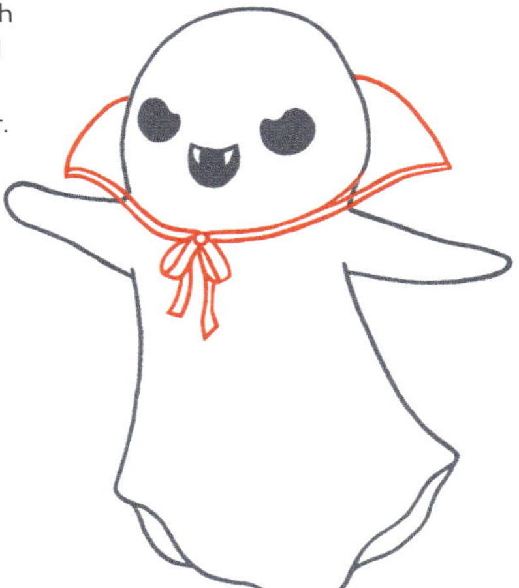

4. Draw the cloak over the shoulders and down the back with wavy lines.

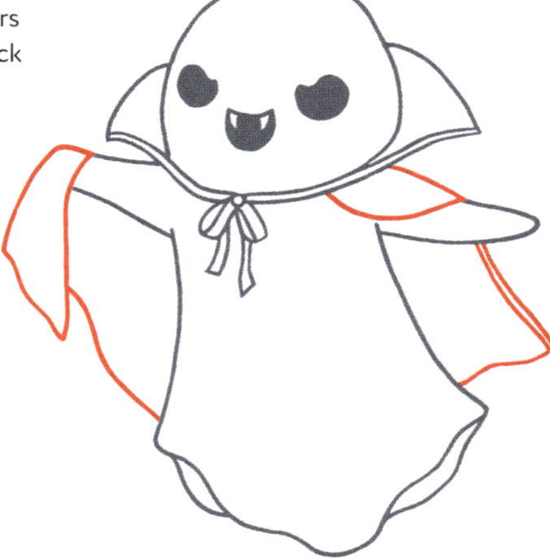

5. Cleanly trace your sketch with pencil on watercolor paper before inking.

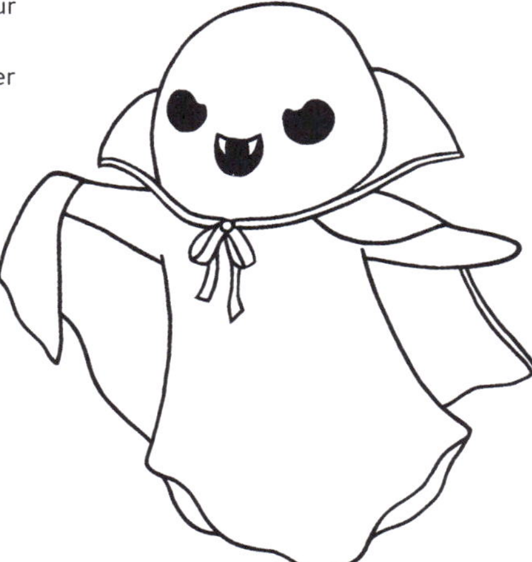

6. I used markers to make the inside of the cloak red and the outside black. I left the ghost and details on the bow white.

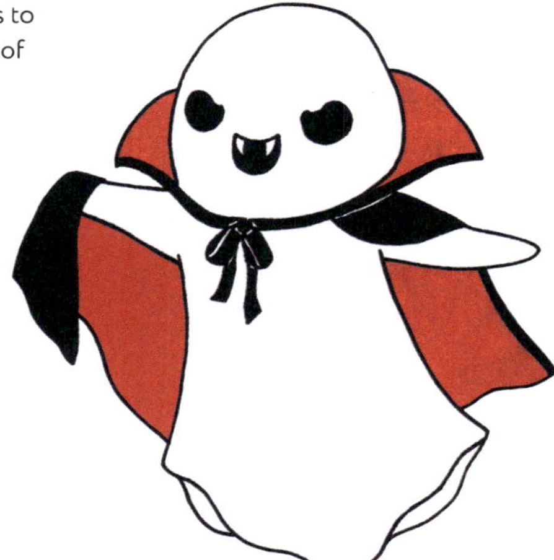

JACK-O'-LANTERN

1. Sketch a rounded trapezoid.

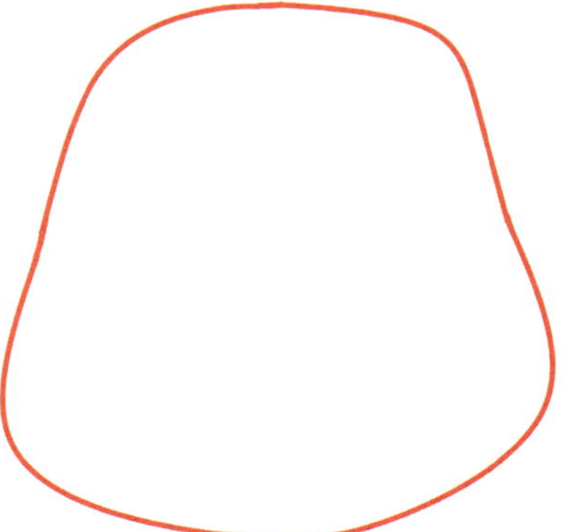

2. Draw the top and bottom ridges of a pumpkin with curved lines.

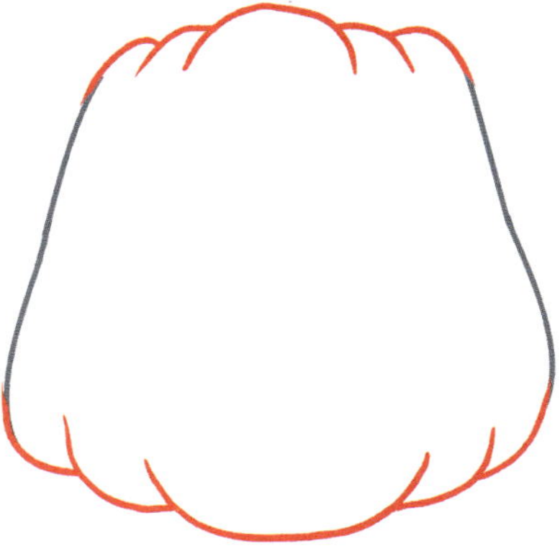

3. Add a curly stem. Add detail with lines inside the stem. Add a face with a triangle nose and eyes and a single-toothed smile.

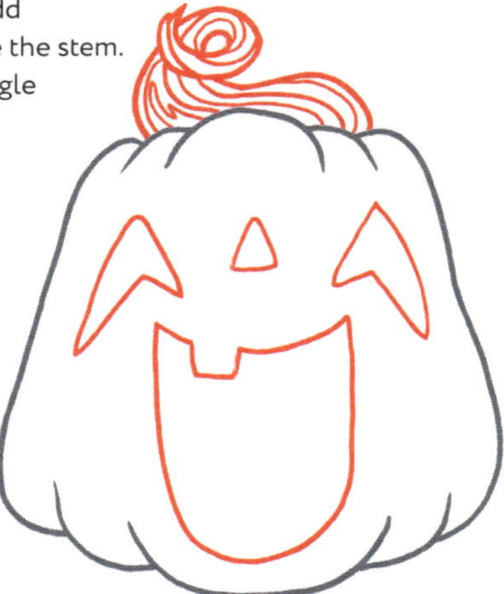

4. Draw lines inside the features to add depth.

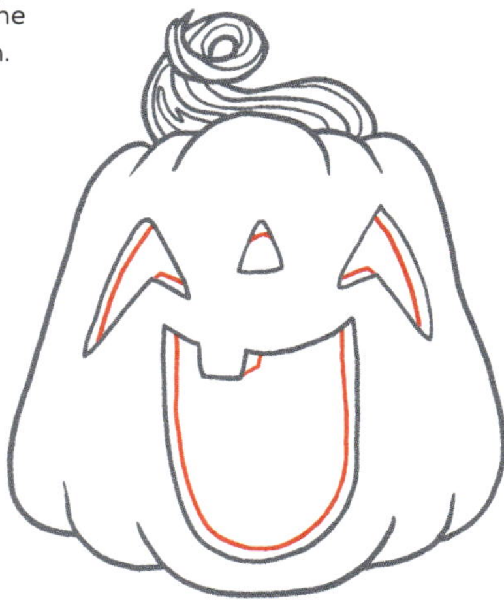

5. Cleanly trace your sketch with pencil on watercolor paper before inking.

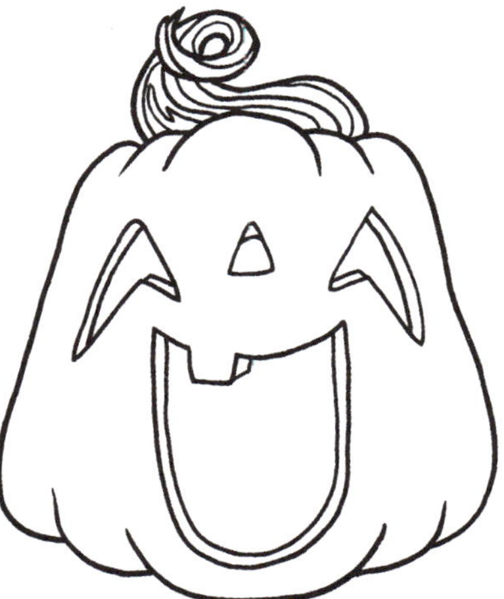

6. I used markers to make the pumpkin a classic orange and the lantern light yellow. The stem is green.

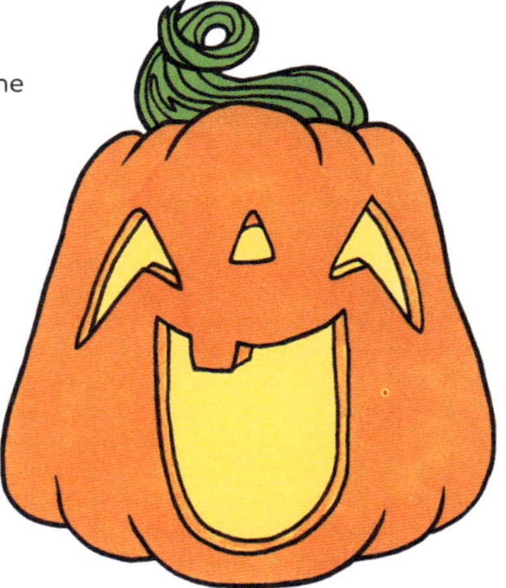

SPOOKMAS STOCKING

1. Draw a Christmas stocking in the shape of a sock with a band at the top. Add a dripping line underneath the band.

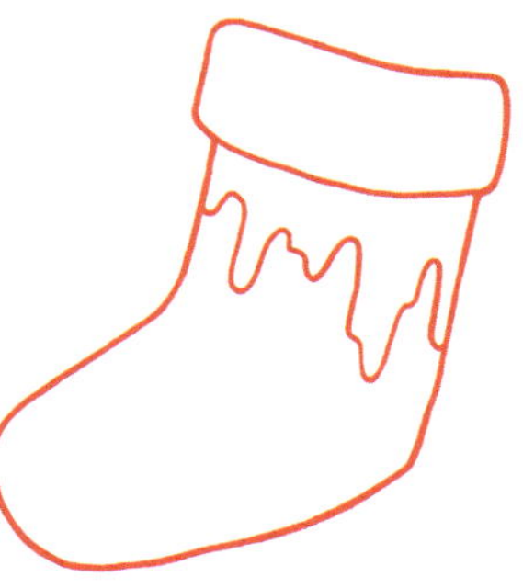

2. Place a stuffed cat toy inside with a round head, triangle ears, and two oval arms. Add a skull face inside the head with circles for the eyes, an upside-down heart for the nose, and triangles for the fangs.

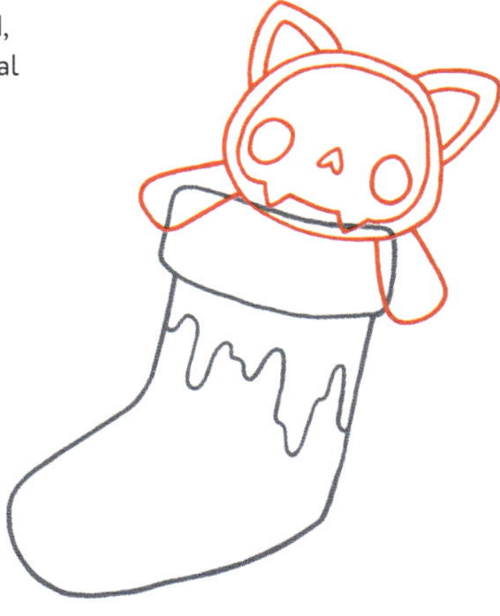

3. Add the top of a candy cane and a bone behind the cat. Draw the stripes of the candy cane.

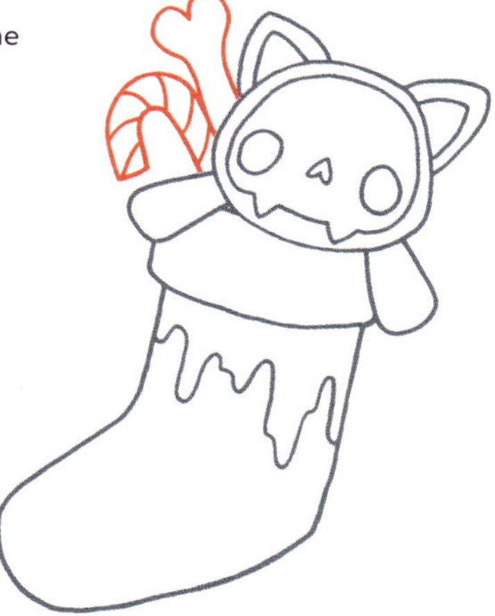

4. Cleanly trace your sketch with pencil on watercolor paper before inking.

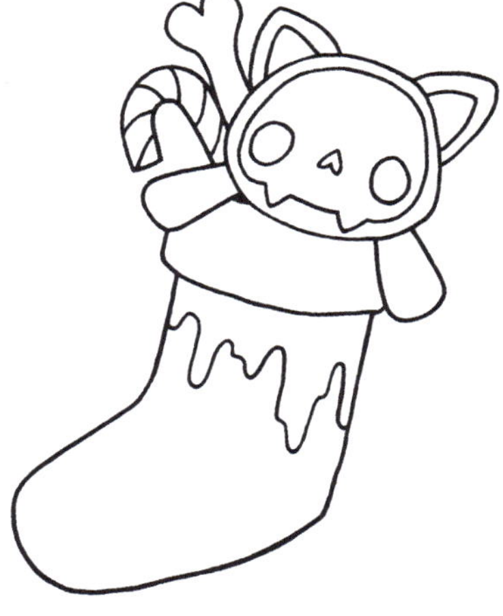

5. I made the stocking and cat black. Then I used red on the candy cane and blood on the stocking.

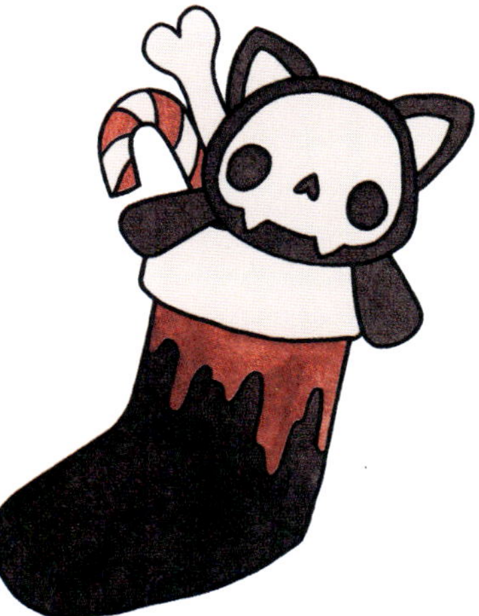

6. With white ink, add some snowflakes on the bottom of the stocking. Create some shading on the bone, candy cane, and under the cat and the band of the stocking.

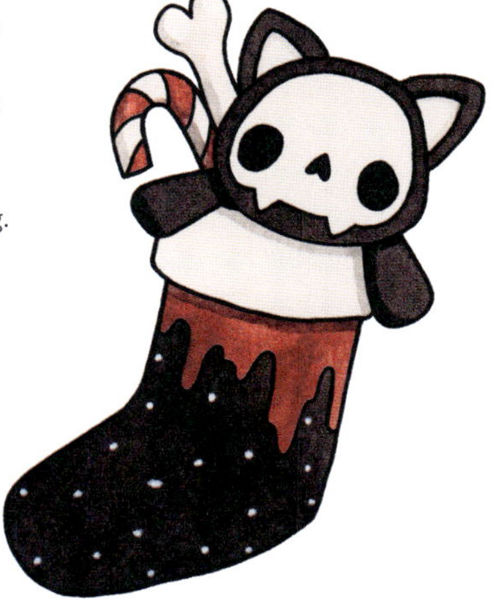

JACK-O'-SNOWMAN

1. Sketch three stacked rounded shapes with a wavy line underneath.

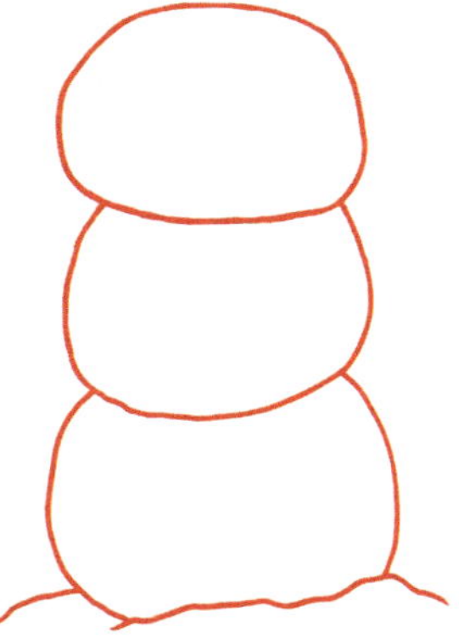

2. Turn the top oval into a jack-o'-lantern. Draw the ridges on the top and bottom and add circle eyes, a triangle nose, and a fanged mouth.

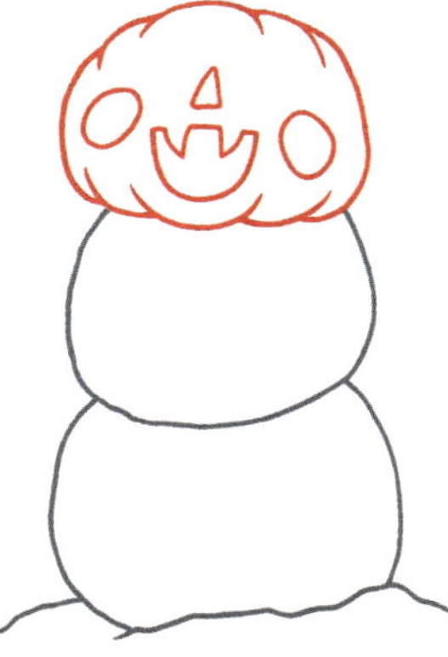

3. Add a winter hat on top with a furry band and pom-pom. Under the jack-o'-lantern, add a scarf with rectangles.

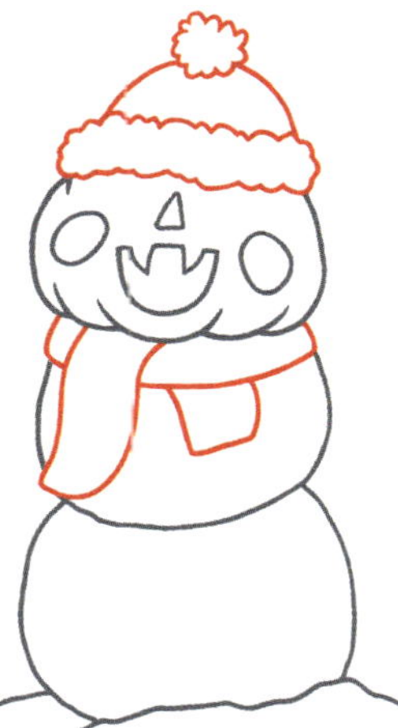

4. Add some round buttons on the middle oval and arms made of pointy sticks on the sides.

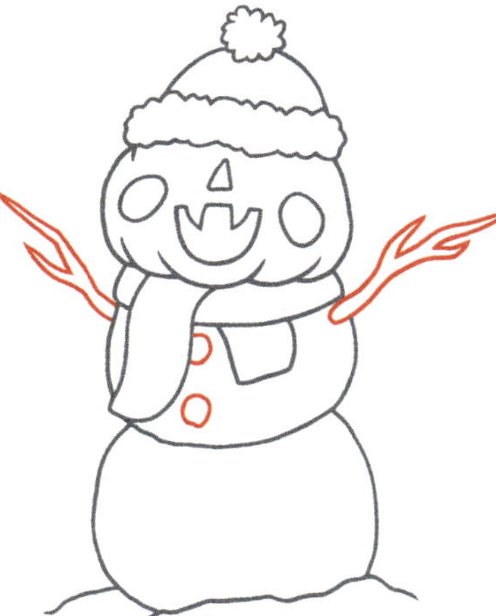

5. Cleanly trace your sketch with pencil on watercolor paper before inking.

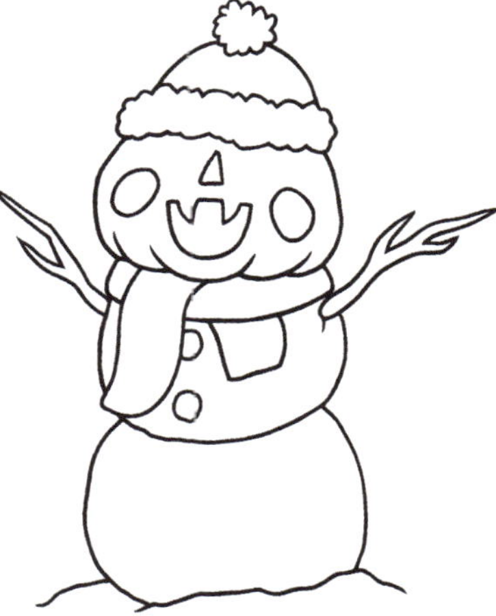

6. I used watercolors to make the hat purple, the head orange, and the scarf, arms, and buttons brown. Add shading with a cool gray color.

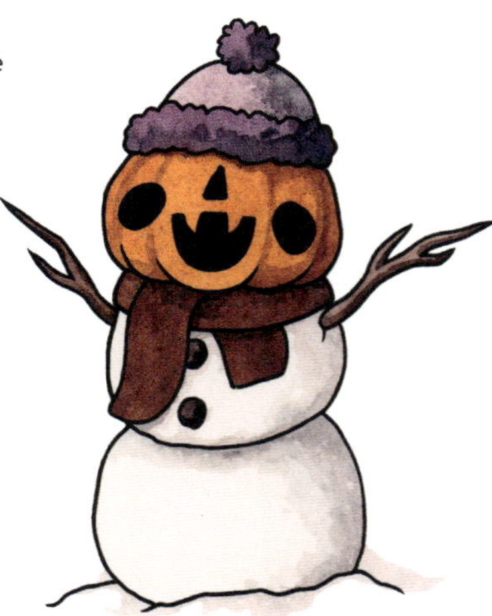

EASTER REAPER

1. Draw a round head and a wavy rectangle body.

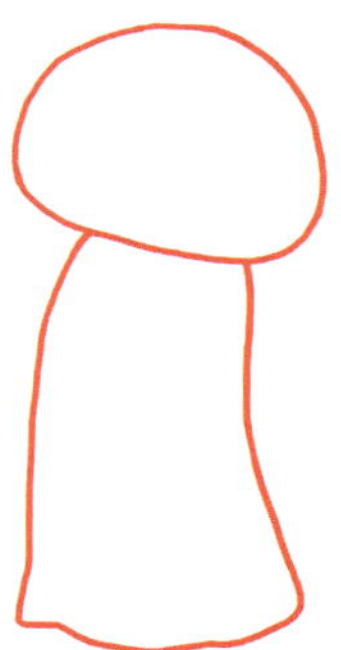

2. Draw a mushroom-shaped skull with a hood curved around it. Add the face with solid circle eyes, an upside-down heart for the nose, and lines for the teeth.

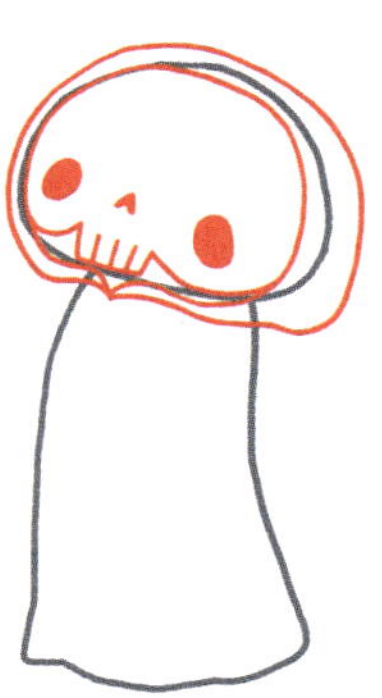

3. Add bunny ears to a headband on top of the hood with tall arches.

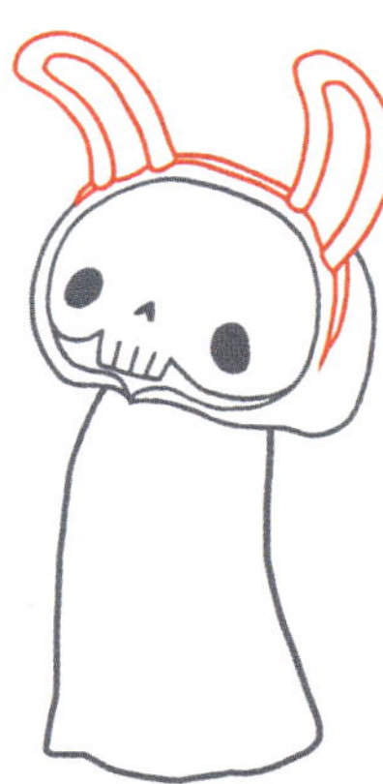

4. Make a basket with a U shape and two circles on top for the rim. Draw curved lines inside the basket for the eggs. Add the reaper's hands on the rim with four fingers each.

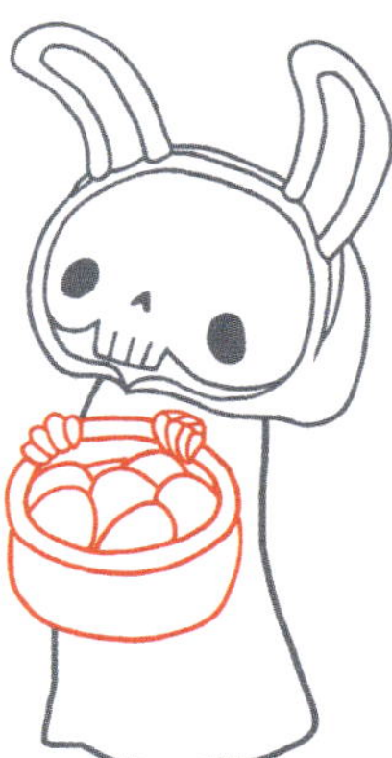

5. Add a twisted trim to the basket with many small, slanted ovals.

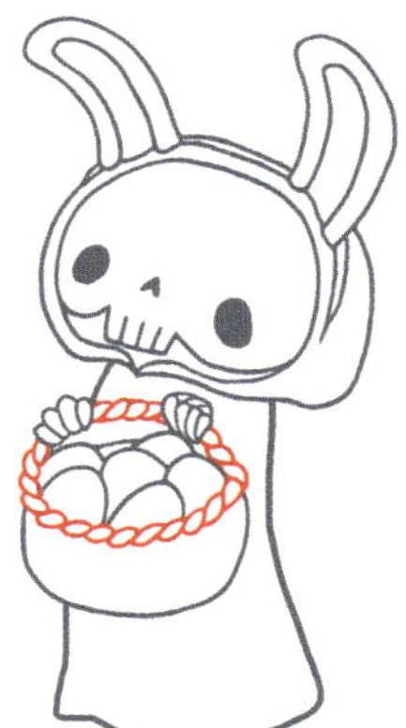

6. Draw the sleeves and shape of the robe.

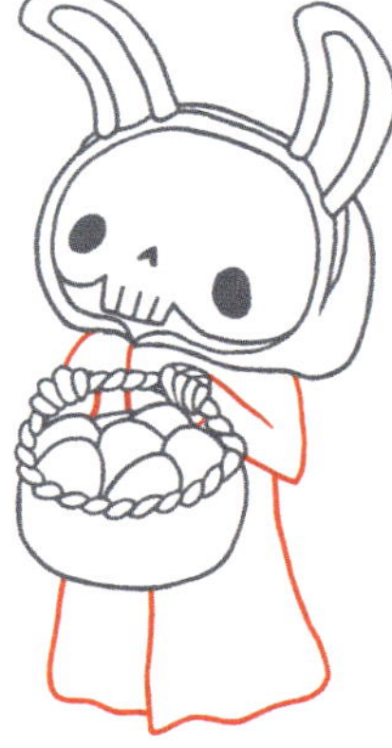

7. Cleanly trace your sketch with pencil on watercolor paper before inking.

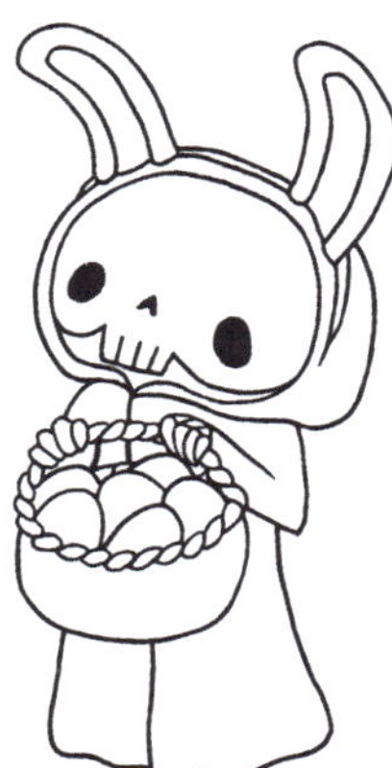

8. I used watercolors in black for the robe and brown for the basket and inner ears. The bunny ears are pink, and the eggs are pink, purple, and yellow.

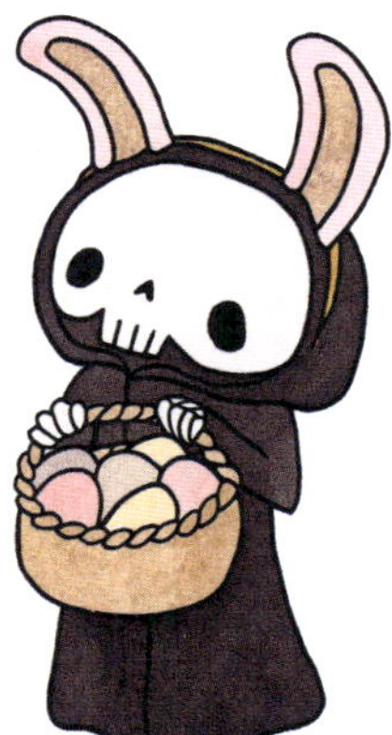

9. Use a thin brush or pen to add a woven pattern to the basket and decorative patterns on the eggs. The light source is on the left, so add shade on the right.

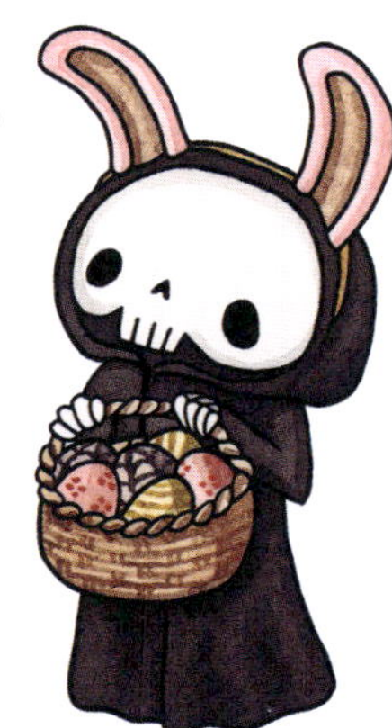

SPOOKY PUPPY

1. Using short lines, draw the shape of a dog's round head and triangle ears.

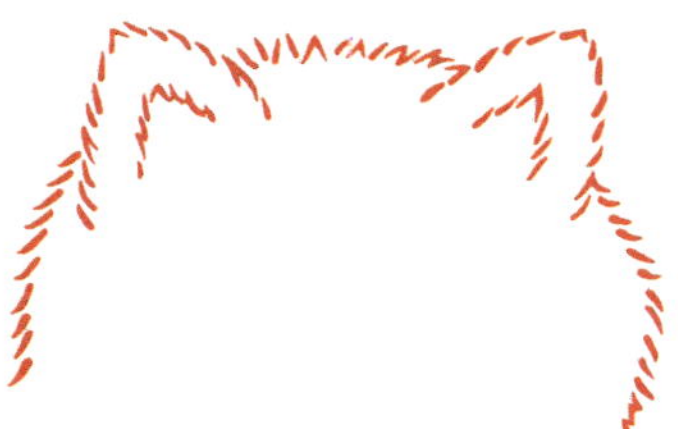

2. Add the face with oval eyes, a mushroom-shaped nose, and three curves for the mouth. Add more short lines around the nose for fur.

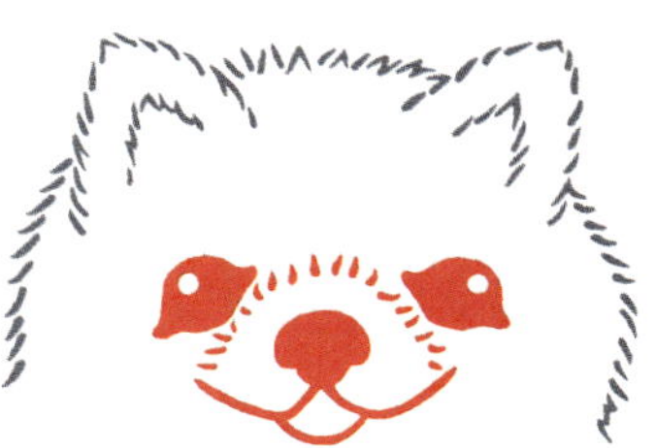

3. Draw a candy bucket in the shape of an oval with two ovals in the top. Add a jack-o'-lantern face. Draw the oval handle gripped in the dog's mouth.

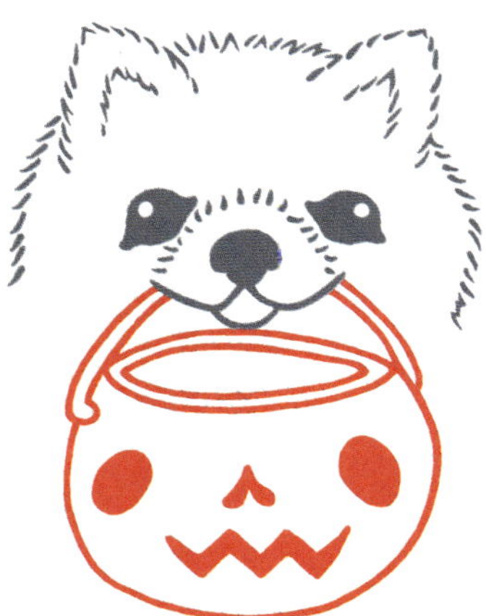

4. Draw two paws with three toes each underneath the bucket. Add furry detail to the legs.

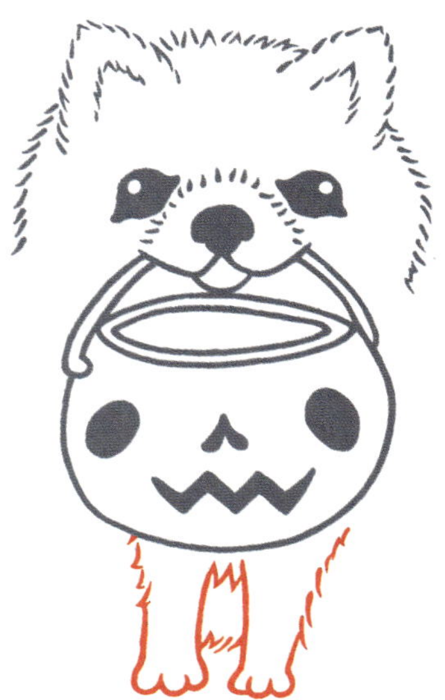

5. Use the short lines again to draw the dog's furry body and curled tail.

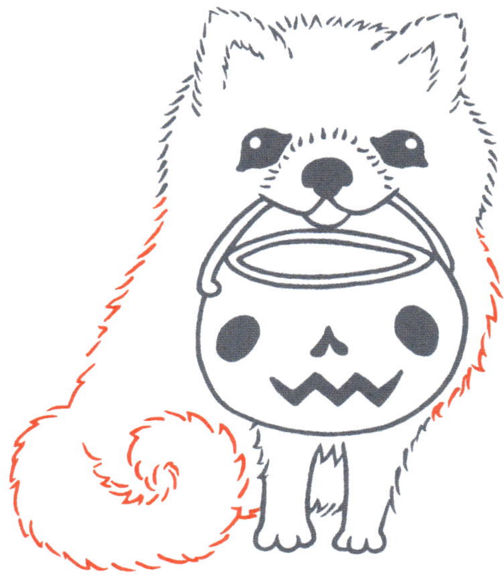

6. Cleanly trace your sketch with pencil on watercolor paper before inking.

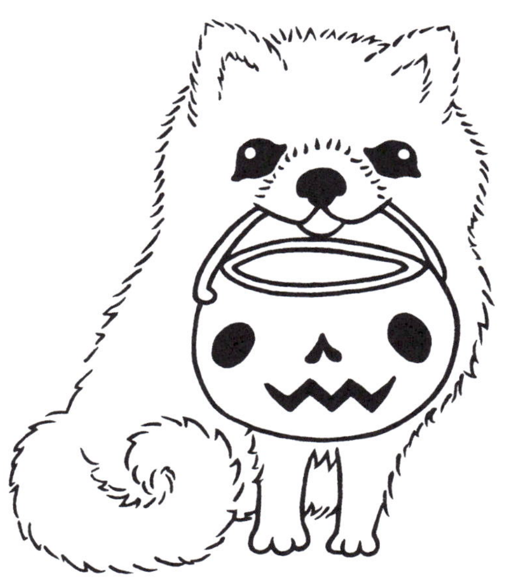

7. I kept the dog white and used markers to make the bucket orange. The inner ears are pink, but you can color it however you'd like!

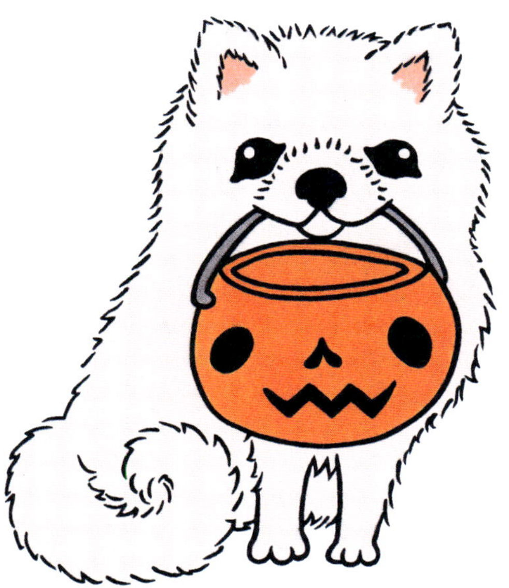

8. Using small overlapping lines, add shading to the dog. Add shading to the edges and inside of the bucket.

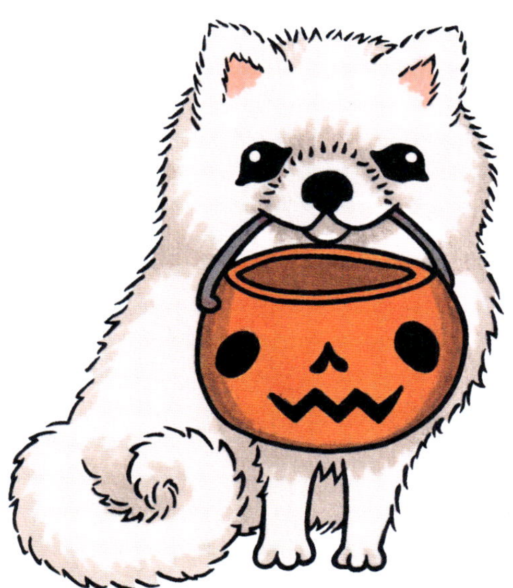

HAUNTED HOT CHOCOLATE

1. Sketch a cauldron with a U shape with a curve at the top. Add a curved line inside the top for the lip.

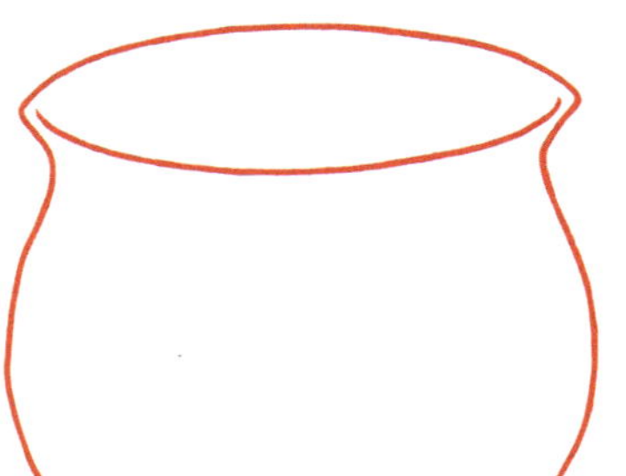

2. Add a decorative handle in a similar shape to a question mark on the right.

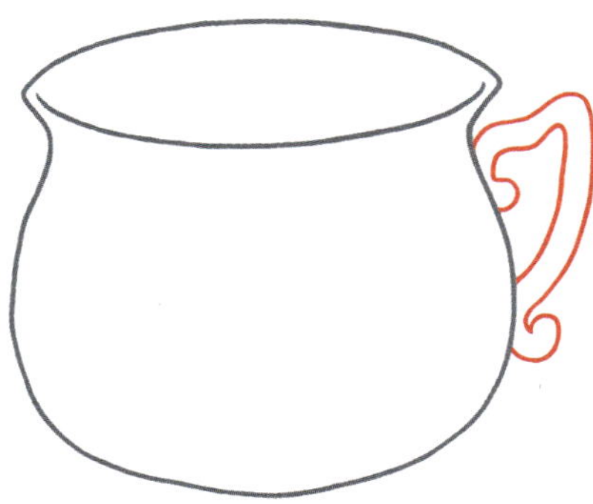

3. Draw a happy jack-o'-lantern face with crescent moons for the eyes, a triangle for the nose, and a smile with one tooth on the top and bottom.

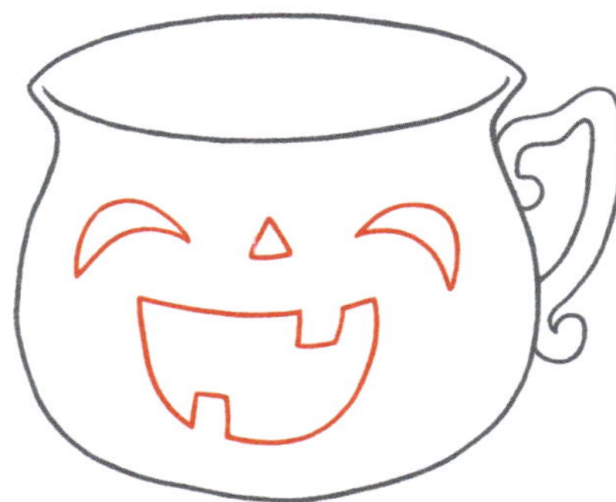

4. Make a large dollop of whipped cream on top with a curved triangle. Add curved lines inside for texture.

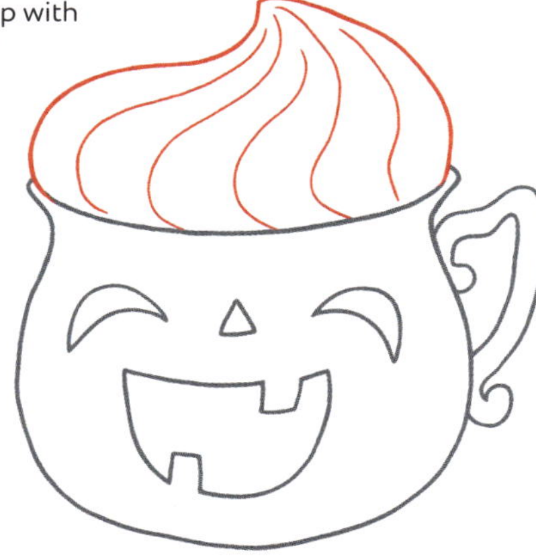

5. Draw a stirrer in the top left of the whipped cream with a bat shape attached to it. Use triangles for the bat's ears, pointed arches for the top of the wings, and a scalloped line for the bottom of the wings.

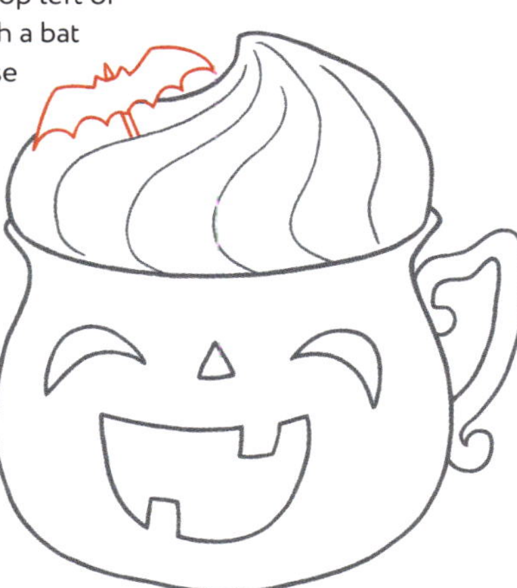

6. Add four cylindrical marshmallows tilted in various directions. Draw a screaming ghost face on each.

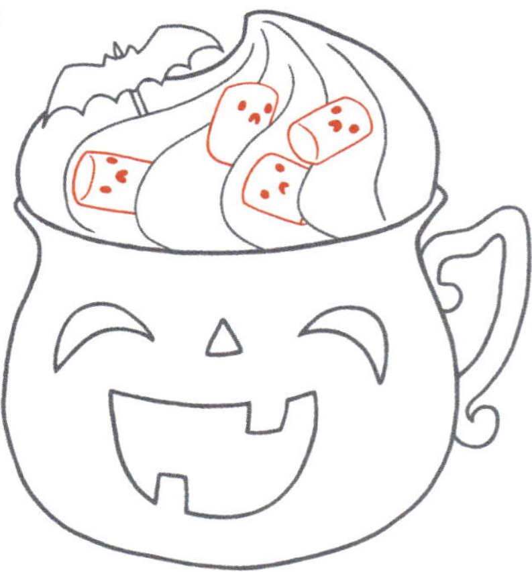

7. Add some star-shaped sprinkles on the whipped cream.

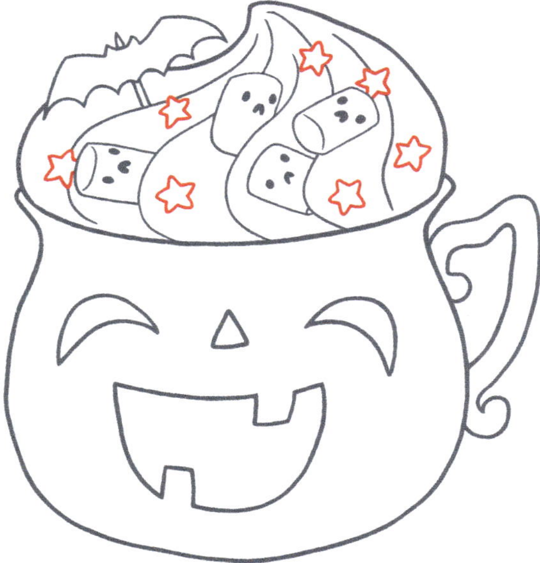

8. Cleanly trace your sketch with pencil on watercolor paper before inking. I used a pencil with a smaller lead point size to trace the marshmallows.

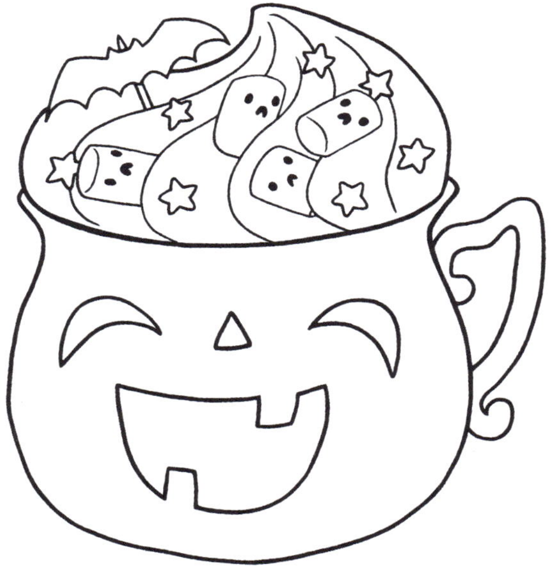

9. I used watercolors in orange for the cup, beige for the whipped cream, brown for the sprinkles, and black for the bat and the cup's handle. Add shading with warm gray on the mug and cool gray on everything else. Use a black marker to color the face of the mug.

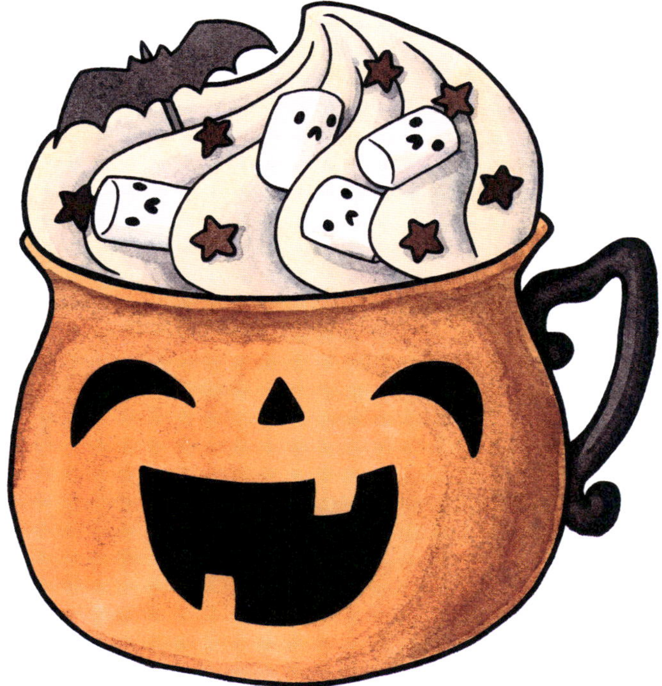

PUMPKIN PATCH PARTY

1. Sketch three ovals in a triangular formation.

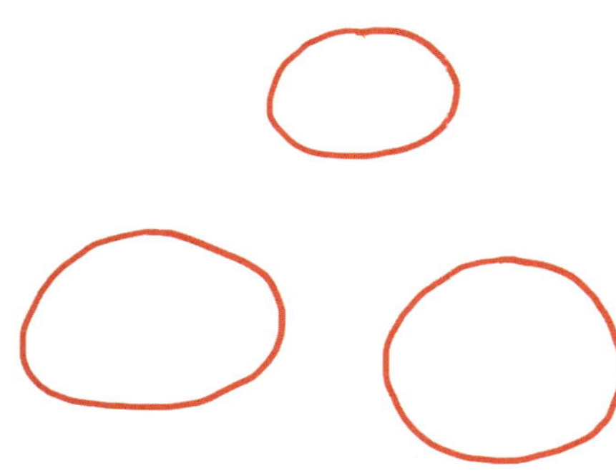

2. Turn the top oval into a lumpy pumpkin with a stem.

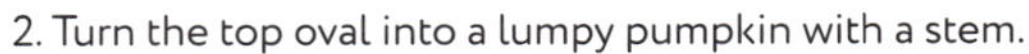

3. Add a sheet ghost behind the pumpkin with hands underneath the pumpkin.

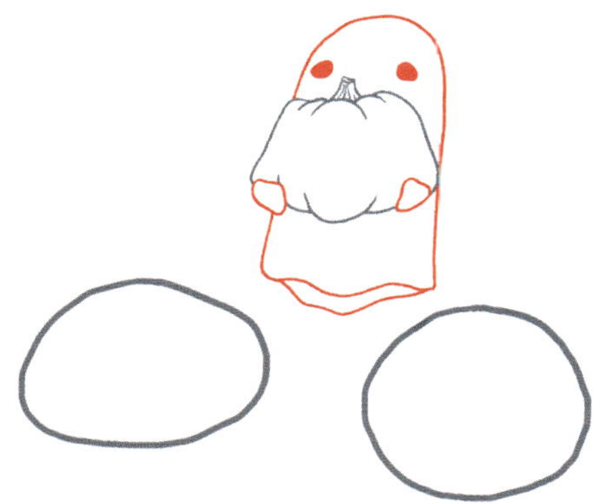

4. Make the left oval a pumpkin with an open top and a curvy stem. Draw a jagged oval on top of the pumpkin for the rim.

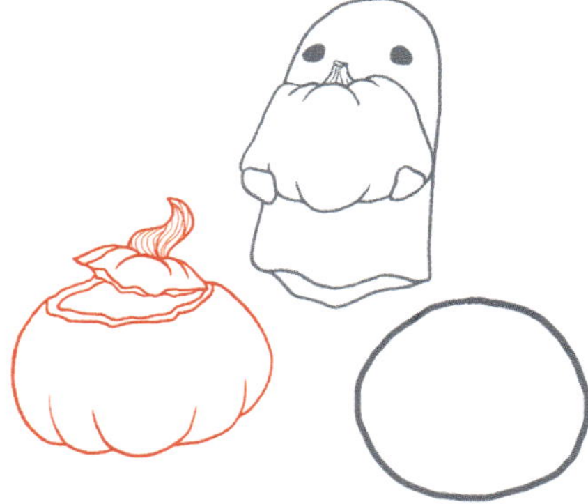
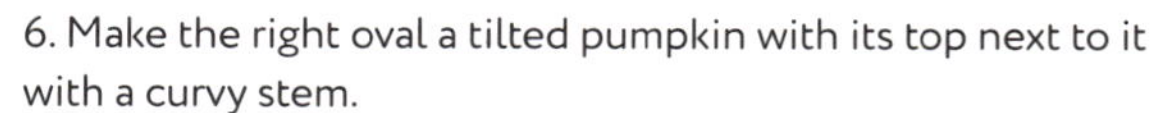

5. Add a ghost behind the left pumpkin with its hand holding the stem.

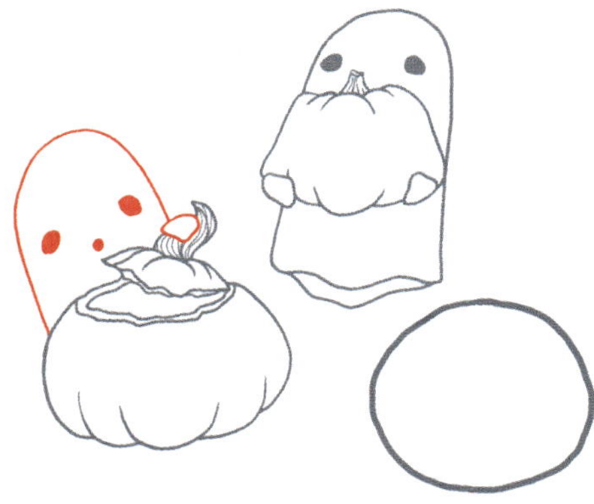

6. Make the right oval a tilted pumpkin with its top next to it with a curvy stem.

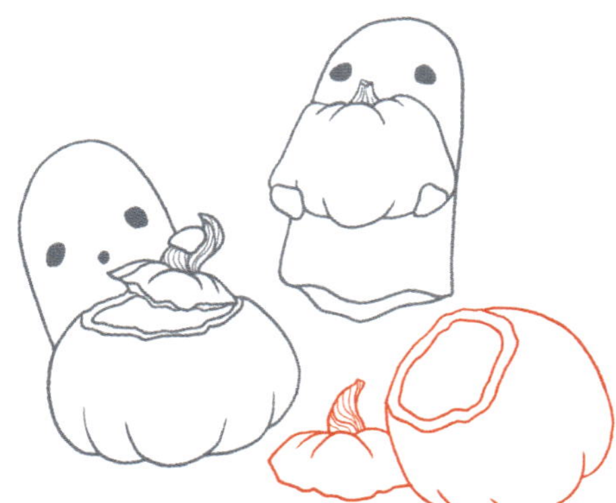

7. Add the profile of a carved face on the bottom-right pumpkin. Draw a ghost's hand holding a knife speared in the pumpkin.

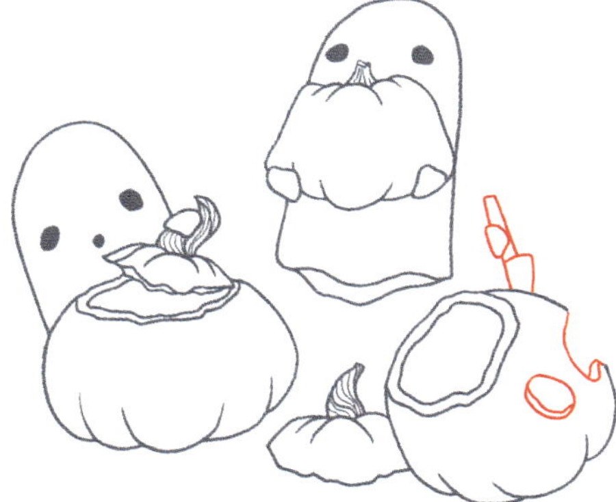

8. Add the final ghost, holding the knife. Let its sheet drape along the ground.

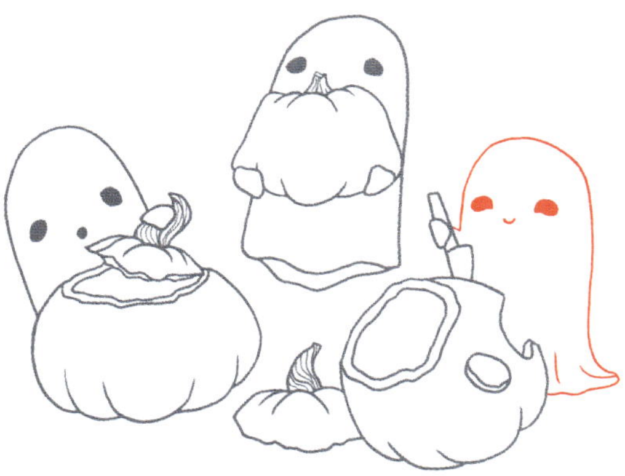

9. Cleanly trace your sketch with pencil on watercolor paper before inking.

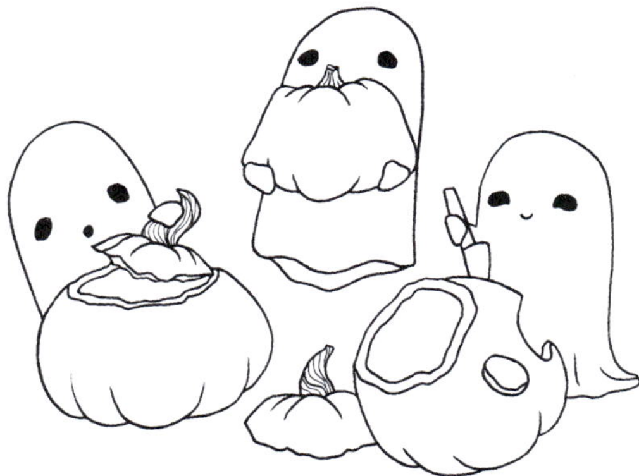

10. I used watercolors in orange for the pumpkins, green for the stems, and red and gray for the knife. Leave the ghosts white. Use stippling to add texture to the pumpkins.

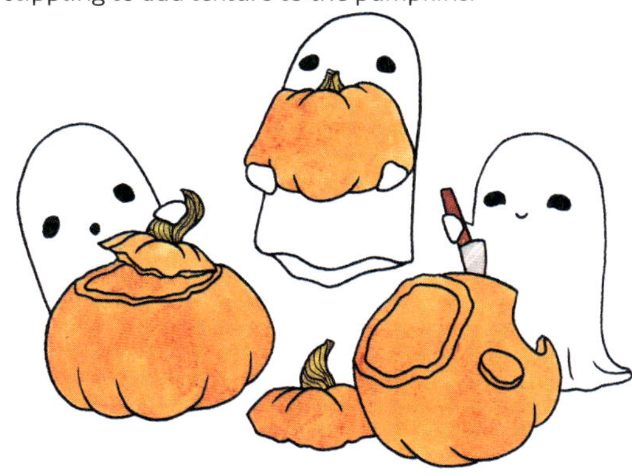

11. Add color to the ghosts and shade any underlayers. Also shade inside the pumpkins and on the stems.

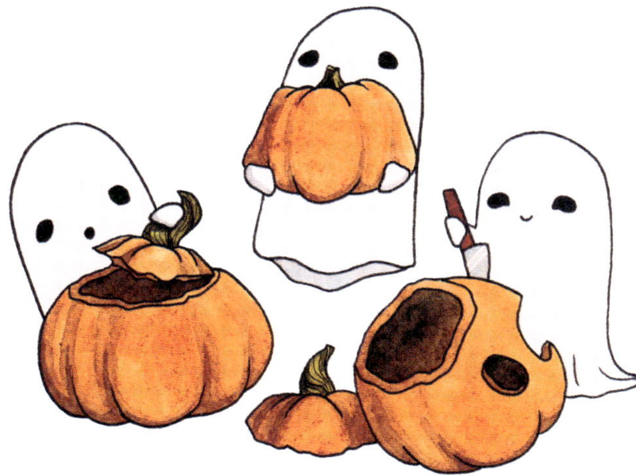

HALLOWEEN PORTRAIT

1. Draw a square with a smaller square in the top part.

2. Draw a mushroom-shaped skull on the right with solid circle eyes, an upside-down heart for the nose, and lines for the teeth.

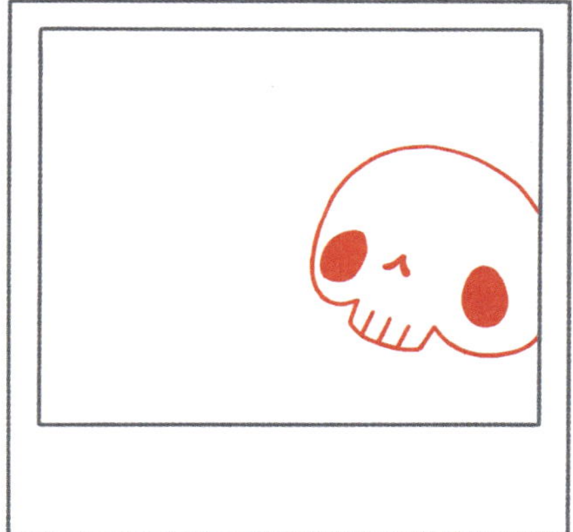

3. Add a bee costume around the skull with ovals and circles for the antennae and curved lines for the shirt.

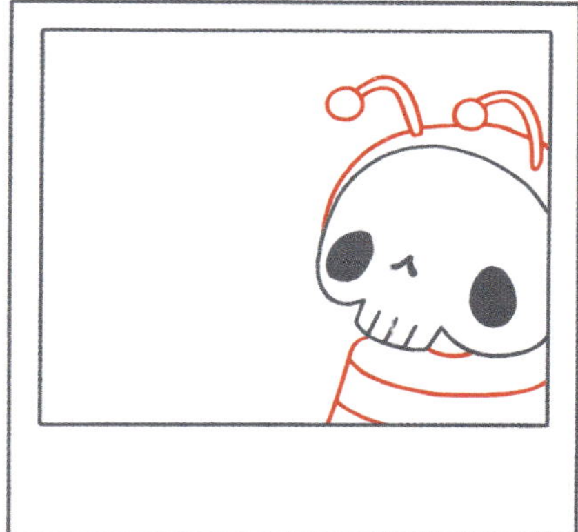

4. On the left, draw a smiling face with fangs.

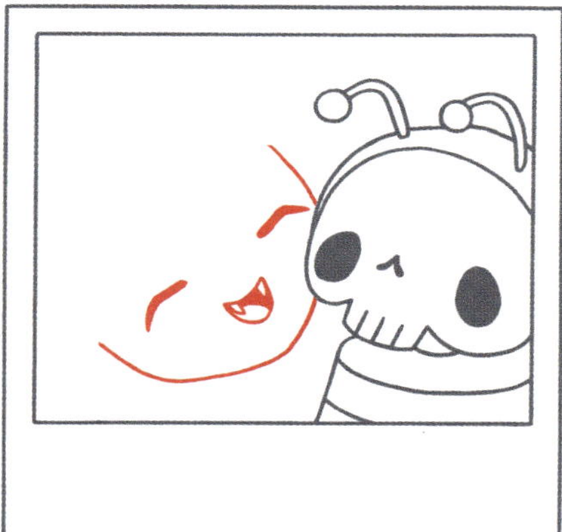

5. To the face, add an ear, round glasses, and lines for the shoulders.

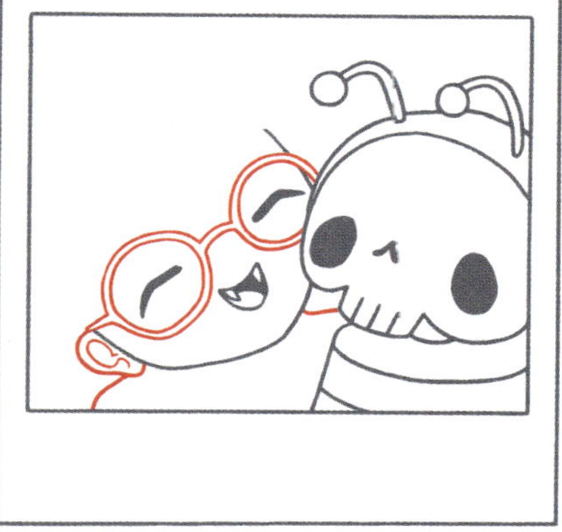

6. Draw slicked-down hair with the bangs curved up. Add two triangle ears on a headband.

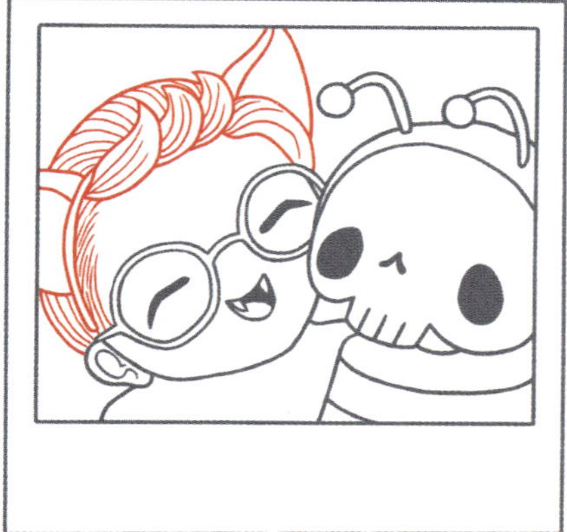

7. Write "Happy Halloween!" on the bottom, underneath the photo.

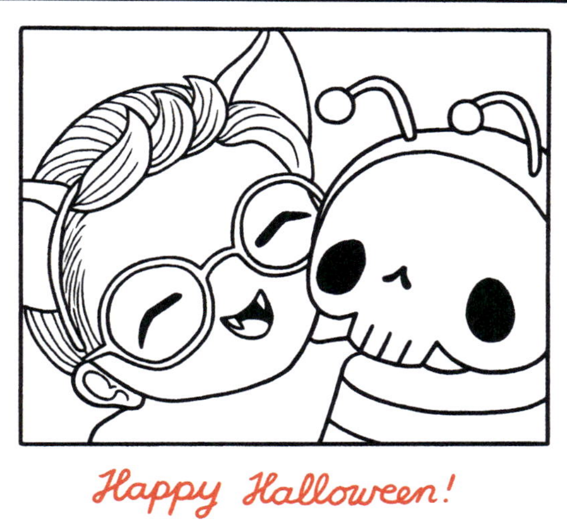

8. Cleanly trace your sketch with pencil on watercolor paper before inking.

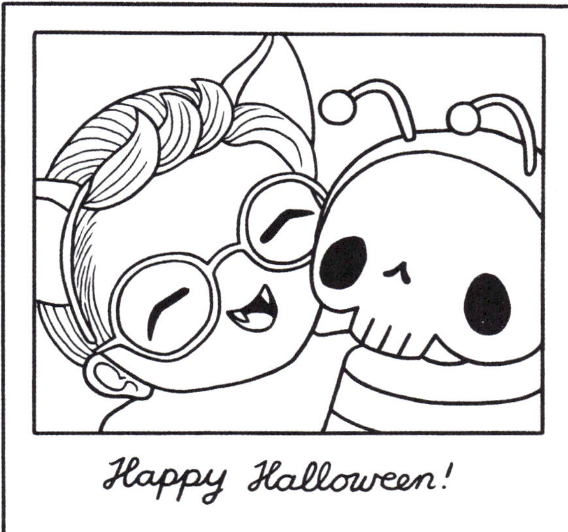

9. I used watercolors to make the background of the photo orange, the bee costume yellow and black, and the boy's cat ears pink, but you can color your drawing however you'd like!

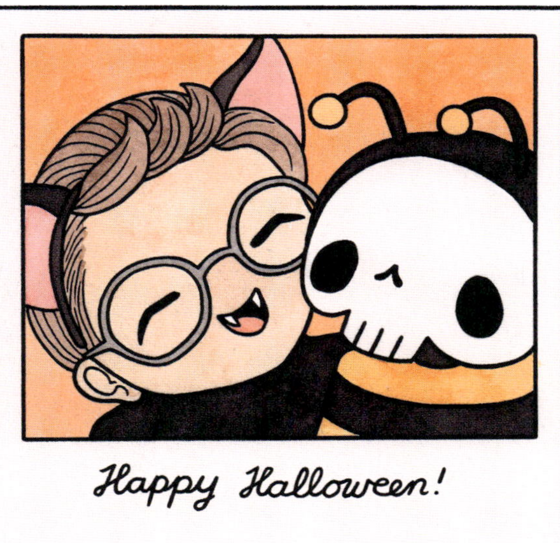

10. Use a thin brush or pen to add lines of texture to the hair. With a grayish-brown color, add shading.

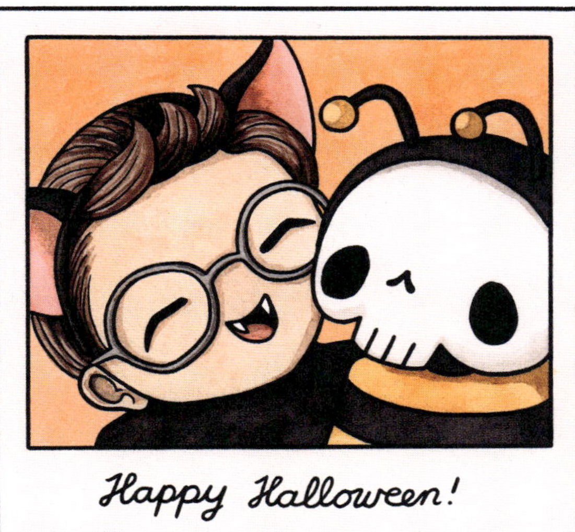

MERRY CREEPMAS

1. Sketch the basic shape of a figure with an oval head and a rectangle body.

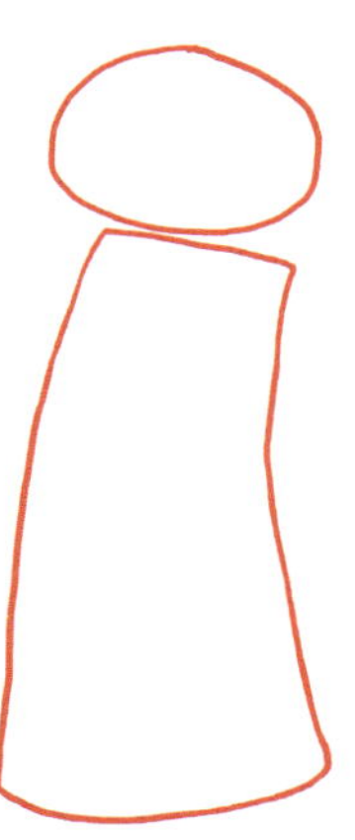

2. Draw the left arm with a curved line and the right arm bent in a V. Add oval hands.

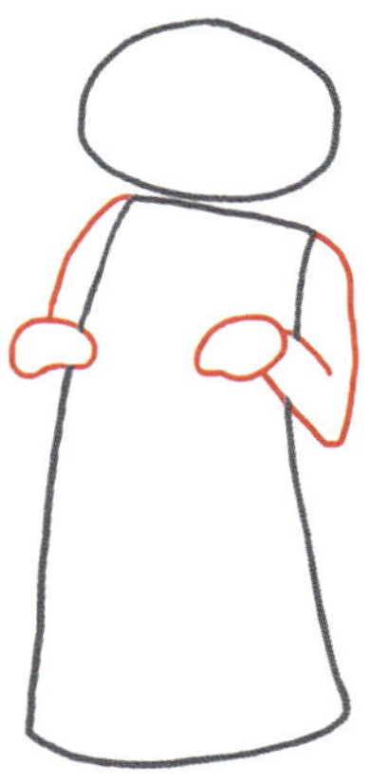

3. Make the face a mushroom-shaped skull. Add solid circle eyes, an upside-down heart for the nose, and lines for the teeth.

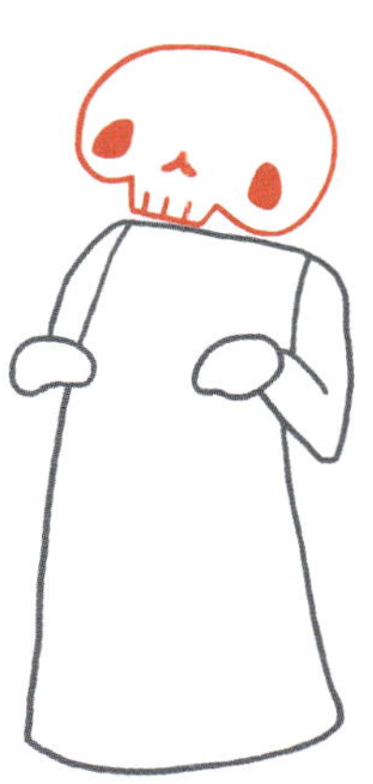

4. Add a floppy Christmas hat with short lines for the furry band and poof at the tip.

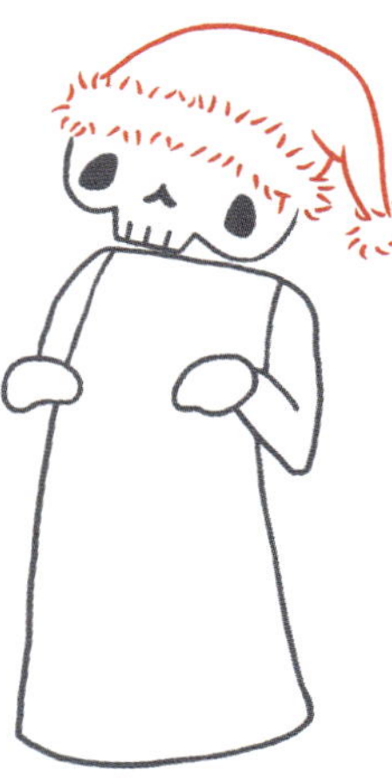

5. Between the hands, draw a long list with a curved rectangle with the ends folded over.

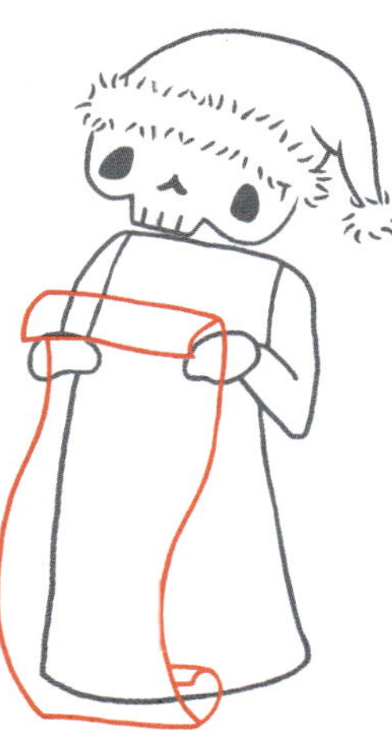

6. Draw bony hands holding the sides of the paper. Remember that each finger is made up of three sections.

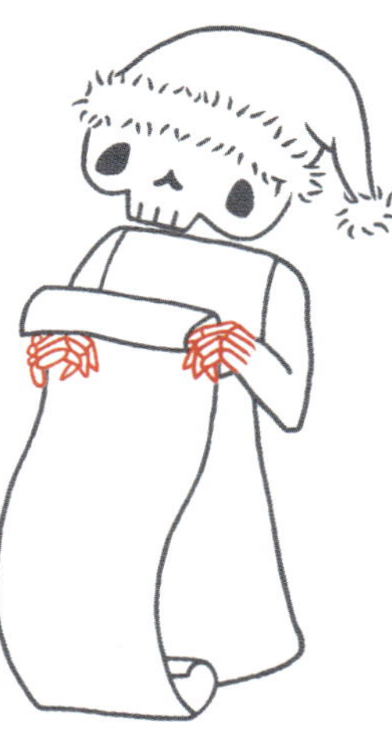

7. Draw sleeves along the arms and add a cloak around the shoulders. Add furry trim to the wrists and on the trim of the cloak.

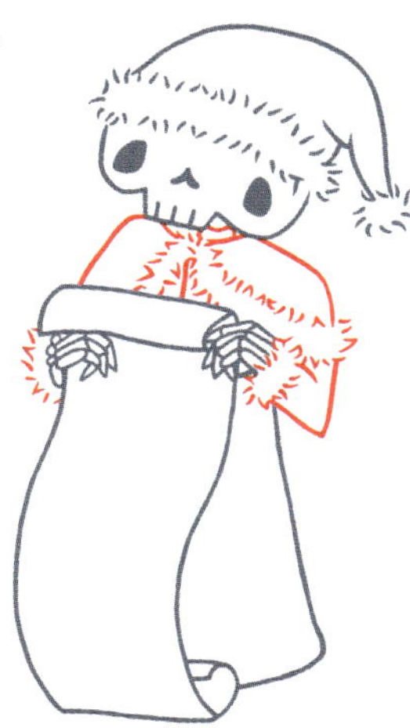

8. Add a belt and the bottom half of the robe with furry trim.

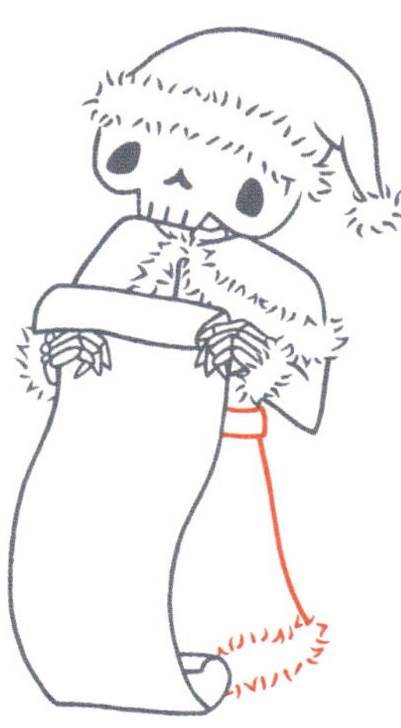

9. Draw a big bag of presents on the right using a lumpy oval with the top cinched by a tie.

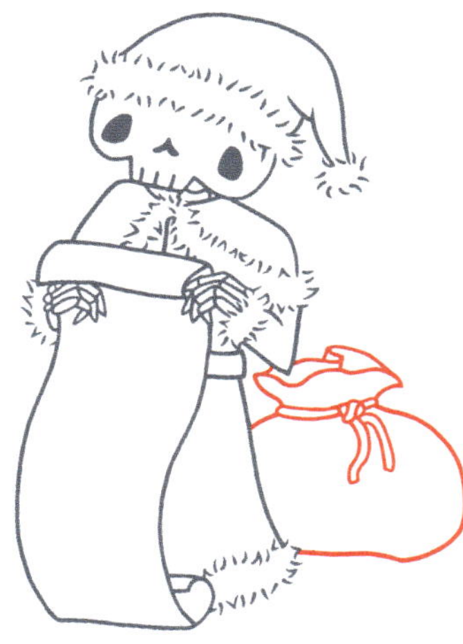

10. Cleanly trace your sketch with pencil on watercolor paper before inking.

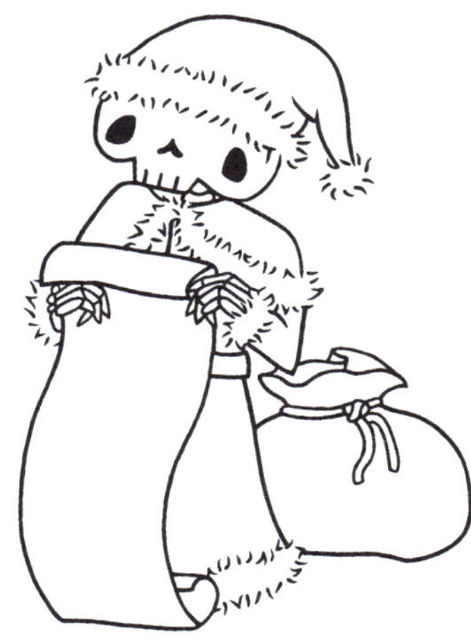

11. I used watercolors in red for the traditional Santa's outfit, cream for the paper, brown for the bag of presents, and yellow for the ribbon. Add shading on the skeleton, paper, and bag.

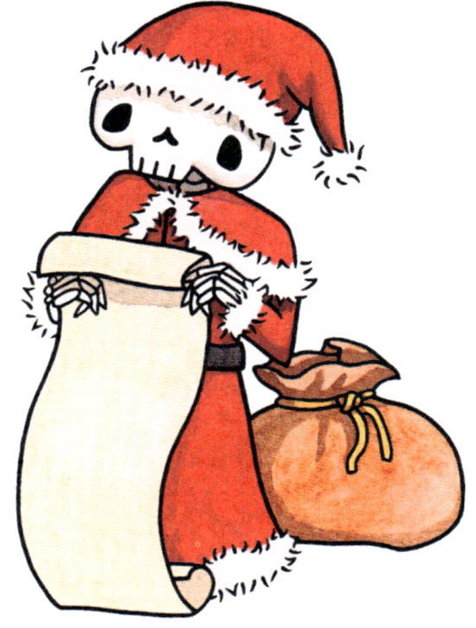

WITCH'S PUMPKIN STACK

1. Draw the basic shapes of three pumpkins with the topmost one tilted and hovering above. Add a witch on the right with a triangle hat on a circle head and two trapezoids for the dress.

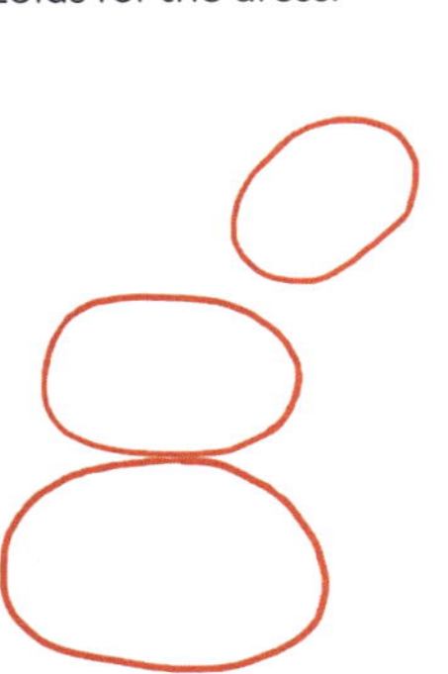 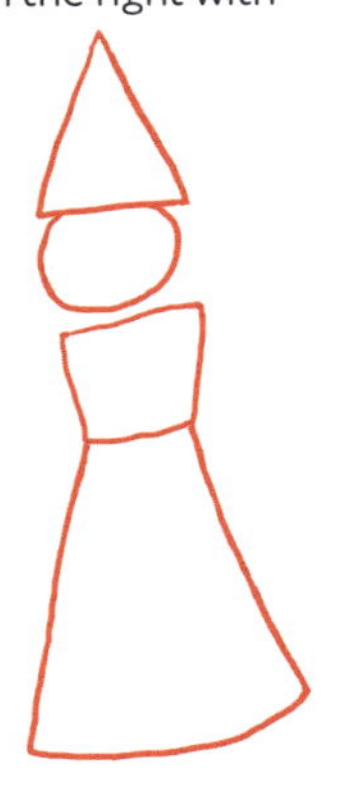

2. Give your witch a face, a wide-rimmed pointy hat, and curly hair. Add pupils to the eyes and fine strands of hair.

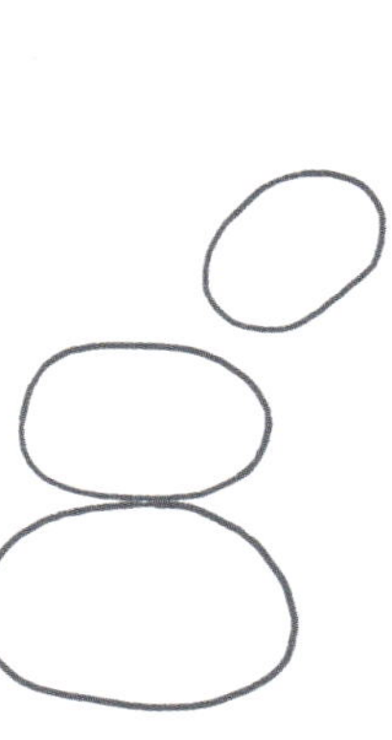 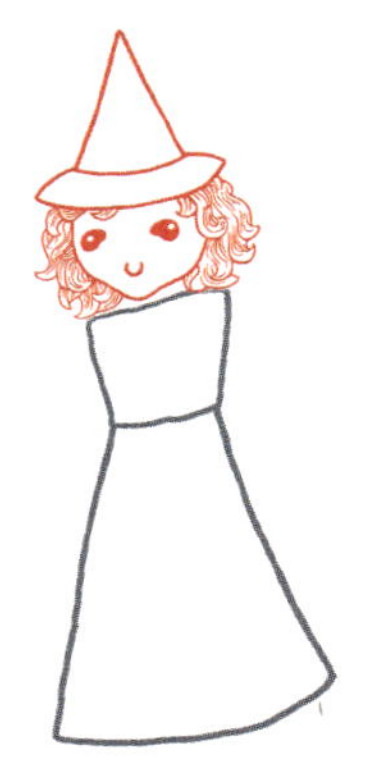

3. Draw the witch's dress with a tank top, a rectangle waistband, and a long skirt with vertical lines for texture.

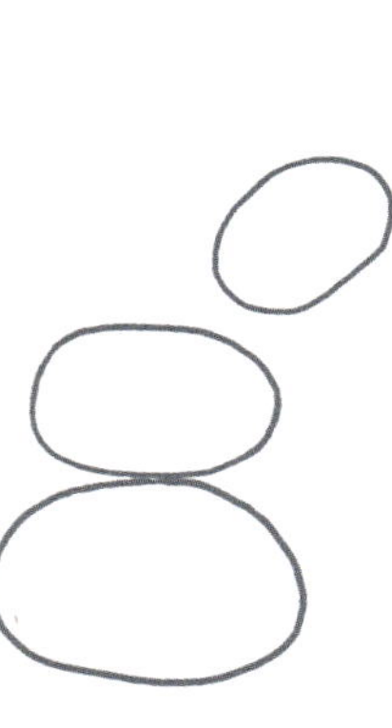 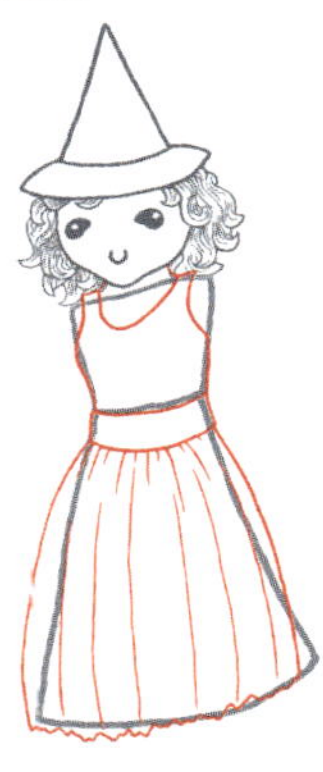

4. Draw the arms and hands. Make the arms bend at the elbow, with the right also bent at the wrist. Draw a simple wand in the left hand, pointed at the pumpkins.

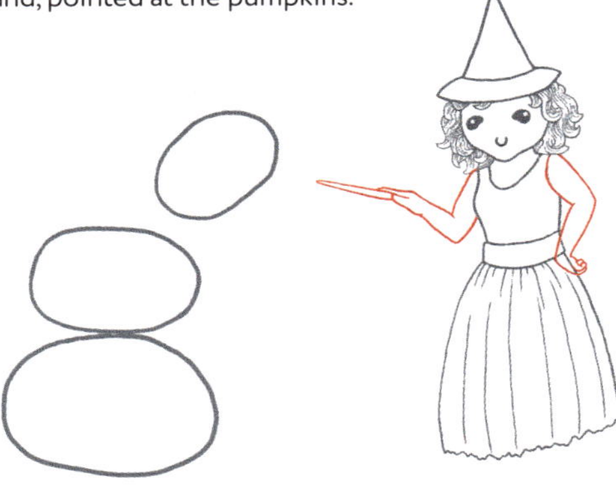

5. Draw lines for the lower legs underneath the skirt with heeled shoes.

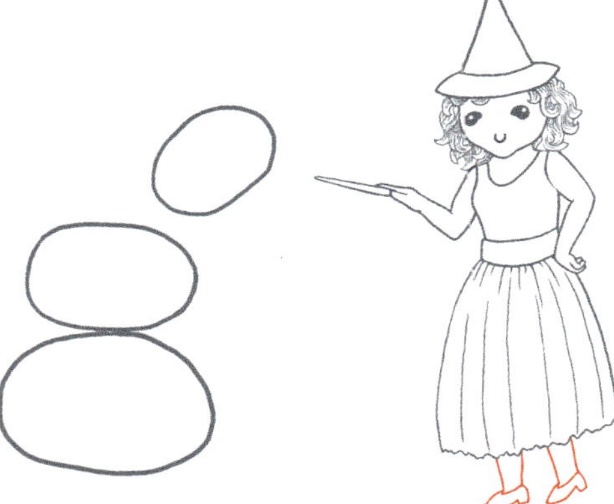

6. Draw the bottom pumpkin with its eyes looking up, a triangle nose, and a jagged mouth.

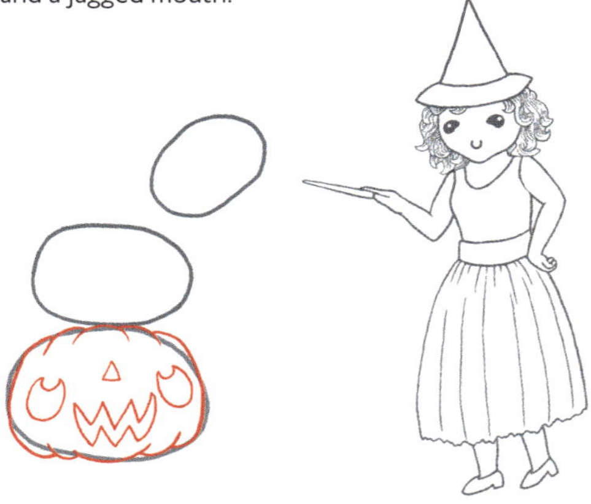

7. Draw the middle pumpkin with two upside-down heart eyes, a fanged smile, and a short stem on top. Add accent marks around the bottom.

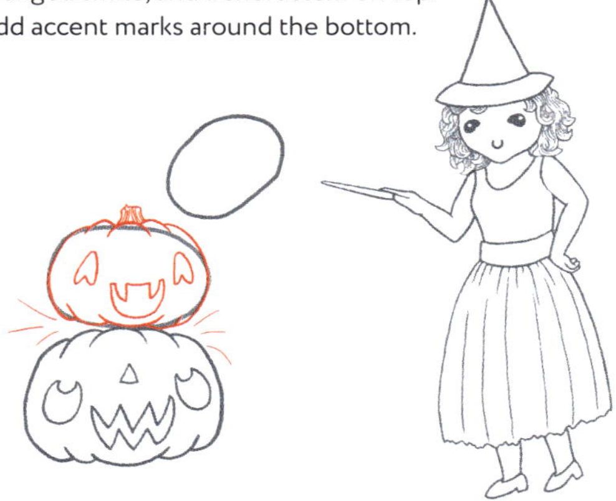

8. Draw the top pumpkin with a scared expression and a curvy stem.

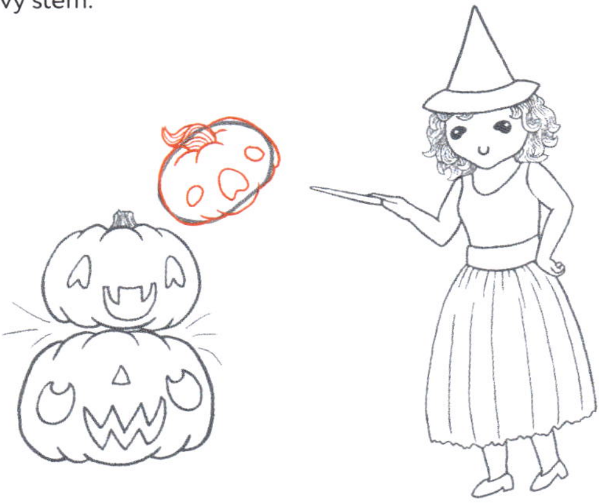

9. Add some bushes to the background with abstract shapes.

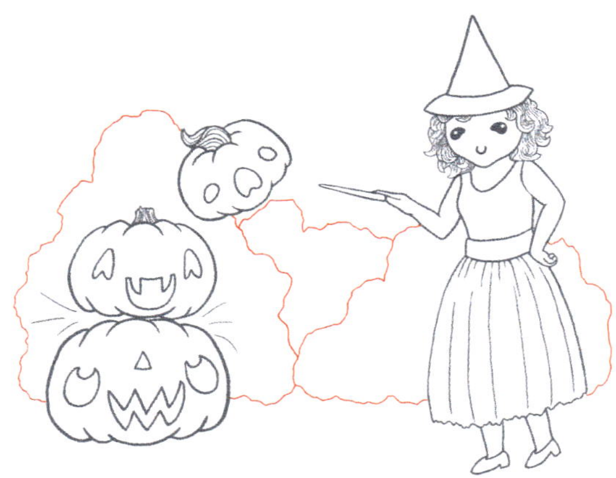

10. Cleanly trace your sketch with pencils of varying lead point sizes on watercolor paper before inking.

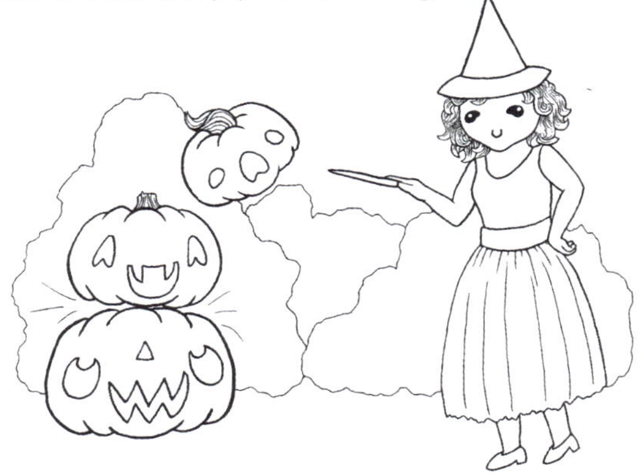

11. Add shading. The light is in the top right so shade on the bottom left of the bushes, witch, and pumpkins with diluted ink or watercolor.

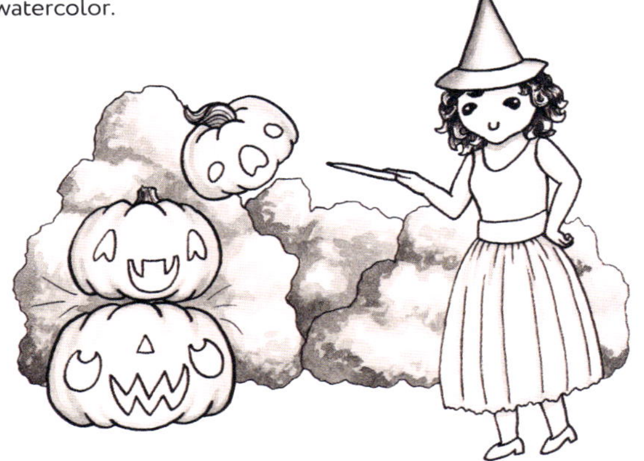

12. I used a bright color palette of pink, green, orange, and yellow to add color, but you can color it however you'd like!

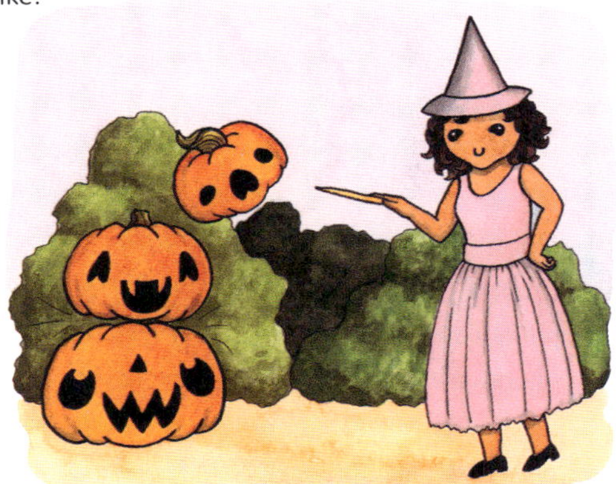

SPOOKMAS TREE

1. Draw a three-tiered Christmas tree that bends slightly to the left. Use one triangle and two rectangles with scalloped bottom edges.

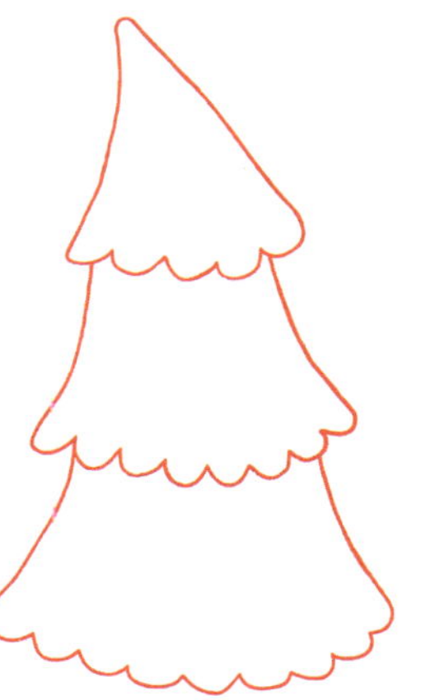

2. On the top, draw a bat ornament using an oval head with a dip in the top, two circle eyes, and two arched wings with a scalloped bottom edge.

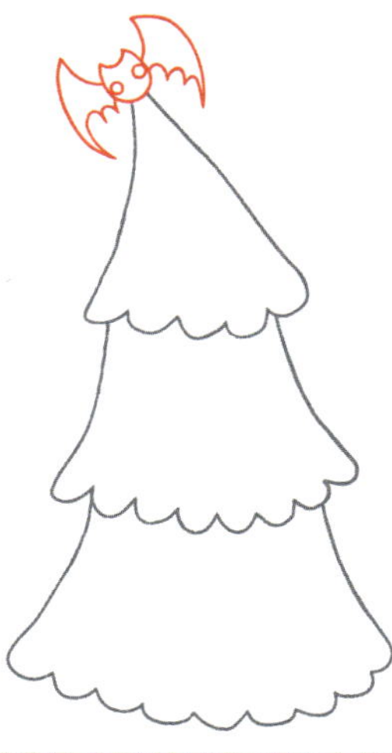

3. Add bone garland laid diagonally on each tier.

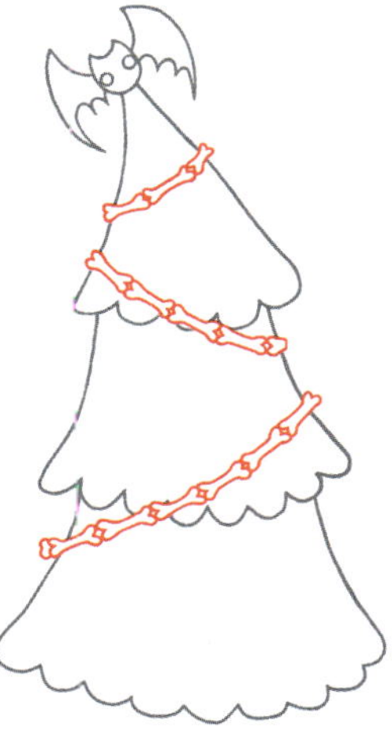

4. Draw strings of lights (minus the lights) laid horizontally on each tier. Add marks for where the lights will go.

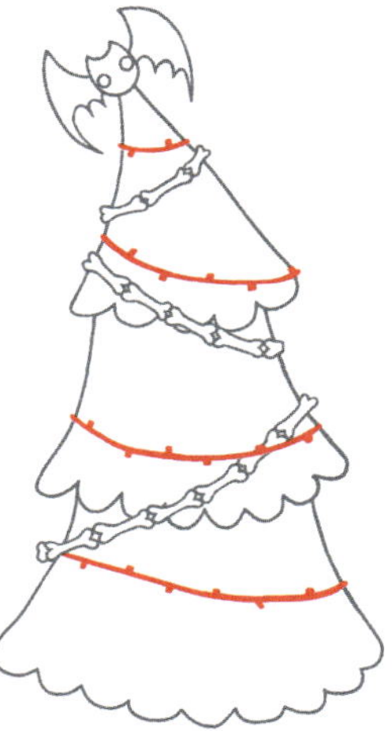

5. Draw a ghost on the left with a happy facial expression. Add an oval arm holding a pumpkin-shaped ornament.

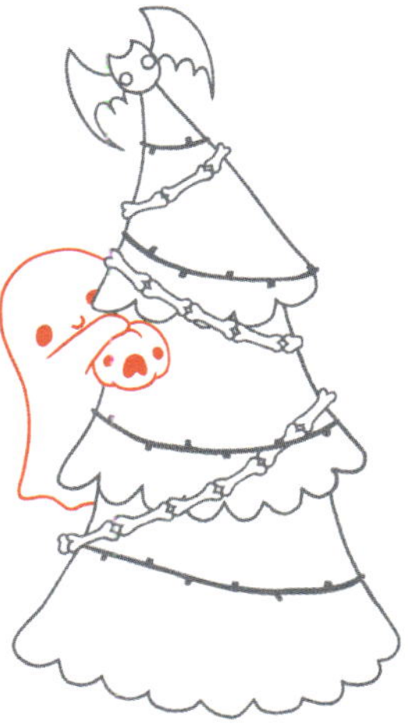

6. Draw a second ghost doing the same on the right but make its back facing us.

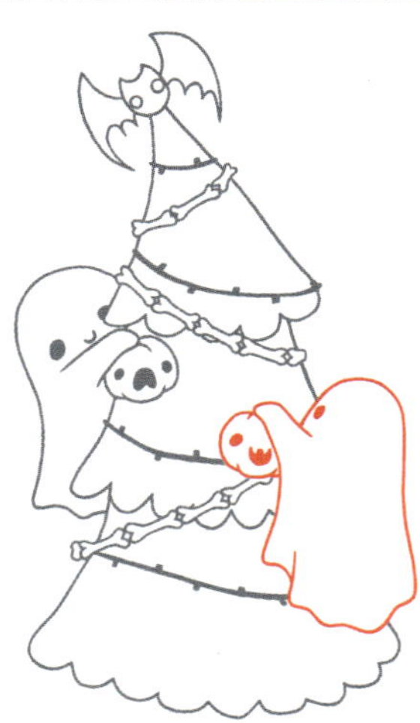

7. Add two more pumpkin ornaments with different facial expressions on the tree.

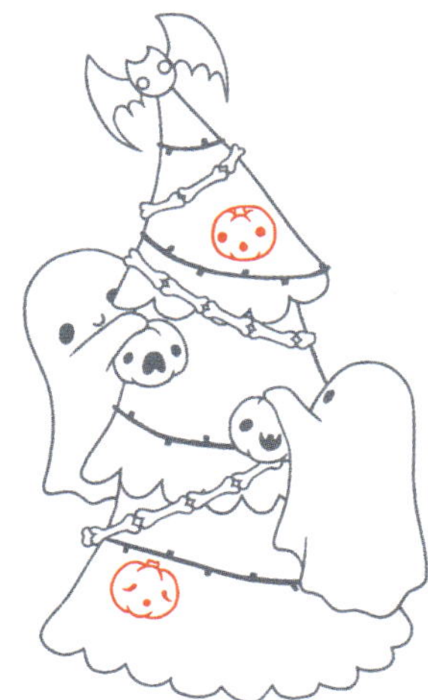

8. Cleanly trace your sketch with pencil on watercolor paper before inking.

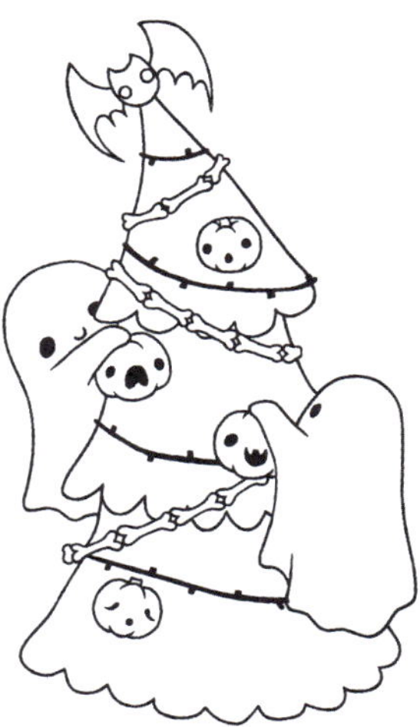

9. I used watercolors to make the pumpkins orange and added purple circles around the marks for the lights.

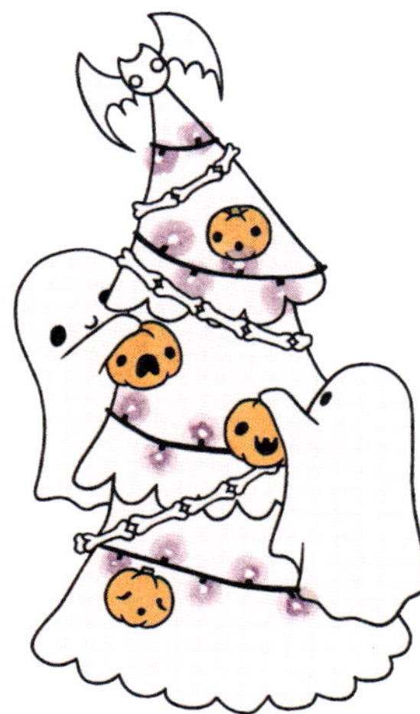

10. I made the tree and bat gray, leaving brighter areas around the lights.

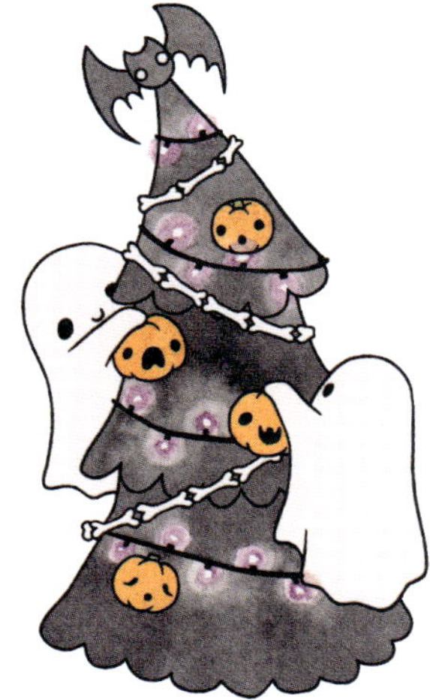

11. Add a striped texture to the tree, again avoiding the light spots. Add stripy shading near the layers of the tree, but keep the shading on the bat, ghosts, and pumpkins smooth.

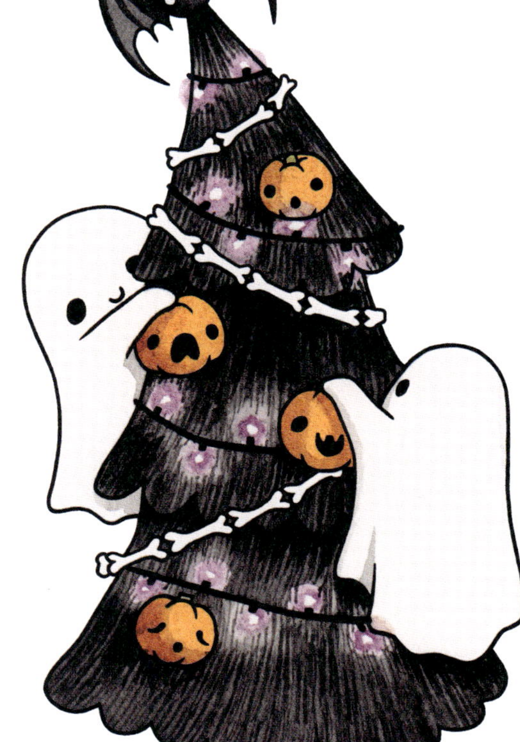

LEAF JUMPERS

1. Use jagged lines to draw a big leaf pile.

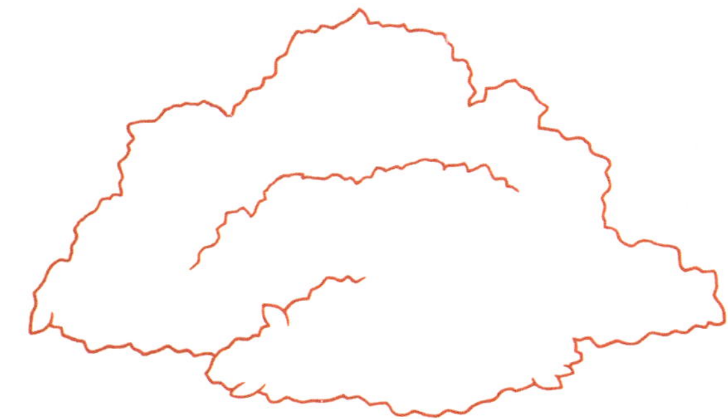

2. Draw a skeleton hiding in the middle with a partial round head, eyes, and hands. Add some leaves on top of the head.

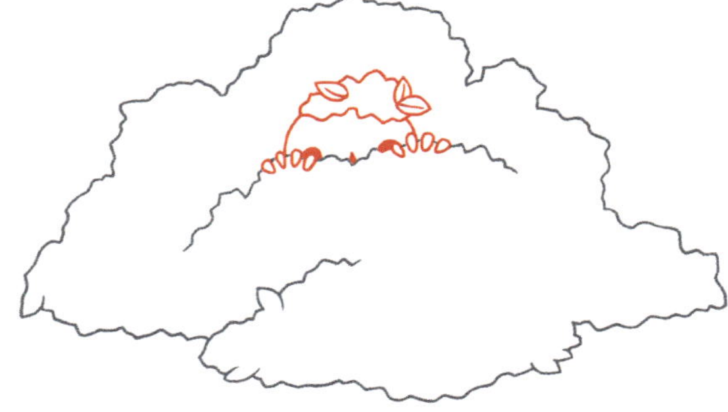

3. Sketch a figure with raised hands in the background with a circle head and lines for the torso, arms, and hands.

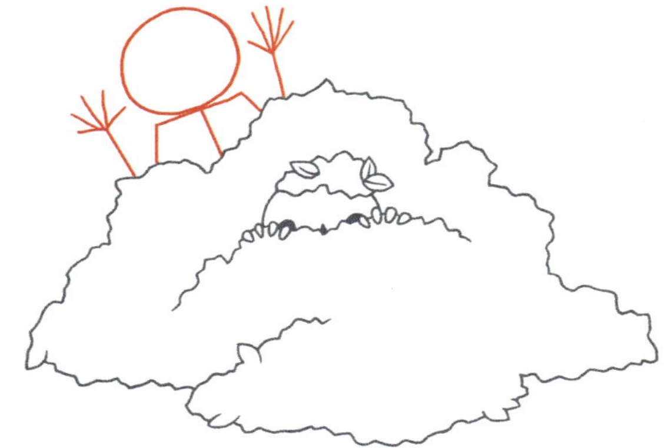

4. Make a mushroom-shaped skull. Add solid circle eyes, an upside-down heart for the nose, and lines for the teeth.

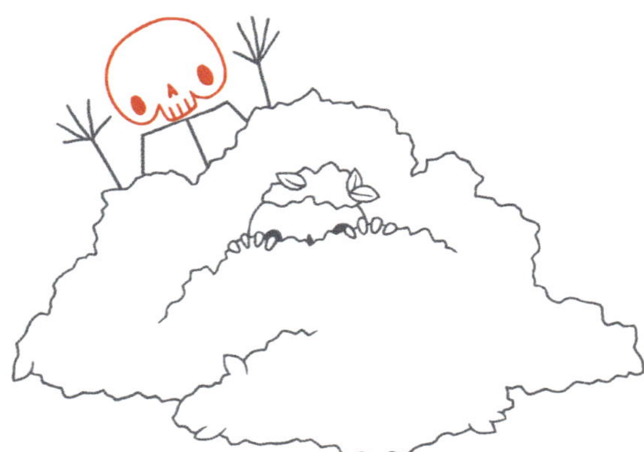

5. Draw a sweater with a thick collar and cuffs at the wrists. Add a rib cage on the front.

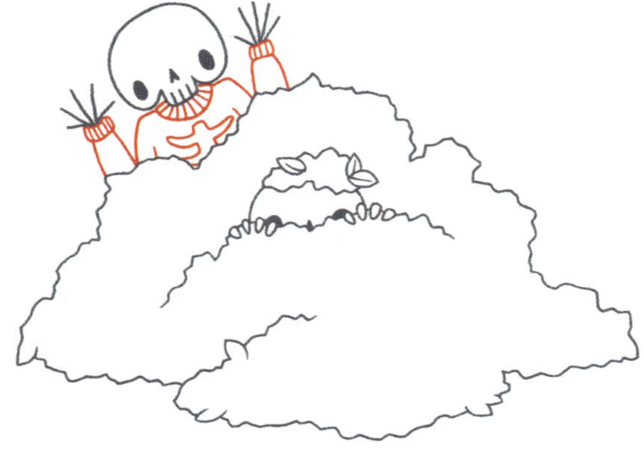

6. Make the hands with five skeletal fingers. Be careful and make the tips short so they look slightly bent like claws.

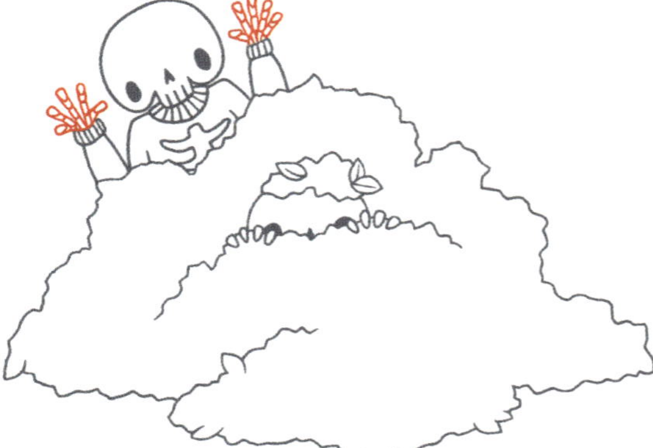

7. Add some detailed leaves to the leaf pile.

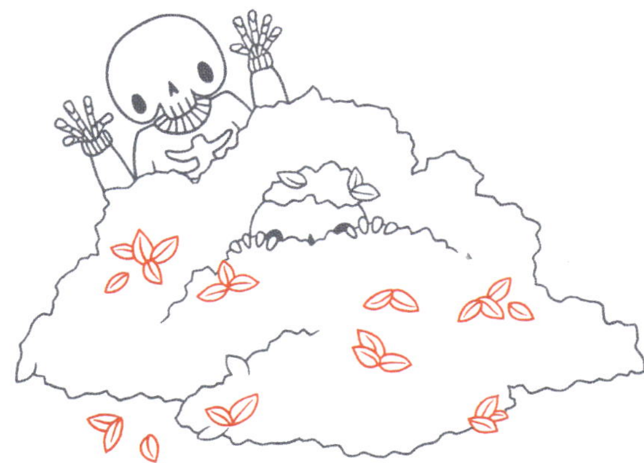

8. Draw an ornate fence on the right with arrowhead spikes and pointed ovals for the bars.

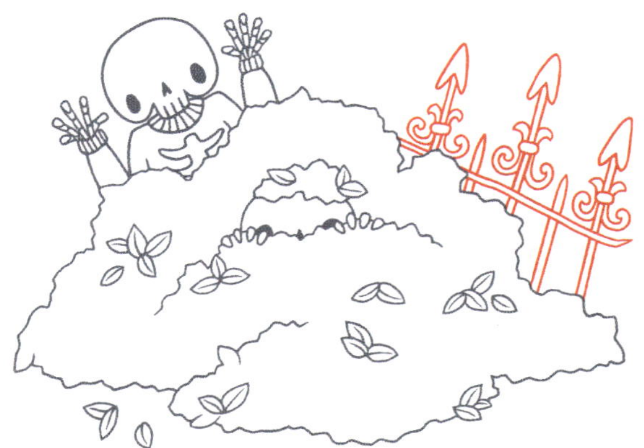

9. Cleanly trace your sketch with pencil on watercolor paper before inking.

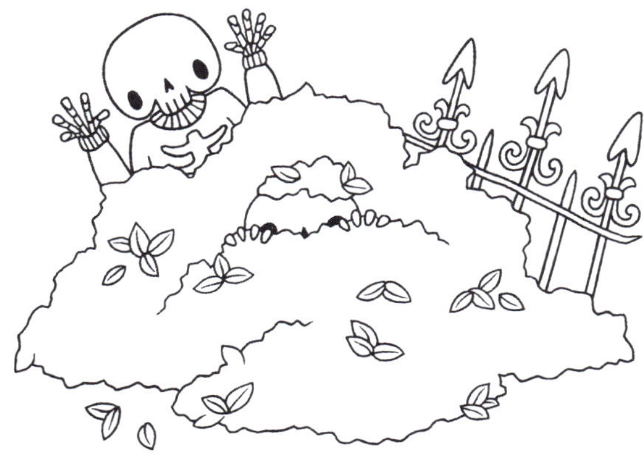

10. I used watercolors to make the leaf pile orange and the skeleton's sweater and the gate black.

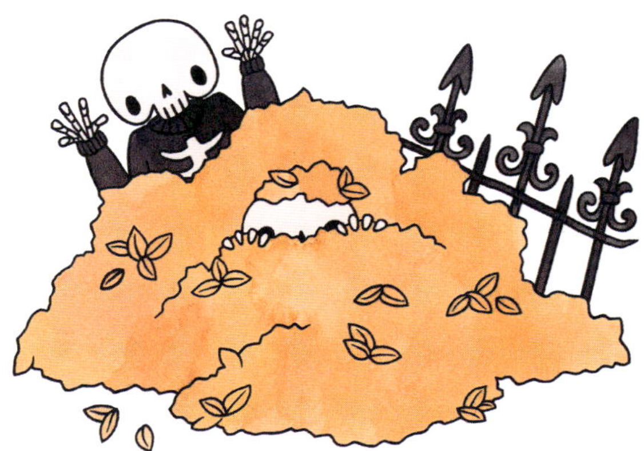

11. With a medium round brush or pen, scribble texture on the leaf pile. Add shading to the gate and skeletons for depth.

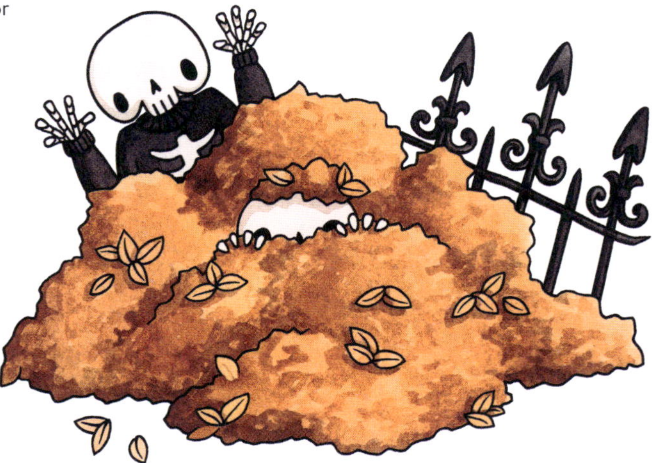

WINDOW WATCHING

1. Draw an arched window. Use two rectangles for the sides, a curved oval for the top, and five rectangles for the bricks on the bottom.

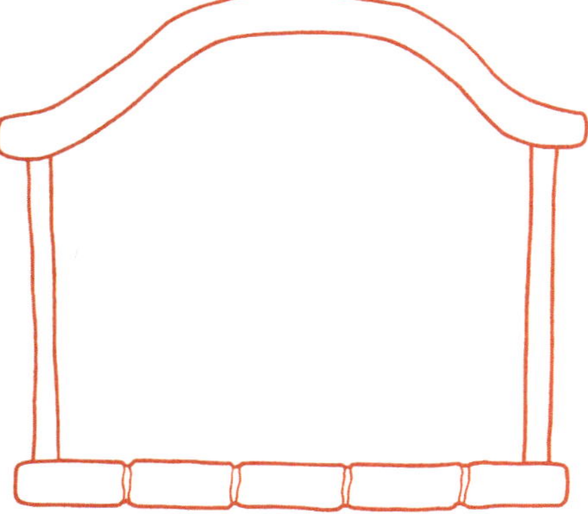

2. Add curtains inside the window using curved lines and a rectangle for a band at the middle.

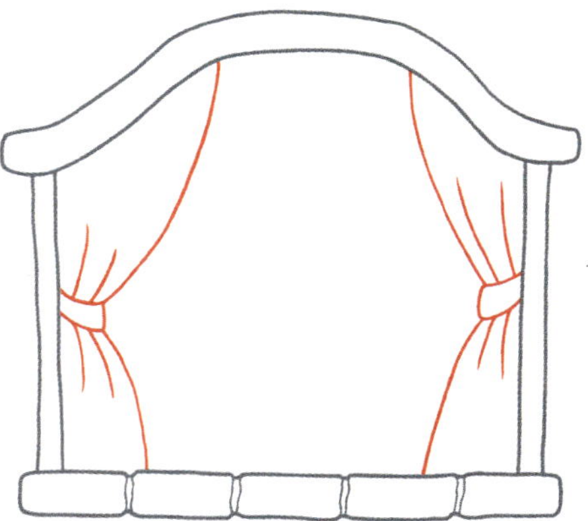

3. Draw a sleeping cat on the windowsill. Give it a rounded head, triangle ears, and a rounded body with the tail lying flat in front of the body.

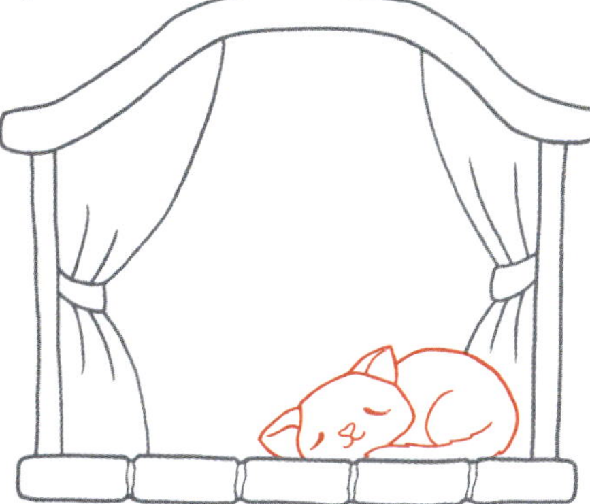

4. Draw two identical ghosts hanging from strings. Give them each two eyes and add a small bow if you'd like!

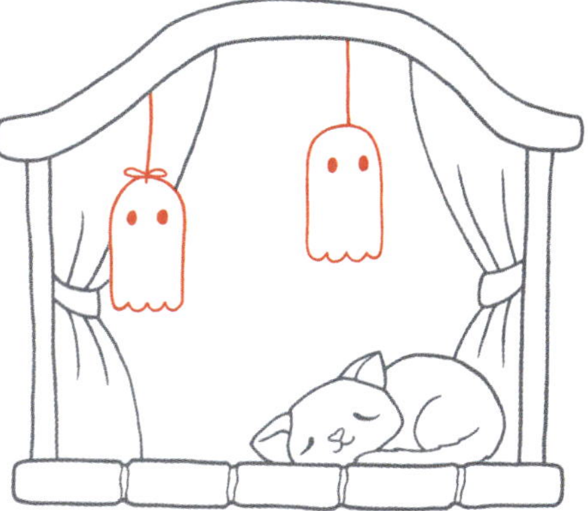

5. Sketch a torso and hips with a raised arm between the hanging ghosts.

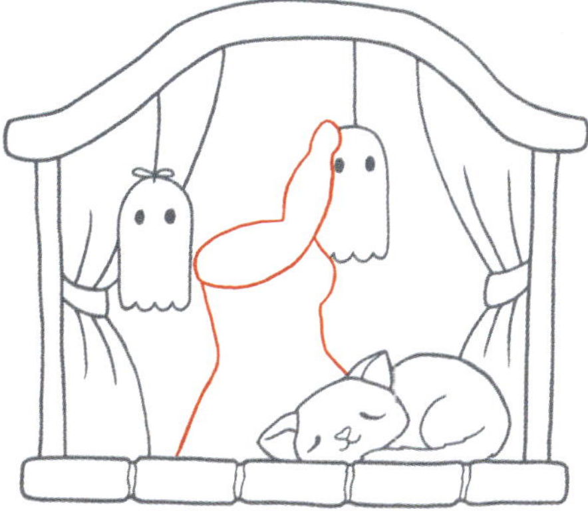

6. Draw a sleeve that has a cuff at the elbow and add detail to the arm and hand. The hand should be pinching a string tied into a bow.

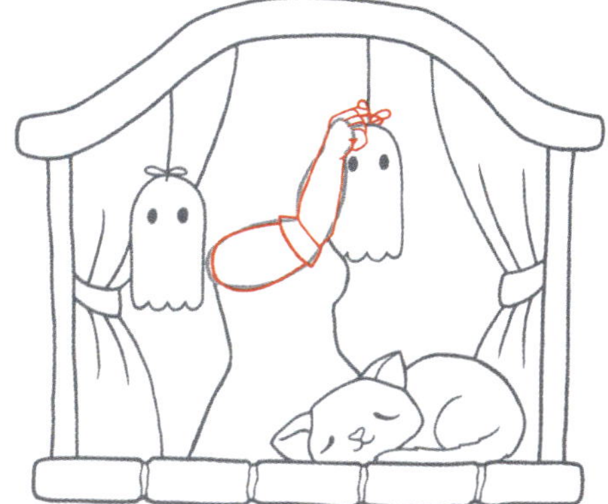

7. Add a head to the body with a smiling face and a witch's hat. Give her some curled bangs and strands down her back.

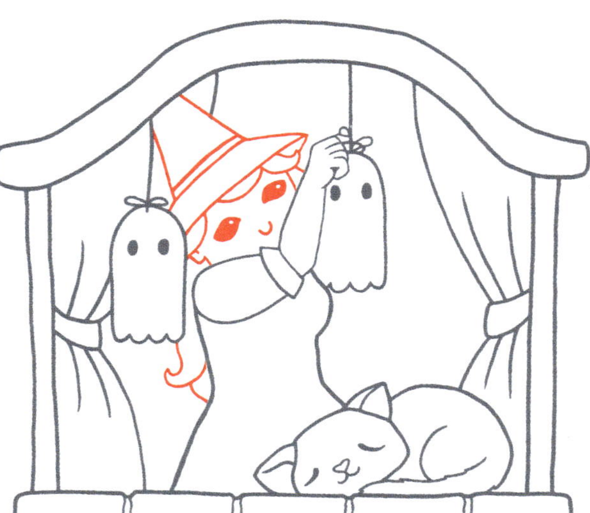

8. Draw a simple dress with a belt.

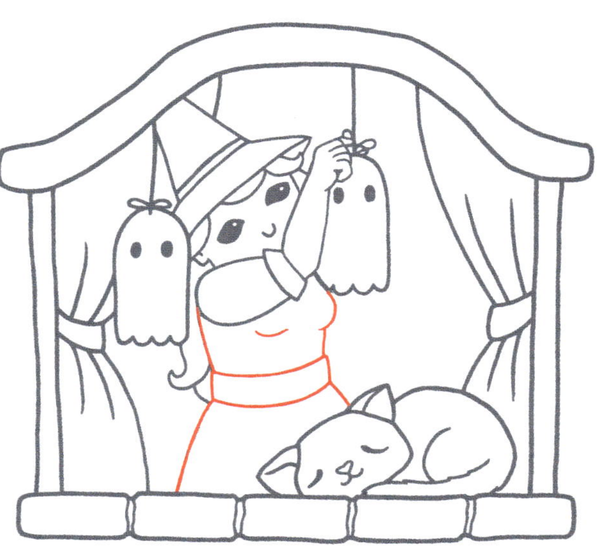

9. Cleanly trace your sketch with pencil on watercolor paper before inking.

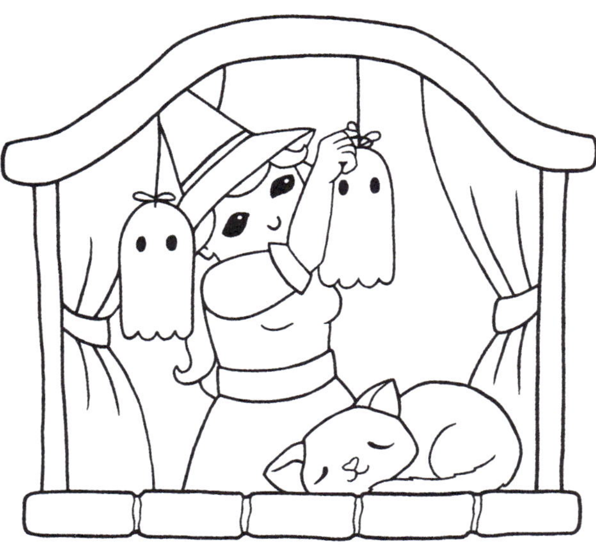

10. I used watercolors to make the witch's outfit black and orange, the curtains purple, and the cat a light yellow. I made the bricks black and the wood frame brown. With a fine brush or pen, add texture to the witch's hair and the cat with light lines. Add shading on the witch, curtains, cat, and window frame.

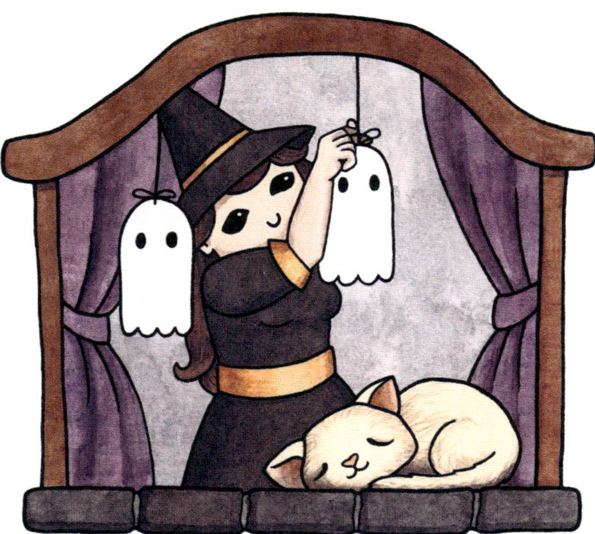

HAUNTED SNOW GLOBE

1. Draw a circle with a curved rectangle underneath.

2. Sketch a house inside the circle with a rectangle base and a trapezoid roof. Add a rectangle with slanted sides for the trim. Then divide the roof into three sections and give the middle section a triangle top.

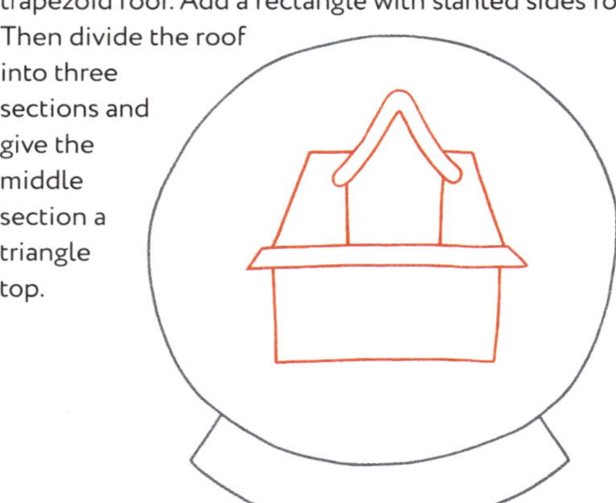

3. Add pillars with lines, a front porch with rectangles, and an arched doorway with double doors. Make one door closed and the other open. Add some details around the door.

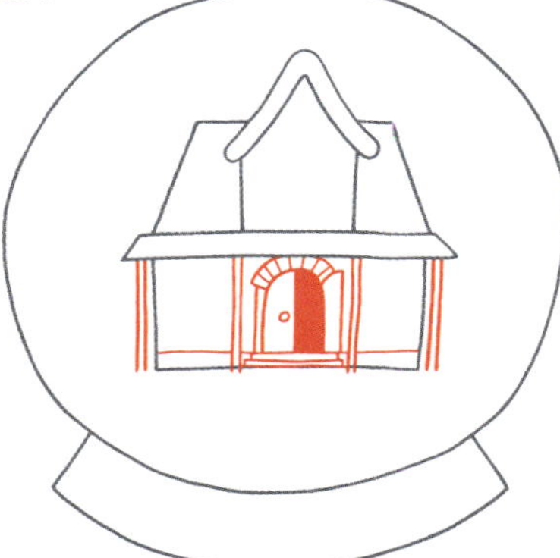

4. Add four arched windows to the house with oval windowsills and square details around the top.

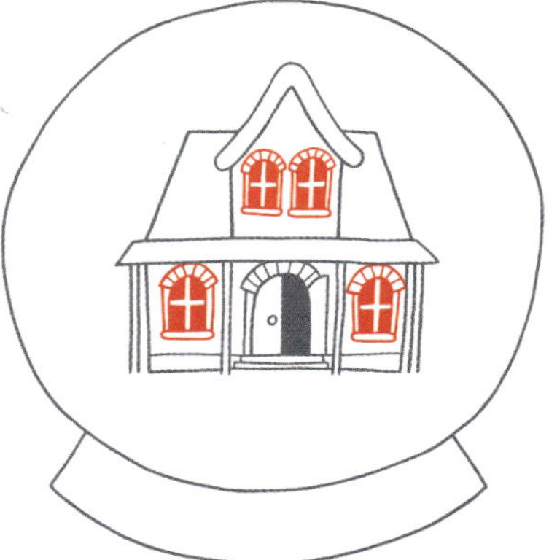

5. Place three pine trees in the background. Make them bend slightly to the sides.

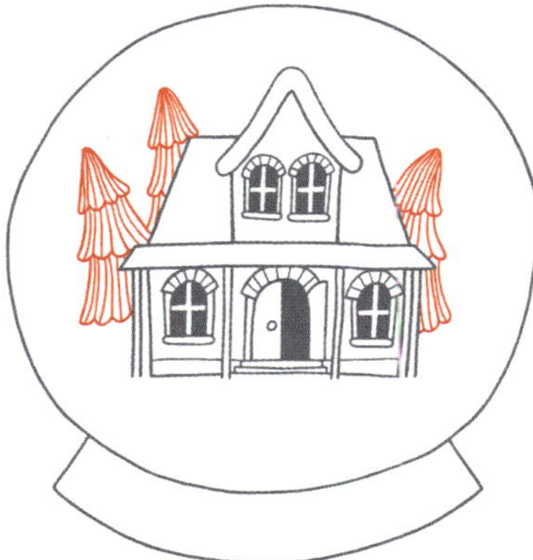

6. Add a wavy horizon line behind the house and a second line at the base of the house.

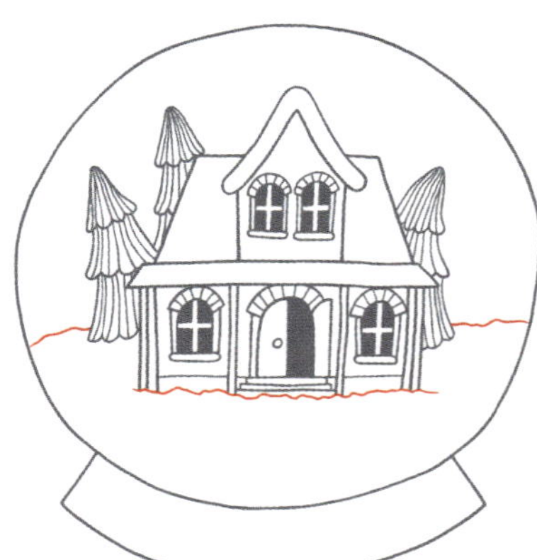

7. Draw piles of snow on top of the house and trees.

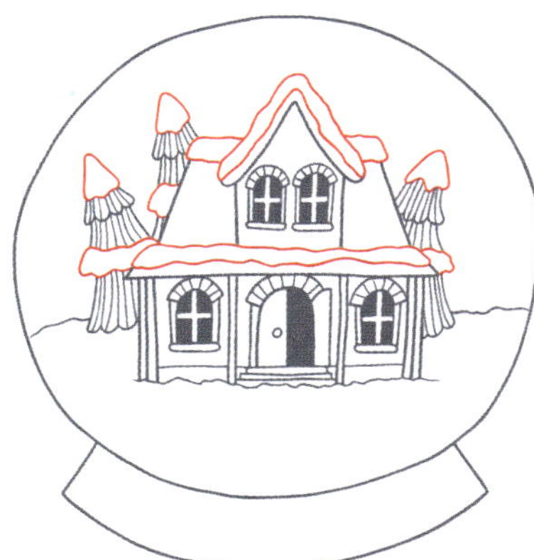

8. Draw three ghosts flying above the house. Make rounded bodies that taper into wisps at the ends.

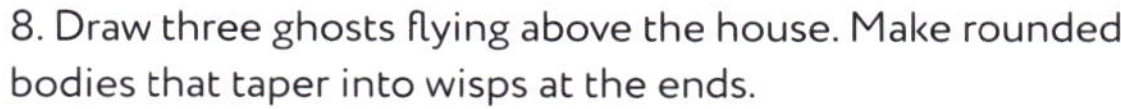
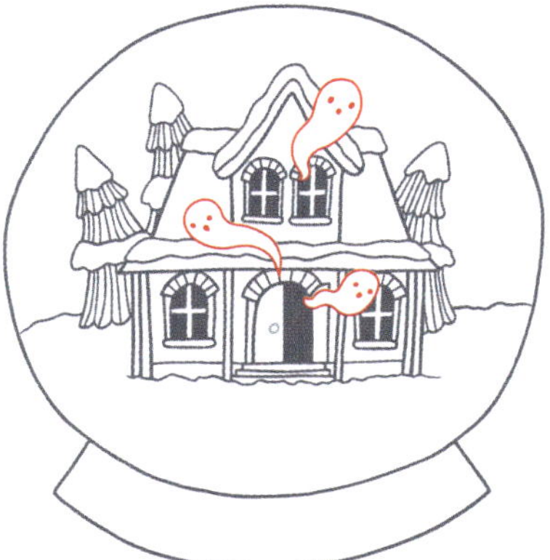

9. Cleanly trace your sketch with pencil on watercolor paper before inking.

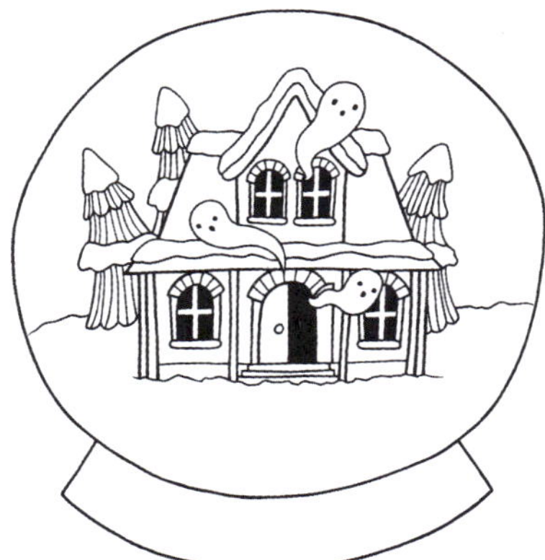

10. Color your drawing with shades of black and gray, leaving the ghosts and snow white.

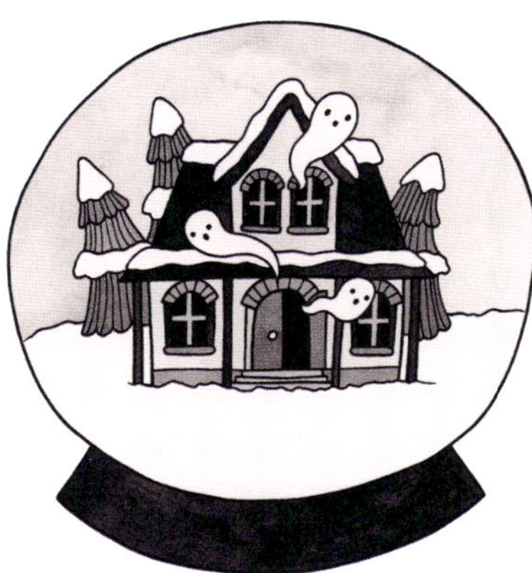

11. With a thin brush or pen, add more lines to the pine trees and detail the door. With white ink, add snowflakes floating around the house. Add shading to the scene inside the globe and around the inner edges of the globe.

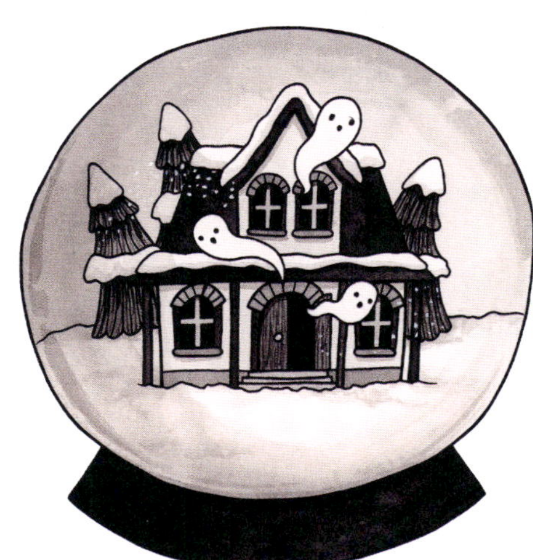

TEETHING TREATS

1. Sketch a round head with a rectangle body and a line for the neck.

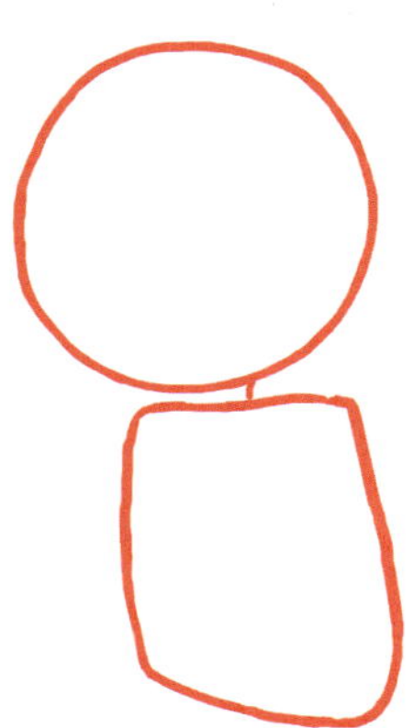

2. Use ovals for the arms, legs, hands, and feet.

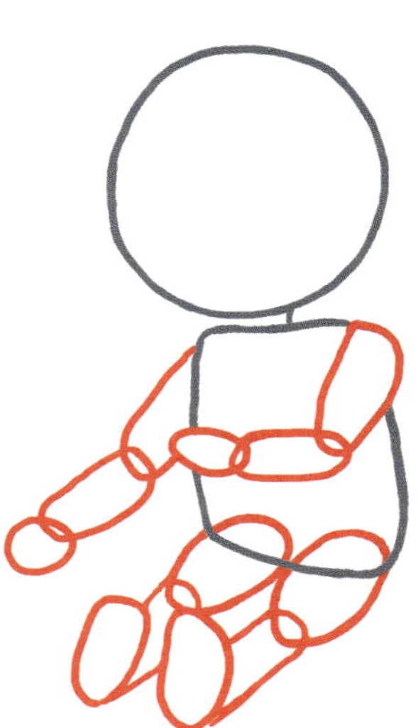

3. Detail the face with a happy, fanged smile. Give her short, straight hair and bangs.

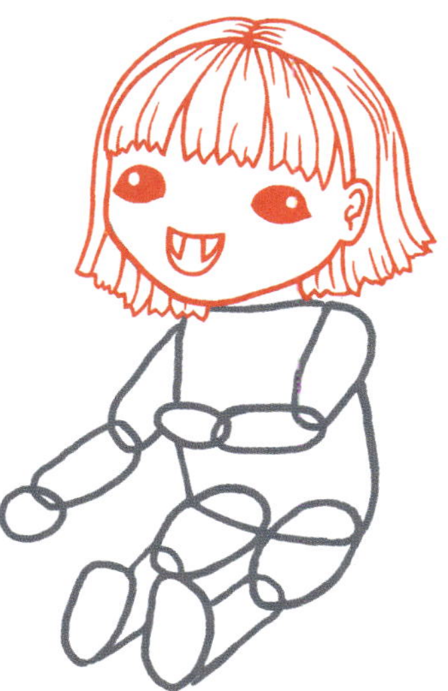

4. Draw the right arm bent to the left and the hand with the fingers slightly curled.

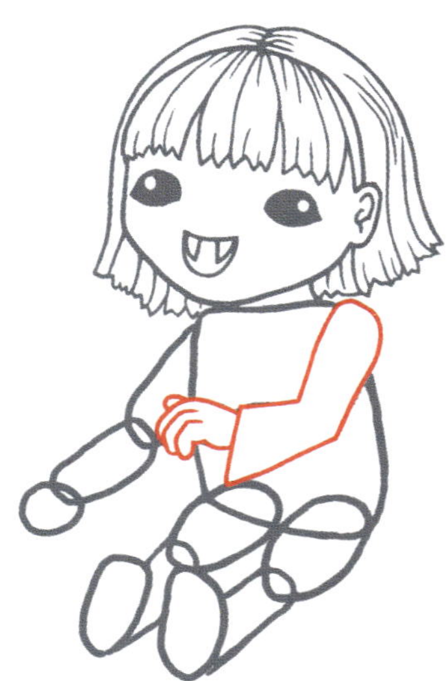

5. Draw a stuffed cat toy with a trapezoid head, triangle ears, rectangle body, and oval arms and legs. Use circles for the eyes and an X for the nose.

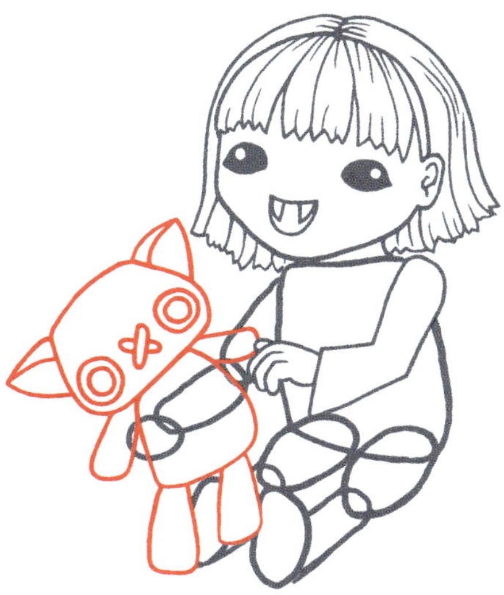

6. Dress the stuffed cat as a witch with a pointed hat, bow tie, and cloak.

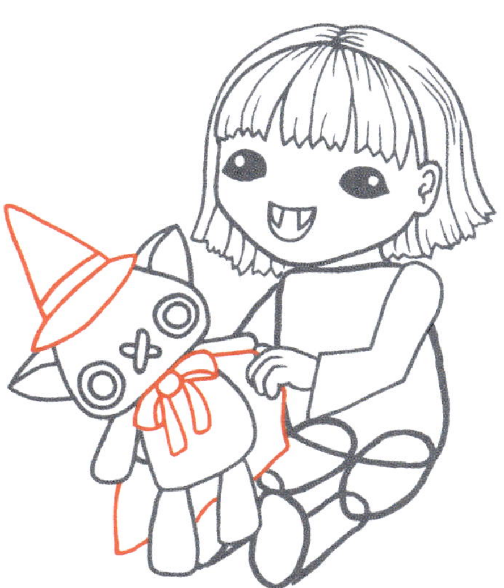

7. Draw the girl's arm and hand holding the toy and a simple dress with a shaped neckline.

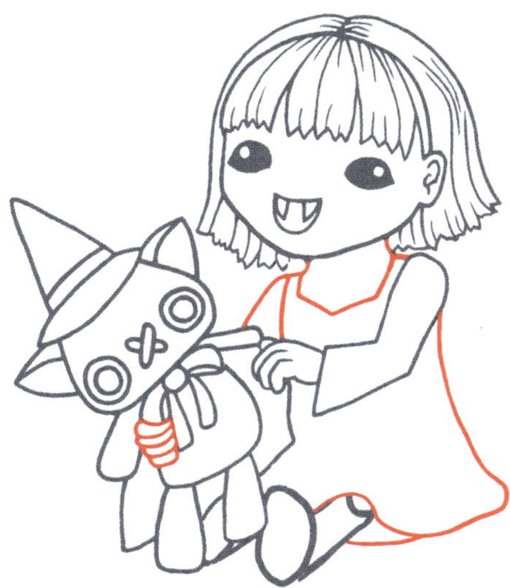

8. Draw her legs and the soles and profiles of the shoes.

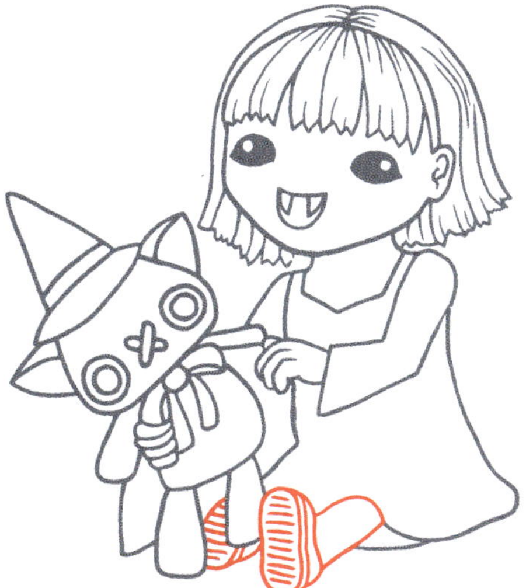

9. Add a bat-ear headband on the girl's head and a wing behind her back.

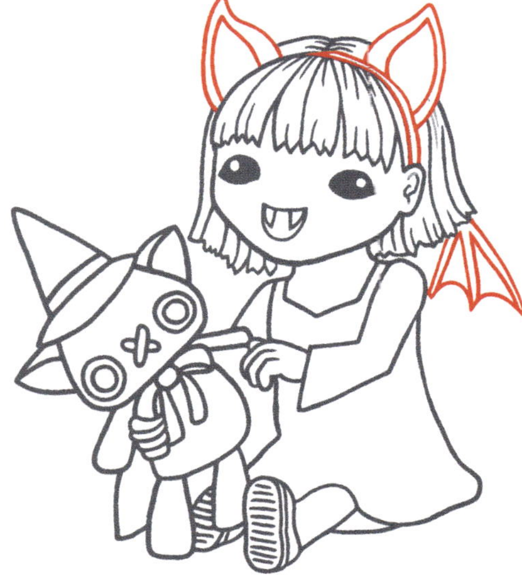

10. On the bottom right, draw a bucket with a U shape and a curve in the top. Draw a vampire face on the bucket, adding a triangle hairline, two circle eyes, a fanged smile, and ears on the sides as handles.

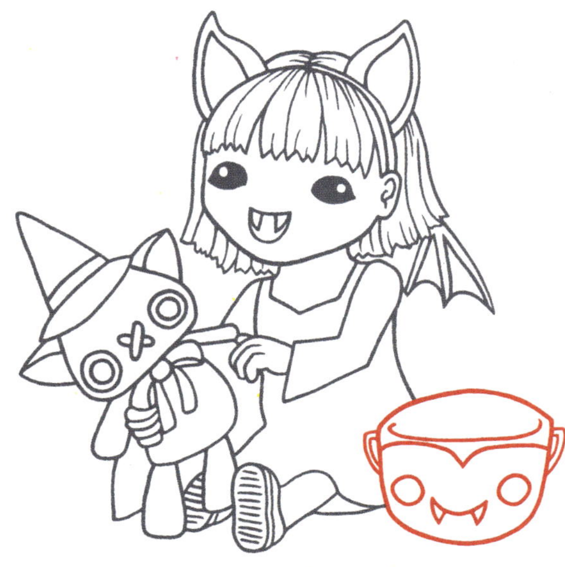

11. Cleanly trace your sketch with pencil on watercolor paper before inking.

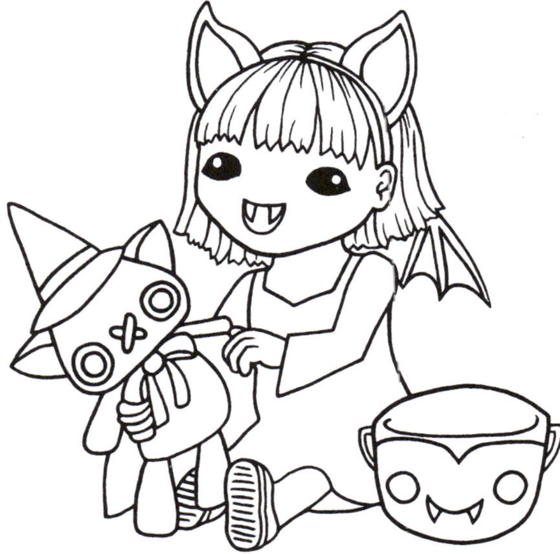

12. I used diluted India ink, leaving part of the hair white for highlights. Add shading on the girl, toy, and bucket.

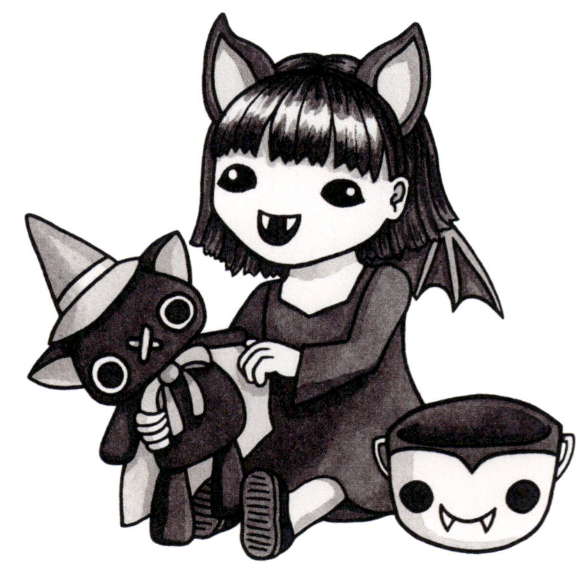

BIRTHDAY SKELETON

1. Sketch three rectangle gift boxes nestled together.

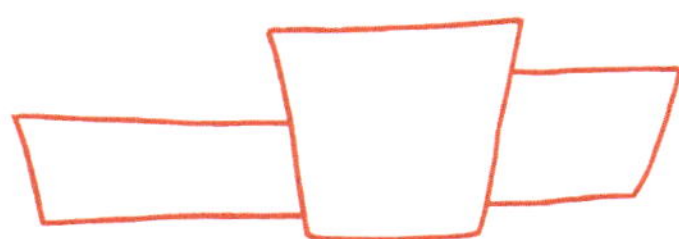

2. Make the boxes 3D by extending the tops with lines.

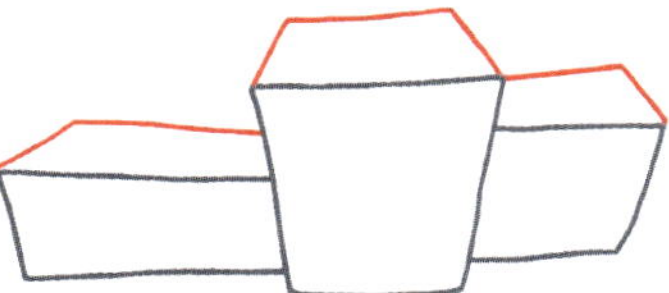

3. Draw the lid of the left box, add a ribbon to the middle box with crossing lines, and add a bow to the right box with connected loops.

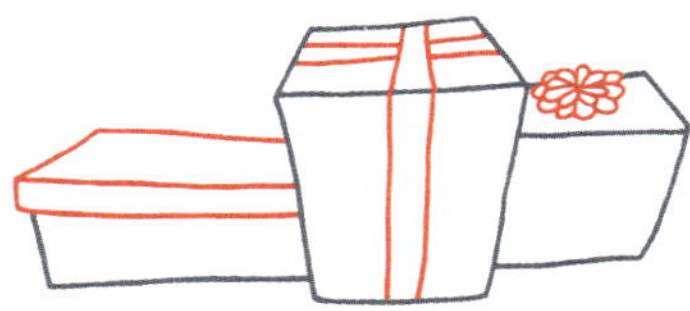

4. Sketch a figure sitting behind the presents. Draw an oval head and hands, and lines for the neck, torso, arms, and legs. Make the arms raised.

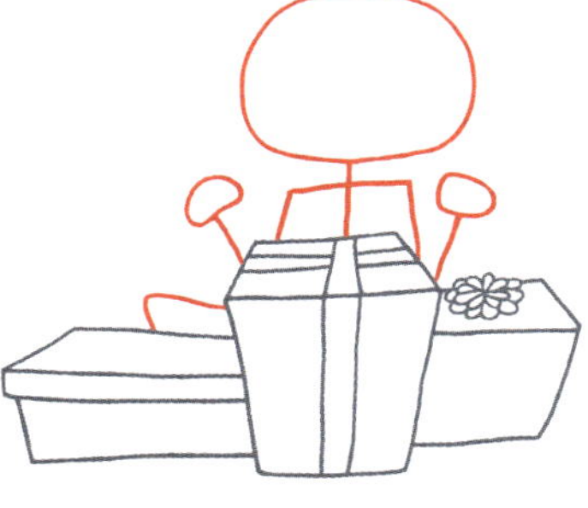

5. Draw a mushroom-shaped skull with two solid oval eyes, an upside-down heart for the nose, and lines for the teeth.

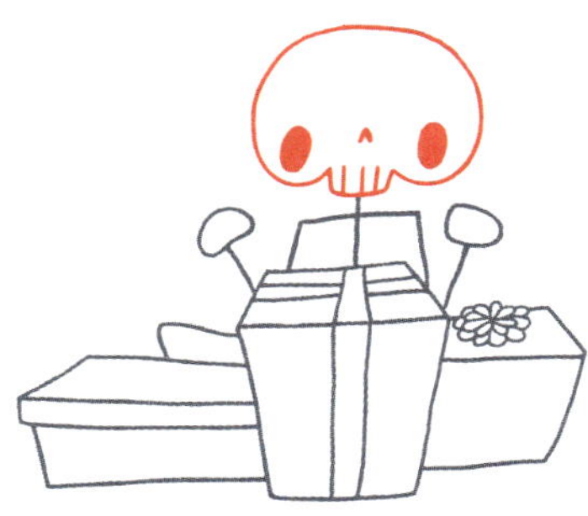

6. Add a party hat on top of the skeleton's head in the shape of a triangle. Decorate it in stripes and a spiky poof at the top.

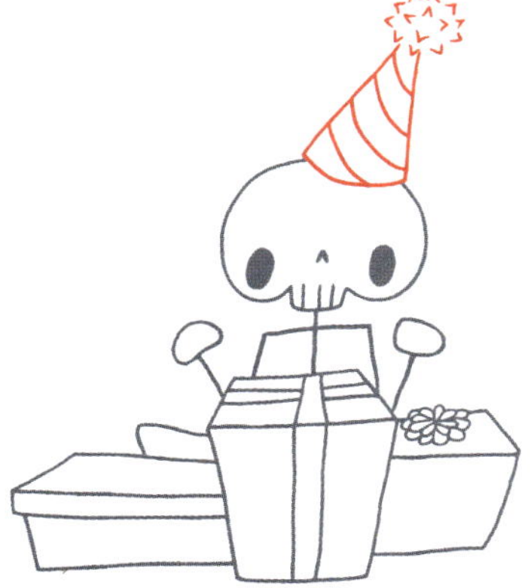

7. Draw the fingers holding a strand of ribbon on the middle present.

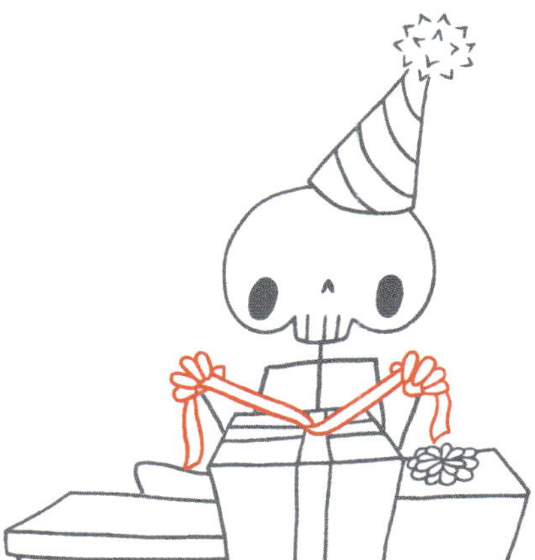

8. Add the skeleton's sweater with a thick-knitted collar and cuffs.

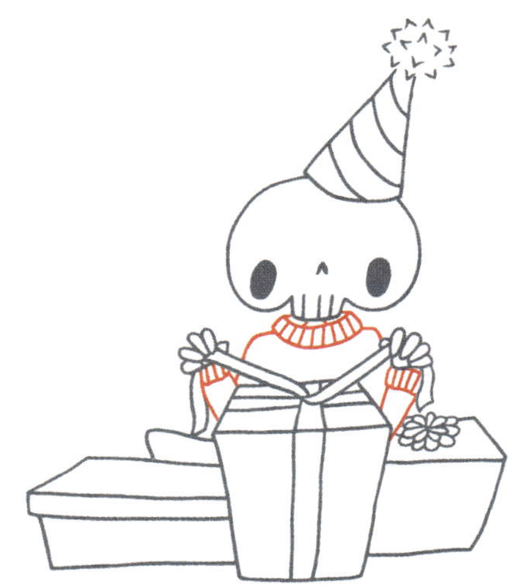

9. On the left, draw a round bag with a big bow tying it closed. Use rectangles in various sizes for the top of the bag.

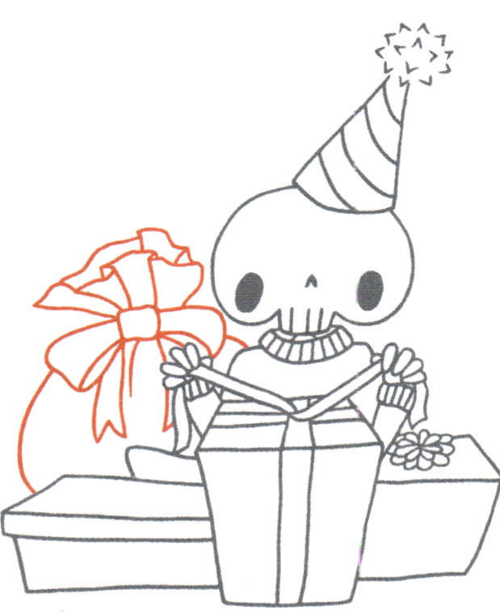

10. Add two more gift boxes on the sides with ovals on top for the bows.

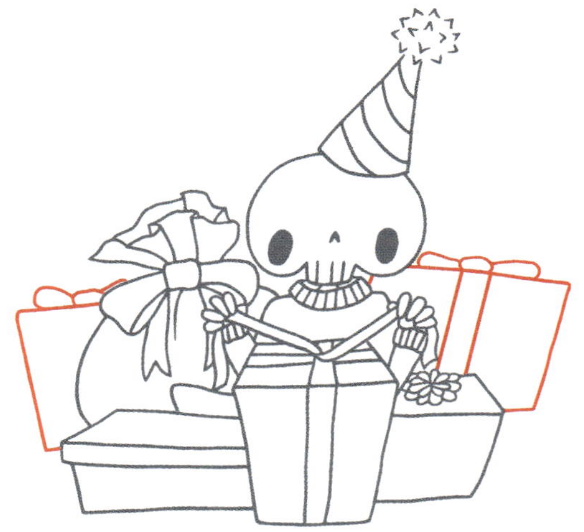

11. Draw triangle bunting above in two curved sections.

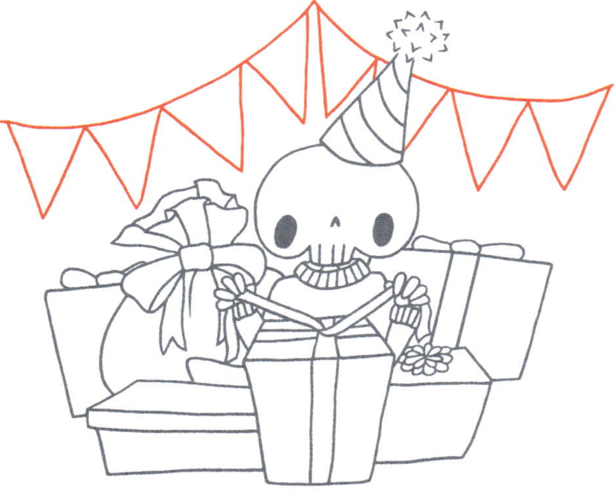

12. Cleanly trace your sketch with pencil on watercolor paper before inking.

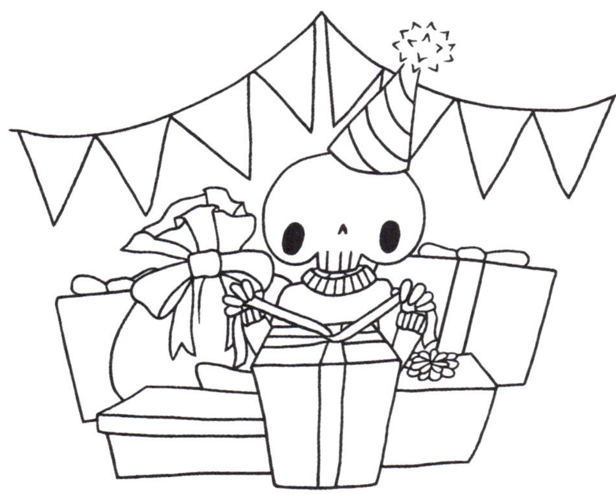

13. I used watercolors to color the scene in shades of black and gray.

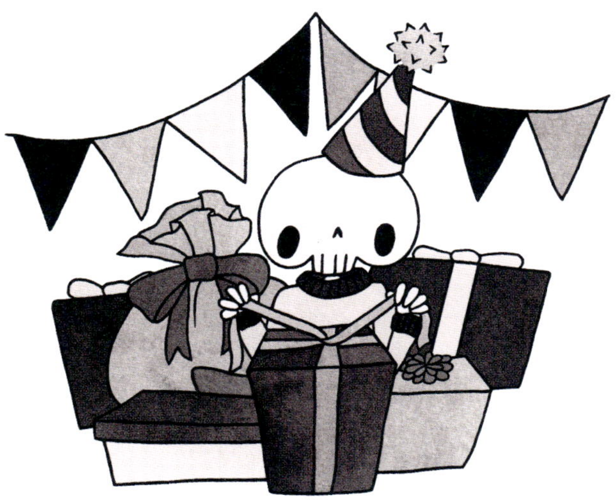

14. Add patterns to the bunting, like spiderwebs, moons, stars, and stripes. Do the same to a few gifts. With white ink or paint, add crossbones to the darkest flags of the bunting. Add shading to everything except the bunting.

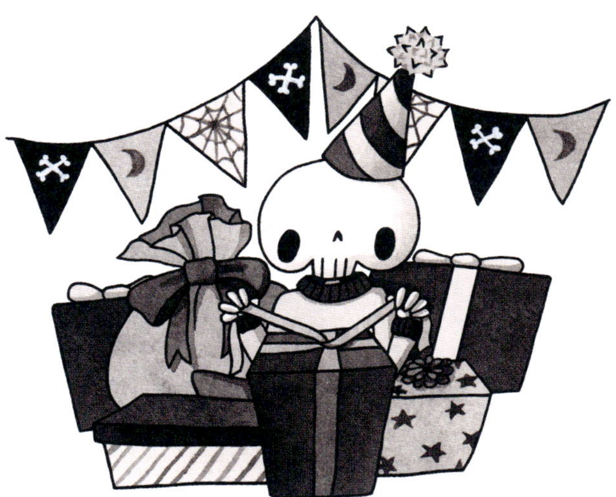

AUTUMNAL SPOOKY SOUP

1. Draw a cauldron with a U shape and a curve inside the top. Add a squiggly line of liquid and some bubbles.

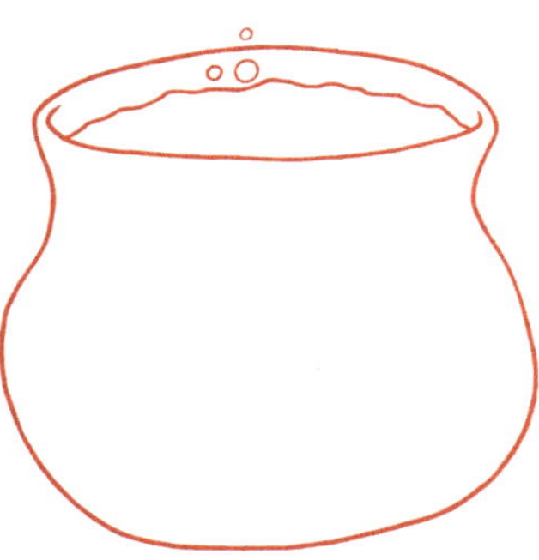

2. Draw some rocks using lumpy ovals around the bottom of the cauldron. Add flames behind the rocks with curving teardrop shapes.

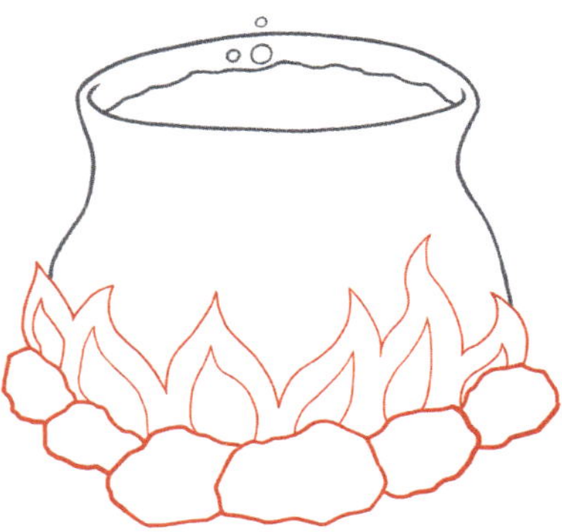

3. Add a partial stool on the right. Draw a circle with a rectangle underneath for depth and an oval leg.

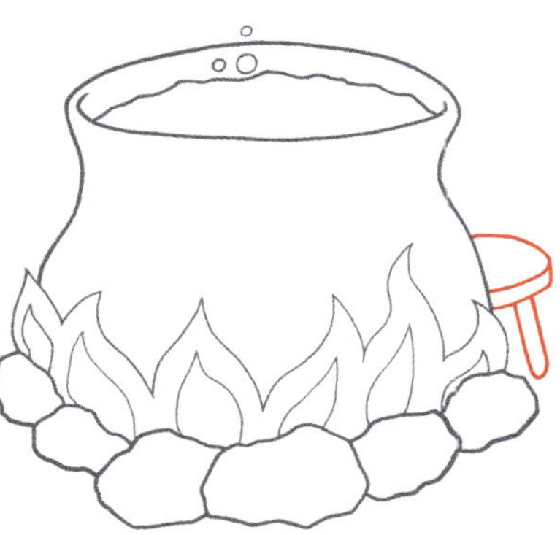

4. Draw a figure standing on the stool. Make a circle head, two lines for the neck, a rectangle torso, and ovals for the arms, leg, and hand.

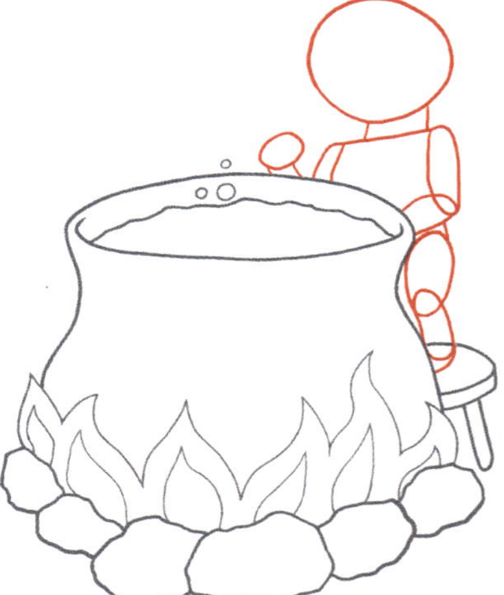

5. Give her face a happy expression. Draw short pigtails and curly bangs underneath a witch's hat.

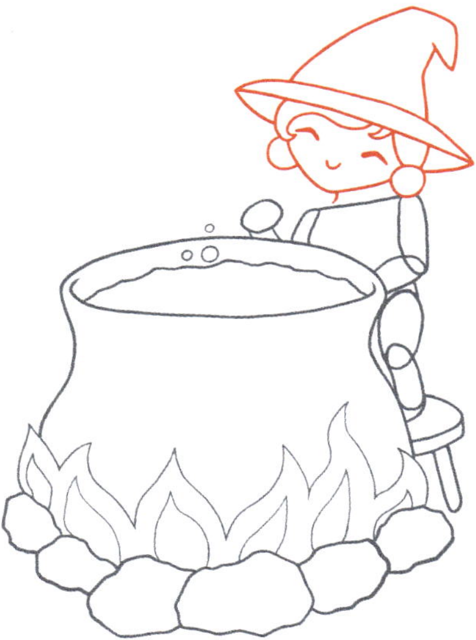

6. Draw a simple dress with a U-shaped neckline and give her a short heeled shoe. Add her arms and leg.

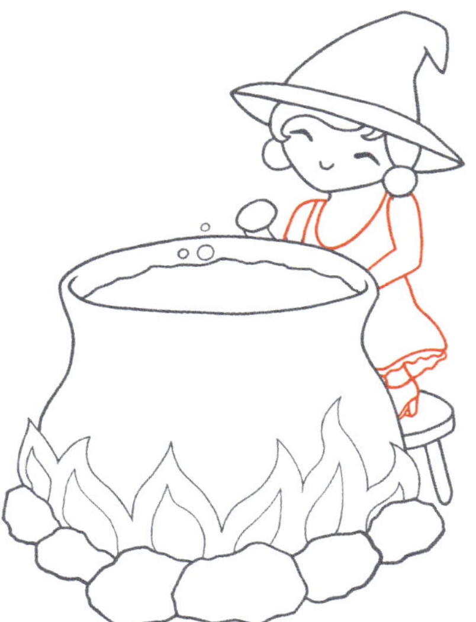

7. Draw her hand holding an oval stick inside the cauldron. Add more water lines around the stick.

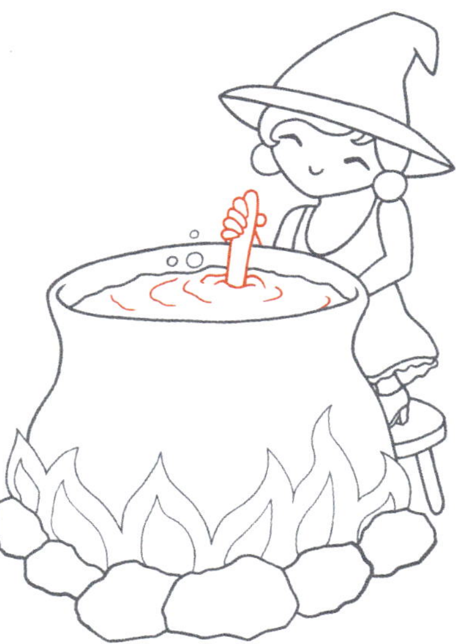

8. Add some bottles on the bottom left in various shapes and sizes.

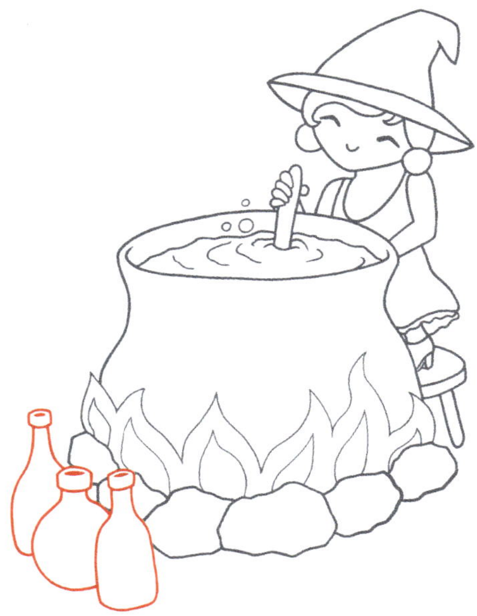

AUTUMNAL SPOOKY SOUP continued

9. Make a U-shaped basket of apples on the bottom right with two arched handles on the sides. Add partial and full circles for the apples.

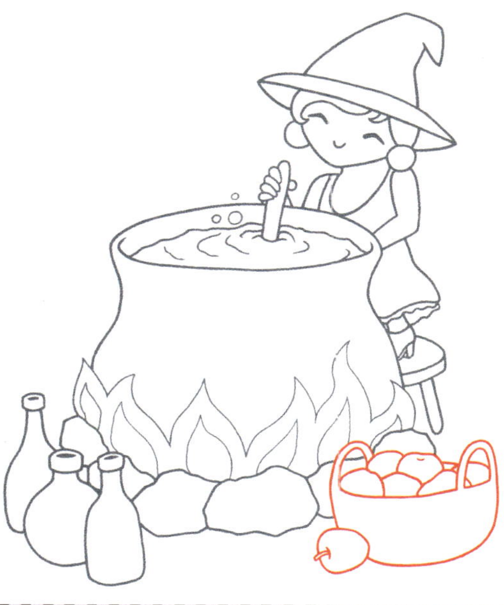

10. In the background, add horizontal lines for the floorboards and wavy lines with ties at the middle for the curtains.

11. Cleanly trace your sketch with pencils of varying lead point sizes on watercolor paper before inking.

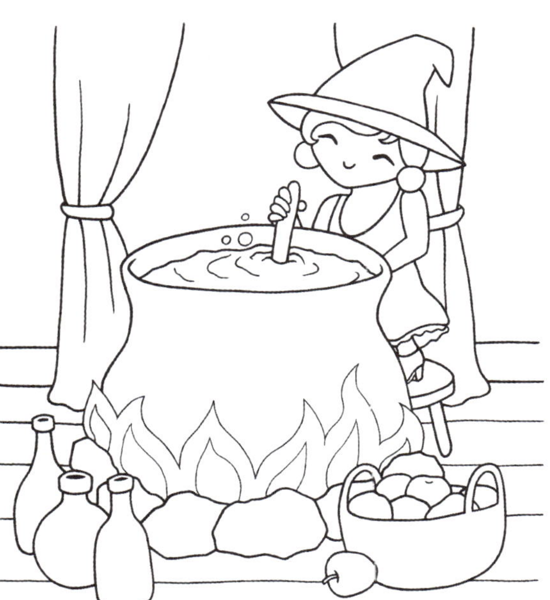

12. I used watercolors in yellow and orange to color the flames around the cauldron.

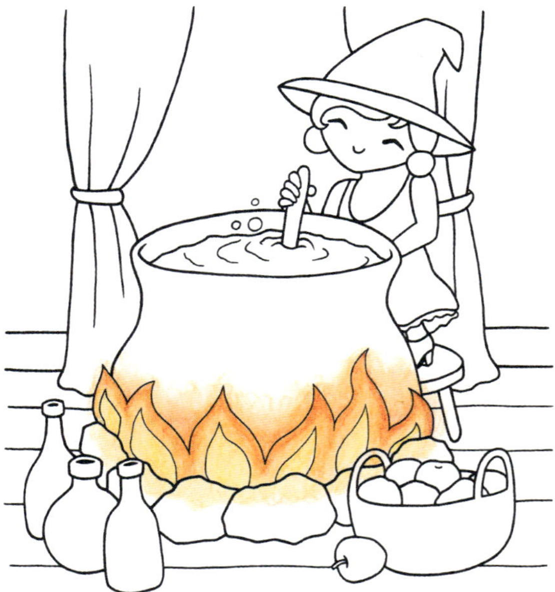

13. I used dark and moody colors of cherry red for the curtains and the witch's dress, black for the hat and cauldron, deep brown for the floors, and dark blue for the sky outside the window. Make sure to keep the area around the fire bright.

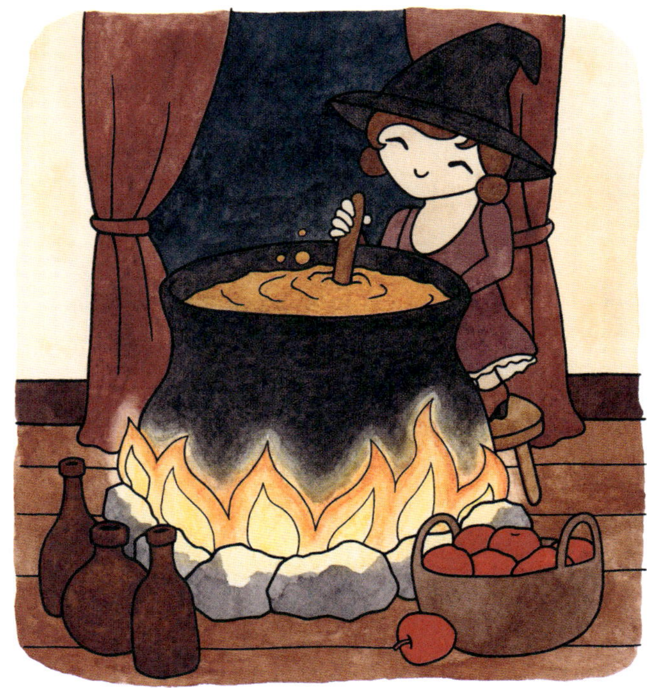

14. With white ink or paint, add stars in the window and highlights on the bottles. Create a braided texture on the basket with long horizontal lines and short diagonal lines. Add shading, noting that the light source is coming from the flames and above.

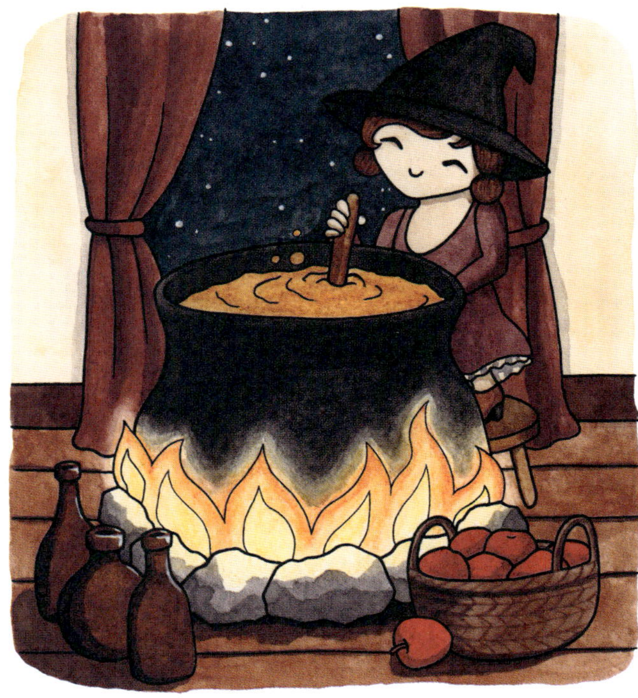

HAPPY HAUNTED HOUSE

1. Sketch a house with a square and an arched oval on top for the roof.

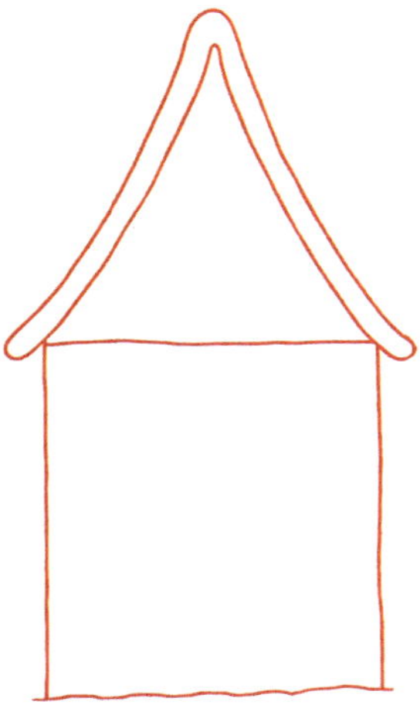

2. Draw two rectangles on the right. Add vertical lines down the top rectangle. Then add two thin rectangles on the top and bottom of the side roof.

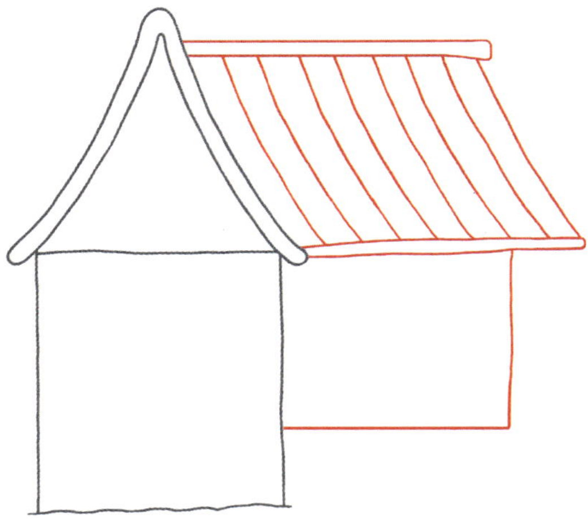

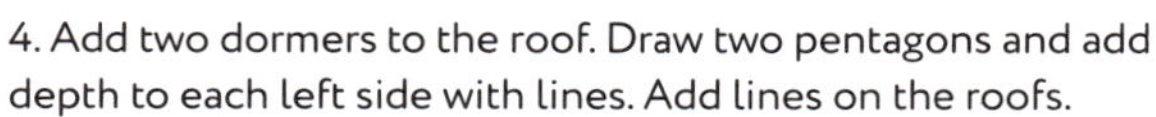

3. Draw more rectangles on the bottom right to make the front porch with three steps.

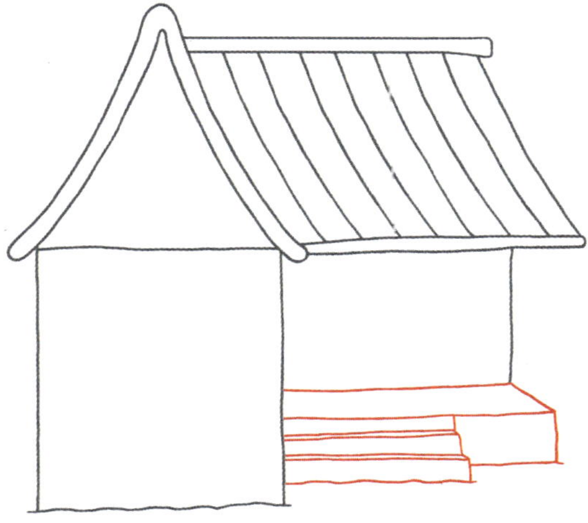

4. Add two dormers to the roof. Draw two pentagons and add depth to each left side with lines. Add lines on the roofs.

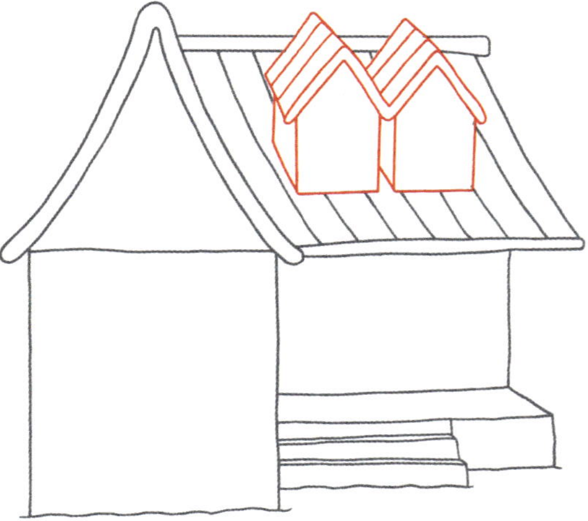

5. Draw a railing on the porch with tall and short ovals. Add an arched door with squares and rectangles and a semicircle window. Don't forget the doorknob.

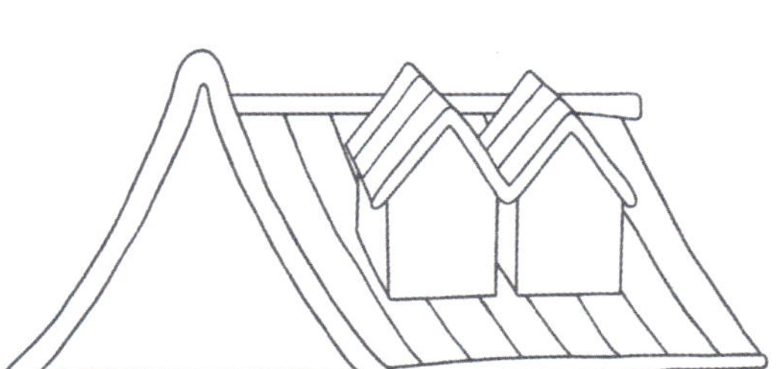

6. Add two windows on the left side of the house and two smaller windows in the dormers. Get creative and decorate them with bats and opened shutters.

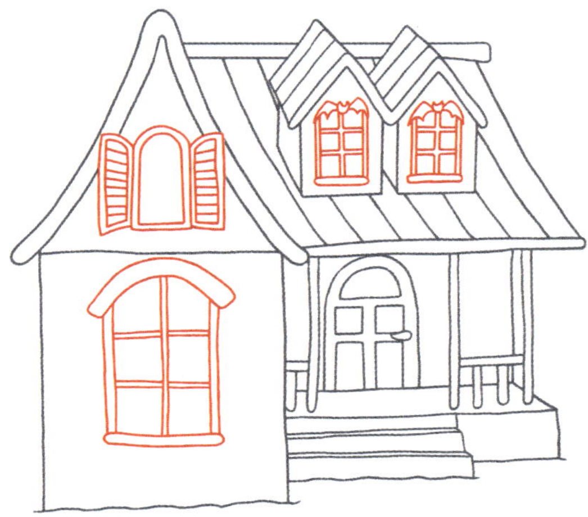

7. Draw a ghost leaning out of the upstairs window. Make a round head and outstretched oval arms.

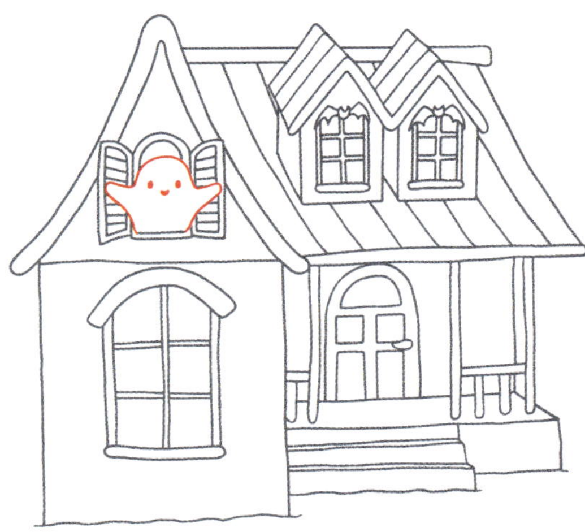

8. Draw another ghost untangling a web decoration on the roof. For the ghost, draw an arch for the body with a wavy bottom edge, and two oval arms. For the web, start with curved lines, then extend horizontal lines in between and connect with more curved lines.

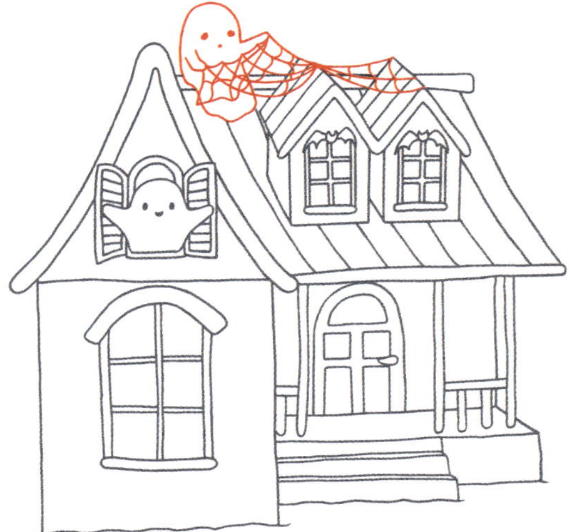

9. Draw a third ghost hanging a line of triangle bunting.

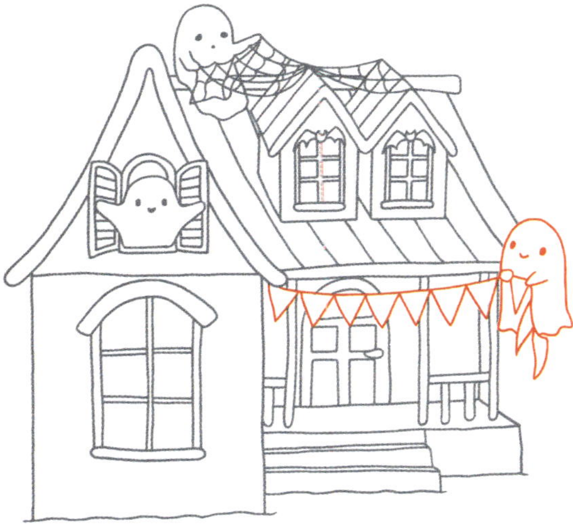

10. Add a paper skeleton behind the big window. Draw an oval head with a creepy face. Add a skeletal arm and hand and some rib bones for the torso.

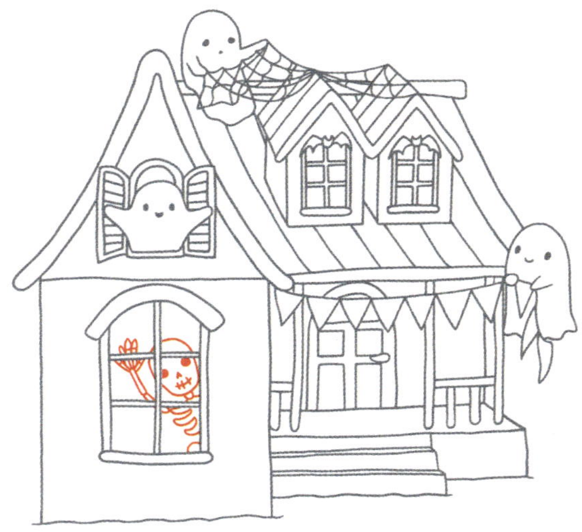

11. Draw tree branches on the side of the house, then draw curving lines of string lights attached to it. Place pumpkins in various shapes and sizes in front of the house.

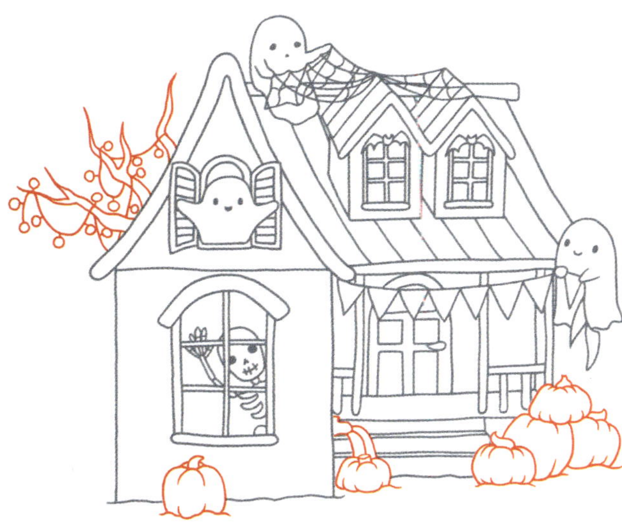

12. On the left, draw a cauldron with a curved U shape and a curve inside the top. Add circles and squares with spiky ends for candy. Also add the end of a broomstick.

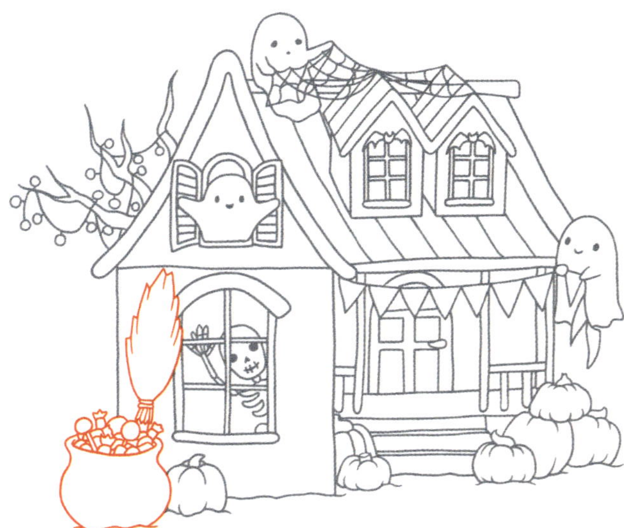

13. Place a witch hat on one of the pumpkins with a triangle and a curved rectangle underneath.

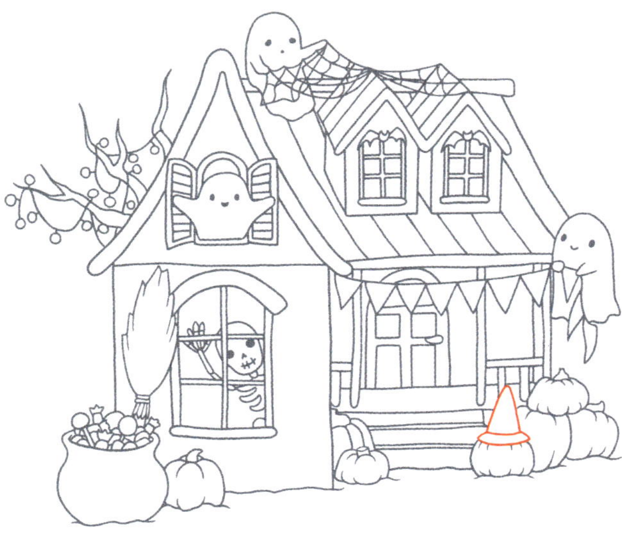

14. Draw a bundle of roses hanging upside down by the big window. Use pointed ovals for the stems with horizontal ovals for the tie. Add leaves and a couple of flowers in abstract shapes.

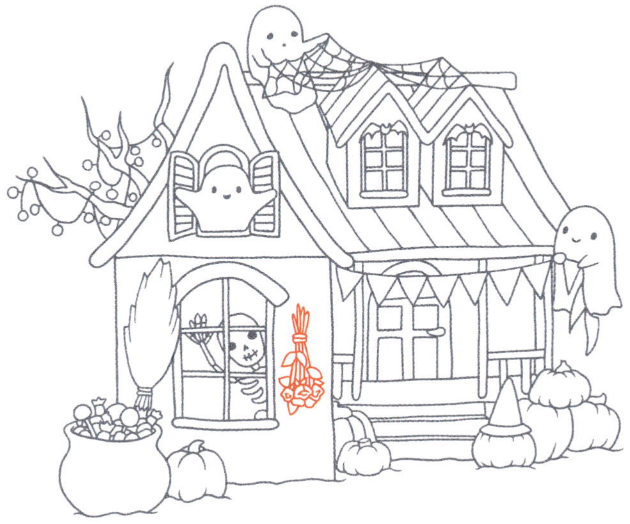

15. Cleanly trace your sketch with pencil on watercolor paper before inking.

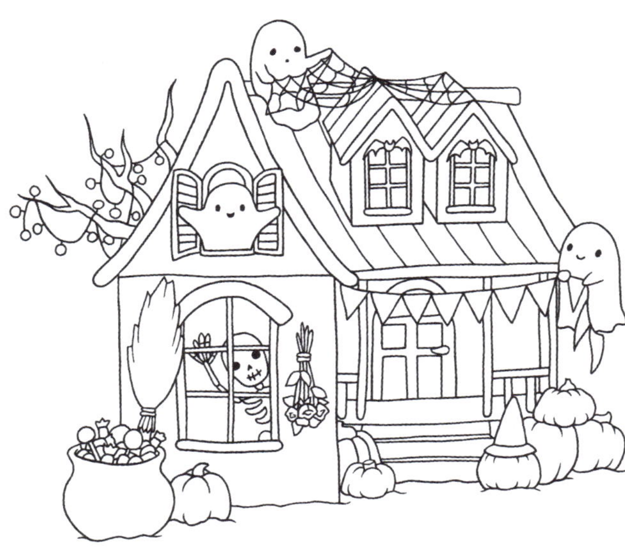

16. I used watercolors in warm colors like oranges and browns, and also green to color my scene, leaving the ghosts and skeleton white. Draw thin lines on the broom and the wooden section on the front of the house. Add shading for depth.

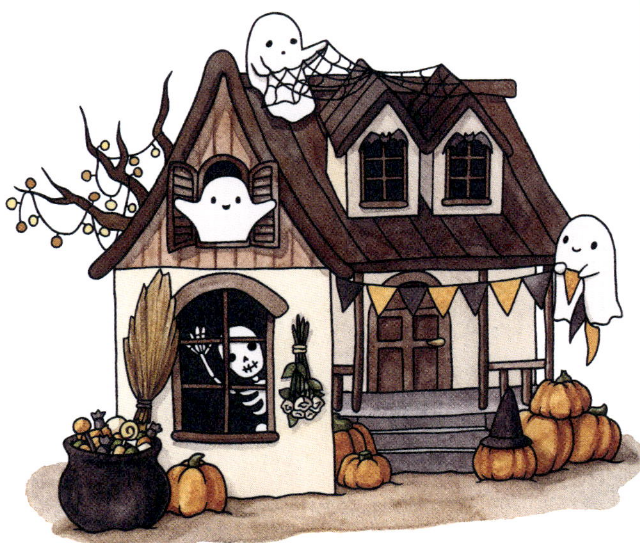

COLORING PAGES

witchy Toad

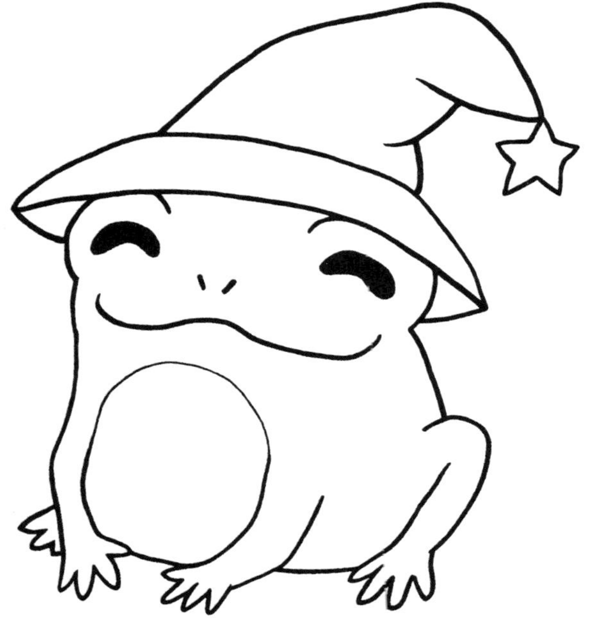

pumpkin peekaboo

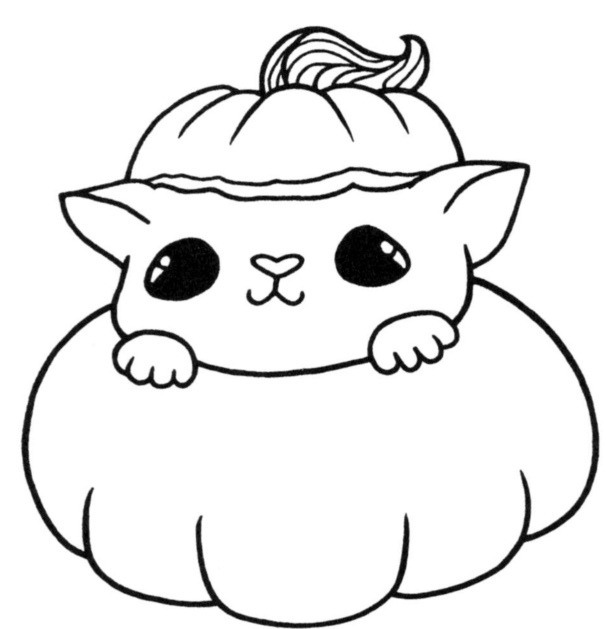

sugar Rush skunk

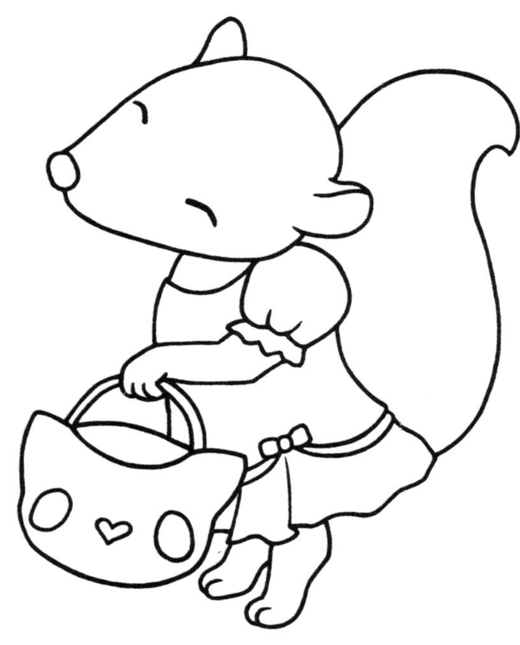

Hocus pocus possum

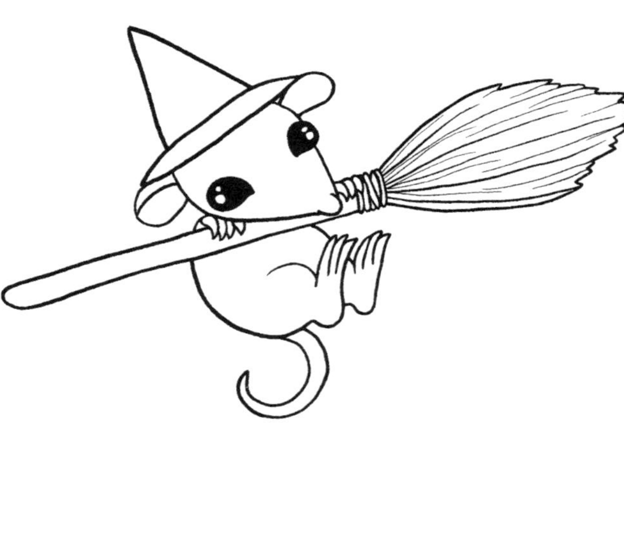

mushroom parasol

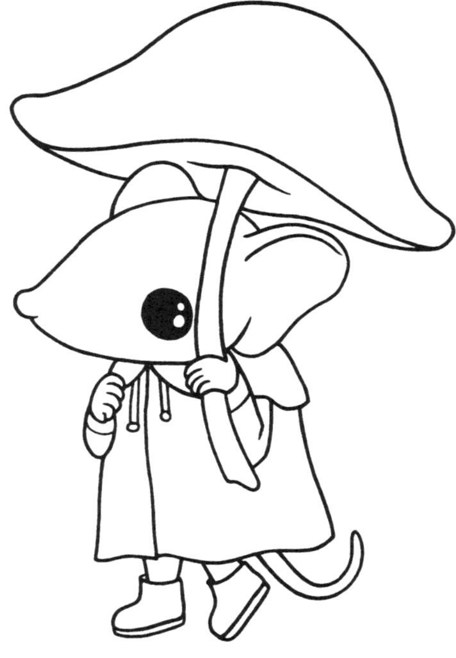

count Bunny

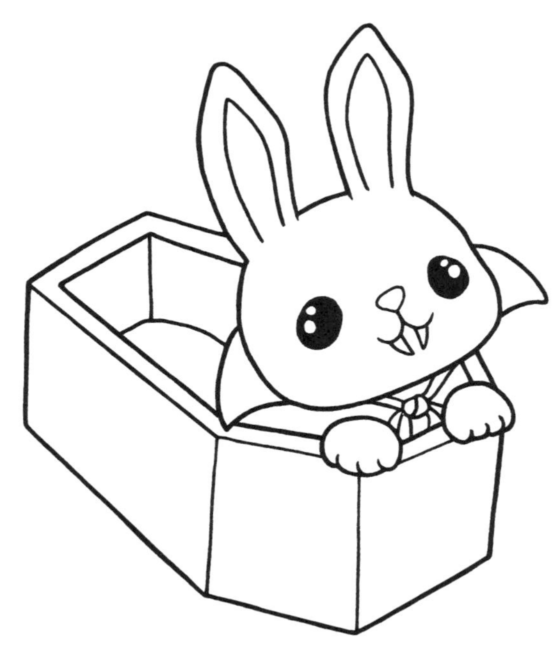

skeleton cat Tree

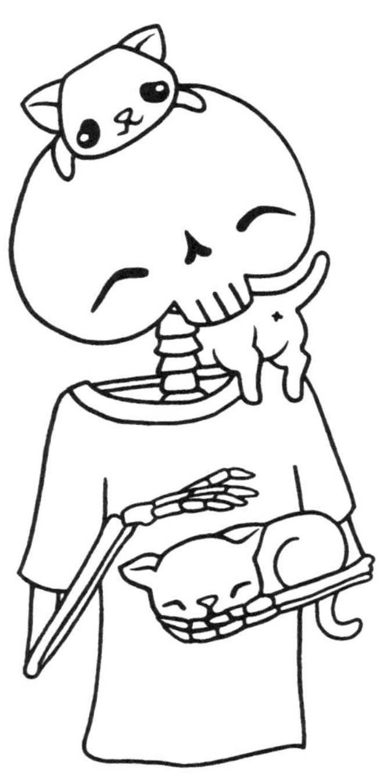

magical Hedgehog

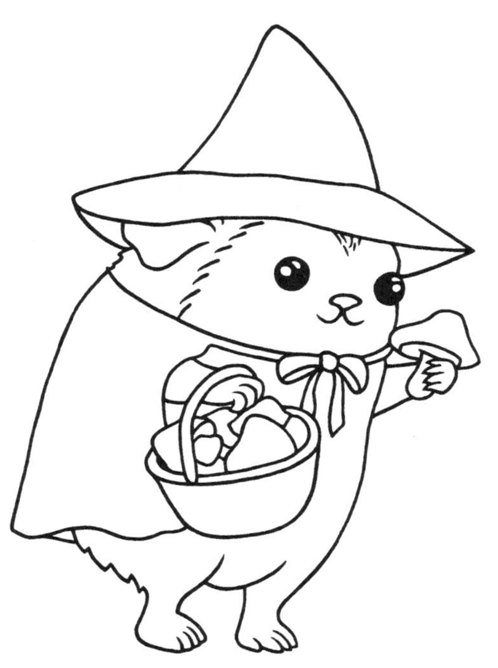

zombie Lemonade stand

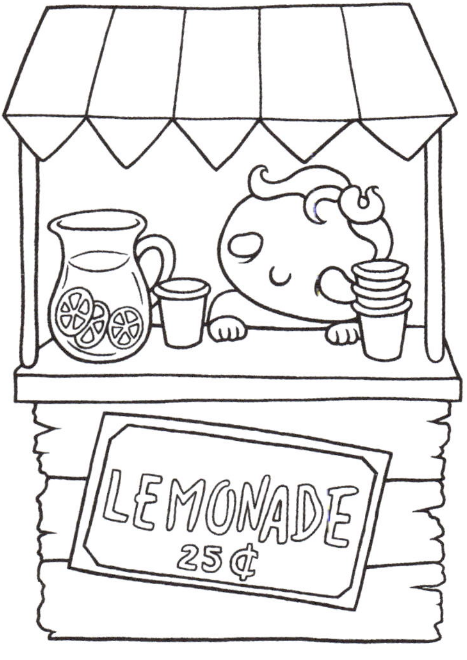

creepy cart

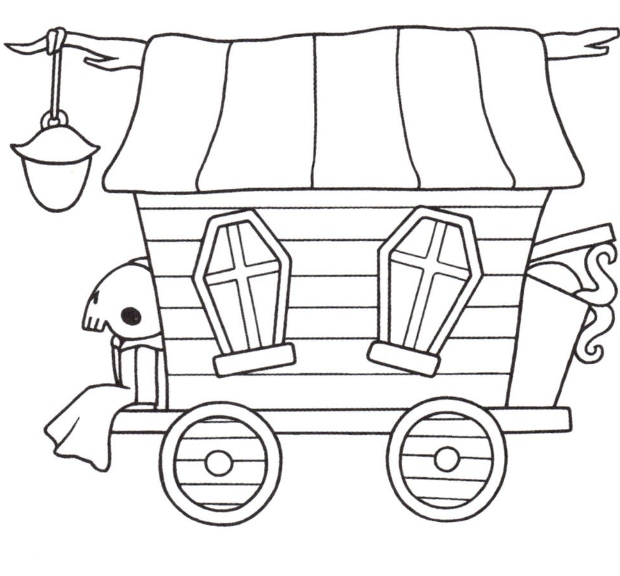

Garden underwraps

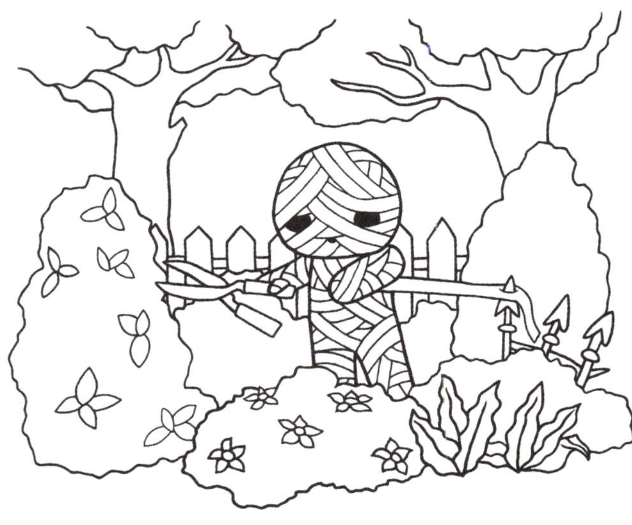

creepy campfire Tales

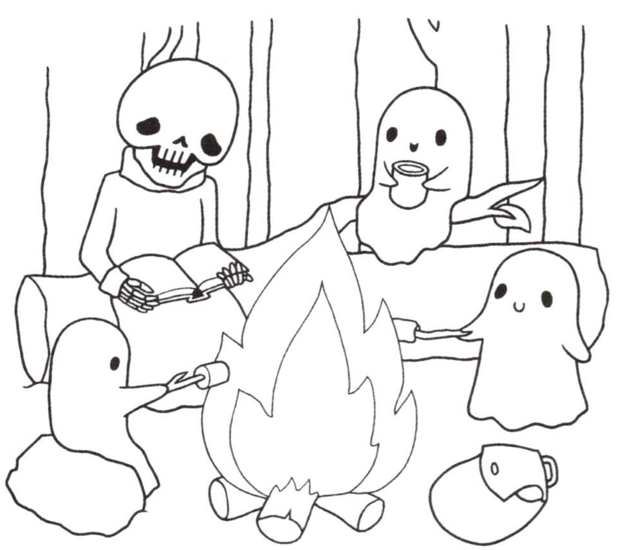

Ghostmade Cookies

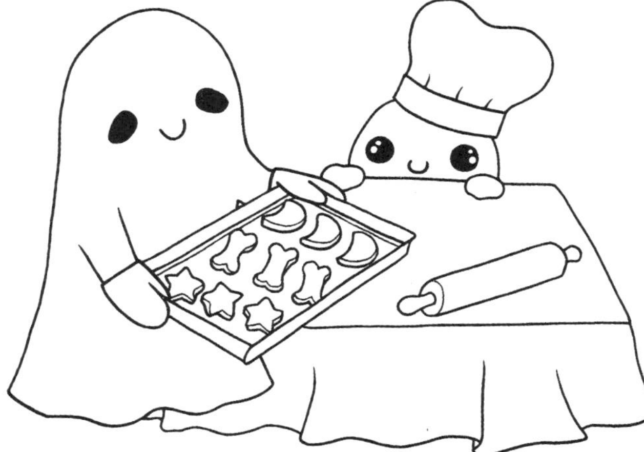

Ghostly Game Room

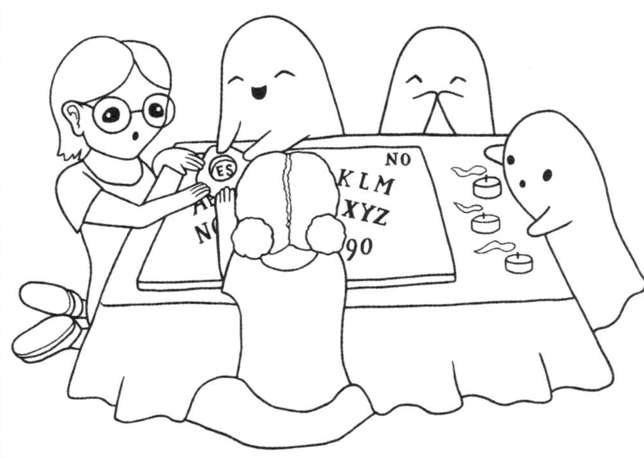

Bedtime Scary Stories

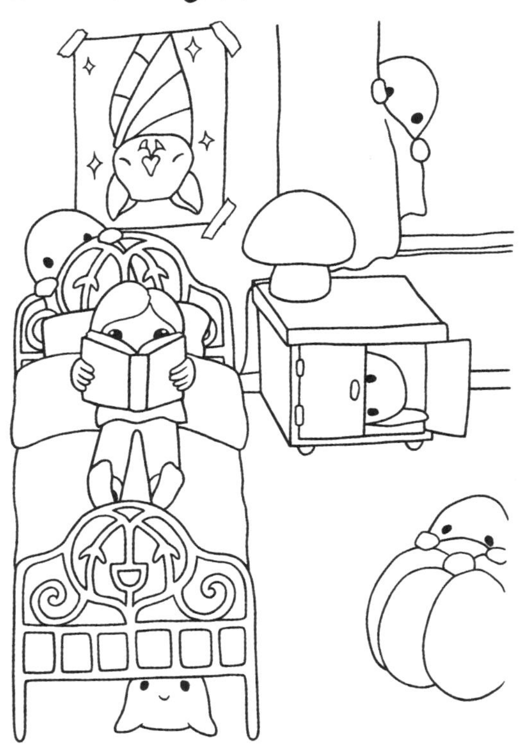

Supernatural Sleepover

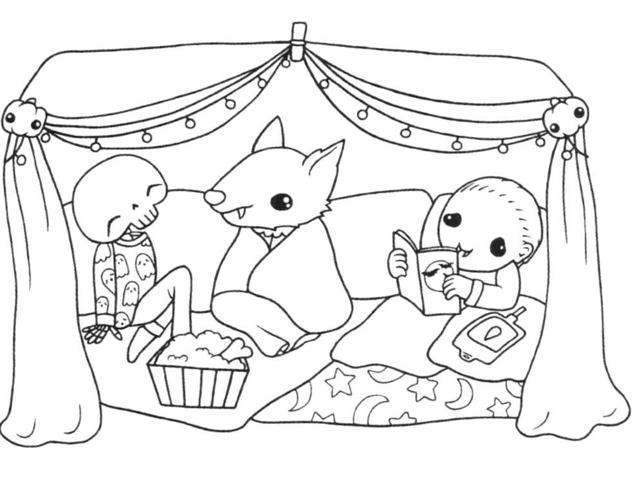

old mulberry House

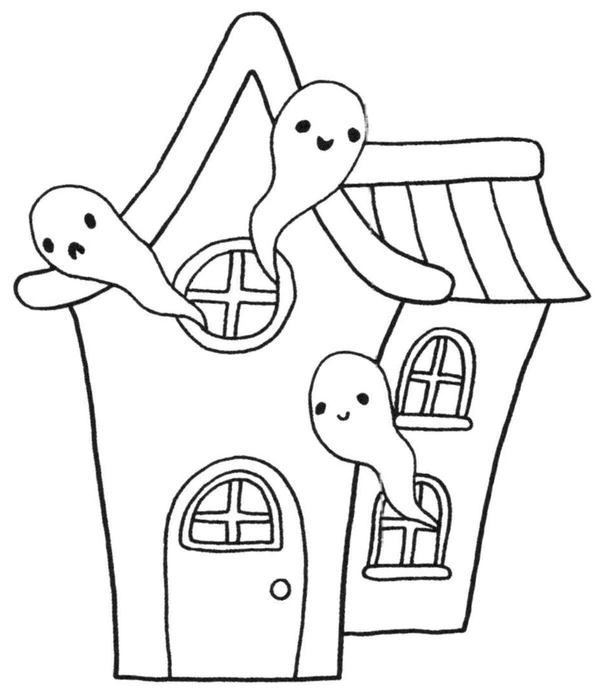

mushroom Lodge

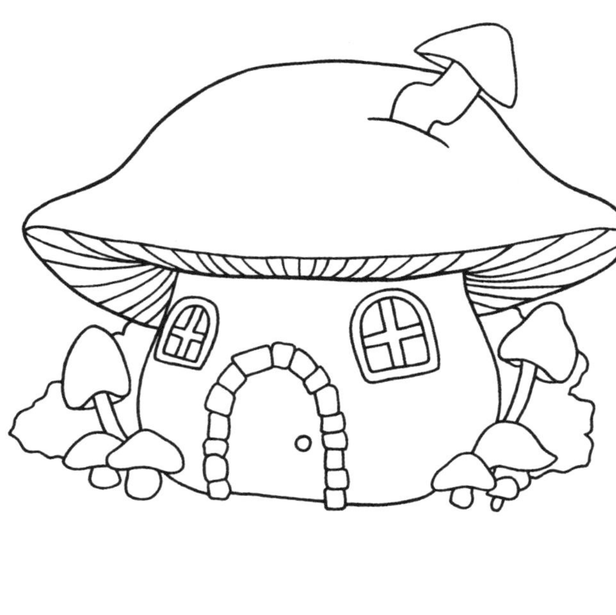

Baba Yaga's Place

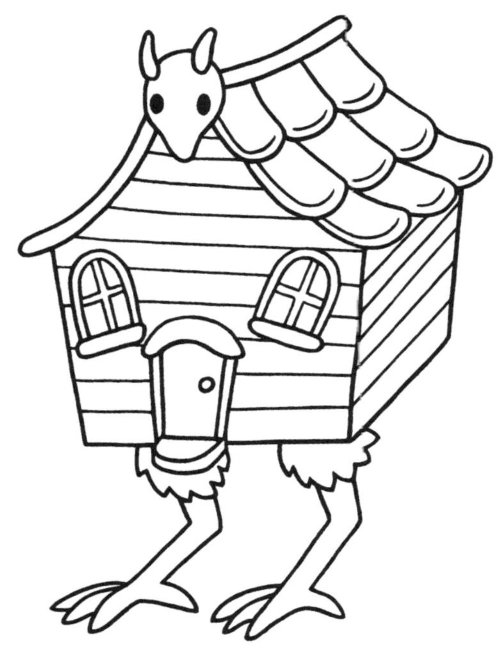

Bootique

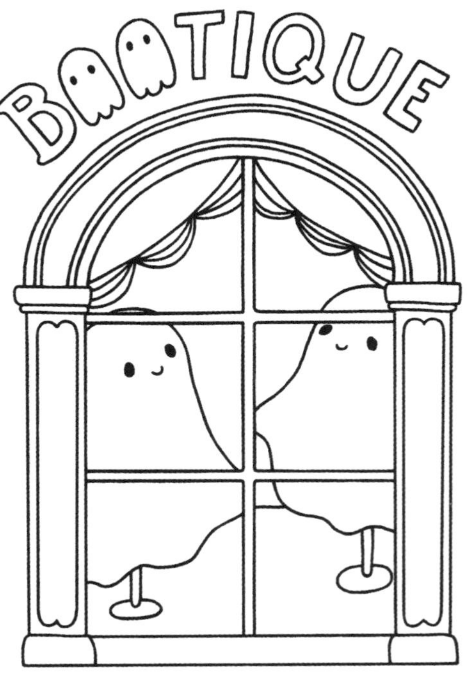

Ghost Roast Café

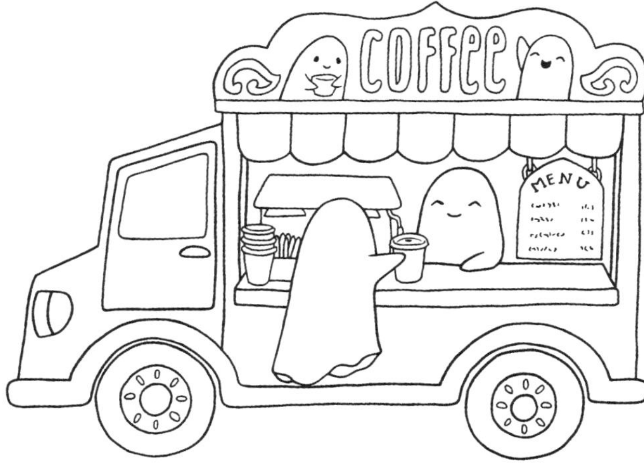

Haunted Hideaway

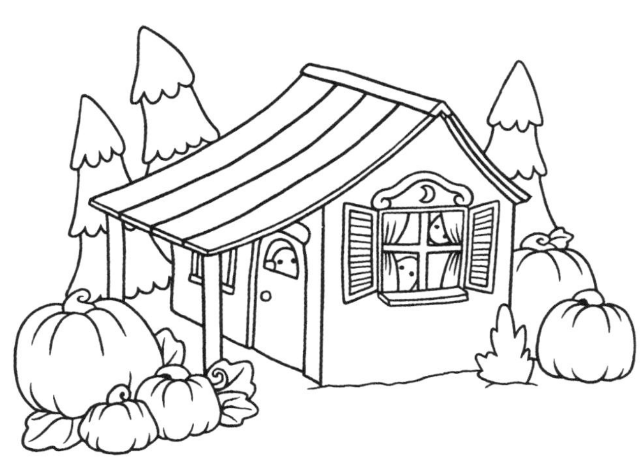

Eerie Eats Confectionery

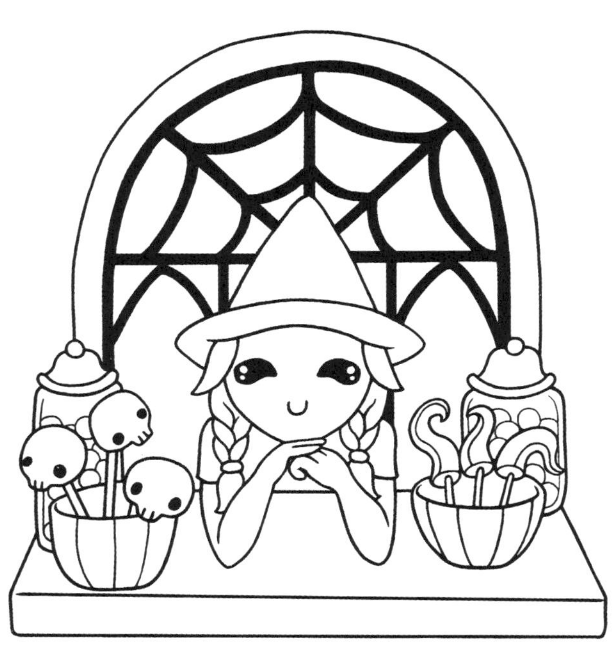

Graveyard Picnic

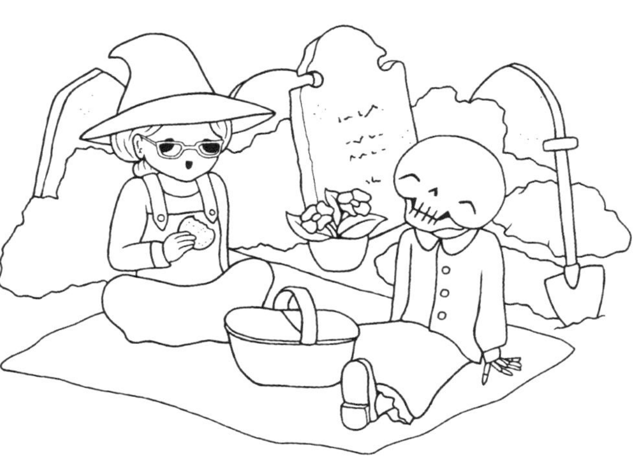

Halloween stamp

Halloween portrait

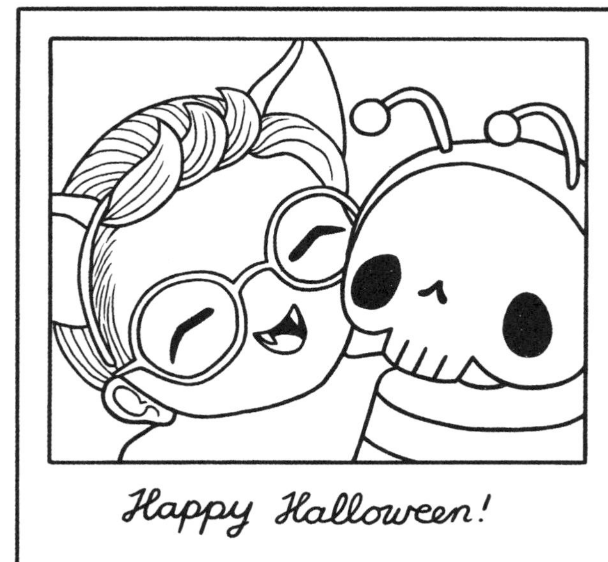

Witch's pumpkin stack

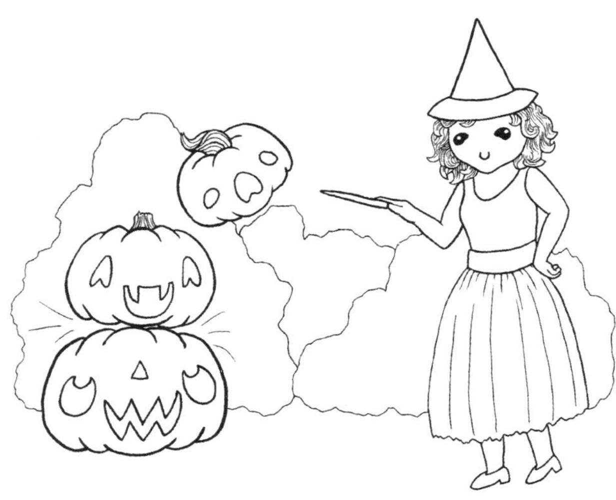

Happy Haunted House

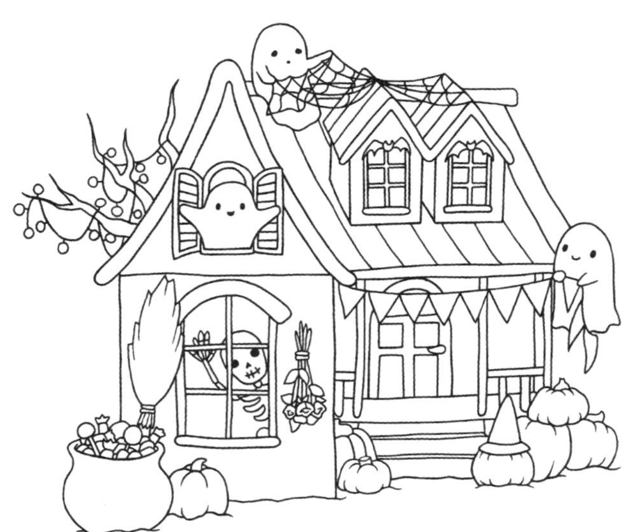

spookmas stocking

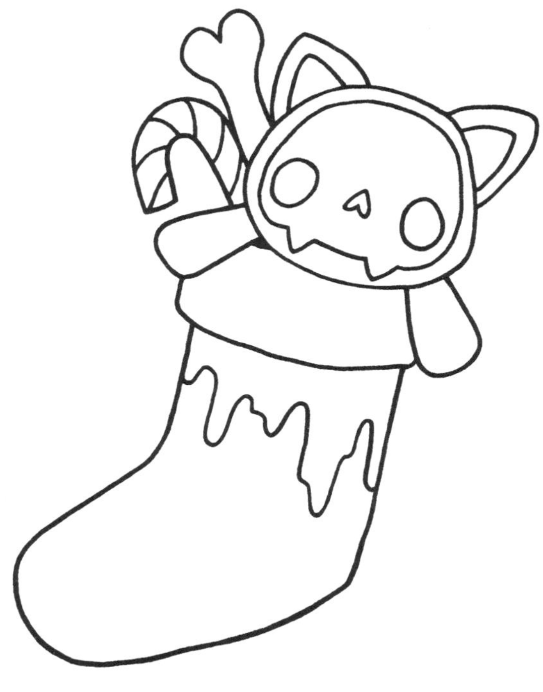

spookmas Tree

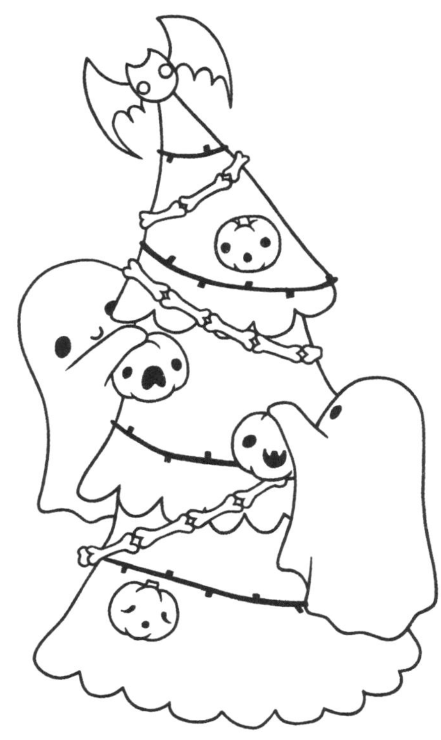

Haunted Hot chocolate

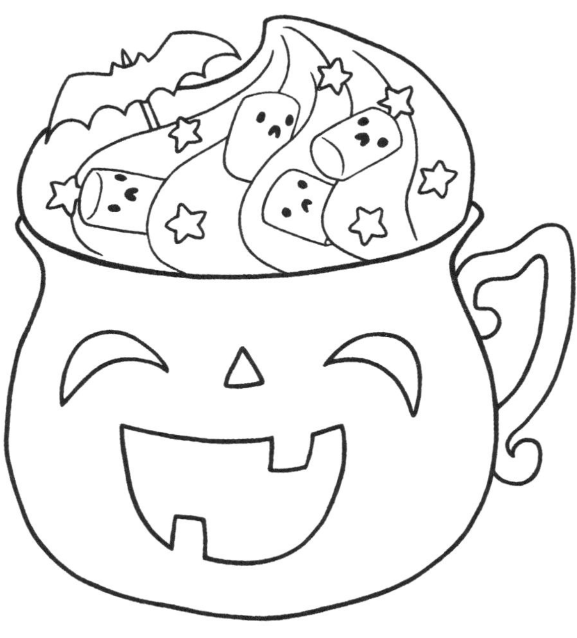

Haunted snow Globe

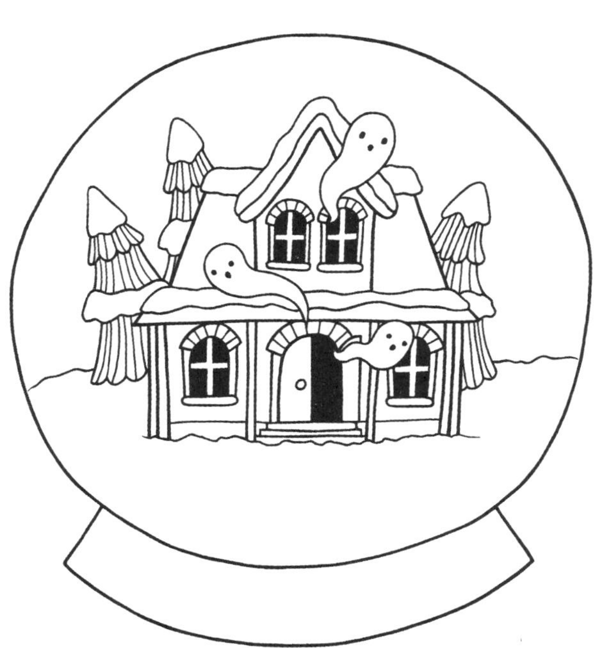

© 2025 by Quarto Publishing Group USA Inc.
Text and Illustrations © 2025 by Maritha Driessen-Veenstra

First published in 2025 by Rock Point, an imprint of
The Quarto Group, 142 West 36th Street, 4th Floor,
New York, NY 10018, USA (212) 779-4972 www.Quarto.com

Rock Point titles are also available at discount for retail,
wholesale, promotional, and bulk purchase. For details,
contact the Special Sales Manager by email at
specialsales@quarto.com or by mail at The Quarto Group,
Attn: Special Sales Manager, 100 Cummings Center Suite
265D, Beverly, MA 01915 USA.

10 9 8 7 6 5 4 3 2 1

ISBN: 978-1-57715-480-8

Digital edition published in 2025
eISBN: 978-0-7603-9303-1

Library of Congress Cataloging-in-Publication Data

Names: Driessen, Marcie, author.
Title: Creepy cute drawing class : learn how to draw 70
   sweetly spooky characters and cozy creatures / Marcie
   Driessen.
Description: New York, NY : Rock Point, 2025.
I Summary: "Whether you're a budding artist or a drawing
   master, Creepy Cute Drawing Class makes drawing your
   favorite creatures of the night fun and easy"-- Provided
   by publisher.
Identifiers: LCCN 2024044393 (print) I LCCN 2024044394
   (ebook) I ISBN 9781577154808 (paperback) I ISBN
   9780760393031 (ebook)
Subjects: LCSH: Drawing--Technique. I Characters and
   characteristics in art.
Classification: LCC NC825.C43 D75 2025 (print) I LCC
   NC825.C43 (ebook) I DDC 743/.87--dc23/eng/20241019
   LC record available at https://lccn.loc.gov/2024044393
   LC ebook record available at https://lccn.loc.
   gov/2024044394

Group Publisher: Rage Kindelsperger
Editorial Director: Erin Canning
Creative Director: Laura Drew
Managing Editor: Cara Donaldson
Editor: Katelynn Abraham
Cover and Interior Design: Beth Middleworth
Interior Layout: Rebecca Pagel

Printed in China

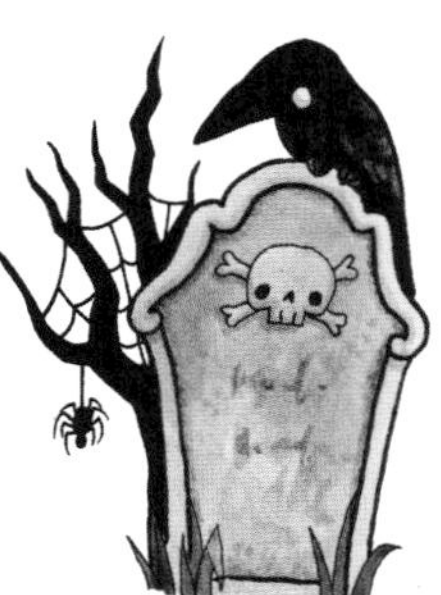